WHITE PEOPLE, INDIANS, AND HIGHLANDERS

WHITE PEOPLE, INDIANS, AND HIGHLANDERS

TRIBAL PEOPLES AND COLONIAL ENCOUNTERS IN SCOTLAND AND AMERICA

COLIN G. CALLOWAY

OXFORD

UNIVERSITY PRESS

2008

OXFORD
UNIVERSITY PRESS

Oxford University Press, Inc., publishes works that further
Oxford University's objective of excellence
in research, scholarship, and education.

Oxford   New York
Auckland   Cape Town   Dar es Salaam   Hong Kong   Karachi
Kuala Lumpur   Madrid   Melbourne   Mexico City   Nairobi
New Delhi   Shanghai   Taipei   Toronto

With offices in
Argentina   Austria   Brazil   Chile   Czech Republic   France   Greece
Guatemala   Hungary   Italy   Japan   Poland   Portugal   Singapore
South Korea   Switzerland   Thailand   Turkey   Ukraine   Vietnam

Library of Congress Cataloging-in-Publication Data
Calloway, Colin G. (Colin Gordon), 1953–
White people, Indians, and Highlanders : tribal peoples and colonial
encounters in Scotland and America / Colin G. Calloway.
p.   cm.
ISBN 978-0-19-534012-9
1. Indians of North America—History. 2. Indians of North America—Social life
and customs. 3. Scots—North America–History. 4. Scots—Social life and customs.
5. Scots—Great Britain—Colonies—History. 6. Great Britain—Colonies—History.
7. North America—History. 8. North America–Ethnic relations. 9. Scotland—History. I. Title.
E77.C15 2008   2007047240

Printed in the United States of America
on acid-free paper

To Marcia, Graeme (my favorite piper), and Meg,
and to all the McLeans of my youth

"Anaether history book, Colin? Aye, well, some of it'll be true, and some of it'll nae."

Jessie McLean (1888–1974)

Map 1. Approximate Locations of Key Highland Clans

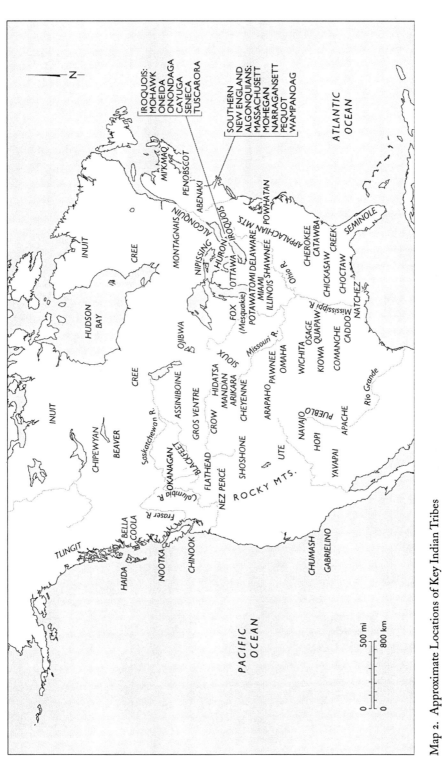

Map 2. Approximate Locations of Key Indian Tribes

Preface

In the 1730s the trustees of Georgia colony recruited Highlanders from the north of Scotland to serve as farmer-soldiers on the frontier against the Spaniards and Indians in Florida. When war broke out between Britain and Spain, General James Oglethorpe raised a corps of Highland Rangers to fight alongside his English colonists and his Creek, Yuchee, and Chickasaw allies. The Highlanders spoke Gaelic, wore kilts, and wielded broadswords. Oglethorpe described his force as "White people[,] Indians and highlanders."[1] He offered no explanation for his comment; pairing American Indians and Celtic Highlanders together as nonwhites made sense to eighteenth-century Englishmen, as it did to many Scottish Lowlanders. This book examines the common ground that Highlanders and Indians shared as tribal peoples living on the edges of an English-speaking Atlantic world, describes their experiences as colonialism and capitalism changed their environments, and explores their interactions in a new American milieu. It considers the ways in which colonialism reconstructed histories and images of Highlanders and Indians, histories and memories of oppression and resistance shaped identities in Britain and America, and Highlanders shed their "nonwhite" status in part by empire-building in North America. Though ultimately divergent, the historical experiences of Highland Scots and American Indians are initially comparative and often connective.

There are thousands of books on Scottish history and Indian history. Scottish studies, like Native American studies, has undergone a florescence in the past generation, and this book benefits from the recent revival, particularly the new attention to the role of Scots in the Atlantic world and the British Empire. In addition, Scottish connections with America and the impact of Scottish individuals, ideas, and influences on American and Canadian culture in particular and the world in general have all received considerable (and sometimes exaggerated) attention. Some works identify people of Scottish origin or ancestry as having had an effect out of proportion to their numbers; others emphasize Celtic influences, especially on the history and culture of the American South.[2] But few works examine relations between Indians and Scots, and fewer still are well grounded in the history of both peoples.

Placing specific encounters in a comparative setting that involves the British Isles, Canada, and the United States, this book illuminates and complicates understandings of Scotland and America, imperialism and Indians. Some studies of empire take a global canvas, and most examine relations between center and periphery. This book does something else: It traces the experiences of two groups of peoples on the fringes of the same empire at roughly the same time and examines how they dealt with one another when they met in multiple American encounters. The stories play out across an ocean and an empire that divided people but also brought them together in new situations and societies that were uniquely American. Tracing the comparative, connected, and divergent experiences of these tribal peoples uncovers varied and ambiguous relationships that sometimes challenge standard depictions of "Indian-White" contact, and reveals diversities in colonial experiences that included participation, as well as victimization.

Unlike Spain, France, and Britain, Scotland as a nation did not pursue policies toward Indians. The Society in Scotland for the Propagation of Christian Knowledge (SSPCK) pursued policies toward both Highlanders and Indians that reflected Lowland and Presbyterian goals that the society associated with the emergence of the Scottish nation, and Highland Scots carved out their own niche in dealing with the Native inhabitants of North America. Nevertheless, Scottish interactions with Indians took place within larger imperial contexts of British-Indian relations and, like all interactions between colonists and Indians, involved a kaleidoscope of relationships shaped by broader historical forces and enduring colonial experiences, as well as a clash between cultures and a conflict over land.

The book follows two central themes within a triangular relationship: It identifies parallels between the experiences of Highlanders and Indians in their respective homelands; it relates multiple stories of encounter between Scots and Indians when they fought, traded, and married in North America, and it does both in the context of relations with colonial power (whether British or American) and far-reaching social, economic, and cultural changes. Chapters are arranged topically. Some deal mainly with parallel experiences; others focus on the shared story of encounter; most do both. Each chapter traces change over time, but the narratives necessarily overlap. The book, then, is an unfinished tapestry of stories, weaving together Highland and Native American threads and loosely framed by colonialism and cultural imperialism. It is a story of American encounters with roots and parallels far beyond America.

* * *

At the end of March 1805 the ice broke on the upper Missouri River. A week later the Lewis and Clark expedition set out from the Mandan villages in present-day North Dakota where they had spent the winter. Anxious to be on his way again to the Pacific, Meriwether Lewis allowed himself an uncharacteristic expression of feeling in his journal. He described the moment of departure as "among the most happy of my life." The voyage had been "a darling project of mine for the last ten years of my life," and he was finally getting on with it.[3] I have had similar feelings about this book. For at least a dozen years I have planned to write a book about the experiences and responses of Highland Scots and American Indians in dealing with colonialism and with one another. Other projects, however pleasurable, got in the way, but this has been "a darling project," and it is overdue.

My credentials for trying to reconstruct the historical experiences of Indian peoples and Highland Scots have less to do with personal identity than with interest and experience. I grew up hearing and reading Scottish history, and I have spent my adult life studying, teaching, and writing about American Indian history. In trying to figure out the history of North America, I have always been an outsider. Not only am I not Native American, but until quite recently, I was not any kind of American. I have tried to be careful and respectful, knowing that for many Indian people a non-Indian doing Indian history represented an intrusion, a presumption, and even a continuation of colonial structures that control historical narratives. In this work, I have closer ties to many of the people involved, but I still write from the position of outsider and claim little inside knowledge or special understanding.

I grew up in Yorkshire. My father was English, and my mother was a Highland Scot from Perthshire. They met at an air force base in the north of

Scotland during the Second World War, at a time when Anglo-Scots marriages were still something of a rarity. ("An Englishman?" my grandmother Jessie McLean said; "I wonder what he'll eat.") My mother's family was large (six sisters, two brothers), so almost all of my many relatives were Scots. I learned from an early age that the McLeans had a boat of their own at the flood and that 150 of the 180 McLeans who fought at Culloden died there. (There was also the story about the McLean who chained his Campbell bride to a rock as the tide was coming in, but we did not dwell on that). My emotional ties and historical interests leaned to Scotland, as did my football (soccer) allegiances in a part of the world where that mattered. But no one in Scotland called me Scottish. I was not born in Scotland, I did not live in Scotland, and my father was English. In the United States, however, the fact that I do not speak like Prince Charles regularly earns me identification as Scottish (or Irish or Welsh or Australian). I feel the same emotional pull to Scotland as do thousands of American and Canadian Scots, but being three thousand miles from home does not make me any more Scottish than I was when I lived in North Britain.

I have found that, like doing Indian history, doing Scottish history involves peeling back myths, identifying their roots, and examining the enduring power of the imagined past in shaping national, tribal, and individual identities. Grappling with the imagined past among American Scots involves layers of myth, memory, and identity on *both* sides of the Atlantic. The histories recounted in this book offer some insights into the mix of cultural persistence and invention of tradition and the issues of identity that come to the fore when, as sometimes happens, Americans of Scots and Indian ancestry participate in both Highland games and powwows.[4]

Acknowledgments

I am grateful to the American Council of Learned Societies for supporting my research with the award of a fellowship for 2004–2005. I have presented aspects of this work to audiences in Edinburgh and Oban, in Vermont, New Hampshire, New York, and New Mexico. I am grateful to the following scholars and colleagues who have shared their work and ideas with me, read parts of the manuscript, and provided valuable assistance: Geoffrey Plank, University of Cincinnati; Margaret Connell Szasz, University of New Mexico; Alison Brown and Marjory Harper, both of the University of Aberdeen; Sherry Farrell Racette, Concordia College; Andrew Hook, professor emeritus, University of Glasgow; Barrie Cox-Dacre of Edinburgh; James H. Merrell, Vassar College; Michael Macdonald, associate editor of *Celtic Heritage* magazine; Michael Newton; Celeste Ray, University of the South; and Mark Simpson-Vos of the University of North Carolina Press.

I am grateful to the anonymous reviewers of the unfinished manuscript and to helpful people at the following institutions for assistance in locating documents and illustrations: Baker and Rauner libraries at Dartmouth College; the Black Watch Regimental Museum Archives; the British Museum; the Buffalo Bill Historical Center, Cody, Wyoming; the Canadian War Museum; Glasgow Museums; the Joslyn Art Museum, Omaha, Nebraska; K. Ross Toole Archives and Special Collections, University of Montana–Missoula; Library and Archives Canada; the McCord Museum, Montreal; the National Archives of Scotland;

the National Gallery of Scotland; the National Library of Scotland; the National Museum of Scotland; the Nova Scotia Museum; the Perth Museum and Art Gallery; the Philbrook Museum, Tulsa, Oklahoma; the Royal Collections, St. James's Palace; Royal Ontario Museum; the Scottish National Portrait Gallery; and the Smithsonian Institution. Special thanks go to Linda M. Welch for her help in organizing the electronic illustrations. As in all of my publications, I have benefited enormously from my colleagues and students in History and Native American Studies at Dartmouth College.

Contents

A Note on Terminology

I have used the terms *Indian* and *Native American* interchangeably. Neither is adequate, and both are problematic in some ways. *First Nations* is the preferred term in Canada, but would stylistically complicate a work like this one in which the same Native groups often feature on both sides of the international border. My preference is to use "Indian people." In referring to particular groups, I have employed the tribal name most commonly used in English rather than the names tribal peoples call themselves in their own language. I use *Scots* to refer to the people who lived north of the English border, distinguishing between *Lowland Scots,* who lived in the south and eastern part of Scotland, and *Highland Scots (Gaels),* who inhabited the Highlands and western islands of Scotland. *Scotch,* which is usually avoided these days as a pejorative term, enjoyed common usage in earlier centuries and appears frequently in quoted material. *Scotch-Irish* or *Scots-Irish* refers to the people of Scots descent who settled first in Ulster and then in North America and who might more accurately be called Ulster Scots. Scots differ from Scots-Irish, who differ from the Irish, and of course they all differ from the English. *British* refers to English and other peoples who constitute "Great" Britain. All English people are British, but not all British people are English. For people of Indian and European parentage generally, I use the term *Métis* rather than "mixed blood." For the descendants of Scottish and Indian parents I use *Scots-Indian* rather than Gaelind, which would refer exclusively to children of Highlanders. In using Highland surnames I have followed the form (MacLean, McLean, Maclean) employed in the source rather than impose my own consistency.

Abbreviations

CO   Colonial Office Records (Public Records Office)
NAC   National Archives of Canada, Ottawa
NAS   National Archives of Scotland, Edinburgh
NLS   National Library of Scotland, Edinburgh
NSAS   New (Second) Statistical Account of Scotland, 15 vols. (Edinburgh
       and London: W. Blackwood and Sons, 1845)
PRO   Public Record Office (now National Archives), Kew, London
SAS   Statistical Account of Scotland (often referred to as the Old or the
       First) by Sir John Sinclair, 21 vols. (Edinburgh: William Creech,
       1791–1799)

WHITE PEOPLE, INDIANS,
AND HIGHLANDERS

Introduction

They were routinely described as wild, savage, barbarous, primitive, lawless, warlike, treacherous, vengeful, lazy, dirty, poor, superstitious, and always in need of instruction and improvement. They were the tribal peoples who inhabited the northern frontiers of Great Britain and the western frontiers of North America. They had more in common than the derogatory terms applied to them.

A Collection of Voyages and Travels published in London in 1745, the year of the last Jacobite rising, contained a frontispiece captioned "Description of the Habits of Most Countries in the World." It depicted the dress of Chinese, Moguls, Persians, Turks, Tartars, Poles, Muscovites, Laplanders, Hungarians, Dutch, Spaniards, Hottentots, Negroes, Moors, and Mexicans. Scottish Highlanders, rather overdressed, shared the bottom of the page with Indians from Virginia and Florida.[1] Some authors identify "a mutual respect and deep affinity" between Highlanders and Indians "based on parallel warrior traditions, a clan-based social structure, and above all a profound independence of spirit."[2] Although this is overstated, there was something to it. According to an account from "a gentleman lately arrived" from New York, published in the *Scots Magazine* and repeated elsewhere, when the Black Watch Regiment arrived in America at the start of the Seven Years' War, Indians reputedly "flocked from all quarters" to see them, "and from a surprising resemblance in the manner of their dress, and the great similitude of their language, the Indians concluded they were anciently one and the same people, and most

3

Frontispiece from *A Collection of Voyages and Travels . . . from the curious and valuable Library of the late Earl of Oxford*, 2 vols. (London: Thomas Osborne, 1745). (Courtesy of the Rauner Library, Dartmouth College.)

cordially received them as brethren."[3] John Campbell, Earl of Loudon and commander in chief of the British forces in North America, said the Black Watch were more likely than any other troops to get along with Indians because "the Indians have an Opinion, that they [the Black Watch] are a kind of Indians." General John Forbes referred to his Highland troops and his Cherokee allies as "cousins."[4] The Cherokee chief Oconostota, or Standing Turkey, was inducted into the Saint Andrews Club of Charles Town, South Carolina, in 1773 and thereby became an honorary Scotsman. British Indian agent Alexander Cameron lived with the Cherokees so long that he had "almost become one of themselves." Countless Scots lived in Indian country, had Indian families, and in effect became Indians.[5] Eighteenth-century Gaelic poems referred to Indians as *coilltich*, "forest folk." A poem reputed to be the first Gaelic song composed in North America said "Tha sinne 'n ar n-Innseannaich cinnteach gu leoir" [We've turned into Indians, sure enough]. (Originally "You are Indians, sure enough," the words of the song seem to have been changed in the nineteenth century as Gaels came to see parallels between their own dispossession and that of Native peoples in America.[6])

By the nineteenth century, in western Canada, eastern New York, and the mountains of Tennessee and Montana one could hear Cree, Mohawk, Cherokee, and Salish spoken with Gaelic accents. In the 1860s a visitor to Fort Pelly, a Hudson Bay Company post west of Lake Winnipegosis, heard Scottish children (whose parents dressed them in their clan tartans every Sunday) "acquiring a fluent use of Indian dialects in addition to their Scottish brogue which is so thick one could 'cut it with a knife.'"[7] Robert MacDougall, who wrote an *Emigrant's Guide to North America* in Gaelic, believed he saw many similarities between Gaels and Indians, particularly in language. The "slow, soft, pleasant speech" he heard among the Algonquians of Canada was, he thought, "merely a branch of the Gaelic language," and he found words with similar sounds and meanings: the Algonquian word *saganash* (white man) and the Gaelic term *Sassanach* (Englishman), for instance.[8] Some observers even commented that Indians had a fondness for the bagpipes.[9]

American historians who simply identify Highland Scots as British, or even, in some cases, English, miss significant cultural distinctions and historical experiences. In their relationships to the land and to one another, Highland Scots often had more in common with the Indians than with the English. Both were known for their attachment to their homeland, and they expressed it in similar ways. "I grow out of this ground," said a man from Skye in the 1770s.[10] "Our Ancestors came out of this very Ground, and their Children have remained here ever since," Canasatego (speaking for the Iroquois) told colonial delegates in 1744.[11] The Highlanders' affections were "more deeply rooted in the soil . . . than any other people except mountaineers equally free," noted a report on emigration in 1803.[12] Highlanders and Indians alike inhabited storied landscapes and shared communal land-holding practices. Even in the twentieth century, some Highlanders retained an attachment to the land that was spiritual and emotional, as well as economic. They "read" the landscape with an understanding born of intimacy across generations and preserved Gaelic place names imbued with mythical, factual, historical, and personal meanings:

> They tell of personal experiences and of community events and activities, both in the past and in the present, and have a richness of meaning that goes far beyond the concern with simple reference to a spatial location or to a single event. In this way, place names bind the landscape with human imagination and experience and inform us about a multiplicity of close associations which thereby blend the human and natural worlds into one.[13]

The passage describes the purpose and persistence of Gaelic place names in the Highlands and islands, but it reads like an extract from Keith Basso's *Wisdom Sits in Places*, which demonstrates how the rich vocabulary of Western Apache place names provides a multilayered link between language and landscape, or from Okanagan novelist, poet, and ecological activist Jeanette Armstrong. For Western Apaches, writes Basso, the past "lies embedded in features of the earth—in canyons and lakes, mountains and arroyos, rocks and vacant fields—which together endow their lands with multiple forms of significance that reach into their lives and shape the way they think." Armstrong's father told her "that it was the land that changed the language because there is special knowledge in each different place. All my elders say that it is land that holds all knowledge of life and death and is a constant teacher. It is said in Okanagan that the land constantly speaks."[14]

Like Highlanders, Indian people inhabited landscapes that were etched with the experiences of generations, held memories of the past, and were alive with the spirits of their ancestors. They read the landscape like a historical text.[15] Mythic tales linked to specific places contained teachings that enabled people to live as true human beings.[16] The lands held stories about the interdependence of people, animals, and the natural world.[17] Tied to place by clan and family memories, stories connected the people to an ancient world whose lessons they must not forget and to the natural world, where they maintained proper relations with other forms of life. Lakota scholar Craig Howe's explanation of how land and identity related to the concept of peoplehood works for Highland Scots, as well as for American Indians: It was "a relationship between a distinct community and their remembered landscape, a relationship often encoded in stories about particular past events that their ancestors experienced."[18] As Rory Stewart was reminded while walking across war-torn Afghanistan in 2002, "places in the Scottish Highlands are also remembered by acts of violence."[19]

American Indians and Highland Scots recorded their histories in song and story and shared their worlds with spirits. Tales told around winter fires explained why things were the way they were, provided moral lessons, and warned of the perils of violating long-established taboos and rituals. Witches could transform themselves into animal shapes, animals could communicate with humans, and certain animals must not be harmed. Birds were messengers of things to come. Omens were to be heeded; nature's powers could be harnessed and propitiated by rituals. Place names recalled mythic encounters with supernatural beings,[20] although civilized folk purported not to believe in such "primitive superstitions."

Landholding practices were not identical, of course. Before the system disintegrated in the eighteenth century, Highland clan chiefs mortgaged or leased the land. Mortgaged lands were known as *wadsets,* and leased lands were called *tacks.* Wadsetters and tacksmen in turn rented the lands they mortgaged or leased to subtenants. The importance of the link between tenant and land in the Highlands was reflected in the Gaelic concept *duthchas,* which expressed the belief that clanspeople had a permanent stake in the clan's homeland.[21] Kinship and clan obligations ensured shared access to cultivable lands and pasture. Under the traditional system of *runrig* farming, Highlanders lived in clustered settlements *(clachans),* held arable lands in common, and reallocated parcels of land. Tenant farmers kept herds of black cattle and other livestock that they drove each spring to the shielings, which were summer pastures in the uplands. The clan chief and tacksmen oversaw the working of the system, levying tribute, displaying generosity and hospitality, and organizing raids and defense. In the eighteenth and nineteenth centuries "improvers" saw the system as an obstacle to progress. As the clan system disintegrated, runrig farming died out, cash rent replaced clan and kinship obligations, and commercial sheep farming drove people to small, individual crofts on marginal lands.[22]

Highland and Indian societies revolved around clan and kinship, although the terms had some different meanings and things worked in dissimilar ways. The Gaelic term *clann* meant children or family and implied a kinship group that claimed descent from a common ancestor. Blood ties between a clan chief and his people might be mythical rather than actual, but the assumption of kinship represented an emotional bond. Kinship bound people together in Native American societies, but there too it often had more to with social relations than with biological connections, governing conduct between individuals and distribution of resources.[23]

Some Native societies, like the Plains Ojibwas, whom Highland settlers met at Red River in Manitoba, were patrilineal, like the Highlanders themselves.[24] However, many of the Indian nations with whom Highlanders interacted traced kinship through women. The clan was the basic unit of Cherokee society. All Cherokees belonged to one of seven matrilineal clans, and all clan members supposedly descended from a common ancestor. Clan membership gave an individual a place in society, and clan ties bound autonomous Cherokee towns together as one nation and one people. Kinship relationships determined both personal and social relations, and clan members were obligated to care for, protect, and if necessary avenge the deaths of clan relatives.[25]

Clans have a deep history in the Highlands, but the clans most prominent in Scottish history—the Campbells, MacDonalds, Frasers, Camerons, and others—emerged from the Middle Ages, when Norman lords moved north and established feudal patterns of landholding that fused with Gaelic tribal traditions to produce a feudal tribalism. Originally based on kinship, clans came to revolve around land distribution and defense. A Highland clan was a group of extended patrilineal families held together by the paternalism and patronage of the *fine* (the elite, the clan chief, and gentry).[26] Duncan Forbes of Culloden described a Highland clan in the mid-eighteenth century as:

a set of men all bearing the same sirname [*sic*], and believing themselves to be related the one to the other, and to be descended from the
same common Stock. In each Clan, there are several subaltern tribes,
who own their dependence on their own immediate Chief; but all agree
in owing allegiance to the Supreme Chief of the Clan or Kindred, and
look upon it to be their duty to support him at all adventures.

Smaller clans sometimes put themselves under the protection of a larger clan.
In the thirteenth century, for instance, the chief of Clan McGillivray put his
people under the protection of Clan Mackintosh. Others followed suit—
MacPhersons, McQueens, McBeans, MacPhails, Frasers, and Shaws—thus
forming the powerful Clan Chattan with the Mackintoshes at the head.
Outsiders could be incorporated into the clan. Sir Walter Scott observed that
"in ancient times, the Highlanders, like the Indians, added prisoners of war
into their tribes," carrying off children whose parents they had killed.[27]

Tribal chiefs on both sides of the Atlantic were expected to act for the
good of their people. Traditionally, they reinforced the allegiance of their followers by giving away rather than accumulating wealth. Thomas Douglas,
Earl of Selkirk, explained it as a function of the precarious nature of property
in a tribal world: Those who acquired it by the sword one day were just as
likely to lose it the next. "Thus among the antient Highlanders, the same
men who made a glory of pillage and rapine, carried the sentiments of hospitality and generosity to a romantic excess," he wrote.[28] "Surplus went to feast,
or gift, or to aid those in trouble," wrote one scholar. She was describing the
communal clan system in the Highlands but could equally well have been
describing common Native American practice.[29] From the liberality with
which Comanches disposed of a chief's effects when he died, said Indian
agent Robert Neighbors, "it would induce the belief that they acquire property merely for the purpose of giving it to others." Chiefs who acquired possessions gained no prestige in Lakota society; in fact, mere possession of
property "could be viewed as disgraceful." Prestige—and followers—came
from giving and sharing whatever one had.[30]

Highlanders retained their faith in their clan chiefs' paternal benevolence
even as those chiefs increasingly put their own interests first. As anthropologist Eric Wolf explained, in such societies chiefs could exploit kinship mech-
anisms and kin-ordered modes of production to increase their power. By
restricting access to resources, controlling social labor, and exacting tribute,
they produced "an aristocracy that utilizes and exhibits kin-ordered ties as a
mark of its distinctiveness and separateness, leaving to the commoner stra-
tum only residual claims. The aristocratic class thus constitutes itself by radi-

cally altering the bonds of kinship in order to promote social distance between rulers and ruled."[31]

Native American societies lacked the feudal aspects of Highland clans. Except in precontact Mississippian chiefdoms and some Northwest Coast societies, leaders rarely possessed the power, paraphernalia, or economic leverage of Highland clan chiefs. Typically, chiefs led by building consensus rather than issuing commands and lacked the means to enforce their will. Scotsman Thomas Nairne, South Carolina's Indian agent in Creek country in the eighteenth century, found "Nothing more contemptible than the authority of these Chiefs, They seldom use any Coercion, only harangue, if by that they can persuade it's well, if not they rarely inforce their orders by sanctions." Each town was "a sort of petty republick," he said. The Shawnees, similarly, were described as "strangers to civil power and authority." They believed that God made them free and "that one man has no natural right to rule over another." Chiefs sometimes had a hereditary claim to leadership but generally people followed them because of their charisma and reputation and because they personified the virtues their society valued—courage, generosity, and concern for the community. "The subjects under discussion in council are at all times open to popular opinion, and the chiefs are the main exponents of it. The democratic principle is strongly implanted in them," Robert Neighbors said of the Comanches. "Each chief is ranked according to his popularity, and his rank is maintained on the same principle."[32] As pressure from outside forces generated changes in leadership in Indian country, as well as in the Highlands, romantic writers likened Highland chiefs to Indian chiefs: Both imbued their speech with metaphorical language, and both represented a nobler past that was disappearing.[33]

Despite differences between clan and tribe, many contemporary observers saw Highland and Indian ways of life as fundamentally similar. They lived in tribal societies with a strong warrior tradition, they inhabited rugged homelands, and they were accustomed to deprivation and inured to hardship.[34] Some people found much to admire in their social bonds. Anne (née MacVicar) Grant lived near Indians when she was growing up and among Highlanders as an adult. As a girl, she spent ten years in America when her father was stationed there with the army. Although she and her mother lived mainly in Albany, they sometimes made their home at Fort Oswego and other more distant locations. When Mohawk families visited the settlements, Anne "delighted to hover about the wigwam," talking with the Indian children, "and we frequently mingled languages." She always remembered the Indians "with kindness." After she returned to Scotland in 1768, she married a Highland minister and learned to speak and read Gaelic. "I insist," she wrote to a friend, "the ties of blood bind stronger, and the duties of relation-ship are better understood, in the Highlands, than anywhere else."[35] Just as Indian people thought (and think) of themselves in relation to their ancestors and to generations yet unborn, so "no Highlander ever once thought of him-self as an individual," wrote Grant. "He considered himself merely with refer-ence to those who had gone before, and those who were to come after him."[36]

* * *

Yet what Highlanders and Indians had in common had less to do with dress, language, and social structure than with their historical experiences as tribal peoples living on the edges of an empire and confronting historical currents at work on both sides of the Atlantic. Although they lived in the centers of their own worlds and often expressed disdain for those who sought to change them, both peoples were treated as tribes in the original sense of the Latin term *tribus:* "barbarians at the borders of the empire."[37] Sir Arthur Chichester, lord deputy of Ireland in the early seventeenth century, described the Gaels of the Scottish Highlands and islands as "proud, obstinate, and disobedient . . . barbarous, irreligious, and headstrong people."[38] Seventeenth-century New Englanders described Indians in identical terms. The Pequots, said Captain John Underhill, were an "insolent and barbarous nation."[39]

In some ways, of course, the histories of Highland Scots and American Indians are so different as to render comparisons superficial. Highland Scots, though belonging to separate clans, constituted a single ethnic group that shared a common culture and language and inhabited a relatively small coun-try. American Indian societies were separated by vast distances and by tre-mendous cultural and linguistic diversity. The bloody chronicles of clan, dynastic, religious, and national struggles, and the wrenching social and eco-nomic changes that constitute Scotland's past, as well as the massive depopu-lation, military subjugation, dispossession, and cultural genocide that characterize much of the Native American past defy easy interpretation as parallel histories. Nevertheless, for Highlanders and American Indians alike, identity was forged not only by land and culture but also by colonial experi-ences and cultural imperialism.

In North Britain and North America, colonial powers and capitalist forces subordinated tribal societies and incorporated tribal resources into new eco-nomic systems. The rise of the nation-state entailed the destruction of kin-based systems of social and political organization.[40] As colonial expansion transformed tribal homelands into contested borderlands, the centers of tribal worlds become someone else's periphery. Whether as place or process, the frontier has exerted an enduring influence on American history, historiography, and mythology. The frontier—a borderland shared with a richer, larger, and sometimes aggressive power to the south—also played a major role in Scottish history.[41] Developments on the northern frontier of Britain affected the western frontiers of America. America's borders attracted displaced peoples from the north of Britain, while resources extracted from American lands fueled developments in Scotland and England.

On both sides of the Atlantic, tribal peoples scrambled to adjust to new colonial relationships, structures, and economic orders. Unfamiliar market forces broke old communal bonds and disrupted established ways of life. Kin-ordered modes of production in which labor was owed gave place to capitalist systems, where wealth controlled labor, means of production, and distribution.[42] Communal landholding practices gave way to commercial management of property. Industrialization and commercialization of agriculture demanded the appropriation and exploitation of land, the main basis of wealth in preindustrial society and the core of tribal life. Reorganizing land required relocating populations. The process accelerated in Britain in the eighteenth century, spread to North America and the rest of Europe in the nineteenth century, and continues to shape economic development in the Third World today.[43]

In the late eighteenth and nineteenth centuries, clan chiefs in the Highlands of Scotland turned their estates over to commercial sheep farming. In what became known as the Highland clearances, people who had lived in the glens from time immemorial were relocated to crofts on the seacoasts, to factory towns in the Lowlands, or to emigrant ships bound for America. Sheep were brought in from the south to graze the lands these people vacated, while mutton and wool from the new Highland flocks were shipped south to industrial England. Indians in the North American fur trade wore woolen blankets made by children in Yorkshire textile mills from the wool of sheep grazing on the lands of displaced Highlanders, some of whom made careers in the North American fur trade. Lowland Scots who invested in sheep farming in the Highlands and later in cattle ranching on the Great Plains helped eradicate tribal pastoralism on communal land on both sides of the Atlantic. Sheep replaced cattle in the Highlands of Scotland, cattle replaced buffalo on the Great Plains.

As Highlanders and Indians endured assaults on their land, resources, and cultures and experienced massive economic and social change, colonial divide-and-rule strategies and competing tribal interests undermined tribal struggles for independence. Colonizing powers tried to replace traditional loyalties to clan and tribe with loyalty to the nation. Some chiefs cozied up to colonial authorities to bolster their own positions, and some readily embraced new commercial values and economic orders. In Scotland, as in North America, "a united people was able to conquer a disunited one."[44]

Given the workings of colonialism, it would be unusual if parallel experiences did *not* emerge. Imperial powers produced similar conditions and responses among very different peoples in various parts of the world.[45] In the eighteenth century, for example, Scotland and the American colonies occupied similar positions and endured comparable peripheral experiences as "cultural provinces" of the English core.[46]

In the depressing film *Trainspotting*, based on Irvine Welsh's novel about heroin addicts in Edinburgh, one of the characters laments (between expletives) that not only was Scotland colonized, but (even worse) it was colonized by the English, a nation of "wankers." Such sentiments may strike Native peoples of North America as odd. Indigenous peoples from America to Australia have encountered Scots as instruments, not victims, of British colonization. Some writers dismiss as fiction or sheer nonsense the notion that Scots were colonized, and Scotland's experience in dealing with England pales in comparison with that of other colonized peoples. Scotland was not conquered, occupied, and controlled in the way that other colonies were; events in Scotland were different even from those in Ireland, and Britain did not establish settler colonies in the Highlands of Scotland as it did in North America, Australia, or parts of Africa. Lowland Scots, the Scottish ruling classes, and Scottish capital played a greater role than English colonists in transforming the Highlands. Many of the changes that affected the Highlands in the eighteenth and nineteenth centuries would have happened anyway, as the old order succumbed to population growth it could not accommodate and new economic forces it could not resist.

Finding opportunities rather than oppression in the British Empire, many Scots became avid colonizers themselves. Moreover, not all Scottish emigrants were Highlanders or poor farmers. Scottish merchants formed commercial cliques and dominated the Indian trade in the southeastern United States and Canada. Scottish educators were prominent in colonial society; Scottish and Scottish-trained ministers dominated the Episcopalian and Presbyterian churches, and more than 150 Scottish doctors migrated to America in the eighteenth century: "Almost the whole of the colonial medical profession was Scottish emigré or Scottish trained."[47] Highland soldiers fought for new territories, and Highland settlers then occupied them. Scotland itself became an imperial nation within the British state.[48]

Likewise, most Americans prefer to think of empire as an entity from which they won independence, not something they themselves constructed in their own country.⁴⁹ America's empire was very different from the British Empire, just as British colonialism in Scotland was unlike that in India. Nevertheless, the Highlands' relationship with both England and the Lowlands had a clear colonial dimension, and the expanding American nation built an empire on Indian lands and colonized Indian people.

Imperialism and colonialism are ill-defined terms. Linda Tuhiwai Smith sees them as interconnected, with colonialism as "but one expression of imperialism." Colonialism was "the fort and the port of imperial outreach," and colonial outposts also served as cultural sites that represented an image of what "civilization" stood for.⁵⁰ Edward Said wrote that imperialism exists "in a kind of general cultural sphere as well as in specific political, ideological, economic, and social practices."⁵¹ Kahnawake Mohawk political theorist Taiaiake Alfred says colonialism is not just a historical era, a theory or a political and economic relationship. "It is a total existence, a way of thinking about oneself and others always in terms of domination and submission that has come to form the very foundation of our individual and collective lives."⁵²

The impact of colonial power on the lives of Native Americans has been pervasive, pernicious, and persistent, not to mention more severe, more devastating, and more enduring than that experienced by Highland Scots. Nevertheless, colonialism offers a useful comparative framework in which to view both peoples' histories. Colonialism is not a one-size-fits-all concept; "nor," as a scholar of northwestern Mexico's colonial frontiers explains, "does it elicit the same meanings in different geographic regions and time periods." Yet insofar as it implies political domination over territories and people, economic control and exploitation of labor and resources, displacement of populations, and the imposition of alien values, beliefs, and structures, as well as cultural dislocation and diverse responses on the part of colonized peoples, colonialism applies to the Highlands, as well as to Indian country.⁵³

A whole nation need not be colonized for colonialism to exist. To say that Highland Scots and American Indians experienced colonialism is not to say that they faced the same colonialism or were subjected to it in all the same ways. Both groups encountered their own brand of internal colonialism: Each one was subjected to political, economic, and cultural integration by the dominant core and suffered marginalization, dislocation, exploitation, and dependency.⁵⁴ Colonization worked along class and regional, as well as racial, lines. Highland Scots fared differently from Lowland Scots, and Highland peasants differently from Highland landlords. Like the children who worked twelve to fourteen hours a day in British textile mills producing inexpensive cloth, the Indians who bought the products of this child labor by overhunting were simultaneously participants in and victims of a colonial system that affected lives on both continents.

Colonial relationships did not always break down neatly into exploiter and exploited. As mercantile and capitalist forces incorporated people and redeployed their bodies and their labor, roles and even identities shifted. "The binary of colonizer/colonized does not take into account, for example, the development of different layerings within each group and across the two groups," notes Linda Tuhiwai Smith. The demands and pressures of colonialism moved people from one area of the empire to another as if they were commodities. "Hence there are large populations in some places of non-indigenous groups, also victims of colonization, whose primary relationship and allegiance is often to the imperial power rather than to the colonized people of the place to which they themselves have been brought."[55]

Tribal peoples developed strategies to deal with colonialism, to maximize their independence in an increasingly dependent relationship, and to manipulate colonial relationships to their own advantage. Sometimes they made a new place for themselves within an empire or between empires, and sometimes they restricted, frustrated, and reshaped imperial projects. Occasionally they responded to the violence and chaos unleashed by colonialism by projecting violence and chaos onto weaker neighbors. The Iroquois in the Northeast, the Osages on the prairies, and the Comanches and Lakotas on the Great Plains demonstrated that Indian peoples were capable of exploiting the conditions created by colonial contacts and competitions to establish "empires" of their own. These Native powers did not set up the structures and edifices associated with Roman or British models of empire, but they built and maintained hegemony, expanded their territorial control, exploited peoples and resources, utilized violence, dominated trade, waged economic warfare, and often incorporated other groups as subordinates in their patterns of power and diplomacy.[56]

Conquest and colonialism entailed more than defeating people, occupying their land, and exploiting their resources. It also involved constructing representations of the colonized peoples and separating them from their languages, their social relations, their ways of understanding the world, and their histories. Colonialism consumed other histories and submerged them in the narratives of the nation-state and colonial education served as an instrument to incorporate "problem peoples" into the state.[57] For a long time, British histories that included Scotland tended to end their coverage with the defeat of Prince Charles Edward Stuart and the Jacobites at Culloden in 1746, as American histories ended their coverage of Indians in New England with the defeat of King Philip in 1676 or, nationally, with the massacre at Wounded Knee in 1890. Scots and Indians mattered only so long as they resisted the growth of the nation. American Indians and Highland Scots preserved their histories in their oral traditions, but in Britain and America tribal histories were ignored, or told from someone else's perspective and written in someone else's language.[58] Today, adult Scots and Native Americans recall learning little or nothing about Scottish or Indian history in the British and American history classes they took at school. Their histories were usually placed on the margins of a larger national narrative rather than at the center of their own story. "Not only was our history largely suppressed but those parts of it which were acknowledged were often taught in such a way that they seemed to appear suddenly out of nowhere. A sense of continuity was difficult to grasp." The writer was Scottish novelist William McIlvanney, citing Mary, Queen of Scots, and Bonnie Prince Charlie as examples of what he calls "the pop-up picture school of history." Pocahontas and Sitting Bull exemplify the same pop-up phenomenon in American history.[59] Prior to the Jacobite rebellion of 1745, wrote Sir Walter Scott, few people in England knew anything about the Highlanders or their history. Most people considered them "complete barbarians" and "cared no more about them than the merchants of New York about the Indians who dwell beyond the Allegheny mountains."[60] Scholars who attempt to reconstruct a fuller picture of the past—in Indian America and in Scotland—therefore have had to wrestle with the challenges of recovering the stories of the voiceless as they attempt to write history "from the bottom up." They also have to try to untangle webs of myth and history woven by colonizers and colonized alike.

* * *

This book looks at Indian country as a whole but only at the Highlands of Scotland. Nevertheless, Lowland Scots crop up repeatedly in the story and appear as colonizers on both sides of the Atlantic. The Highlands and western islands (the Hebrides) of Scotland form a cultural as well as a geographic region. The rugged Highlands are separated from the rest of Britain by the "Highland line," the boundary fault that runs from the mouth of the Clyde on the west coast, through Perthshire and Angus northeastward to the North Sea. The line was cultural and linguistic, as well as geographic, marking the *Gàidhealtachd,* the Gaelic-speaking area beyond it. It ran through my mother's hometown, Crieff, which stands at the edge of the Highlands and was burned during the 1715 Jacobite rising. Crieff's minister in the late eighteenth century described his parish as divided into Highland and Lowland parts, with Gaelic spoken in the former, Scottish-dialect English in the latter. It was the site of a great cattle fair, where drovers from the Highlands brought their black cattle for sale and export to the Lowlands and England.[61]

The Highland-Lowland divide was not such a racial gulf as Sir Walter Scott and others portrayed it, but the differences ran deep.[62] In the four-teenth century Scots chronicler John of Fordun described Scotland as a country of two halves. The Lowlands were inhabited by law-abiding, peace-ful, and industrious citizens. "The highlanders and people of the islands, on the other hand, are a savage and untamed nation, rude and independent, given to rapine, ease-loving, of a docile and warm disposition, comely in per-son but unsightly in dress, hostile to the English people and language and owing to diversity of speech, even to their own nation, and exceedingly cruel."[63] According to sixteenth-century chronicler John Major, foreigners called Lowlanders "householding Scots" and Highlanders "Wild Scots."[64]

The distinction held in the eighteenth century: The Lowlands were regarded as relatively civilized; the Highlands were regarded, by Englishmen, Lowland Scots, and foreign travelers, as a separate country, a land of savagery in need of civilization.[65] The "fiery and ferocious" Highlanders seemed "a very distinct species" from their "cool and circumspect" Lowland neighbors.[66] General George Wade—an Irishman—said Highlanders held Lowlanders "in the utmost Contempt, imagining them inferior to themselves in Courage, Resolution, and the Use of Arms, and accuse them of being Proud, Avaricious, and Breakers of their Word." Highland clans that agreed on little else shared a common contempt for Lowlanders, he said.[67] Moreover, Dr. Samuel Johnson said Lowlanders and Highlanders maintained a mutual dislike, and each regarded the other's way of life with contempt. The Highland Scots he met who spoke English spoke it well because they had learned it from the English, not from Lowland Scots, by whom they refused to be taught, "for they have long considered them as a mean and degenerate race."[68] Visitors from the continent noted the distinction: A merchant from Lisbon said Highlanders "call themselves the ancient *Scots,*" while Lowlanders were a mix-ture of ancient Scots, Picts, Danes, English, French, and others; an eighteen-year-old French aristocrat who spent five weeks in Scotland in 1786 said the Highlanders "are a people apart, and act as though they are entirely different from the rest of the Scots."[69]

This book focuses on the Highland strain of the huge Celtic movement to North America, but other people from Britain's Celtic borderlands created new Celtic settlements on North American frontiers. Protestant Scots-Irish migrated to these regions in great numbers, cut repeated swaths through Indian country, and earned an enduring reputation as shock troops of colonialism. Like other people moving to America from Britain's border areas, they carried with them a frontier heritage of their own.[70]

*　*　*

Scots held no monopoly on mixing and mingling with Indians. By the eighteenth century, large stretches of Indian country had become crossroads of exchange and culture, where members of different Indian and European nations interacted regularly. In the babel of languages that resulted, Gaelic was just one of many tongues. In Creek country, U.S. Indian agent Benjamin Hawkins told Thomas Jefferson, "I hear the language of Scotch, French, Spanish, English, Africans, Creeks, and Uchees."[71]

In such contexts, claims for a special affinity between a particular nation and Native Americans usually do not stand up to close scrutiny. Within each national group, individuals' characters, experiences, and attitudes affected relations with outsiders, as did the circumstances in which they met. The French earned a reputation for cultivating good relations with Indian peoples, but they did so largely because they had to. In the early seventeenth century Samuel de Champlain set the French on a course of intercultural cooperation as they built an empire on the fur trade; in the eighteenth century, outnumbered by English rivals, France depended on a network of Indian alliances.[72] Individual Frenchmen lived with Indian people, and French-Indian communities grew up in many places. However, when Indians frustrated French colonial designs, Frenchmen slaughtered Mesquakies (Foxes), Natchez, and Choctaws as readily as Englishmen slaughtered Pequots or Americans gunned down Cheyennes and Sioux. Many Germans have long demonstrated a romantic fascination with Native American cultures and portrayed themselves as "the Indians of Europe," but few Indian people reciprocate the fascination. Indeed, Germans looking to expand eastward depicted the Poles and other Slavs as the Indians of Europe: Savage, "history-less" people, they were doomed to ruin and should give up their lands to the march of progress. In the German East, the Nazis emulated the conquest and colonization of the American West. They dispossessed and destroyed indigenous people and proclaimed it a civilizing mission. "There is only one task," Hitler declared: "To set about the Germanization of the land by bringing in Germans and to regard the indigenous inhabitants as Indians."[73]

Highland Scots and American Indians met within larger contexts of cultural collision and colonial encounter that governed their interactions. Having been colonized and "civilized" themselves, Highland Scots sometimes identified and sympathized with Indian people they saw going through the kind of hard experiences they or their parents had suffered, but Highland traders, soldiers, and settlers often displayed the same prejudices, sentiments, and behavior as other European traders, soldiers and settlers when dealing with Indians, and Scots sometimes took on the role of colonizing and civilizing Indians with zeal. Highland governors, soldiers, and traders were probably just as likely as their English or American counterparts to exploit, shoot, and cheat Indians, and Highland settlers proved as eager as anyone else to occupy Indian land. Indians in turn knew that Scots came to their country as part of a colonial endeavor that always subordinated and sometimes sacrificed Indian interests to British benefit.[74] The notion that peoples were less prone to abuse or kill each other because they shared similar tribal structures does not stand up to historical scrutiny anywhere in the world.

Nevertheless, the British were not a homogenous group. Highland Scots and Englishmen had different ideas about what it meant to be British, had dissimilar experiences of colonial power, and did not necessarily share a common vision of empire. Many Scots "went native," that is, they lived in Indian communities and identified with their adopted people. Arthur Herman contends that the Scottish Enlightenment's insistence that people of different places and periods shared a common humanity, a universal human nature shaped by environment and development, rendered them "largely immune to racial theories of White supremacy" (though not of cultural supremacy). This was not a phenomenon unique to North America. "In one colonial setting after another, Scots proved themselves far better able to get along with people of another culture and color than their English counterparts."[75] In India, according to Simon Schama, Scots were "the most phenomenally knowledgeable and culturally tolerant" of the British imperial administrators." They took to India the lessons of the Scottish Enlightenment, an appreciation of the need to understand the people and culture they were dealing with, and a determination not to repeat in Asia the mistakes England had made in Scotland.[76] Michael Fry, no misty-eyed romantic when it comes to the Scots' role in imperialism, also notes the legendary adaptability of Scots in other cultures:

> While in the pages of Rudyard Kipling or John Buchan we can read legends of Scotsmen who turned themselves into Asian khans or gods on Pacific Islands, in real life there was nothing more striking than this affinity of the Scots and Native Americans. The parallels in their martial values, oral culture and social structure do not perhaps fully account for it. Somehow, the generosity and freedom in both peoples made a mutual appeal to them across the racial barrier (which they, of course, did not acknowledge).[77]

John Buchan, expatriate Scot, governor of Canada, and novelist (who on occasion had himself photographed wearing a Plains Indian headdress and clothing) had one of his fictional characters declare that "the truth is we are the only race on earth that can produce men capable of getting inside the skins of remote people. Perhaps the Scots are better than the English, but we're all a thousand per cent better than anybody else."[78]

Highland Scots were not unique in the range and nature of their interactions with Indian peoples but, in the vast colonial encounter that is American history, Highlanders and Indians came together in unusually large numbers and across huge stretches of the continent. They brought to their encounters their own stories, mythologies, memories, and experiences, and they developed intricate and sometimes intimate relations. They fought in colonial conflicts, clashed over lands, and met and married in the fur trade. They wove tangled webs of family and allegiance, and their offspring often forged roles for themselves as mediators and culture brokers.

They also built new societies together. Highlanders met Indians on the peripheries of empire, and where they lived and slept side by side, they created fluid communities held together by shared experiences and interests, children, and ties of kinship rather than allegiance to the state. For a time, Michael Fry suggests, Highlanders and Indians offered "an alternative model of American development." As occurred in South America, an incoming group integrated with the indigenous people and achieved "a mestizo culture . . . a fresh amalgam contain[ing] something of both." But it was a road not taken. In Britain, eighteenth-century ideas that culture and environment explained human difference and determined human potential give way to less flexible racial explanations that placed whites and nonwhites in permanently separate categories.[79] In the United States, nation building demanded the displacement and destruction of Indian peoples to make way for white populations and white culture. "[T]he sharply drawn American frontier," says Fry, "cut across the fluid and porous Scottish idea of a frontier." In the late nineteenth century, government and settlers intended to transform the Canadian West into a modern agrarian society of white peoples, not to perpetuate the old fur trade society, where Highlanders and Indians mixed and mingled.[80] Communities and families that contained Scots and Indians—and where one could be both Scot and Indian—did not figure in the American and Canadian vision of the future. It was that vision that most Highland Scots in North America ultimately embraced as they took their place on the white side of the racial divide.

1

Cycles of Conquest and Colonization

Colonial powers took over tribal lands in Britain and America and, as they saw it, brought civilization to tribal peoples. The second effort was clearly subordinate to the first, but the dual assault produced brutal and bloody histories on both sides of the Atlantic. The Highlands of Scotland and Indian country had to be "pacified" before the Native peoples could be "civilized," and civilization justified barbarous measures of pacification. In North Britain and North America, Englishmen rooted out savagery with fire and sword. Even at nineteen, Anne MacVicar (later Grant), who had known Indians as well as Highlanders, recognized how colonial powers dehumanized tribal peoples: "It is but calling people savages," she wrote to a friend, "and then their blood is of no value, and their lives of no consequence."[1]

Colonial forces crushed tribal resistance with the assistance of tribal allies. Highlanders fought against each other and the Scottish kings as often as they battled the English; American Indians resisted Europeans and simultaneously sustained long-standing conflicts against Native enemies. Sometimes, working with rather than fighting a colonizing power offered the best chance to survive and succeed in a perilous world. Colonial powers fomented and exploited divisions between and within tribes, undermined the tribal chiefs' authority, dismantled tribal social structures, and disrupted tribal economies. Tribal peoples competed for their own advantage and tried to maintain their independence in colonial relationships predicated on dependence. Chiefs generally pursued clan and tribal interests rather than broader national or racial goals. They followed their own agendas rather than colonial plans, which prompted colonizers to describe them as fickle. Indian nations often survived by playing rival colonizers against each other and sometimes cultivated relations with more than one power simultaneously. Scots apparently had a reputation for doing something similar. At the height of Pontiac's war in August 1763, a New York merchant complained that some of Pontiac's Ottawa nation were negotiating with the British: "Like Scotch policy one half of these people disclaim the measures of the other."[2]

Patterns, practices, policies, and philosophies of conquest and colonization that developed in the British Isles were repeated in North America. Highland Scots, many of whom had experienced defeat and dispossession themselves, in turn took a heavy toll on American Indian life, land, and culture. They were "the poor foot soldiers of the empire of emigration," in the words of Eric Richards, but "they were as heavily implicated in the quasi-genocidal aspects of American and Australian empire as any other group from the British Isles."[3]

North Britain

In the summer of 1772 Thomas Pennant passed by the Roman road that ran through Inerpeffray in Perthshire.[4] As children growing up in Inerpeffray, a tiny community with a one-room school and a public library dating from 1680, my mother and her five sisters played on that road. Years later, during summer visits, my brother and I played around the earthwork remains of a fortified Roman encampment at the entry to the Sma' Glen, just outside Crieff. The road and the camp are visible reminders of one empire's attempt to conquer the north of Britain—and its failure to subdue the Highlands.

The Roman general Agricola defeated the "Caledonians" in a pitched battle in AD 83 near the Grampian Mountains. Prior to the battle, according to Tacitus (who probably invented the speech), Calgacus, leader of the Caledonians, exhorted his followers to remember that they were "the most distant dwellers upon earth, the last of the free." The Romans were "pillagers of the world," Tacitus had him say. "They create a desolation and call it peace."[5] Resistance to imperial Rome was not constant and ubiquitous—indeed, as in the eighteenth and nineteenth centuries, some inhabitants of North Britain found that an empire offered opportunities for those willing to cooperate and participate.[6] Nevertheless, the Romans were unable to establish a foothold beyond the Highland line.[7] Emperor Antoninus Pius took the title "Lord of All the World,"[8] but his global dominion stopped short of the Highlands: The Antonine Wall marking the northern extent of Rome's empire ran from the Clyde to the Forth. Centuries later, English and Scottish kings and generals tried to do what the Romans had failed to do and emulated Roman tactics in their efforts to conquer, colonize, and control the tribal peoples in the north.

It is often said that Scotland was "born fighting." Different peoples met, waged war, and merged, creating a complicated history in which writers over the centuries have tried to find the origins and identity of the Scottish nation.[9] In the centuries following Rome's withdrawal, "Scotland's native culture was attacked, appropriated, infiltrated and occasionally overwhelmed by outsiders, peoples who sailed across the eastern and western seas."[10] Around the fourth century, descendants of the Gaelic branch of the Celts (who had moved across Europe and settled in Ireland) crossed the narrow sea into the west of Scotland and established their own Gaelic culture. The Romans called them Scotti. For centuries they displaced or absorbed the Picts until Gaelic was spoken across most of Scotland. In the ninth century, Norsemen from Scandinavia raided and then settled the Shetlands, Orkneys, Sutherland, and parts of the Western Isles. The first "Scottish" king, Kenneth MacAlpine, established his dynasty and his "country," Alba, by expanding from Argyll and fighting Norse enemies, but local chiefs in the western Highlands and islands were more concerned with preserving their own independence than with whether Scotland or Norway governed.

For centuries the Scottish and the English states endeavored to absorb the Highlands and islands; Gaels resisted the threats posed to both their freedom and their way of life, although rarely with much internal unity. The Highland geography checked the advance of English-speaking people who moved into the eastern regions of Scotland and settled the fertile Lowlands. After William of Normandy seized the crown of England in 1066, he granted Scottish lands to Norman nobles. These nobles—Bruce, Comyn, Stewart, Douglas, Murray, and others—colonized their new lands, brought feudalism north, and changed the Scottish political world into one dominated by "a court-oriented Anglo-Norman-Gaelic elite."[11] Once established as "marcher lords," however, they often put their own interests and independence above loyalty to a distant king. Over time they "went native" and became Scots.

Scotland's clash with England was on some levels a clash between two expanding monarchies.[12] While the English crown was establishing supremacy over Wales and Ireland, the Scottish crown extended its reach over all of modern-day Scotland (except Orkney and Shetland, which remained Norwegian

dependencies until the fifteenth century). Alexander III defeated the
Norwegians and made the Western Isles part of the Kingdom of Scotland,
something Scottish historians have labeled "the winning of the west."[13]
However, effective royal authority in the area remained limited, and
Alexander's untimely death in 1286 produced a succession crisis. Edward I of
England, known as "the Hammer of the Scots" for his ruthless campaigns
north of the border, seized the opportunity to establish the Scottish king as
his vassal.

Descendants of Norman nobles in Scotland now fought to prevent
Edward's assertion of English authority. William Wallace (a Lowlander, not
a Highlander, despite Mel Gibson's depiction in *Braveheart)* spearheaded
resistance, and Robert Bruce led Scots to victory at Bannockburn in 1314,
although the slaughter of a Scottish army at Halidon Hill in 1333 revived the
threat of English dominance, and border conflicts continued. The wars
against England helped fuse Lowlanders into a single people who identified
with an emergent Scottish nation. Highlanders also fought in the wars, but
that did not mean they were prepared to accept the authority of a Scottish
crown. Clan chiefs in the West wanted independence from Edinburgh, as
well as from London.[14]

In the fourteenth century a branch of the MacDonalds set themselves up
as lords of the isles. They acted as an autonomous power and on occasion
even allied with the king of England to help fend off the crown of Scotland.
James IV of Scotland destroyed the power of the Clan Donald chiefs, and in
1493 the Scottish parliament declared the lordship ended, but the crown was
unable to fill the resulting power vacuum. For the next 250 years, the government, first in Edinburgh and then in London, tried to bring the Highlands
and islands within the orbit of the state and the Gaels within the orbit of
"civilization." Meanwhile, clans jostled for power and position, and new economic forces that would ultimately undermine the independence of the chiefs
penetrated the region.[15]

Although the Lowlands were perceived to be "more civilized," violence
plagued North Britain's borderland as much as the Scottish Highlands. As
historian T. C. Smout has observed, Highland life and border life were actually very similar in the sixteenth century "and for the same reasons that the
land was hilly and the king remote."[16] Tribes, clans, and families on both
sides of the border engaged in raids and blood feuds. English and Scottish
armies launched periodic cross-border invasions, one of which ended in the
slaughter of James IV and his Scottish army at Flodden in 1513. Family ven-
dettas between Elliotts, Scotts, Kerrs, Armstrongs, Grahams, Irvines,
Maxwells, and Johnstones were as bitter as those between Campbells and

MacDonalds in the Highlands, between Pequots and Mohegans in New England, or between Hatfields and McCoys in nineteenth-century Appalachia.[17]

Like intertribal conflicts in North America, internecine feuding in the Highlands and western islands involved fighting for honor and revenge, as well as raiding and jostling for power. Clans waged age-old feuds. They raided, killed, and on occasion massacred each other, and clan bards commemorated the carnage in song and story. "Lifting" cattle in the Highlands was as common as horse raiding on the Great Plains and served some similar purposes. In a region of scarce resources, rustling cattle, stealing grain, and burning fields enhanced a clan chief's ability to support and feast his followers and reduced a rival's capacity to do the same. On the edges of the Lowlands, bounties for recovering stolen livestock gave clans like the MacFarlanes and Farquarhsons additional economic opportunities, although Lowland landlords' efforts to hire Highlanders to "watch" against raiding often led to little more than a Highland protection racket (the term "blackmail" derives from this region).[18] Sixteenth-century commentators attributed these bloody feuds to the fact that wild Highlanders, like wild Indians, owed allegiance to kin, not to the state. They lay outside the body politic and had to be brought into it for their own good as well as that of society.[19]

Claiming dominion over Scotland and Ireland, Henry VIII aggressively pushed the idea of an empire within Britain. Indeed, notes historian David Armitage, "the very language of British imperial ideology"—" Great Britain," "empire," and "colony" (meaning a settlement from a parent state in a foreign country)—sprang from Anglo-Scottish relations in the late 1540s.[20] Donald Dubh, who led a rebellion to try to restore the lordship of the isles in 1545, actually made an alliance with Henry VIII against James V of Scotland.[21]

Clan chiefs had little allegiance to a Scottish nation or a common Highland cause; they acted according to personal rivalries, clan loyalties, and the ebb and flow of political fortunes. The inhabitants of the Western Isles and of Ulster shared a common culture of herding, seafaring, and warring, and western clan chiefs enjoyed closer relations with allies in Ireland than with the king in Edinburgh. Clans who supported the Scottish crown likely as not saw it as an ally against rival clans; clans who withheld support often did so because rival clans offered it. Hugh MacDonald of Skye, compiling a history of his clan in the seventeenth century, drew breath from the litany of killings, plots, and treacheries to comment: "There are few names in Scotland who have not been some time or other guilty of treason." Clan chiefs cultivated their own power bases, closely watched the royal court, as well as developments in the next glen, and kept an eye on their main chance.[22] Weakened by long and repeated periods of minority rule (for almost two hundred years every Scottish monarch came to the throne as a minor) and internecine struggles at court, the Scottish crown lacked the power to enforce its authority on the clans of the West.

* * *

The accession of James VI of Scotland as James I of England in 1603 changed things. Now, instead of constituting about one half of an independent kingdom, the Highlands became "the outlier of a composite, soon imperial monarchy." The royal court moved from Edinburgh to London, and so did the attentions of Scottish statesmen. Subduing the Gaels of Ireland and Scotland, which had formerly been separate challenges for the English and Scottish monarchs, now became a single challenge for the new "British" monarchy. With the English navy at his disposal, James formally annexed Orkney and Shetland and sent Scots to colonize Ulster, thereby driving a wedge between Gaelic Ireland and Gaelic Scotland. Transplanting hundreds of Scots from the Lowlands and the southwest Highlands to settle in Ulster removed a disruptive element from his now united kingdom and established a buffer zone against the "wild Irish." It was a step in building a "British" empire, and it was also the Scots' first experience in founding a colony beyond their own borders.[23]

James took steps to curb "the proude rebellion, defection and dissobedience of the inhabitants of the Ilis and hielandis" and to assimilate them into Lowland society. He dispatched several military expeditions and threatened to send others. The privy council summoned Highland chieftains to Edinburgh each year. Clan chiefs captured by deceit were compelled to sign the Statutes of Iona in 1609, which limited their military retinues, restricted the carrying of firearms, and suppressed the bards, who celebrated and perpetuated the Gaelic warrior culture. In addition, the statutes required every gentleman or yeoman in the Western Isles to send his oldest son (or, if he had no sons, his eldest daughter) to school in the Lowlands to learn English. Though rarely enforced, the statutes took to another level the assault on the clan chiefs' political and cultural autonomy. Many began to develop "a dual persona": Highland chiefs at home, British gentlemen when in Edinburgh.[24]

Colonizers portrayed tribal worlds as inherently violent, but colonialism brought new kinds and levels of violence. Colonizers fueled existing conflicts and employed tactics just as barbaric as those of the people they professed to be civilizing, sometimes more so. The crown issued commissions of fire and sword, which rendered progovernment clans immune from legal sanction.

Clans accustomed to raiding and feuding now faced more sustained forms of aggression.[25] King James used the Mackenzies against the MacLeods on the Isle of Lewis. He outlawed the MacGregors, notorious raiders on the Lowlands borders, in 1603, and they became targeted for systematic persecution. The earls of Argyll and Clan Campbell eagerly pursued the work of eviction. The Earl of Argyll received lands in Kintyre as reward for service against the MacGregors in 1607; four years later, the crown granted him commission of fire and sword "to lay mercie asyed, and by justice and the sword ruit out and extirpat all of that race." Campbells drove MacGregors from their ancestral homelands in Glen Orchy, Glen Lochy, and Glen Strae. The MacGregors were proscribed again after the 1689 Jacobite rising. A "murderous clan, infamous for excesses of all kinds," they were "hunted down like wild beasts; their very name suppressed by act of council; so that the remnant," noted Thomas Pennant in 1769, "now dispersed like Jews, dare not even sign it to any deed." The laws outlawing Clan MacGregor were not lifted until 1774. Sir Walter Scott made the clan famous in the early nineteenth century with his novel *Rob Roy*, whom he portrayed as "blending the wild virtues, the subtle policy, and unrestrained license of an American Indian."[26]

The English Civil War was a civil war for Scotland as well, and its effects north of the border were devastating. Many clans supported the king, Charles Stuart. Of one thousand men raised by Sir Hector Maclean of Duart, seven hundred fell with their chief at the Battle of Inverkeithing in 1650. The Macleods of Dunvegan suffered huge casualties when Oliver Cromwell defeated the Scots at Worcester, and Cromwell transported hundreds of Scots prisoners as indentured servants to Virginia and the West Indies.[27] Cromwell invaded Scotland in 1650 and 1651 and built a fort at Inverness "to preserve the peace of the country, and keep the highlands in awe, which they effectually did all his time," wrote Daniel Defoe, who toured the region in the 1720s. Fifty years later Dr. Samuel Johnson noted that Cromwell was a hated name (as it was in Ireland after the massacre at Drogheda in 1649). Like the Romans, he built forts and roads, said Johnson, and "what the Romans did to other nations, was in great degree done by Cromwell to the Scots; he civilized them by conquest, and introduced by useful violence the arts of peace." Defoe and Johnson both commented that the soldiers of the garrison at Inverness mingled with the townsfolk and "left the English accent upon their tongues." At the end of the century, people in the Inverness region were still noted for speaking perfect English, although the prevalence of English over Gaelic owed much to the town's role as a center of trade.[28]

The expulsion of Catholic James II/VII and the accession of Protestant William III of Orange to the throne in the "Glorious Revolution" of 1688 added another layer to Anglo-Scots conflicts and added urgency to the government's efforts to control the clans. The exiled king and his descendants became the focus of Jacobite (from the Latin *Jacobus* or James) efforts to restore a Stuart to the thrones of England and Scotland. William defeated James's Scottish supporters in the first Jacobite "rebellion" in 1689 and beat James himself the next year at the battle of the Boyne in Ireland. Pacifying the Highlands was now vital to national security. William and his successors extended Cromwell's policy of garrisoning the region. The fort at Inverness, which had been demolished, was rebuilt. Fort William, "the first of a new generation of forts," was constructed at the southwestern end of the Great Glen (in the heart of the Jacobite Lochaber region) to check the Camerons, a clan "greatly addicted to plunder, and strongly inclined to rebellion."[29] Extending English rule meant curbing the power of the clan chiefs, imposing law and order in a lawless region, and rooting out recalcitrant tribes.

Clan Campbell and the earls of Argyll stood ready to assist. Attaching their fortunes to the English government, they destroyed their rivals. "My family had always taken the side of the Crown in its contests to secure a central and national government," wrote George Douglas Campbell, eighth Duke of Argyll in the nineteenth century. "The natural and legitimate reward was grants of the lands of the rebellious and defeated chiefs."[30] In this way they "laid claim to the headship of the Gael, once held by Clan Donald."[31]

Although Campbells and MacDonalds fought on the same side at Bannockburn in 1314, their bitter rivalry continued for 450 years. Most histories of Scotland "focus on the concept of nation and wade into emotional quicksands as it ebbs and flows," but for the most part, notes Oliver Thomson in his study of this feud, the Campbells and the MacDonalds fought for their own interests and "regarded the idea of Scotland as an irrelevance."[32] After they backed Robert Bruce, the earls of Argyll grew in power and influence. Clan Donald also supported Bruce but began losing power in the fifteenth century. The MacLeans and the MacLeods, once vassals of Clan Donald, asserted their independence as distinct clans. Clan Donald itself fragmented as Glencoe MacDonalds and Glengarry MacDonalds, and others followed their own chiefs and went their separate ways. Meanwhile, the Scottish crown relied on the Campbells to quell the disorders that occurred during recurrent periods of minority rule, and the earls of Argyll arranged strategic marriage alliances and exploited feuds between and within rival clans. For example, the MacDonalds of Dunyvaeg and the Glens defeated the MacLeans of Duart in 1598. The MacLeans were then forced to accept the Earl of Argyll as their feudal superior, and in the 1670s the earl dispossessed them of their lands in Mull, Morvern, and Tiree in what James Hunter characterizes as "an all-out war of conquest." Internal quarrels divided the MacDonalds, and the Campbells of Cawdor took over Islay, once the heartland of Clan Donald. The earls of Argyll took possession of Kintyre and Jura and settled the lands with Lowland Presbyterians. The Catholic MacDonalds backed the Stuart dynasty partly to check the power of the earls of Argyll, as well as "the rampant imperialism of Clan Campbell."[33]

The Campbell-MacDonald rivalry played out in tragedy and treachery at Glencoe in 1692. When Alastair MacIain MacDonald, chief of the Glencoe MacDonalds, failed to meet the January 1 deadline for taking an oath of loyalty to King William III, the authorities seized on the opportunity to make an example of his clan. "I am glad Glencoe did not come on the time prescribed," wrote John Dalrymple, the Earl of Stair and secretary of state for Scotland; "it were of great advantage to the nation that thieving tribe were rooted out and cut off. It must be quietly done." Orders filtered down to Captain Robert Campbell of Glenlyon of the Argyll Regiment to "put all to the sword under seventy." Campbell had been sent to Glencoe with 150 men ten days earlier and had enjoyed MacDonald hospitality, but he carried out his orders. Thirty-eight MacDonalds were killed, and more died of exposure in the snow. Three hundred escaped. Compared with other Scottish bloodlettings, the death toll was relatively small, but Glencoe became infamous as an act of "murder under trust." Paul Hopkins observes: "The Massacre, carried out by one group of Scottish highlanders upon another, upon orders given by a Scottish Secretary and countersigned by a Dutch king, is something for which, naturally, no true Scot will ever forgive the English."[34]

* * *

The Treaty of Union with England in 1707, by which the Scottish parliament merged with the English parliament at Westminster, has been a source of controversy for three hundred years. Tainted with allegations—and evidence—of bribery and corruption, it benefited Scotland's political classes and brought Lowland merchants and ports into the empire and the burgeoning commerce of the Atlantic world. Scotland was now governed from Westminster. Many Scots, then and since, felt they were "bought and sold for English gold."[35] The Highlands and islands were now obstacles to a united nation, as well as to progress, and the Campbells continued to assist in bringing them into line. In 1701 the tenth Earl of Argyll was granted a dukedom for raising a regiment for the crown. After the Hanoverian succession brought a German prince to the throne, more than twenty thousand Scots "willingly or unwillingly" joined the Jacobite rising of 1715, but the rebellion petered out after the second Duke of Argyll held the rebel army to a stalemate at Sheriffmuir. More than six hundred Jacobite prisoners were transported, some to the Caribbean, but most (nearly five hundred) to the North American colonies as indentured servants. The governor of South Carolina bought the indentures of many of the prisoners, armed them, and dispatched them to the frontier to fight the Yamassee Indians, with whom the colony was at war.[36]

Successive dukes of Argyll continued to exploit their relationship with the crown to expand their power and patronage as the political managers of Scotland. They were "Highland chiefs, Lowland magnates and, crucially, seasoned players at the Court." They were simultaneously powerful marcher lords and loyal subjects.[37] "The greatest part of the Western Highlands may be said to be subject, or in some respect belong to the House of Argyle, or to speak more properly, to the family or clan of the Campbells," wrote Daniel Defoe, who traveled through the area in the 1720s.[38]

Nevertheless, in the 1720s General Wade reckoned twelve thousand Highland clansmen were hostile to the Hanoverian government, a formidable force if mobilized.[39] To facilitate the movement of troops, Wade constructed a system of roads connecting Crieff and Dunkeld in the south to Fort William, Fort Augustus, and Inverness.[40] The chain of British garrisons presented an ominous presence in the Highlands, as would British forts in Indian country.[41] Nineteen-year-old Anne MacVicar said Fort William looked "just like a place to kill people in."[42]

In 1745 Charles Edward Stuart made a dramatic bid to regain the throne his grandfather had lost. Landing on the west coast of Scotland with a handful of followers and hopes of French support, Charles called on clan chiefs to rally to his cause. They did, but with some hesitation. Although the rising began and ended in the Highlands, Lowlanders made up a large proportion of the so-called Highland army.[43] Moving quickly along Wade's roads, the army headed for Edinburgh. At Prestonpans the Highland charge routed an English army, and the prince entered Edinburgh in triumph. Marching south, he reached Derby, about 120 miles from London. However, the anticipated rising of supporters in England failed to materialize, as did a French landing. (As in Indian country, the English government worried that its enemies would find ready allies in the French.[44]) The Jacobite army turned back, much to the relief of Londoners, who were petrified at the thought of a tartan horde entering the capital.

That horde was in many ways a conventional army, but the '45 rebellion had many of the characteristics of a tribal war. A charismatic leader held together a loose and fragile alliance that scored initial victories but succumbed to division, logistical problems, and the superior numbers, organization, and firepower of the nation-state. The Jacobites won another victory at Falkirk, but their numbers dwindled as men departed for their homes and families. When the Duke of Cumberland caught up with them at Culloden in April 1746, they were dispirited and divided, and many of them were scattered across the countryside searching for food.[45]

Poorly led, hungry, cold, and depleted, they withstood murderous fire from the Hanoverian artillery before they launched their charge. Advancing across unfavorable ground ("running on in their wild manner," Cumberland called it), with wind and sleet in their faces, most never even reached the red-coat lines. Those who did confronted ranks bristling with steel and soldiers who had been trained to thrust to their right and catch attackers under their raised sword arm rather than strike the shield of the man directly in front of them: "Our men fairly beat them with their Bayonets," Cumberland reported. Campbells on the flanks poured a raking fire into their old enemies and settled some old scores. When the Highlanders broke, the English cavalry rode them down. The battle became a killing field: The dead "lay in Heaps," an officer wrote to a friend in Edinburgh two days after the battle.[46]

The Duke of Cumberland and the Hanoverian government regarded the Highlands and the clan-based warrior culture as the breeding ground of Jacobitism. Distinguished by their Gaelic language, kilts, broadswords, and ferocious charges, Highlanders were savages as well as rebels. The aftermath of Culloden offered an opportunity to simultaneously root out savagery and punish treason. Unrestrained violence was justified, especially since Cumberland announced that the Highlanders had orders to give no quarter.[47] Cumberland denied the rebels the rights of war, which were reserved for civilized enemies fighting in a legitimate cause, and determined to consolidate his victory "by eradicating the social roots of resistance." It was, notes Christopher Duffy, "pacification, not peace."[48] Cumberland's troops ranged the Highlands with fire and sword and drove off the Highlanders' cattle. John Prebble noted the parallels with the American slaughter of the buffalo herds that formed the cultural and economic base of Plains Indian society: "Cumberland knew, as General Sherman was to learn in the American west a century later, that a warlike people may be more easily starved than fought."[49]

Cumberland's butchery was followed by measures to reduce the clan chiefs' power, to outlaw the symbols of treason, and to tighten military control of the Highlands. Some rebels were tried and executed; many others forfeited their estates to the crown.[50] Some were transported as prisoners to labor in North America and the Caribbean, although proposals to send entire Highland communities into exile got nowhere: Colonial authorities were alarmed at the prospect of relocating Highland "savages" near Indian "savages" on their frontiers at a time of Anglo-French conflict.[51] North American colonists expressed relief at Cumberland's victory by naming forts, towns, counties, and a river in his honor.[52]

The Jacobite rebellions bore more resemblance to civil wars than to national uprisings. Clan fought clan, and Highlanders fought on both sides. In the '45, Campbells, Mackays, Munros, and Sutherlands backed the government; others either offered no support to the Jacobites or hedged their bets. Some clans and even some families were deeply divided. Roderick Chisholm of Chisholm had supported the Jacobites in 1715, but he stayed out of the fray in '45. His youngest son, who had the same name, led the clan out and died at Culloden. Two other sons fought on the government side at Culloden, serving with the Royal Scots Fusiliers. A fourth son was a surgeon in the British army.[53]

In an effort to ensure that the family estate would not be confiscated should the rebellion fail, some of the clan chiefs embraced the prince's cause but willed their estates to sons who did not. Murdoch MacDonald, who by then was minister of Kilmore in Argyll, wrote in his diary that "the unnatural Rebellion" and the threat of a Jacobite "invasion" threw his parishioners into a panic, "like Reeds shaken with the wind, hiding all their portable Effects, and at a loss what to do with themselves." News of Culloden brought welcome relief. "[O]ur Friends have greatly got the better of our Enemies," wrote MacDonald, saying nothing about the many MacDonalds who perished there. "'Tis thought that the remaining part of that Wretched set of men can't long Survive."[54]

Simon Fraser, Lord Lovat, had fought for George I in the 1715 rebellion, but many Frasers joined the Jacobites in 1745. Now seventy-eight, Fraser denied rallying his clan to the prince's cause and claimed that his clansmen followed his nineteen-year-old son, also called Simon. In August 1746 the younger Simon Fraser surrendered to John Campbell, Earl of Loudon, who had raised a regiment, fought for the government, and participated in the ravaging of the Highlands. Donald Cameron of Lochiel held Loudon personally responsible for the scorched-earth tactics used in Cameron country, although other officers surpassed Loudon in the zeal with which they applied them.[55] Fraser expressed suitable remorse for his actions and named names of prominent Jacobites. Loudon even persuaded him to give evidence against his father, who was convicted of treason and executed at the Tower of London, the last man to be beheaded in Britain. The son went free. Loudon's demonstrated loyalty to the Hanoverian regime helped secure him the position of commander in chief of the British forces in North America during the Seven Years' War, where his firsthand experience with scorched-earth tactics would serve him well. Simon Fraser proved his loyalty by raising a regiment to fight in North America, where he served alongside Loudon.[56]

John 4th Earl of Loudoun Capt Genl of H Ms Forces in N America.

Figure 1.1. John Campbell, Earl of Loudon, by Allan Ramsay (from a Private Collection). Loudon fought against Highlanders in the 1745 rising and against Indians as commander in chief of British forces in North America in 1756. Although he believed Indians had an affinity for Highlanders, he had little use for Indian allies.

The defeat of the '45 rising confirmed the Campbells' dominance. Archibald Campbell, Earl of Islay (who limped from a wound sustained in the 1715 rising) became third Duke of Argyll after his brother died in 1743. He emphasized the Campbells' role as the leading Highland allies of the Hanoverian government and used his English political connections (particularly with Sir Robert Walpole) to build his power base. He became Scotland's lord justice general and for almost forty years managed Scotland through a network of patronage.[57]

Britain increased its military presence in the Highlands. To prevent the clans from mobilizing and to bring law and order to this breeding ground of rebellion, parties of soldiers "after the Roman manner . . . Spread over the Country and encamp'd chiefly at the passes and places of Danger."[58] Wade's system of military roads was extended until it measured more than a thousand miles by 1767. Fort George, the great fortress east of Inverness, was completed by 1769, a permanent bastion to prevent any further insurrections.[59] As in Indian country, military defeat was the prelude to a sustained assault on tribal ways of life.

Wrenching social and economic changes in the century after Culloden sent thousands of Highlanders across the Atlantic to North America. There they participated in the conquest and colonization of other tribal peoples. They donned the king's red coat and fought his wars. They also dominated the fur trade, extending Britain's economic imperialism deep into Indian country, from Hudson Bay to the Gulf of Mexico, from the Saint Lawrence to the Columbia River. Moreover, they settled on Indian lands. Whether of Lowland or Highland origin, Scots brought experiences of contested borderlands to America. Governor James Glen of South Carolina, for example, a Lowlander, had lived near enough to the Highlands to be aware of the dynamics of cultural encounter in a frontier environment, and he drew on that knowledge in the southeastern Indian trade and in winning over Indian allies from the French and Spaniards. Scotland may have offered a "forcing ground" for expertise in dealing with indigenous peoples in frontier zones.[60]

North America

When Frenchman Jacques Cartier sailed up the Saint Lawrence River in the 1530s, his cartographer, Jean Rotz, was evidently the son of a Scotsman. However, European colonization was well under way before Highland Scots arrived in North America in significant numbers. Relative to France and

Spain, the English too were latecomers to America, but they were not new to colonization. By the time they began settling the Chesapeake region and New England, they were entrenching colonial and cultural frontiers in Scotland and Ireland and had formed opinions about how to deal with people "beyond the pale."

English colonizers developed attitudes and policies in subjugating the Irish that they subsequently applied to Indians. After a period of trial and error in Ireland, the English developed a harsh, Anglocentric style of rule and then exported this system across the Atlantic—the barbaric and pagan customs of the Irish and the Indians justified such a colonial scheme. English experiences in Ireland fueled interest in American exploration and provided a model for transatlantic exploits. The same personalities, including Sir Walter Raleigh, Sir Humphrey Gilbert, and the Calvert and Penn families, promoted both Irish and American colonization. Funding for expeditions to both locations often came from the same pockets. Ireland showed the English what resources were necessary to run a colony successfully and demonstrated that the "new colonies should consist of such men as were most unlike to fall to the barbarous customs" of the Natives. In theory, the Englishmen selected to go to North America were thus chosen on the basis of their ability to plant the seeds of civilization. In King James's eyes, wrote David Quinn, "the new capital of Jamestown and the older capital of Dublin had a very similar colonial character. Each was a door through which English and Scottish colonists could enter, and thereafter the old inhabitants, whether they were Irishmen or Powhatan Indians, would take second place to the imperial colonists."[61] Colonial writers frequently made cross-cultural references to Irish and Indians and depicted them in similarly retarded stages of cultural development: They were dirty, lazy, uncivilized, and desperately in need of Anglicization. Such attitudes justified taking their land. The first "reservations" were established in Ireland.[62] The ideology and rhetoric of American colonization and even the metaphors of colonial extermination—"nits make lice"—had origins in Ireland.[63]

Seventeenth-century Englishmen believed that Indians, like the wild Irish and Scots, would accept English dominion and English civilization once they were made to see the superiority of the English. They expected to obtain the submission of Indian chiefs just as the crown had brought about the capitulation of Gaelic chiefs. At Jamestown, few in number and inept in their new environment, the English cannot have seemed much of a threat to the powerful chiefdom of Powhatan, which embraced some thirty tribes and extended across most of eastern Virginia. Captain John Smith tried to obtain Powhatan's submission but Powhatan may have tried to get Smith to submit to him.[64]

Like their Gaelic counterparts, Indian peoples experienced new concepts of total war imported by those who carried out the work of civilization with fire and sword and bible. After the Pequot Indians of southern Connecticut suffered staggering losses to smallpox in 1633 and 1634, the English went to war against them in 1636. The fighting stemmed from disputes over trade, tribute, and land among various Indian tribes, Dutch traders, and the English, but English Puritans transformed it into a mythic struggle between savagery and civilization: Pequots were wild and violent people who had to be eradicated.[65] In 1637 a Puritan army attacked a Pequot village on the Mystic River, surrounded it, and set the lodges ablaze. "Those that scaped the fire were slaine with the sword; some hewed to peeces, others rune throw with their rapiers, so as they were quickly dispatchte, and very few escaped," wrote Governor William Bradford of Plymouth Plantation. "It was conceived they thus destroyed about 400." Despite the horrible "stinck & sente" of burning flesh, "the victory seemed a sweete sacrifice . . . over so proud & insulting an enimie."[66] According to historian William Christie MacLeod, John Mason, the commander of the Puritan army and the officer who ordered the burning, had "learned his butcher's trade in warring on Scotch clansmen."[67]

The English thanked God and hunted down the survivors. As Cromwell did in Scotland and Ireland, they sold many into slavery in the West Indies. They handed others to the Mohegans and Narragansetts who had assisted them in the war. At the Treaty of Hartford in 1638, the English terminated Pequot sovereignty and outlawed the use of the tribal name. In his history of the British colonies, published in the mid-eighteenth century, William Douglass wondered whether "some Expedient of this Nature might be used with Regard to some of the incorrigible Clans of Highlanders in the Northern and Western Parts of Scotland."[68] In fact, the MacGregors were already being persecuted and outlawed by the time of the Pequot War.

As the Campbells helped harass the MacGregors, so the Mohegans assisted in the demise of the Pequots. Like the earls of Argyll, Uncas of the Mohegans saw cultivating an English alliance as the way to elevate his own power and that of his tribe at the expense of rival neighbors. Like the earls of Argyll, Uncas extended and maintained political power by developing kinship networks through strategic intertribal marriages. Uncas broke off from the Pequot confederation and led a Mohegan confederation from the 1630s until his death in 1683. He and his warriors participated in the Pequot massacre. He sided with the English against the Narragansetts of Rhode Island, and when the Narragansett chief Miantonomi was captured in 1643, the English turned him over to Uncas and the Mohegans for execution. Uncas was no pawn—he died without converting to Christianity and adhered to

Mohegan, not English, ways and interests. He built a Native power base and secured the core of the Mohegans' Thames River valley homeland during calamitous times of war and epidemic, even as colonial population and the colonial system began to engulf the Mohegan world. It is perhaps too much to see the Mohegans as the Campbells of New England, but Uncas pursued goals and strategies that the earls of Argyll would have understood.[69]

Uncas supported the English again during King Philip's War. As the English encroached on Wampanoag land and placed increasing restrictions on Indian sovereignty, Wampanoags had to fight or submit to English domination. Wampanoag leader Metacom, known to the English as King Philip, forged a multitribal coalition, and in 1675 Indians and colonists fell on each other in a brutal and bloody conflict that severed the ties they had developed over the previous half-century.[70] When the Narragansetts declared their intention to remain neutral, many of Metacom's followers sent their women and children to take refuge with them. The English interpreted Narragansett sanctuary to noncombatants as an act of hostility. An English army of more than one thousand men marched through deep snow and attacked the main Narragansett stronghold near Kingston, Rhode Island. Hundreds of Narragansett men, women, and children died in what became known as the Great Swamp Fight. The survivors joined Metacom's war of resistance. In April 1676 the English captured the Narragansett sachem Canonchet and handed him over to Uncas and the Mohegans for execution. In August an Indian soldier fighting with the English shot and killed Metacom. Canonchet and Metacom both received the treatment reserved for traitors. Like William Wallace, their bodies were drawn and quartered, and the parts were stuck on posts as a grisly reminder of the punishment for treason. Mohegans fought again as English allies in the "French and Indian wars" in the mid-eighteenth century.

By then immigrants from Britain's borderlands were moving into every part of the American colonies. As many as three hundred thousand Scots-Irish migrated to America, and many of them pushed to the frontiers. Philadelphia became a major port of entry, and Pennsylvania became the gateway for Scots-Irish invasion and settlement of large areas of Indian country. Mostly Protestant and poor farmers, the Scots-Irish joined Germans, English, and others traveling the Great Philadelphia Wagon Road, which followed old Indian trails from Pennsylvania to Georgia, and they crossed the Appalachians. James Logan, provincial secretary of Pennsylvania, expressed alarm at the influx, noting that the new immigrants "crowd in where they are not wanted," boldly squatting "on any spot of vacant land they find." When the authorities tried to expel them and burned down their cabins, the Scots-Irish simply moved on and squatted again. The Indians were "alarmed at the swarms of strangers."[71]

Pennsylvania colonial authorities regarded the Scots-Irish in the eighteenth century much as King James had regarded them in the seventeenth: Formerly a barrier against the wild Irish, they now provided a barrier against "untamed" Indians. Encouraged to settle on the western frontiers as a first line of defense or as shock troops, they became "hard neighbors to the Indians." Their mobility and their expectations of access to Indian land disrupted British policies of frontier regulation and fueled escalating Indian-white conflicts. By 1790 more than half the people living in the backcountry regions of southwestern Pennsylvania, western Maryland and Virginia, North and South Carolina, Georgia, Kentucky, and Tennessee came from Scotland, Ireland, and northern England.[72]

People who had been colonized by England on the Celtic fringes of the British Isles brooked little restraint when they themselves became colonizers and carved out new borderlands in North America. Families of Ulster Scots, with names like Crockett, Calhoun, Jackson, Houston, and Carson, who figured prominently in the defeat and dispossession of tribal peoples in America, had plenty of frontier experience before they crossed the Atlantic and the Appalachians. In David Hackett Fischer's interpretation, immigrants from the borderlands of Britain came from a violent region and were at home in a hostile and anarchic environment, "which was well suited to their family system, their warrior ethic, their farming and herding economy, their attitudes toward land and wealth and their ideas of work and power."[73] The dilemma of trying to convert Indians to an "orderly" and "civilized" way of life in frontier environments noted for the absence of order and civility plagued British and Indian relations until the Revolution and beleaguered U.S.-Indian relations until the 1830s, when the government "resolved" the dilemma by removing the Indians.[74]

When Indian wars erupted in the eighteenth century, the first settlers to die were often Scots-Irish. After midcentury, the first British soldiers on the scene were often Highland Scots. The contest between Britain and France for North American hegemony culminated in the so-called French and Indian War, when Indians first met Highland regiments as enemies and allies. As in the Highlands, waging war against "savages" freed European soldiers from the normal constraints of "civilized warfare." Confronted with warrior societies fighting in their own country, British soldiers adapted to unconventional warfare. Although British officers are commonly depicted as bewigged martinets out of their element in North America, many had experience with guerilla warfare in Europe and in the Highlands of Scotland and understood well the importance of irregular skirmishing on the periphery of more conventional campaigns. Loudon in particular promoted the training of British regulars for forest fighting and supplemented regular troops with rangers, who would, he hoped, "be able to deal with the Indians in their own way."[75] Robert Rogers's Rangers, who specialized in guerilla warfare, included a heavy component of Scots-Irish fighters.[76] Highlanders who had seen scorched-earth tactics applied to their homelands in 1746 applied them in Cherokee country in 1760 and 1761.

By 1763, after more than half a century of conflict with France, Britain emerged victorious in North America. British redcoats took over French forts in Indian country and built others. Fort Pitt loomed over the forks of the Ohio as Fort William loomed over Loch Lihnne. English and Scots-Irish settlers flooded onto Indian lands. In Pontiac's war, tribes in the Great Lakes and the Ohio Valley rallied against the British and drove the redcoats back on almost every front until the usual combination of European military superiority and European disease turned the tide. In western Pennsylvania, Scots-Irish frontiersmen (calling themselves the Paxton Boys) massacred peaceful Conestoga Indians.

The British attempted to regulate the turbulent frontier by prohibiting settlement west of the Appalachian Mountains. Nonetheless, the Royal Proclamation that attempted to separate Indians and colonists set the colonies on the road to the American Revolution. Many colonials felt cheated of the fruits of victory. Land speculators (like George Washington) who had investments in the West began to protest against the empire they had formerly served. Many Scots-Irish and other settlers simply ignored the proclamation. Like Indian chiefs who were unable to control their young men, the British government was unable to prevent its subjects from encroaching on Indian lands.

Irishman Sir William Johnson built a fortune on Mohawk lands in New York and encouraged emigrants from the Highlands of Scotland to settle on his estates. At the Treaty of Fort Stanwix in 1768 Johnson purchased a huge tract of land from Iroquois delegates, who deftly diverted colonial expansion south of the Ohio River by ceding hunting territory that belonged to the Shawnees and Cherokees. Colonists swarmed into Kentucky, confident that the lands had been ceded and came into open conflict with Shawnee and Cherokee warriors determined to defend their hunting grounds against trespassers. In 1774 John Murray, Lord Dunmore, the Scottish governor of Virginia whose family had sympathized with the Jacobites, led his colony to victory against the Shawnees. This made him, for a moment, "as popular as a Scotsman can be among weak prejudiced people."[77] But hostilities had hardly ceased before the American Revolution broke out, a conflict that ousted Dunmore and drove many Highland Scots and Indians into alliance and exile.

Indians and Highlanders fought for their freedom in the Revolution just as much as the American patriots, but they had different understandings of what that freedom meant and where it lay.[78] For the most part, Indians sided with the British. American land hunger convinced them that their best hopes of survival lay in supporting the crown. Doing so placed them alongside Highland Scots, who generally remained loyal to the king (although there were regional variations, notably in Virginia and South Carolina), and pitched them into continued conflict with Scots-Irish, who typically did not. (As David Armitage points out, "the supposed Celtic affinity between Scots and Scots-Irish is, in large part, a later invention. Political and religious identities, not indefinable ties of ethnicity, determined the allegiances of different groups."[79]) Highland Scots and Ulster Scots clashed in the vicious battle at King's Mountain in 1780.

Not all former Jacobites fought for the king. Nineteen-year-old Hugh Mercer served as assistant surgeon in Prince Charles's army, witnessed the carnage at Culloden, and fled to Philadelphia in 1747. He became a frontier doctor and served as captain of Pennsylvania militia in the attack on the Delaware town of Kittanning in 1756, led by Lieutenant Colonel John Armstrong (an emigrant from the north of Ireland). In the Revolution, Mercer espoused the rebel cause for the second time in his life and rose to the rank of brigadier general in the Continental Army. Having escaped the British bayonets at Culloden, he bled to death from multiple bayonet wounds sustained at the battle of Princeton.[80]

Americans were quick to apply the tactics the British and other colonial powers had used when fighting tribal enemies: Burn their homes and food supplies. Armies from Virginia, Georgia, and the Carolinas burned Cherokee towns and cornfields; George Washington dispatched General John Sullivan on a scorched-earth campaign through Iroquois country, where he reduced to ashes forty towns, millions of bushels of corn, and orchards; Kentucky militia launched regular attacks across the Ohio against Shawnee villages. Determined to root out all Indians, America militia in 1781 slaughtered ninety-six pacifist Delaware men, women, and children who had converted to the Moravian religion.

Once the United States had won its liberty from the British Empire, it began to build its own empire in the territory Britain had transferred—everything south of the Great Lakes, east of the Mississippi, and north of Florida. Indians were neither represented nor included in the peace treaty that ended the war. The United States regarded them as defeated enemies who had forfeited their lands and rights and regarded its own expansion as inevitable, even divinely ordained. The Northwest Ordinance of 1787 proclaimed that the United States would observe "the utmost good faith" in its dealings with Indian people and that the Indians' lands would not be invaded or taken from them except in "just and lawful wars authorized by Congress." However, the ordinance also laid out a blueprint for national expansion. Congress also passed the Indian Trade and Intercourse Act in 1790, stipulating that no transfers of Indian land were valid without congressional approval. But, like Britain after 1763, the U.S. government could not to control its own citizens on distant frontiers. Individual states, resentful of the federal government's attempts to interfere in their affairs, frequently made treaties that never received congressional approval. Squatters and land speculators ignored the laws. It was "open season" on Indian lands.

The Iroquois, Hurons, Delawares, Shawnees, Ottawas, Ojibwas, Potawatomis, Miamis, and Wabash River tribes united to resist American settlement northwest of the Ohio. In 1790 they defeated an invasion by General Josiah Harmar and routed an army under General Arthur St. Clair a year later. However, American agents fomented and fueled divisions within and among the tribes. When General Anthony Wayne advanced into Indian country in 1794, like the Duke of Cumberland in 1746, he confronted a tribal alliance weakened by old and new rivalries, divided councils, and hunger. On the eve of the battle of Fallen Timbers, as on the eve of Culloden, many warriors dispersed in search of food. At Culloden and at Fallen Timbers, the cannon, bayonets, and cavalry of the nation-state's army prevailed. Like the Jacobites, the Indians were disappointed in their expectations of foreign support. The British had no intention of getting embroiled in another war in America at a time when they were preoccupied with revolutionary France. When Indians sought refuge at Fort Miami after the battle, the British commander, Major William Campbell, closed the gates and denied them entrance. The following year at the Treaty of Greenville, Indian delegates ceded to the United States two-thirds of present-day Ohio.

Like their counterparts in the Highlands, many Indian chiefs now opted for cooperation. However, in the first decade of the nineteenth century, Tecumseh, a Shawnee war chief who built on a movement of spiritual revitalization led by his brother Tenskwatawa, revived united resistance among the tribes to any cessions of land. He denounced older chiefs who signed away tribal territory and carried his message of Indian unity from the Great Lakes to the Gulf of Mexico. In 1811 American firepower and bayonets prevailed again in a Pyrrhic victory over Tenskwatawa's warriors at Tippecanoe. When war broke out between Britain and the United States the next year, Tecumseh sided with the redcoats in a last attempt to stem the tide of American expansion, but Indian unity east of the Mississippi died when he was killed at the battle of the Thames in 1813.

Figure 1.2. *An Incident in the Rebellion of 1745* (*Battle of Culloden*) by David Morier (fl. 1705–1750). (Royal Collection, © 2007, Her Majesty Queen Elizabeth II.)

Figure 1.3. *The Battle of Tippecanoe* by Alonzo Chappel. From Henry B. Dawson, *Battles of the United States by Sea and Land* (New York: Johnson, Fry, 1859).

In the southeastern region of the United States, the sons of Scots traders who married Creek women generated far-reaching and ultimately disruptive changes in Creek society.[81] The Creeks were a loose confederacy of about fifty autonomous towns in Georgia and Alabama and spoke several distinct languages. When conflicts within the confederacy spilled over into attacks on American settlers, the United States responded with swift military action. In the Creek War of 1813–1814, Andrew Jackson waged a series of devastating campaigns that culminated in the slaughter of some eight hundred Creek warriors at the battle of Tohopeka or Horseshoe Bend on the Tallapoosa River in March 1814. "It was dark before we finished killing them," Jackson wrote his wife, and he justified the carnage as necessary in dealing with such a barbarous and savage foe.[82]

About five hundred Cherokees and one hundred Lower Creeks helped Jackson win his victory. Red-haired William Weatherford, one of a number of Creek chiefs with Scots ancestry, surrendered to Jackson. The Treaty of Fort Jackson divested the Creek nation of fourteen million acres, mostly lands belonging to Jackson's Creek allies. It was the single largest cession of territory ever made in the Southeast and initiated a boom in land sales and cotton production in Alabama and Mississippi. Plans by Scottish admiral Alexander Cochrane to use Indians in concert with British troops to conquer Florida and Louisiana and thus provide a diversion for Canada came to nothing,[83] but Jackson feared British agents and activities in Indian country. When he raided into Spanish-held Florida in 1817, he arrested and executed two Scottish traders, Alexander Arbuthnott and Robert Ambrister.

In the next two decades, Jackson became the arch exponent of ethnic cleansing. While Highland clan chiefs implemented programs that cleared people out of their glens and moved them across the Atlantic, the United States adopted a policy of uprooting Indians from their homelands and moving them west across the Mississippi. Among the people who walked the emigrant trails were Indians with Highland surnames. Their fathers had left Scotland to escape colonial pressures and entered Indian country to pursue colonial opportunities. People bearing Highland names found themselves on both sides of the cultural divide as cycles of conquest and colonization familiar in the Highlands were repeated in Indian country.

2

Scots and Indians in a Changing World

American Indians and Highland Scots encountered colonizers, as well as each other, in eras of massive change on both sides of the Atlantic. New market forces swept the Atlantic world, bringing innovation and disruption, driving colonial projects, undermining tribal independence, and altering indigenous ways of life. Economic transformation worked alongside government programs in effecting change; in Scotland it did more than garrisons and parliamentary legislation to integrate the Highlands into a greater Britain.[1] The Highlands of Scotland and Indian country both felt the reverberations of the industrial revolution occurring in England and the Lowlands. New developments created tensions and conflicts within Highland and Indian societies as people confronted unfamiliar pressures, took advantage of new opportunities, and tried to balance innovation and tradition as their world changed around them.

Historians of Indian America have often chastised other historians for depicting Indians in static terms, as if the societies that European colonists encountered had existed without change for centuries before contact. Yet we have not always practiced what we preach when considering the European side of the encounter. One sometimes gets the impression that European colonists arrived in full possession of the same values and beliefs their descendants displayed in later centuries. In reality, European societies were experiencing changes of their own that reshaped their world and people's understanding of it. Few European societies experienced more changes more rapidly than did Scotland.

As Simon Schama points out, in the late seventeenth century "the crucial conflict was taking place *within* Scotland between two cultures: one based on the ancient obligations of honour and kinship, the other on the aggressive pursuit of interest and profit."[2] The Lowland Scots' vision of a united Scottish nation depended on the removal of Gaelic difference and disorderliness. Law and order had to be established beyond the Highland line before commerce and industry could take hold. In North Britain and North America, conflicts between and within clans and tribes involved more than just ancient grievances; they also revolved about the future and who should shape it.[3]

* * *

On both sides of the Atlantic, new forces assaulted "a practiced and lived tradition" that had connected "people to land and people to people through kin and community."[4] Before the intrusion of capitalist forces, Highlanders and Indians lived off the land and close to it. They occupied rough shelters, gathered around smoky fires, often shared their lodgings with their animals, and had few material possessions. People lived in kin-based societies and operated within a redistributive economy in which generosity and reciprocity were expected and essential. "[G]ive them a fine gun, coat, or other thing," William Penn said of Indians, "it may pass twenty hands before it sticks; . . . wealth circulateth like blood, all parts partake."[5] Civilized people shook their heads at such "improvidence."

In the early sixteenth century, it was said, the people of the Highlands had "na repair with marchandis of uncouth [foreign] realms."[6] Scotland traded with Ireland and across the North Sea with Norway, Denmark, Holland, Danzig, and Poland, but the Highlands were remote from the centers of power and prosperity in the south. Things changed in the seventeenth century, and the union of 1707 made Scotland part of Britain's emerging economic empire. Located at the northwestern periphery of Europe, Scotland was well positioned to take advantage of developing Atlantic commercial networks. Some Scots had migrated to America in the 1600s, and Scots established their first American colony in East Jersey with about one thousand settlers before the end of the century.[7] Many educated and professional Scots migrated temporarily to places like Jamaica and the Chesapeake, with the goal and expectation of making their fortunes and returning home.[8] Some Highland clans became involved in transatlantic ventures: The Camerons of Lochiel joined Bristol merchants dabbling in the New Jersey land market in the late seventeenth century, and by the 1730s they had an interest in a Jamaican plantation.[9]

Even after General Wade constructed a network of military roads in the 1720s, travelers to the Highlands got around on horseback over poor roads and rugged mountain terrain.[10] However, by the end of the eighteenth century, travel by coach between Edinburgh and London was cut from thirteen to two and a half days, and the upper Clyde River, once unnavigable, was transformed into "one of the world's best ship canals."[11] In 1803 Thomas Telford and his colleagues began a parliamentary program of road and bridge construction. Fifteen years later a traveler returning from the Highlands declared that "where within the memory of man neither a good road nor a good inn were to be found, the roads are now among the best and the inns among the most convenient and comfortable in the whole world." Stage coaches began to run between Perth and Inverness in 1809, two or three times a week; a dozen years later seven coaches a day passed to and from Inverness. In 1826 the chief inspector of roads proclaimed that since 1803 new roads and bridges had effected "a change in the state of the Highlands, perhaps unparalleled in the same space of time in the history of any country." The sixty-two mile long Caledonian Canal, which poet Robert Southey saw under construction and pronounced "the greatest work of its kind that has ever been undertaken in ancient or modern times," was opened in 1822, linking the east coast near Inverness to the west coast near Fort William. In 1861 Parliament passed the Highland Railway Bill. The railway reached Inverness the same year.[12]

As transportation improved, new goods and influences flowed north. Highlanders began to experience a consumer revolution. They exported more cattle to the south and imported increasing supplies of meal from grain-rich areas to help stave off recurrent harvest failures.[13] Mass-produced glass, ceramic vessels, and other items manufactured in Lowland or Midland factories spread to remote regions of the Highlands and Hebrides, where inhabitants also began to savor imports from Britain's expanding colonies—tea, tobacco, sugar, and molasses. Touring Scotland in 1819, Robert Southey was surprised (at Clashmore in "the wilds of Caithness") to be served breakfast on "a tasteful and handsome set of Worcester china."[14] Some chiefs began to timber their forests to provide fuel for industry, wood for building, and masts for the growing demands of the Royal Navy, which also looked to the forests of Canada and northern New England for its supplies. A cash economy appeared alongside (and in some cases replaced) traditional systems of agricultural barter and owed labor.

Industrializing Britain placed insatiable demands for food and raw materials on the rural economy, and the transformation of rural society occurred more rapidly in Scotland than anywhere else in Europe.[15] The rationalism of the Scottish Enlightenment taught that nature could be improved by planned and systematic intervention. In *The Wealth of Nations,* published in 1776, Adam Smith, a Lowlander, depicted the Highlands as a backward, isolated, and poverty-stricken society in which peasants employed primitive farming methods on poor land and gave compulsory service and feudal deference to their chiefs. Progress in the Highlands, Smith argued, depended on consolidating the land, specializing labor, and converting the region to market economics—in short, changing from feudalism to capitalism.[16]

Between 1755 and 1820 Scotland's population grew by two-thirds. The populations of Glasgow and Edinburgh grew so fast that by 1800, according to one estimate, Scotland had become one of the five most urbanized societies in Western Europe. Displaced Highlanders accounted for a substantial part of that urban growth: As many as twenty percent of the population of Greenock and Glasgow in the late eighteenth and early nineteenth century may have been born in the Highlands. Even as thousands left for the industrial towns in the south or for America, population in the Highlands increased twenty percent from the middle to the end of the eighteenth century, owing largely to the introduction of potatoes from the 1740s and smallpox inoculation from the 1780s. Highland population did not show a decline until the census of 1851. For historian Eric Richards, population growth "was the single most important fact of life in the fate of the region throughout the turmoil." For James Hunter, the commercialization of agriculture was "the great fact of eighteenth century Highland history," from which everything else followed. The two developments were inextricably linked.[17]

Growing populations in Glasgow, Edinburgh, Perth, and Dundee, as well as in England, and military demand for salt beef produced an expansion in Highland cattle droving in the late seventeenth century, when thousands of cattle were sold at the markets in Crieff and Falkirk. A century later cattle could not keep pace with the demands of the mushrooming population in the south nor with the tastes and expenses of the clan gentry. Enclosures and sheep farming had already transformed the Lowlands; as England and the Lowlands became more heavily industrial and urban, pressure to commercialize Highland agriculture accelerated dramatically. Sheep were introduced into the Highlands; wool and mutton were then shipped south to Yorkshire textile mills and hungry factory towns. By 1825 Scotland supplied forty percent of British wool.[18] Rents increased, and ties to the land became more tenuous. Heavy sheep grazing affected vegetation, degraded the environment, and pushed more Highlanders to the cities.[19]

The forces that transformed the Atlantic world spread deep into Indian country as well, and their impact was often dramatic and devastating. As demand for wool in Britain generated change and disruption in the Highlands of Scotland, Europe's demand for beaver pelts and deerskins did the same in Indian country. Indian peoples exchanged their resources for Europe's commodities and became enmeshed in the market webs of the Atlantic economy. The fur and deerskin trades produced massive destruction of animal populations as hides and pelts from Indian hunting grounds were shipped in vast quantities to European markets. Most of the deerskins harvested in the southeastern Indian trade went to London to feed the tanning and leather-dressing industry, which was extensive in the late eighteenth century. In exchange, Indians received the products of Europe's mills and factories. By the time Highland Scots arrived in numbers in North America, most of the Indian people they met had been trading with Europeans and trying out their commodities for generations.

In addition to guns, steel-edged weapons, iron tools, and woolen clothing, Indian people obtained an inventory of manufactured goods that included combs, scissors, linen shirts, hats, books, paper, pewter, glassware, china, lace, silk, buckles, shoes, and glass beads from Italy and Czechoslovakia. By the middle of the eighteenth century, according to one old chief, the Cherokees had become dependent on the English for guns, ammunition, and clothing: "Every necessary Thing in Life we must have from the white People," he told the governor of South Carolina.[20] He probably exaggerated—pleading poverty to secure more trade or better rates was a common practice—but not by much. Trade with Europeans was a major part of Indian life. Archaeologists working on eighteenth-century sites in the eastern United States sometimes have difficulty determining whether they are excavating an Indian or a European settlement.[21] By the time of the American Revolution, some Oneida Indians in upstate New York lived in frame houses with chimneys and windows, drank from teacups and punchbowls, used silk handkerchiefs, wore white flannel breeches, and combed their hair with ivory combs while looking in glass mirrors. Some were skilled farmers and carpenters, some spoke and read English, and many attended Presbyterian church services.[22] Many American Indians by this time enjoyed a material standard of living higher than that of common people in the Highlands of Scotland. The Earl of Selkirk described Saint Regis (now Akwesasne) on the Saint Lawrence in 1804 as a village of about two hundred warriors (perhaps one thousand people), whose minister, Father Roderick Macdonell, was "a good soul." They lived in log houses with chimneys, stoves, and glass windows and were "on the whole not worse lodged than the generality of labourers in Scotland & even in many parts of England."[23] Like the Highlands and islands of Scotland, Indian country was becoming part of an Atlantic economy and experienced a growing consumer revolution that shaped people's tastes, their lives, and the world they inhabited.[24]

Europeans also brought concepts of land use and ownership that would forever change the face of North America. They introduced new plants and crops like rice, wheat, barley, and oats; new grasses and weeds; and domesticated animals such as horses, cattle, sheep, goats, and pigs, which trod down native grasses, trampled Indian cornfields, and drove away wild game. Colonists' axes cleared forests to make way for farmland.[25] African slaves were hauled across the ocean in chains to work the cotton, tobacco, and rice fields of the South and the sugar plantations of the West Indies. British factory workers, stimulated and diverted by sugar and rum from the West Indies, produced guns, steel weapons, cotton clothing (from buds picked by African slaves on lands formerly held by Indians), and woolen clothing (from the sheep that replaced people in the Highlands) for the trade in Indian country. In a dangerous new world of international and intertribal competition, Indians needed guns and other European merchandise as much as Europeans needed their resources.[26]

* * *

Indians also experienced the Atlantic world's diseases. Europeans carried germs and viruses that exploded into epidemics among Native American populations, who had not acquired immunity to diseases that were all too common in Europe, Asia, and Africa. Smallpox, measles, bubonic plague, influenza, cholera, whooping cough, and other killer illnesses spread like wildfire through Indian societies, which were simultaneously experiencing bouts of famine, escalating warfare, cultural disruptions, and other associated traumas of colonization. Mortality rates reached as high as ninety percent, and in some cases entire populations perished. Sometimes populations recovered or even increased as they incorporated refugees from other areas, but sooner or later imported diseases struck all of the Native populations. Recurrent epidemics and numerous chronic afflictions contributed to the continual attrition of Indian numbers from the fifteenth to the twentieth century.[27]

Smallpox was a particularly vicious killer. According to Governor William Bradford of Plymouth Plantation, a smallpox epidemic among the Indians on the Connecticut River in 1633 and 1634 killed ninety-five percent of the population.[28] At the time of the American Revolution, a huge smallpox pandemic killed thousands of Indian peoples in the West. Breaking out in Mexico City in 1779, the scourge spread in all directions, traveling through the southwest, north across the Great Plains and Rocky Mountains, and deep into the forests of Canada by 1783. Perhaps half of the people on the plains died.[29] In the nineteenth century smallpox struck repeatedly. The Mandans on the upper Missouri may once have numbered as many as fifteen thousand but declined steadily under recurrent outbreaks of disease. They probably had no more than two thousand people when smallpox broke out in 1837. When it was over, 138 remained. The sickness spread across the plains, killing thousands of people.[30] In 1869 smallpox hit the northern plains again. Cholera, measles, and scarlet fever added to the death toll in Indian villages. The American conquest of the West took place in the wake of biological disasters that rocked Indian communities and reduced their capacity to resist.

Because Europeans had had longer exposure and thus developed some resistance, killer diseases struck Indian populations with greater virulence, but Europeans were not immune to epidemiological tragedy and demographic catastrophe. The Black Death of 1348–1350 had killed a third to one half of Britain's population, and recurrent outbreaks—Scotland suffered eight plague years between 1349 and 1420—kept the population low well into the sixteenth century.[31] Scotland's population rose steadily in the eighteenth and nineteenth centuries, while Indian populations collapsed, but the deadly diseases brought devastation, heartbreak, and despair to Highland as well as Indian communities.

As in Indian country, smallpox was for centuries the most deadly epidemic in Scotland. It was so common and recurrent in eighteenth-century Scotland that it was mainly a childhood disease: By one contemporary estimate one out of every six children born died of smallpox, which amounted to about 8,000 out of 48,000–50,000 births.[32] "The Small Pox are on their March towards us, making Execution as they travel through the Country," Murdoch MacDonald, minister of Durness in Sutherland, wrote in his diary: "There are three of my Children yet unvisited by that formidable Emissary of an offended God" (and therefore vulnerable to infection).[33] Visiting the isle of Saint Kilda in June 1760, Richard Pococke noted that disease had followed hard on the heels of Christianity, as sometimes happened in Indian country when germs followed missionaries: "They were about 160 souls, but the small pox coming among them the infection of which was brought in some cloaths, a great number of them died, so that now there are not above 70 or 80 souls."[34] Smallpox mortality rates seem to have ranged from eighteen to forty percent in the cities of eighteenth-century Britain; in the last two decades of the century smallpox accounted for ten percent of all deaths in London and for twenty percent in Glasgow. Statistics for the Highlands are lacking. By the end of the eighteenth century, inoculation was common in the region, but distrust of the procedure among some segments of the population meant that children continued to die. There were severe outbreaks of smallpox in the Western Isles in 1784 and 1792 and the Isle of Lewis in the 1820s.[35]

Smallpox in Scotland was also a hazard for Indian visitors. In 1768 John and Tobias Shattuck, two Narragansett Indians who traveled to Britain with a petition for the king to prevent the selling of tribal lands, fell victim to smallpox while they were in Edinburgh. Twenty-six-year-old Tobias was described as a young man who had "won the Hearts of Boath English, and Indians," and "a Person Devoted to do Good among Man-kind in General." Despite the best medical attention available ("we live in a City where the best help is to be had of any place in Brittain") and the presence of the future eminent physician Benjamin Rush of Philadelphia, who was studying at Edinburgh's renowned medical college, Tobias succumbed to the dread disease. John survived and made it home to Rhode Island, where he died of consumption (tuberculosis) two years later. He was twenty-four.[36] Dugald Buchanan, a renowned Highland bard and schoolmaster who was in Edinburgh and had met Benjamin Rush, left just about the time the Shattuck brothers arrived. He was called home to Loch Rannoch in Perthshire, where his family was suffering from an epidemic of fever. Buchanan himself caught the fever and died in June 1768.[37]

Dysentery, "the flux," was a ferocious killer. It carried off many of Murdoch MacDonald's parishioners in a matter of days. "The Death and Mortality still increasing," he wrote in his diary in June 1741. "Lord! God of Hosts, thy hand is up: hard to know where or when it may stop." Then he received "the Alarming News of the Death of Mr. George McKay, a man ordain'd, married, and dead, in less than a month's time." MacDonald himself fell ill and feared the worst, but he was one of the lucky ones and survived.[38]

Highland men, women, and children who migrated to Glasgow and other cities suffered the kinds of illnesses associated with poor living and working conditions—typhus, tuberculosis, and other lung-related diseases—as well as measles and smallpox. Average life expectancy in Glasgow dropped to twenty-seven years in 1841.[39] International communications brought new illnesses to Britain as well as to Indian country. Cholera from Asia reached England and Scotland in 1832, killing hundreds of thousands, particularly infants, in the crowded and unsanitary cities; "how meney has been taken Awe this last year by a pestlenc [sic] that the lord Sent Among us," a Scottish sister wrote in a letter she hoped would find its way to her brother on a Hudson's Bay Company ship on the Northwest Coast of America. By 1833, the cholera epidemic had spread to the Indians of the Great Plains. Cholera struck Scotland again in 1849—"the cholora [sic] is reaging verry much in

Inverness," a correspondent wrote his brother at Vancouver Island; "their is a great number dying ever day"—and wagon trains heading for Oregon and California the same year carried it to Indian people on the plains.[40]

Highland children died of smallpox in Scotland; they died of smallpox on the emigrant ships to America; and they died of smallpox in America. Twenty-five children succumbed to smallpox during the six-week voyage of the *Pearl*, which carried Glengarry settlers to New York in the fall of 1773; thirty-nine children perished aboard the *Sarah* and the *Dove*, which sailed from Fort William to Pictou, Nova Scotia, in the summer of 1801.[41] Both smallpox and dysentery broke out on the *Hector* during its voyage to Nova Scotia in 1773, and eighteen children died. Eighty-one passengers, fifty of them children, died on the *Nancy*, which left Sutherland with 250 passengers for New York the same year.[42] When the brig *Stephen Wright* arrived at Cape Breton from Tobermory, Isle of Mull, in 1827, 40 of the 170 passengers had smallpox, so the ship was quarantined.[43]

Famine was a recurrent visitor in the Highlands, rendering the population vulnerable to greater devastation when disease followed. Thousands died in the famines of the 1690s, and the population in some areas fell by as much as a third as residents succumbed or fled.[44] In times of famine in the eighteenth century, some parents sold their children to shipmasters, who in turn sold them to plantation owners in the American colonies. The transaction relieved anxious parents of extra mouths to feed, offered children (they hoped) a better future, and gave plantation owners a cheap source of labor. When the famine eased, the trade dried up, but the demand for cheap young labor remained. Aberdeen became center of a trade in which kidnapped children were sold to plantation owners in America.[45] Famine hit Scotland again in 1836; and again when the potato crop failed in the 1840s.

* * *

As diseases reached tribal communities via increasingly active trade and transportation routes, different ways of thinking about the world came on new intellectual currents. New ideas, beliefs, and ways of conveying them reached into Indian country and the Scottish Highlands. Missionaries utilized books and Bibles in their campaigns to convert Indians. Soon Indians recognized that writing constituted not only an efficient mode of communication but also an effective tool of dispossession in the hands of colonists insistent on obtaining lands by deed and treaty—one chief described writing as "pen and ink witch-craft, which they can make to speak things we never intended." Some Indians acquired the power inherent in print by becoming literate themselves. Books and writing were not new to Scotland, but the explosion of print in the eighteenth century facilitated the spread from Edinburgh into the Highlands and across the Atlantic of ideas, views, and values that were fundamental in constructing the modern age.[46]

Indian country and the Highlands of Scotland both felt the reverberations of religious contests and the repercussions of religious change. In North America, Christian missionaries often led the cultural assault. Indian people responded in multiple ways to the new teachings and insistent efforts to save their souls from eternal damnation. Many refused to listen; many listened politely and carried on as before; many adopted outward forms of Christianity but kept their core beliefs; many combined traditional and Christian beliefs and practices; many accepted Christianity completely; and some became ministers and missionaries themselves. Debates over Christianity split some communities and generated new ones. New England Algonquians who embraced John Eliot's Puritan teachings in the mid-seventeenth century left their old ways of life and took up residence in praying towns; Delawares who converted to the Moravian faith in the eighteenth century lived in separate communities. Some Mohawks left their Mohawk Valley homeland and moved north to the Saint Lawrence to live in French Catholic mission villages, while other Mohawks maintained ties to the British and the Church of England. Beginning in the 1730s and 1740s, people felt the call of the emotionally intense religious revival known as the Great Awakening on both sides of the Atlantic. "When I was 16 years of age," Mohegan Samson Occom recalled, "we heard a Strange Rumor among the English, that there were Extraordinary Ministers Preaching from Place to Place and a Strange Concern among the White People." After converting, Occom devoted his life to spreading God's word to his "Poor Brethren," a commitment that took him to Scotland in the 1760s.[47] By the time of the American Revolution, many Oneidas espoused a Presbyterian/Congregationalist religion, sided with the Americans, and came into open conflict with Anglican Mohawks. After the Revolution, the Seneca prophet Handsome Lake merged Christian and traditional Iroquoian teachings to produce the Longhouse Religion, which met his people's spiritual needs in a time of deep crisis.

Scotland too felt the currents and conflicts of religious change. Christianity had reached Iona during the so-called Dark Ages, and prior to 1560 all of Scotland was Roman Catholic. But after the Reformation, the Lowlands became more quickly and completely Protestant than did the Highlands, where pockets of Catholicism survived. Protestant Lowlanders regarded the Highlands as a backward world where people lived in the grip of Catholicism and superstition, much as Puritan New Englanders regarded the regions to their north as a savage place where Jesuit teachings and influences corrupted and controlled the Indians. By the eighteenth century, whereas the Lowlands of Scotland were predominantly Presbyterian, most Highland clans were Episcopalian, and some remained Catholic. These divisions contributed to instability in the Highlands and the rest of Scotland. Most Jacobites were Episcopalian.[48]

The influence of the Great Awakening and the dispatch of missionaries by the Scottish Society for the Propagation of Christian Knowledge into the Highlands in the eighteenth century produced further changes and generated additional responses. Like Indian peoples, Highlanders sometimes fashioned a variety of syncretic responses that worked for them. Many had held on to old Celtic beliefs when they adopted Christianity; now many maintained their Episcopalian or Roman Catholic beliefs as they accommodated the Presbyterian teachings of SSPCK missionary-teachers. In some instances, pre-Christian beliefs and rituals survived the conversion to Christianity, and Catholic observances outlived the change to Protestantism.[49] Gaelic poet Hugh MacDiarmid captured some of the diversity of responses in his description of a twentieth-century funeral in the Western Isles. The mourners included believers and unbelievers, and many steered a middle course, being "priest-ridden by convention" but "pagan by conviction."[50]

* * *

Taking a long view, the Highlands and islands had been adjusting to social and economic changes since the collapse of the lordship of the isles around the end of the fifteenth century. As market forces and values penetrated the region, clan chiefs acquired new tastes and developed different codes of behavior. They obtained more goods from the outside world, and by the eighteenth century many Highland chiefs had even seen some of it; they had been educated in Edinburgh, France, Holland, or England, and some could speak several languages. Chiefs who had formerly been most concerned with the number of their followers and the "social product" of their lands increasingly focused on maximizing production. Chiefs who adopted expensive new lifestyles had to raise rents and sometimes even sell lands. They became more like landlords and were sometimes absentee landlords; tacksmen became estate managers; and clanspeople became mere tenants. Financial considerations and commercial connections undermined both kinship obligations and the chiefly prerogatives of feasting, feuding, and controlling redistributive exchanges.[51]

Long-term economic, demographic, and cultural factors were pushing clanship into decline well before the Jacobite rising of 1745, but the abolition of heritable jurisdictions and military obligations in the wake of Culloden accelerated the pace of change. Clan chiefs now circumvented their tacksmen and rented directly to the subtenants, often at greatly increased rents. As a result, tacksmen felt betrayed, and tenants felt oppressed.

The dukes of Argyll, who took the lead in supporting the extension of government authority in the Highlands, also took a primary role in shifting Scottish agriculture toward increased commercialization. They restructured their estates to meet the demands of the market, developed extractive industries in coal, lime, and slate quarrying, and promoted forestation.[52] In the 1750s the third Duke of Argyll began a rebuilding program to transform Inverary castle into a stately home and turn the medieval burgh of Inverary into a modern town.[53]

In Allan Macinnes's words, the period after Culloden represented "the final convulsion" of Gaeldom. State-sponsored terror gave way to state-sponsored improvement. Progress, political economy, and the needs of the British Empire demanded that the Highlands shift "from resource-management under clanship to demand-management under commercial landlordism," which in turn necessitated the reform and relocation of the tribal peoples of the Highlands.[54] Only those few chiefs who had actively supported the Jacobites were exiled or executed, and in 1784 even their lands were restored to their families. Clan chiefs placed economic realities before clan loyalties and flocked to sheep in far greater number than they had rallied to Bonnie Prince Charlie. The British government was able to pursue its policy of modernizing the Highlands, "not by expropriating the Gaelic aristocracy, as had been done in Ireland, but by winning the upper rank of the old order to its side."[55] Greedy landlords and sycophantic clan chiefs would be blamed for the worst of the upheaval, which culminated in the infamous Highland clearances, but they were responding to irresistible forces of change that swept Western Europe.[56]

New kinds of chiefs emerged in North America as well, where recurrent warfare produced repercussions on social and political structures. European policies and influences both consolidated and fragmented power in ways that undermined traditional patterns of leadership. Most Indian societies in the eastern woodlands had two classes of chiefs: older civil or village chiefs, whose influence guided the community in daily affairs and in reaching consensus on issues of importance, and younger chiefs with impressive or growing military records, who led warriors on campaign but relinquished authority when they returned to the village. As war became a normal state of affairs and war parties came and went with increasing regularity, war chiefs exerted more influence in tribal councils. European allies bolstered war chiefs with supplies of guns and gifts of medals and uniforms. On the other hand, civil or peace chiefs saw their influence decline. In 1747 "the old men at the Fire at Onondaga," the central council fire of the Iroquois League, advised against war, but in the Ohio country "the Young Indians, the Warriors, and the [war] Captains consulted together and resolved to take up the English Hatchet against the will of their old People, and to lay their old People aside as of no use but in time of Peace." In 1762 Seneca warriors told the British superintendent of Indian affairs, Sir William Johnson, that now they, not the sachems, were making the decisions; the sachems, they said, were "a parcell of Old People who say Much, but who Mean or Act very little." As sachems lost the ability to restrain the headstrong young warriors, an important generational balance was eradicated. "Formerly the Warriors were governed by the wisdom of their uncles the Sachems," said an Onondaga chief, "but now they take their own way & dispose of themselves without consulting their uncles the Sachems."[57] In 1776, Scottish Indian agents Henry Stuart and Alexander Cameron watched helplessly as younger warriors in the Cherokee council house at Chota seized the initiative from older chiefs and led the Cherokees into war against the Americans.[58] In Indian communities the voices for war grew louder and less restrained, fueling the stereotype of warlike Indians that Europeans and Americans invoked to justify treating them as "savages."

In a world where war and trade increasingly dominated life, some Indian chiefs became dependent on European traders and officials to supply them with the guns and other goods they now needed to command a following, and Europeans could direct the supply to those chiefs they favored. Europeans began to "appoint" chiefs, designating their European-derived status with medals they hung around the chiefs' necks.[59] Europeans' preoccupation with issues of war and trade—areas of male responsibility—often caused them to ignore or dismiss the leadership roles occupied by Indian women, thereby undermining gendered divisions of responsibilities that had helped ensure balance in many Indian societies, just as they undercut generational divisions of responsibilities.[60]

As in the Highlands, the debts some chiefs accumulated resulted in sales of tribal lands. In eighteenth-century Rhode Island, the Ninigret family of Narragansett sachems curried favor with the English colonial authorities and repeatedly sold off tribal lands to finance their efforts to live like English gentry. Hoping to persuade George III to prohibit Thomas Ninigret from selling any more, John and Tobias Shattuck sailed across the Atlantic—which was why they found themselves in Edinburgh in 1768.[61]

Novel forms of chieftainship and new kinds of leaders emerged, some of them the product of Scots and Indian intercourse. In Creek country, in the late eighteenth and early nineteenth centuries, sons of Scottish traders often attained leadership positions among their Indian mother's people and accumulated unprecedented wealth and power. Attuned to commercial practices themselves, they reoriented Native society toward a market economy and promoted "a new order of things."[62] The changes they introduced into Creek society were paralleled by similar transformations back in the Highlands, where clan chiefs were also embracing a new order of things, becoming prosperous, and reorienting clan society to the market economy. Like some clan chiefs after Culloden, a number of Indian chiefs adopted new strategies in the wake of defeat. Men like Little Turtle of the Miamis and Black Hoof of the Shawnees, who had fought against American expansion for twenty years, made their peace with the United States after the battle of Fallen Timbers and followed a path of accommodation rather than resistance. Living both alongside and like their American neighbors was a hard choice but it offered a way to survive in the new world the Americans were creating.

* * *

The changes in their worlds set people in motion. Before the union with England, Scottish emigration went almost entirely across the North Sea. War and trade in foreign lands offered opportunities lacking at home. In the fourteenth century, there were "whole streets" of Scots in Paris. Thousands of Scots went as soldiers and peddlers to Prussia, Denmark, Sweden, and especially Poland, to which as many as forty thousand Scots migrated in the first half of the seventeenth century. In the same period, another forty thousand took advantage of King James's offer of low rents and religious toleration and migrated to Ulster. Oliver Cromwell continued the policy, and more followed after the battle of the Boyne. When Scottish harvests failed in the late 1690s, Scots by the thousands—contemporaries said by the tens of thousands—migrated to Ireland. Some estimates reckoned as many as one hundred thousand Scots had moved to Ireland by 1700.[63] The sheer volume of the Scottish migration to Ireland in the seventeenth century delayed Scottish emigration to America.[64]

Highland Scots traditionally practiced seasonal and temporary migration, moving between upland pastures and valley crops. However, as the traditional Highlands economy became inadequate to the task of feeding and employing its own growing population (let alone meeting the increasing demands on its resources from outside), many people traveled south for seasonal employment, work to "tide them over," or more permanent jobs. "The most industrious" people from Strathnaver on the north coast of Sutherland were reported to "migrate to the south for employment, during the spring and summer seasons, and return with the savings of their labour to pass the winter at home with their families," while "the more idle class remain at home during the whole year, in poverty, idleness and wickedness; their chief employment (if it deserves the appellation) being angling, or shooting." One parish minister complained that young people who took seasonal harvest work in the south spent their wages "on superfluous finery" and brought home diseases such as smallpox, measles, and typhus.[65]

As the Lowlands became increasingly urban and industrial in the eighteenth and early nineteenth centuries, many Highlanders gravitated to Glasgow and Edinburgh, to coal mines and mill towns. "[T]he mills are occupied mostly by the children that come from the Highlands," a Perth mill owner testified to a parliamentary committee in 1834.[66] By this time, however, Highland migration to Lowland mill towns was dwarfed by Irish immigration. In a reversal of early seventeenth-century population movements when Protestant Scots had migrated to Ireland, both Catholic and Protestant Irish migrated in large numbers to the Clyde. By 1851, after the great potato famine, seven percent of Scotland's population were Irish born, most of them concentrated in Glasgow and other western towns.[67] Scots continued to move to Ireland and England, but as the population grew at home, Scottish migration needed a different outlet. Migrant Scots thus turned increasingly to North America.[68]

In Britain, replacing subsistence economy with market-oriented production was regarded as fundamental, both to integrate the Highlands into the larger national economy and to advance the social improvement and "civilization" of the Highlanders.[69] Clan chiefs removed people to render their lands more profitable. In North America, traditional subsistence economies became untenable as animal populations declined and the environment became degraded. Tribal leaders were coerced into selling tribal homelands for American farmlands, and their people moved west. "Common property and civilization cannot co-exist," declared T. Hartley Crawford, commissioner of Indian affairs in 1838.[70] He spoke at a time when the Highland clearances and Indian removals were both in full swing, and he could have been speaking for attitudes on both sides of the Atlantic.

Like Highland Scots before the clearances, Indians were on the move long before the removals of the 1830s. Tribal traditions and origin stories recall migrations from lower worlds to this one and from other regions of the continent to historic homelands. Choctaw and Chickasaw traditions relate that people moved from a land of darkness in the West to new lives on the east bank of the Mississippi. Anishinabe peoples around the Great Lakes recalled migrating from the Saint Lawrence Valley. In some cases migration changed the people as they journeyed into a new identity. People moved down the Ohio River, crossed the Mississippi, and separated to become the historic Osages, Quapaws, Otos, Omahas, and Poncas. Arikaras separated from the Pawnees and moved up the Missouri River; some of the Hidatsas split off from their relatives on the upper Missouri, moved onto the northern Great Plains and the Yellowstone Basin, and remerged as the Crows. The Cheyennes, Kiowas, and Comanches moved south into the heart of the Great Plains and became equestrian buffalo hunters. Creeks who moved from Alabama into northern Florida in the eighteenth century developed a new identity as Seminoles.[71] Indians traveled enormous distances along well-traveled trails, canoe routes, and trade networks. Many communities practiced cyclic migration—from cornfields to hunting grounds to fishing sites—to take advantage of seasonal abundance.

In the wake of European invasion, the scope and tempo of movement increased. Groups moved to make the most of new trade and allies and to escape new diseases and enemies. Escalating intertribal contests, recurrent colonial wars, and increasing racial conflicts pushed many groups deeper into Indian country and frequently generated repercussions there. Indians from the eastern woodlands moved west beyond the Mississippi to escape British domination after the defeat of the French in 1763 and American control after the overthrow of the British twenty years later. The stream of westward migration continued as the new nation intensified the pressure on Indian lands and cultures.

As European colonists and their animals and market forces disrupted traditional Native American economies, Indian people relocated in response. Some moved away; others went to new towns and cities for work, returning to their home communities at certain times of year to continue traditional subsistence practices, participate in community rituals, and maintain family obligations. Seasonal wage labor began to play an important role in many Indian economies and cultures as it did in the Highlands.[72] For some people, seasonal work and regular movement was a way to maintain a place in their old world as they made a place in a new one. Indians sometimes lived in and around colonial settlements and profited from the new economic opportunities they found there even as those same settlements curtailed their mobility and restricted their traditional economy. They worked for cash, labored on colonial plantations alongside African slaves, and enlisted in colonial armies. Indian men traded beaver pelts and deerskins; Indian women traded the corn they grew, the baskets they wove, and the moccasins they sewed. In eighteenth-century New England many Indian men took to the seas, signing on for whaling voyages that sometimes took them away from home for years at a time. In nineteenth-century New England, many Indian women became mill workers.[73]

The first cotton mill in Scotland was built in 1778; by 1795 there were 91; in 1812, 120.[74] While young women from the Hebrides were traveling south to work in these mills, young Abenaki women from northern New England were traveling south to find work in the cotton mills of Lowell and Lawrence, Massachusetts, and Manchester, New Hampshire. There they were likely to work on Scottish looms alongside immigrant Scottish women who had been recruited for the mills.[75] Southern cotton grown on Indian lands seized by Andrew Jackson (and also, as we will see, acquired by Scottish merchants) supplied mills in Scotland, as well as in England and New England and provided employment for Highland and Indian women at a time when their traditional economies were disintegrating.

Highlanders and Indians were becoming participants in the economy of the Atlantic world and part of its labor force. At the same time, people on both sides of the Atlantic were striving to make them a part of civil society.

3

Savage Peoples and Civilizing Powers

As James Boswell and sixty-three-year-old Samuel Johnson traveled by boat in the Western Isles, "Dr. Johnson got into one of his fits of railing at the Scots." He declared they displayed no signs of civilization until the union with England in 1707. "We have taught you," he lectured his Lowland Scot companion, "and we'll do the same in time to all barbarous nations, to the Cherokees . . ."[1] People who regarded themselves as civilized tried to improve Highlanders, Indians, and everyone else. Colonizers made determined efforts to change the way tribal people lived and understood the world. They would raise them up from their "savage state" and give them their religion. They would educate the children by teaching them the English language and English ways. The English initiated such efforts, Lowland Scots continued them, and the United States incorporated them into national policy. The teachings of the Scottish Enlightenment provided a prescription for change in the Highlands of Scotland and in the wilds of America. If tribal people were to survive in the new worlds emerging in North Britain and North America, they would have to be remade in the image of their colonizers.

Depicting Savage Life

Before they romanticized them in the nineteenth century, outsiders regarded Indian country and the Highlands of Scotland as lands of savagery and trackless wilderness. French historian Fernand Braudel's comments about the place of highland societies in world history apply equally to the Scottish Highlands and to Indian country: "The mountains are as a rule a world apart from civilizations, which are an urban and lowland achievement. Their history is to have none, to remain almost always on the fringe of the great waves of civilization, which may spread over great distances in the horizontal plane but are powerless to move vertically when faced with an obstacle of a few hundred metres."[2]

John of Fordun described the Highlands in the fourteenth century as impassable on horseback, except in a few places, and difficult to negotiate even on foot, except in summer.[3] Few travelers made excursions into the Highlands before the mid-eighteenth century. Martin Martin and Edmund Burt were exceptions, and Martin was a native from the Isle of Skye.[4] Daniel Defoe, traveling through Lochaber in the 1720s, described it as "indeed a frightful country full of hideous desert mountains and unpassable [sic], except to the Highlanders who possess the precipices. Here in spite of the most vigorous pursuit, the highland robbers, such as the famous Rob Roy in the late disturbances, find such retreats as none can pretend to follow them into, nor could he ever be taken."[5] General Wade agreed: Without roads and bridges, regular troops were at a distinct disadvantage when fighting Highlanders.[6] Real and fictional travelers described the Highlands as "a wild, uncivilized land," "amazingly wild," with "a most stupendous appearance of savage nature."[7] For Boswell and Johnson, traveling the Highlands and islands, often on small ponies, was an adventure, as well as an odyssey: They were "going where nobody goes, and seeing what nobody sees." Leaving the Isle of Skye on a dark, wet evening, their boatmen "seemed so like wild Indians, that very little imagination was needed to give one an impression of being upon an American river."[8] During a six-week tour of Scotland in 1803, Dorothy and William Wordsworth and poet Samuel Taylor Coleridge were astonished at their Highland guide's ability to find a mountain track where none was visible to them. "It reminded us," wrote Dorothy, "of what we read of the Hottentots and other savages."[9]

The Celtic fringes of the British Isles had been centers for the preservation of classical learning during the so-called Dark Ages.[10] However, to English people and Lowlanders, the Highlands were primitive places inhabited by backward people whose "notions of virtue and vice, are very different, from the more Civiliz'd part of Mankind."[11] The deeper one went into the Highlands, the more savage the inhabitants, wrote William Cross, professor of law at Glasgow University, in 1748: "They who live near the skirt of low country on the East side, are more civilized, But they who are remov'd and lye more to the west, are wild & Barbarous beyond expression, having no intercourse with the low country." Even after 1750, travelers to the Highlands felt themselves in a different world as much as did easterners venturing into the "backwoods" of North America. Duncan Forbes of Culloden said the mountains, coupled with the lack of roads and inns and the ferocity of the inhabitants, prevented the free flow of art, industry, and law from the south and preserved the Highlanders' barbarous customs.[12] Doctor Johnson agreed: "As mountains are long before they are conquered, they are likewise long before they are civilized."[13] Travelers who crossed the Proclamation line in America, like travelers who traversed the Highland line in Scotland, entered "a savage unexplor'd country; without roads; without posts."[14] Travelers to the "wilds" of Scotland regularly described the "manners and customs" of the inhabitants in terms very similar to those applied by travelers in America to the residents of the backcountry, whether Indians or Scots-Irish migrants who perpetuated their Celtic ways in new locations.[15] Highlanders who migrated to America did not immediately shed their tribal ways, and some took on Indian traits, so even in their new homes they sometimes were described as wild and savage people.

Nontribal people generally viewed tribal life with contempt. Their opinions and attitudes rested on preconceptions about savagery and civilization as much as on observation of people's lives. "Civilization" usually meant living a settled, ordered, and agricultural way of life, displaying proper "Christian" modes of behavior and dress, possessing material comforts, practicing the Protestant religion, speaking English, and demonstrating a degree of literacy. The rich oral literatures of Highland and Indian societies did not register with people who expressed their opinions of those societies in writing. When they found the attributes of civility lacking, they resorted to a list of negative traits to describe Highlanders and Indians. As Robert Berkhofer explained in his classic study of white images of Indians, "description by deficiency" led to "characterization by evaluation" and examinations of moral character.[16] In civil society, clothing said much about one's status; lack of clothing thus signified a lack of civility. "Savage" people went around naked or half-naked.[17] Indian loincloths and leggings, as well as kilts that left bare the Highlanders' knees and part of the thighs, were deemed "very indecent."[18]

The languages of race and class were interconnected in the discourse of English colonialism: "The colonized abroad and the poor at home occupied similar moral space," and it was a space reserved for "heathens."[19] The towns of Georgian England and colonial America were not known for health and cleanliness, and the cities that mushroomed during the industrial revolution created horrific conditions for those who lived and worked there, yet travelers expressed disgust about the dirt they saw in Highland and Indian life.[20] Highlanders and Indians lived hard lives in a hard land. Most observers agreed that they lived in wretched habitations and ate a monotonous diet.[21] Daniel Gookin, who had "often lodged in their wigwams," found the lodgings of New England Algonquians "as warm as the best English houses,"[22] but few shared his experience or assessment. Even fewer English visitors said as much for Highland homes.

The typical Highland village was a collection of bothies, which were smoky one- or two-room huts made of mud and stones, with dirt floors and thatched or turf-covered roofs. At the end of the eighteenth century Thomas Garnett described cottages on the Isle of Mull as "extremely poor indeed, being little, if at all, better than the cabins of the South Seas islands, or the wigwams of the American Indians." The Rev. Edward Clark went further: "The pig sties of England are palaces [compared] to the huts of Mull," he wrote. Highland homes were likely to house animals, as well as humans. In this, they resembled the earth lodges of the Mandans, Hidatsas, and other peoples on the banks of the Missouri River, but in fact Highlanders were much poorer.[23] Prior to their devastation by smallpox and Sioux, the Mandans and Hidatsas were prosperous, their villages the center of a thriving trade network built around the surpluses of corn produced by Mandan and Hidatsa women. Dorothy Wordsworth regularly complained about the dirt and poverty of Highland dwellings; she described woodsmen's dwellings as "like savages' huts," and William Wordsworth thought one home so dirty it could only be described as "quite Hottentotish."[24]

Thinking themselves industrious and energetic, English and Americans regarded Highlanders and Indians as lazy, except when it came to fighting or hunting. "They are much addicted to idleness, especially the men, who are disposed to hunting, fishing, and the war, when there is cause," wrote Gookin in the seventeenth century. "The sole occupations of an Indian life, are hunting, and warring abroad, and lazying at home," wrote Lieutenant Henry Timberlake in the eighteenth century. "Nothing can induce him to resort to labor, unless compelled to do so by a stern necessity," said Indian Commissioner William Medill in the nineteenth century. Highland fur traders leveled the same complaints against their Indian customers, but their words matched many descriptions of Highlanders.[25]

While the men seemed to do little except hunt and fight, the women worked hard and aged early.[26] Anne MacVicar Grant, from her observations of Mohawk society as a child and of Highlanders as an adult, described the gendered division of labor in each group in almost identical terms. Because the wild and warlike men thought farming beneath them, the burden of agricultural labor fell on Iroquoian and Highland women. "Wherever man is a mere hunter, woman is a mere slave," she concluded.[27] Women were commonly described as unattractive and indecent and as having loose morals or none at all. "The Indian women are not so good-looking as the men," wrote Lowland trader Robert Ballantyne, who

Figure 3.1. *Interior of a Weaver's Cottage, Islay, 1772,* by Thomas Pennant, from *A Tour in Scotland and Voyage to the Hebrides,* 1774. (Trustees of the National Library of Scotland.)

worked in Cree country. "They have an awkward, slouching gait, and a downcast look—arising, probably, from the rude treatment they experience from their husbands; for the North American Indians, like all other savages, make complete drudges of their women, obliging them to do all the laborious and dirty work, while they reserve the pleasures of the chase for themselves." Ballantyne found Cree women "anything but attractive."[28]

A Scottish minister who had lived in Canada for thirty-six years wrote that he had Indians "in my house, and often encamped about my farm all night, and never missed anything." But those who did not know them accounted Highlanders and Indian great thieves. Highlanders "are always busy'd in grazing & defending their own, or attacking & carrying off the cattle belonging to their Neighbours," wrote William Cross. "To be an adroit & Clever Thief is with them (as with the Spartans of Old) held in high esteem & veneration."[29]

European and American writers agreed that tribal men were proud, their honor was easily slighted, and they were dangerous once crossed. Indians were "very vengeful" and sure to take their revenge when they had the opportunity, "though it be a long time after the offence was committed."[30] Highland trader Duncan

Figure 3.2. *Interior of a Mandan Earth Lodge* by Karl Bodmer. (Joslyn Art Museum, Omaha, Nebraska.)

McGillivray said an Indian would wait "with the most astonishing patience, and if he cannot attack without risking his own life he restrains his resentment 'till another occasion." Fellow trader Alexander Ross said much the same thing.[31] Edmund Burt said Highlanders "are, for the most Part, civil when they are kindly used, but most mischievous when much offended, and will hardly ever forgive a Provocation, but seek some open or secret Revenge, and generally speaking, the latter of the two."[32]

Clan and kin loyalties demanded vengeance. "If any murther, or other great wrong upon any of their relations or kindred, be committed," wrote Gookin, "all of that stock and consanguinity look upon themselves concerned to revenge that wrong." "They are so nearly connected together," said trader Alexander Henry, "that to injure one is to injure the whole tribe."[33] Others said much the same thing about Highland clan vengeance: "Great Barbarities are often committed by One, to revenge the Quarrels of Another."[34] Duncan McGillivray generalized: "It is a universal maxim among Savages that Blood must pay for Blood."[35]

Highland Scots who encountered clan retaliation in Indian country would have understood it better than other Europeans, but some of its dimensions would likely have been new to them. What outsiders saw as random violence and treachery, tribal members understood as retributive and even restorative justice. In the absence of a centralized judicial or penal system, clan vengeance served to regulate homicide and prevent violence from escalating into open clan warfare. In Cherokee society, it also helped restore order to the cosmic balance that was disrupted when someone was killed. Once someone from the same clan as the victim had exacted retribution, "both clans involved considered the matter settled because harmony had been restored."[36]

When outsiders offered positive descriptions of tribal society, they tended to express admiration for a simpler way of life, especially when it was about to be lost. "And now I'm leaving these people whom I truly love," wrote young French traveler Alexandre de La Rochefoucauld, adding "I'm perhaps biased towards them by their beauty and the simplicity of their manners."[37]

Though they had little to give, Highlanders and Indians earned a reputation for hospitality. Observers made almost identical comments about both. "If any strangers come to their houses, they will give him the best lodging and diet they have," Gookin said of the Indians in New England.[38] "I have never seen them deny hospitality and generosity," Robert MacDougall wrote about Highlanders in Canada.[39]

Even as colonial powers worked to reduce tribal peoples to dependence, commentators noted their fierce independence and love of freedom. Some admired the fact that tribal societies combined individual liberty with care for the poor and the weak and that they governed themselves by kinship and custom rather than by state coercion.[40] "The idea of liberty makes them live," one said about Highlanders.[41] "The Iroquois laugh when you talk to them of obedience to kings," said another, "for they cannot reconcile the idea of submission with the dignity of man. Each individual is a sovereign in his own mind."[42]

Of course, Highlanders and Indians had their own ideas about who was civilized. "The poorest and most despicable Creature of the name of MacDonald looks upon himself as a Gentleman of far Superior Quality than a man of England of £1,000 a year," noted one commentator.[43] Indians likewise regularly made it clear that they did not regard themselves as inferior to whites (quite the contrary). Trader Duncan Cameron said that Indians thought themselves "the wisest, happiest and the most independent of men; the greatest compliment they can bestow on a white man is to compare him to an Indian."[44] Not surprisingly, they often expressed disdain for those who sought to change them.

To Raise Them Up

In America and Britain well-meaning and not so well-meaning individuals organized themselves to root out tribal ways, to promote the moral, educational, and spiritual rehabilitation of Indians and Highlanders, and to teach them English. Fueled on both sides of the Atlantic by the religious revivalism of the Great Awakening and then by the philosophies of the Scottish Enlightenment, missionaries, teachers, and reformers endeavored to "raise up" Indians and Gaels by refashioning them to resemble their superiors. The thrust to change Highlanders as a precondition to absorbing them into a unified state came from Edinburgh as much as from London, and Lowlanders took an active role in transforming "barbarous nations" on both sides of the Atlantic. Philosophers of colonization believed that the people beyond the frontiers in North Britain and North America occupied a lower stage on a scale of human and social development. Nonetheless, they were humans who would surely see—or must be made to see—the inferiority of their ways when shown the English example.[45] In the late sixteenth century, artist John White depicted Virginian Algonquians and fanciful Picts in very similar ways, and many writers likened Indians and Highlanders to the ancient Britons at the time of the Roman invasion. Wild Indians, like wild Scots and wild Irish, could be induced to adopt English standards of civility and thereby make up for their delayed development, just as the Romans had tamed the ancient Britons. The process was good for colonizer and colonized, even if force was necessary to convince the natives of the need to change.[46]

James VI/I set out to eradicate the cultural independence of the Highlands. In 1609 the Statutes of Iona required island chiefs who owned more than sixty head of cattle to send their sons to be educated in the Lowlands; seven years later the Privy Council extended the provision to include all children of Highland chiefs. The decrees also tried to suppress the Gaelic bards as carriers of Highland warrior culture and to undermine the chiefs' status in feasting and redistributive exchange by banning the sale of wine and whiskey.[47] In 1616 the Scottish Parliament passed an education act that required each parish to establish a school where the young would be "trained up in civility, godliness, knowledge and learning." There the children would be taught English instead of Gaelic, which, as "one of the chief and principal causes of the continuance of barbarity and incivility among the inhabitants of the Isles and the Highlands, may be abolished and removed." Since most parishes covered more than four hundred square miles, the law had little effect in many sparsely populated areas.[48]

In 1701, the same year the Church of England formed the Society for the Propagation of the Gospel in Foreign Parts, "a few private gentlemen in Edinburgh" who were "deeply affected by the unhappy situation of their countrymen in the Highlands and islands, sunk in ignorance, and destitute of all means of improvement," opened a subscription to establish schools in the Highlands. They raised £1,000 and began lobbying the general assembly

Figure 3.3. John White, *Pictish Man*. (Courtesy of the British Museum.)

The manner of their attire and
painting them selues when
they goe to their generall
huntings, or at theire
Solemne feasts.

Figure 3.4. John White, *Indian in Body Paint*. (Courtesy of the British Museum.)

of the Church of Scotland. In 1709 Queen Anne approved the Presbyterian Society in Scotland for Propagating Christian Knowledge in the Highlands and Islands and the Foreign Parts of the World. The SSPCK opened schools and sent "warrior schoolmasters" into the Highlands and islands to provide a basic education for the people by means of mobile instruction, working one community after another. They taught English language, inculcated Lowland values, and promoted the Presbyterian religion. The first schoolmasters were Lowlanders, but subsequently the teachers were often Highlanders. The SSPCK reflected typical Lowland attitudes toward their northern neighbors: The Gaels were barbarous, backward, and in dire need of instruction and salvation. Unreformed, the Highlands threatened the cultural unity of Scotland and the political stability of the British union. To transform Highlanders from crude rebels to loyal subjects, their language, religion, clan system, economy, and isolation all had to be changed. As "the single most important instrument of anglicization in the 1700s," the SSPCK was committed to erasing Gaelic and replacing it with English as the language of progress. The SSPCK also endeavored to replace Episcopalian and Roman Catholic clergy with ministers of the Church of Scotland.[49]

Englishmen and Lowland Scots saw civilizing the Highlands as vital to both national security and the stability of the Hanoverian regime, as well as for the good of the people themselves. Inhabited by heathens living under the thumb of tyrannical warrior chiefs, the lawless Highlands provided a breeding ground for Jacobitism: "Considering that they are trained up from their infancy in principles destructive to Society and are early taught by their parents a slavish dependence on their Chiefs, and that Robbery and theft are no ways criminal its no wonder to see them making depredations on others and blindly following their Chiefs into every Rebellion." "All the Rebellions in this Country have taken their rise in the Highlands of Scotland, a Country not Subject to Law," wrote William Cross in 1748; the remedy was clear: "Civilize this small corner of the Island, and we shall see no more rebellions from that Quarter, & consequently from no other part of the Country." It was no use conquering the country with military power and then removing that power; the government must establish law and order. Civilization required maintaining garrisons throughout the Highlands, stamping out cattle raiding, enforcing the laws with swift and strict punishment, encouraging industry and husbandry to combat laziness, and sending in "Resolute and diligent Ministers and Schoolmasters," supported by troops if necessary, to drive out Catholic priests who tampered with the common people and instilled in their minds "such Hellish Tenets as may Invigorate the Spirit of Jacobitism."[50]

After the 1745 rising, a way of life that had aroused contempt, suspicion, and fear was treated with open hostility and targeted for eradication. The state's reprisals against the clans were presented as a policy of replacing barbarism with civilization.[51] The clan system had to be broken for the good of the Highlanders. Repressive and punitive measures were justified as necessary to free people "from bonds which, oddly enough, did not seem to irk [them]."[52] Having been defeated militarily, Highlanders were now to be remade to resemble the rest of Scotland, just as defeated American Indians would be targeted for transformation into "Americans." "The way to civilization was thus fairly thrown open to the natives of Caledonia."[53]

Not only Englishmen and Lowland Scots advocated "civilizing" the Highlands. Duncan Forbes of Culloden (1685–1747) supported the Hanoverian government during the '45 and worked to dissuade clan chiefs from joining the Jacobite cause. Like William Cross, he believed that, as long as the clan system survived, the Highlands would remain violent and economically backward. Disarming the Highlanders was the necessary first step. In words that anticipated Thomas Jefferson's plans to convert Indians from hunters to farmers, Forbes wrote:

> When the Highlanders are deprived of their Arms, and thereby that diversion which is the greatest incentive to their idleness, i.e. hunting, is cut off, it is to be hoped the advantages which they must see in their neighbourhood acrueing [sic] from industry, may naturally lead them to it, or, at least, may induce them to send their children to the nearest stations, to be instructed in husbandry, and the other arts and manufactures that may be there acquired.[54]

Pacifying the Highlands was the first step in civilizing them. A government minister described the Disarming Act as a measure for "disarming and undressing those savages."[55] The state understood the political and ethnic symbolism of clothing. Tartan was outlawed—although bagpipes evidently were not—as a vestige of a Gaelic culture that had fomented treason. British troops stationed in the Highlands arrested those they caught wearing Highland dress.[56] The Gaelic language was to be eradicated.

"The children of savages," the *Westminster Journal* pronounced in the wake of Culloden, "are as capable of as much improvement as the children of

Englishmen."[57] In addition to teaching reading and writing in English, the SSPCK schools now added an industrial component, teaching spinning, weaving, and other crafts. The society initially operated to assist the Church of Scotland in ridding the Highlands of Catholicism and savagery by establishing charity schools to supplement the church's parochial schools. Since teaching the Scriptures in English made little impression on students who understood only Gaelic and who, like Indian children in Catholic mission schools, simply mouthed scriptural passages, the SSPCK worked with the established church to replace Gaelic with English. Students who were caught speaking Gaelic were chastised (Latin was also banned as the language of Roman Catholicism). However, like Jesuit missionaries in America, the SSPCK realized that tolerating native language could help facilitate religious instruction and ease the transition to English. The society continued to ban Gaelic from its classrooms and from student conversations, but in 1767 it published the New Testament in Gaelic and distributed thousands of copies. Translation of the Old Testament was completed in 1801.[58] English was the language of education, commerce, and culture, but people still prayed in Gaelic and spoke it at home; it was, said one parish minister, "their fireside language, and the language of their devotions." Even schoolmaster and catechist Dugald Buchanan said "he always prayed and dreamed in his native language." Now the SSPCK policy aimed to teach Highlanders English as the common language of the nation and "teach them to read the Word of God in their own language."[59]

The shift in policy provided little reprieve, however. Gaelic acquired a new legitimacy and respectability "as the language of God and church," but the secular attractions of English as the language of education and economic opportunity in the modern world ensured Gaelic's continued decline.[60] In reports to the general assembly of the Kirk of Scotland, the Rev. John Walker argued that the Highlands and islands were cut off "from the more enlightened parts of the kingdom" by language as much as by distance. Spreading the English language over the Highlands was "at once the most effectual means for the religious instruction of the inhabitants, and the improvement of the country."[61]

Well before the eighteenth century, English had been regarded as the language of status and Gaelic as the language of Highland common people. The language policies of the eighteenth century and Gaelic's association with failed rebellions and declining clan systems emphasized the gulf. Like Indian parents who sent their children to government boarding schools, Highland parents understood that speaking and reading English would help their children cope in a changing world. Despite revived interest in the language by

Gaelic societies formed in the nineteenth century, many schoolteachers continued to punish students who spoke it. Reports from parish clergy in the *Statistical Account of Scotland* in the 1790s and in the *New Statistical Account of Scotland* half a century later documented the steady inroads of English in formerly Gaelic-speaking communities and predicted Gaelic's impending extinction.[62] English was making the same inroads at the same time in Native American communities in New England and producing the same predictions of language extinction.[63]

Additionally, SSPCK-style evangelism sought to bring social as well as spiritual reform to the Highlands and islands. Evangelicals worked zealously to eradicate the "immoral" music, dancing, drunkenness, and fighting that often accompanied supposedly solemn occasions (e.g., baptisms, marriages, funerals) and to curb sexual laxity.[64] They apparently made an impact: In the nineteenth century the Gaels developed a reputation as sober, God-fearing folk, and the Highlands ceased to be a mission field.[65]

The '45 rebellion, noted a report on emigration from the Highlands at the beginning of the nineteenth century, "completed the Civilization, and has hastened the dispersion of the Highlanders; and will probably annihilate the genuine Stock."[66] Most visitors to the Highlands arrived after the mid-eighteenth century, and they saw a culture under siege and a way of life slipping away. Doctor Johnson observed in 1773:

> There was perhaps never any change of national manners so quick, so great, and so general, as that which has operated in the Highlands, by the last conquest, and the subsequent laws. We came thither too late to see what we expected, a people of peculiar appearances, and a system of antiquated life. The clans retain little now of their original character, their ferocity of temper is softened, their military ardor is extinguished, their dignity of independence is depressed, their contempt of government is subdued, and their reverence for their chiefs abated. Of what they had before the late conquest of their country, there remain only their language and their poverty. Their language is attacked on every side. Schools are erected, in which English only is taught, and there were lately some who thought it reasonable to refuse them a version of the holy scriptures, that they might have no monument to their mother tongue.[67]

Alexandre de La Rochefoucauld and his tutor Maximilien de Lazowski also observed "the great changes that time, and civilisation, have brought about."

As English replaced Gaelic and breeches replaced kilts, it seemed that all of the Highlanders' "ancient customs were at stake. They faced becoming a former people."[68]

* * *

To the SSPCK and other evangelizing organizations, the rugged lands of the Scottish Highlands and North America were both spiritually destitute, and both constituted "foreign mission fields." The SSPCK saw these areas as part of a "North Atlantic circuit" in which it endeavored to evangelize peoples who were culturally distinct from English-speaking Britain. It supported missionary activities and educational colonialism in both places, and its work among Highlanders and Indians followed some parallel courses.[69]

With two decades of educational missionary work in the Highlands under its belt, the society was ready to extend its efforts to other "heathen and infidel lands" and began to support missionary work among the Indians. James MacGregor of Saint Fillans in Perthshire, who became the first Gaelic-speaking Protestant minister in Nova Scotia when he emigrated in 1786, wrote a number of hymns in Gaelic about spreading the gospel west "to America and the wild Indians" to lift them out of blindness and ignorance just as the Gaels had been elevated.[70] Carrying its work across the Atlantic, the SSPCK joined the growing movement to remake American Indians and save them from themselves. It also worked to save them from others: As the SSPCK sought to defend Britain at home by converting Highlanders who might be seduced by Catholic Jacobites, so it endeavored to defend Britain in America by converting Indians who might be won over by the Catholic French.

Twenty years after it was founded, the SSPCK set up boards of correspondents in Boston and New York through which it subsidized projects. It sent missionaries to Indians in Connecticut and Long Island. The SSPCK's "utmost ambition," according to a committee report in 1796, "was to *seize* upon young untutored minds, as yet undepraved by vicious habits and examples, but utterly destitute of all means of cultivation; to rescue from savage ignorance, superstition, and vice; to furnish them with the means of knowledge and grace, and to train them up into fitness for being useful members of the church, as well as of human society." The goal was not just to teach children to read English and do numbers: "It is the SALVATION OF SOULS."[71]

Ironically, as the SSPCK dispatched ministers to spread Lowland values and faith, it sometimes found that the untamed Highlanders it was trying to reform in Scotland had beaten them to Indian country, and the ministers went to work in an existing Highland-Indian context. The SSPCK provided Oglethorpe's colony in Georgia with a Gaelic-speaking missionary, John Macleod of Skye, who was to serve as minister to the Highland settlers, as well as to their Indian neighbors; in 1741 it planned to send a missionary to North Carolina who would minister to both the Highland colonists and the local Indians.[72] In 1743, when the society sent David Brainerd to live with a Mahican community at Kaunameek, midway between Stockbridge and Albany, Brainerd complained: "I live in the most lonesome wilderness." The only person with whom he could converse in English was his Indian interpreter. "Most of the talk I hear is either Highland Scotch, or Indian."[73] The society sent Brainerd to work among the Delawares, where he died of tuberculosis in 1747.

The SSPCK also supported missionaries to the Cherokees, dispatched Samuel Kirkland as missionary to the Oneidas, people whom Kirkland described as "in plain English, filthy, dirty, nasty creatures, a few families excepted," and supported a proposal to build a school in Iroquois country.[74] But it focused its primary efforts on the Algonquian tribes of the Northeast. As in the Highlands, the society endeavored to recruit and train native teachers and missionaries to carry on its work. That meant sending former students like Delawares David and Jacob Fowler and Hezekiah Calvin into Iroquois country, a journey of some three hundred miles into a linguistically, culturally, and politically different landscape. As Margaret Connell Szasz aptly suggests, "the shock they received upon their arrival in Oneida or Mohawk villages could easily have paralleled that of early Lowland school masters arriving on the Isle of Harris or the Strath of Kildonan or Fort Augustus." The Algonquian teachers struggled in Iroquois villages, and by 1769 the society stopped sending new schoolmasters to Iroquois country. By 1772 only Samuel Kirkland remained in Oneida, where he exerted his influence in the developing split from Britain and the Church of England.[75]

The SSPCK believed that savagery and Christianity were incompatible "& that men must cease to be Savage before they can be truly converted to the truth of the Gospel."[76] However, as in the Highlands, the society modified its strategy and shifted its emphasis by employing the native language to help bring salvation rather than eradicating it as a step toward civilization. (With the help of an Indian translator and an Indian printer, missionary John Eliot had produced a Bible in the Massachusett Algonquian dialect a hundred years before the SSPCK translated the Bible into Gaelic.[77]) After 1760 the SSPCK encouraged its missionaries to learn Indian languages and even advocated sending English-speaking youths to live with the Indians to learn their tongues. It subsidized Eleazar Wheelock's educational efforts among Indians, first at Moor's Charity School in Connecticut and then at Dartmouth College in New Hampshire. The SSPCK also provided funds for John Sergeant's school at the Indian mission town of Stockbridge in western Massachusetts. In Sergeant's words, the goal of educating Indian children was to "change their whole Habit of thinking and acting; and raise them, as far as possible, into the Condition of a civil industrous and polish'd People." Unlike students in the Highlands and islands, Indian students did not get to go home at the end of the school day, but in many other ways their journeys to school and their experiences there were comparable. "The omnipresent instruction of the Reformed Protestant faith, which provided the matrix of learning for both Gaelic and Native scholars in their respective charity schools, created a rather somber tone." Every day began with prayer and catechism. It is no coincidence that the colonial institutions' goals for Indian students sound almost identical to the SSPCK's goals for Highlanders. Highlanders and Indians—and Irish—were part of the same evangelizing program to bring civilization and Protestant Christianity to the barbaric edges of the British Empire.[78]

Eleazar Wheelock wanted to establish his own regional board of correspondents for the SSPCK, and in 1764 the society approved it. The SSPCK also arranged part of Nathaniel Whitaker and Mohegan minister Samson Occom's 1766–1767 visit to Britain to raise money for Wheelock to build a new Indian school, the future Dartmouth College. During his fund-raising tour, Occom visited and preached in Edinburgh, Aberdeen, and other places. He was, reported the *Scots Magazine,* "the first Indian minister that was ever in Britain." Ironically, as Margaret Connell Szasz has noted, Dugald Buchanan, who was promoting reform for his fellow Highlanders, was in Edinburgh at the same time, supervising the printing of the Gaelic New Testament. If the two met, they would have found much in common: both Reformed Protestant ministers, both from a tribal society and an oral culture, both speaking English as a second language, and both functioning as spiritual intermediaries for their people during a time of profound change. The general assembly of the Church of Scotland did not respond favorably to Occom's plea for financial support, but Occom and Whitaker raised £2,529 in the course of their two-month tour in Scotland, "proportionate to the population of the country, a larger sum of money" than the £9,497 they collected in twenty-eight months in all of England and Wales.[79]

By 1775 Wheelock had spent the money Occom had raised in England, but few Indian students attended his new school. The SSPCK kept a tighter grip on its share of the funds, holding the capital and insisting, to the frustration of Wheelock and subsequent Dartmouth presidents, that the revenue be used strictly for its intended purpose: educating Indian missionaries.[80] The SSPCK also withdrew its support of Samuel Kirkland's mission, citing negative reports of its limited success.[81] It provided financial support to some Indian students at Hampton Institute in Virginia.[82]

* * *

In the second half of the eighteenth century, Edinburgh developed from being a backwater town notorious for dirt and disease and became, at least for a moment, one of the intellectual capitals of Europe, an Athens of the North. It produced and attracted a galaxy of writers, scientists, poets, and thinkers—Adam Smith, James Black, Robert Burns, James Boswell, David Hume, Adam Ferguson, and others. Tobias Smollett called Edinburgh "a hot-bed of genius," and the city sustained a book trade that "transform[ed] this intellectual activity into print."[83] Scottish Enlightenment thinkers changed the way people understood and explained the world. They saw human beings as essentially the same, regardless of time, place, and culture; physical and human environments explained their different behaviors. In an age where travel reports from America and elsewhere were coming off the presses thick and fast, and the Seven Years' War made information about Indians available as never before, the men of the Scottish Enlightenment attempted to explain what distinguished civil society from "rude" and primitive societies. They "preferred to point out how they resembled the Spartan or the Iroquois in thought or feeling rather than how they differed from the Spartan or the Iroquois in behavior." Philosophical historians like William Robertson and Adam Ferguson explained human development according to diverse modes of subsistence. Societies moved gradually through four basic stages: "savage" (hunting and fishing); "barbarian" (pastoral herding or shepherding), a first phase of "civilized," based on agriculture; and "fully civilized," based on commerce and manufacturing. This model of stadial development was warmly received and widely accepted. "The Great Map of Mankind is unrolld [sic] at once," exclaimed Edmund Burke, writing to congratulate William Robertson on his new *History of America*, published in 1777.[84]

Both the Highlands of Scotland and Indian country offered testing grounds for the philosophical historians' theories. Clans and tribes were societies in their infancy. Indians were primarily hunters and therefore "savage"; Gaelic-speaking Scottish Highlanders were pastoral herders and occupied the next rung on the stadial ladder, but they were still "barbaric" and had not yet attained the level of progress of the English and the more anglicized, pro-union Lowlanders. More than just "curiosities living at the periphery of the empire," Indians were "living windows on Europeans' past"; by observing Indian societies one could see "the first footsteps of the human race." Adam

Ferguson, the only Highlander and Gaelic speaker among the Edinburgh luminaries, wrote that Indians "in their present condition," presented "as in a mirrour, the features of our own progenitors." A former chaplain to the Black Watch Regiment in Flanders in the 1740s, Ferguson published his "Essay on the History of Civil Society" in 1768. Drawing liberally on Kames, Hume, Rousseau, and Smith, Ferguson's work contained passages in praise of primitive peoples, especially in North America and the ancient world. He may have "found in them what he had found in his Highland regiment: honor, integrity, and courage, which commercial society with its over specialization and mental mutilation, destroyed." Scottish Enlightenment thinking influenced both Sir Walter Scott and James Fenimore Cooper, whose writings established enduring images of Highland Scots and American Indians.[85]

In fact, wrote Roy Harvey Pearce, "American theorizing about the Indian owed its greatest debt to a group of eighteenth-century Scottish writers on man and society." William Robertson was as renowned as Edward Gibbon and Voltaire in his day. As principal of the University of Edinburgh, he transformed it from a northern town college into a leading European university. Robertson's histories—of Scotland up to the union of the crowns, Europe during the reign of Charles V, Spanish discoveries and conquests in America, and early contacts with India—comprise a major historical narrative that traces the emergence of Britain, the growth of European nation-states, and the beginnings of European empire. Although he had never seen Indians, his *History of America* fit them into the rationale of progress by depicting them as primitives (with both the virtues and the vices of that condition): They lived off the bounty of the land, but unlike "civilized" people they did not transform it by their labor. "In all his histories," notes Owen Dudley Edwards, "we will only understand him if we see that behind his comments on early Scotland, or post-Roman Europe, or pre-conquistador America, he is thinking of his not-too-distant Highland cousins in the present or, at best, very recent times."[86]

Robertson shaped the way American leaders thought about Indians. By the late eighteenth century, the books of the Scottish Enlightenment were not only being read in America; they were also being printed and reprinted in America, as well as in Edinburgh and London. Americans who were in process of building a new society found great appeal in the sociology of progress the Scottish Enlightenment thinkers constructed. They could interpret the American Revolution as a phase of social evolution rather than a violent political upheaval. The Scots thinkers were not only read and taught in American colleges: "Their thinking became American thinking." Thomas Jefferson (who was tutored by a Scot, William Small) knew the Scottish school of thinkers well. He was familiar with Robertson's writings and shared the school's assumptions about human progress, the Indians' inferiority, and the future they faced: "There was only one way forward for North American Indians. It was a path of unconditional assimilation conceived as stadial progression, and if they did not take it the fault was theirs." Robertson may have "set in concrete" the assumptions that men like Jefferson shared with him and in doing so, argues Bruce Lenman, "has his place among the architects of Indian removal in the North American republic and that ultimate pathway paved with good intentions, the Trail of Tears."[87]

Jefferson was a leading advocate of bringing Indians to "civilization." As his writings on human rights and his record on slavery famously demonstrate, Jefferson was a man of many contradictions. As a scholar, he admired Indian character and customs. He recorded their languages, excavated an Indian burial mound near his home in Monticello, and instructed Lewis and Clark to gather all of the information they could about Indians during their expedition to the Pacific. He believed that Indians were culturally inferior but that, with proper guidance and instruction, they were capable of improvement, of becoming "civilized." In many public utterances Jefferson appeared a concerned friend of the Indians and a champion of their rights. However, he also speculated in Indian lands, and, when he became president, he was far more concerned with dispossessing Indians than with civilizing them. He was the architect of policies that would eventually result in their forced removal from the eastern United States beyond the Mississippi. Taking Indian lands was for the their own good, Jefferson told himself, because it would compel them to give up hunting and become farmers. In Jefferson's vision of the future, this was the Indians' only alternative to extinction. Giving Indians "civilization" in return for land allowed the United States to expand with honor. The United States needed Indian lands in order to grow; the Indians needed American civilization in order to survive. It was a fair exchange, he believed. Indians who refused to change (and sell) were doomed, which was lamentable but inevitable. As Anthony F. C. Wallace put it, "the Jeffersonian vision of the destiny of the Americas had no place for Indians as Indians."[88]

The United States imposed programs of massive change. Men like Benjamin Hawkins, U.S. agent to the Creek Indians from 1796 to 1816, attempted to impose a social, economic, and gender revolution in Indian country and base Indian life around intensive agriculture. Like most other eastern woodland peoples, the Creeks and Cherokees had farmed for centuries, but women grew the crops. Now men were to give up hunting for a life behind a plow, and women were to take up spinning, weaving, and other "domestic chores." As Indians spent less time hunting, they would need less land and could sell the "surplus" to the United States. As men spent more time at home, the nuclear family, with the male at its head, would supplant the matrilineal clans. As families acquired more property, they would learn to adopt Anglo-American principles of ownership and inheritance.[89]

In 1819 Congress passed the Civilization Fund Act, which provided for an annual appropriation of $10,000 to introduce "the habits and arts of civilization" among the Indians by employing "capable persons of good moral character, to instruct them in the mode of agriculture suited to their situation; and to teach their children in reading, writing, and arithmetic." The act was not a one-time measure but a commitment to permanent involvement in Indian education; by 1900 the figure appropriated was $3 million.[90] Like Highlanders, Indians were deemed capable of improvement, and the changes made by the Cherokees and other tribes in adopting the trappings of civilization furnished evidence to support that view.

Many Cherokees accommodated to American ways, wore European styles of clothing, plowed fields and fenced lands, and cultivated corn and cotton. They owned looms and spinning wheels, saw mills and grist mills, cattle, pigs, and sheep. Some held slaves; some were Christian. In 1827 the Cherokees restructured their tribal government into a constitutional republic modeled after that of the United States, with a written constitution, an independent judiciary, a supreme court, a principal chief, and a two-house legislature. Sequoyah devoted a dozen years to developing a written version of the Cherokee language. In 1828 the Cherokees established a newspaper, the *Cherokee Phoenix*, published in both Cherokee and English. Some Cherokees were literate in two languages. John Ridge and his cousin Elias Boudinot, who edited the *Cherokee Phoenix*, attended the American Board's Foreign Mission School in Cornwall, Connecticut. "You asked us to throw off the hunter and warrior state," Ridge said in a speech in Philadelphia in 1832. "We did so—you asked us to form a republican government: We did so—adopting your own as a model. You asked us to cultivate the earth, and learn the mechanic arts: We did so. You asked us to learn to read: We did so. You asked us to cast away our idols, and worship your God: We did so."[91]

However, in America as in Scotland, the drive to acquire land outpaced the determination to change the people living on it. Advocates of rapid change increasingly came to believe that Indians and Highlanders were doomed to extinction unless they stopped being Indians and Highlanders. In the nineteenth century they showed decreased patience and increased contempt for those who clung to their old ways; such cultural resistance demonstrated that they were, in fact, incapable of becoming civilized. Missionaries and teachers had made heroic efforts to instruct Indians "in agriculture and the mechanic arts, as well as in the principles of morality and religion," but "what tribe has been civilized by all this expenditure of treasure, and labor, and care?" asked Governor Lewis Cass of Michigan Territory in 1830. "The cause of this total failure cannot be attributed to the nature of the experiment, nor to the character, qualifications, or conduct of those who have directed it." The fault lay with the Indians. A few Cherokees had made significant progress, but in general there was not "a more wretched race than the Cherokees" on the face of the globe. Two centuries of contact with Europeans had brought no improvement in their condition. Clearly, it was the will of God that Americans should reclaim the earth from a state of nature and cultivate it. Likewise, eighteenth-century Enlightenment thinkers had faith in the Highlanders' ability to ascend the stadial ladder, but Highlanders who faced starvation in the nineteenth century despite all the "improvements" made must be inferior by nature and should be moved off the land. Backward people who were unwilling or unable to ascend the stadial ladder of development must not stem the march of progress.[92]

Crossing Cultures, Competing Cultures

If people could ascend the ladder of human progress, they could also descend it, something that worried observers and commentators when Europeans went native. Where tribal and modern societies met, some individuals moved easily—and some not so easily—between them. Some moved between Indian country and Scotland. Indians, as well as people who had lived with them, visited or returned to Scotland. As we will see, many Highland Scots lived with Indians, and some effectively became Indians. Passing between Highland and Indian cultures constituted a crossing, not an ascent or a descent.

Scots made such crossings for various reasons. Between 1740 and 1745 some five hundred boys were abducted (with the apparent connivance of town officials) from the Aberdeen area for servitude in America. One kidnap victim, Peter Williamson, was captured by Delaware Indians, lived with them, and returned to Scotland, where he published an account of his experiences. The Aberdeen magistrates seized the book and had it burned, and Williamson was thrown in jail but escaped to Edinburgh. From there "Indian Peter" sued and won damages from the Aberdeen officials who had conspired in his kidnapping. His autobiography went through numerous editions, and "Indian Peter" became quite a celebrity. The frontispiece of the 1762 edition of Williamson's book showed him dressed as a Delaware.[93] Some Scots found that the ties they forged in Indian country proved stronger than those to home. Lowlander David Ramsay lived with the Indians in Upper Canada, although he did not marry. When he returned to

Scotland, his sister refused to acknowledge him as her brother because he was dressed like an Indian; subsequently, he returned to America.[94]

Highland travelers in Indian country saw evidence of change, borrowing, and adaptation to new circumstances just as travelers witnessed the same phenomena in the Highlands. Patrick Campbell, a former soldier from Fort William in Inverness, set out from the Highlands of Scotland in 1791 "with an intention to explore the interior inhabited parts of North America, attended with an old faithful servant, a Dog, and gun only." As he made his way across Canada, from New Brunswick to Niagara and back across New York State, Campbell met Highland settlers virtually everywhere and enjoyed their hospitality. But nothing compared with his reception at Grand River, Ontario, home of the famous Mohawk chief, Joseph Brant. Brant had been educated at Wheelock's school and had twice visited England, where he had befriended and gone carousing with the Prince of Wales. He was "well acquainted with European manners," and his home was an elegantly furnished mansion. The other Indians lived in humbler style, but Campbell found them "more comfortably lodged than the generality of the poor farmers in my country." Brant's two black servants, wearing buckled shoes, ruffled shirts, and livery, served tea and dinner with china, crystal, and silver and offered a selection of port and Madeira wines after the repast. A young Indian played a hand organ, and when Campbell attended a service at the Indian church, he "never saw more decorum or attention paid in any church in all my life." Brant engaged Campbell in a theological discussion, but Campbell seemed more impressed by the singing of the Indian women—they "sung most charmingly," he wrote. Campbell made a speech in Gaelic, "the Indian language of my country."

Campbell was quite taken with the Mohawk women. From the moment he arrived he was impressed by the handsome appearance of Brant's wife. The highlight of his visit was an evening of dancing, drinking, and flirting with the girls. Brant had his young men stage a war dance for his guest, after which Campbell joined in their "native and civil" dances. Then "we began to [do] Scotch reels, and I was much surprised to see how neatly they danced them." The women were attractive, the wine and rum flowed freely, and Campbell "got tipsy," although he could barely get the women to touch a drop. He suggested to Brant that in Scotland "it was customary to kiss both before and after every dance," but Brant replied that "it would never do here," no doubt to Campbell's disappointment. The dancing continued until dawn when, "fatigued with drinking and dancing, we retired to rest." "I do not remember I ever passed a night in all my life I enjoyed more," wrote Campbell.[95]

John Norton, also known as Teyoninhokerawen, traveled between Indian country and Scotland. Norton claimed he was the son of a Cherokee father

Figure 3.5. Patrick Campbell. Miniature portrait from Patrick Campbell, *Travels in the Interior Inhabited Parts of North America*. (Courtesy of the Champlain Society.)

(who appears to have been rescued as a boy by a British officer when redcoats destroyed Keowee in 1760 and taken to Scotland) and a Scottish mother. Norton went to Canada in the army, taught school for a time, and then became a trader. He became a Mohawk by adoption, as a nephew of Joseph Brant. In the early nineteenth century he made several visits to Britain and became something of a celebrity in Georgian society. At the request of the British and Foreign Bible Society, he translated the Gospel of John into Mohawk. He wrote a journal of his thousand-mile travels in America, together with a history of the Indian tribes. Dedicated to the Duke of Northumberland, it was "an Indian book, but addressed to contemporary readers in England and Scotland." In 1814 Thomas Scott, stationed in Quebec, wrote to his brother, Walter, about Norton. He was, he said, "a man who makes you almost wish to be an Indian chief." "What do you think of a man speaking the language of about twelve Indian nations, English, French, German and Spanish, all well, being in possession of all modern literature—having read with delight your Lady of the Lake, and translated the same, together with the Scriptures, into Mohawk?" Thomas assured his brother that Norton dressed, painted, and wielded a scalping knife like an Indian. He added that Norton was apprehensive that the *Edinburgh Review* would be hard on his book. Norton traveled to London in 1815 with his Indian wife and son, also named John, but he spent most of his visit in Scotland. Both his wife and son went to school in Dunfermline, and the son remained there when his parents returned to Quebec in 1816. Four years later, John Jr. was said to be marrying a Scots girl, a "Miss MacDonald." During his time in Britain, Norton became the personal friend of Sir Walter Scott, William Wilberforce, the Duke of Northumberland, and other influential literary and political figures.[96]

The poet Thomas Campbell, who saw Norton on his first visit to England in 1805, considered him a fraud "who whoops the war-whoop to ladies in drawing rooms" and "palms a number of old Scotch tunes (he was educated in the woods by a Scotchwoman), for Indian opera airs, on his discerning audience." Scholar Tim Fulford is more lenient: "Teyoninhokarawen's Scots songs were not frauds but the fruits of a hybrid culture arising from colonial encounters."[97]

Walter Scott also interested himself in the visit to England and Scotland in 1823 and 1824 of a "white Indian," John Dunn Hunter. Like other visitors from the forests of North America, Hunter spoke of the Indians' plight, noted the social evils and inequities of industrial Britain, and had great appeal for philanthropists and romantics who feared the loss of community in their own country. Like the Highland chieftains Scott lionized in his novels, Hunter would have seemed a brave champion of a disappearing way of life.[98]

Figure 3.6. Solomon Williams, *Portrait of Major John Norton* (*Teyoninhokarawen*). (Beaverbrook Collection of War Art, AN 199950096–001, © Canadian War Museum.)

Natives and some nonnatives worried about the effects of imposing "civilized ways" on tribal peoples. Indian leaders regularly reminded Europeans and Americans that "your ways are not our ways" and that native people lived according to their own moral codes. Some Indians were quick to point out hypocrisy, as when Seneca chief Red Jacket asked missionaries why they were so sure theirs was the one true religion. Indians might be more inclined to accept Christianity, he said, if Christians offered them better examples than lying, cheating, drunkenness, and theft.[99]

Many people argued that Indian life and civilized life did not mix and that tribal people who were exposed to civilization acquired all of its vices and none of its virtues. Fur trader Alexander Ross expressed a commonly held opinion: "The Indian in his natural state is happy; with the trader he is happy; but the moment he begins to walk the path of the white man his happiness is at an end."[100] The rapidity of change in the eighteenth-century Highlands, as well as the upheavals it produced, caused some commentators to question the benefits of "progress" elsewhere. Connections with the aggressive capitalist society to the south generated love of money in place of attachment to kin, clan chiefs became oppressors rather than protectors of their people, and whole communities were uprooted. "If civilization be said to bring blessings among a people," wrote one critic, "the case of the Highlands furnishes a melancholy exception."[101]

Scots who were schooled in the Enlightenment theory of the development of human societies thought seriously about the implications of living in Indian country. There were doubts too about the relative benefits of "civilized" and "savage" life and ample evidence that the gulf between the two ways of life was not as clear as some might like to think. Strange as it seemed to would-be reformers, "savage life" sometimes exerted a magnetic attraction for "civilized" people, as Benjamin Franklin, Hector St. Jean de Crèvecoeur, and others realized. "There must be in their social bond something singularly captivating, and far superior to anything to be boasted of among us," wrote Crèvecoeur; "for thousands of Europeans are Indians, and we have no examples of even one of those Aborigines having from choice become Europeans! There must be something more congenial to our native dispositions than the fictitious society in which we live."[102] Charles Mackenzie traded widely in Indian country, married an Indian, and had several children with her. Advised to retire from Indian country, he replied, "It does not require much to reconcile a civilized being to the Indian life, but a mighty task to reconcile an Indian to civilized life and thinking; there is nothing for me better than remaining where I am." Mackenzie lived the rest of his life with his family at Red River in Manitoba.[103]

The upward path of human progress was steep and unsteady. Would-be reformers and missionaries knew that "savages" stumbled and fell backward if not tended:

"O all of you who are sending Bibles and honest missionaries
To the Indians so far away
Will you not send some of them into all of the Gaelic islands . . . ?"

wrote a Baptist minister and Gaelic poet in the early nineteenth century.[104] They also feared the effects of environment. What would become of Highland Scots who went to North America, where they would live in isolation, perhaps even in Indian country? Recently emerged from "barbarism," Highlanders might be more prone than others who came into contact with Indians to slip back down the ladder of progress; they might fall even further—even back into "savagery." In a sermon delivered and published in Dundee in 1831, John Jaffrey launched "An Appeal on Behalf of the Scottish Settlers in British North America," in which he reminded his audience that brotherly love and Christian duty required that they raise money to send ministers to Scottish settlers in Canada, as well as to heathens in foreign lands.[105] Highland Scots, once considered wild and savage in North Britain, now needed to be saved from wildness and savagery in North America. Once subjects for civilization, they now also became instruments of civilization.

4

Warriors and Soldiers

In the summer of 1763 Colonel Henry Bouquet cobbled together a force of 465 soldiers to march to the relief of Fort Pitt. It was the height of Pontiac's War, and the Indians had captured every British fort in the West except Niagara, Detroit, and Fort Pitt, to which they laid siege. Most of Bouquet's soldiers—390 of them—were Highlanders, battle-hardened veterans of the Black Watch, with a detachment of Montgomery's Highlanders and another from the 60th Regiment. Early in the afternoon of August 5, after they had already marched seventeen miles that day, the army was ambushed by Shawnee, Delaware, and Mingo warriors. By nightfall, when the fighting subsided, the soldiers had suffered more than sixty casualties. Surrounded and outnumbered, they hunkered down behind hastily constructed ramparts of flour sacks on the crest of a hill. They expected to be overrun come daybreak. But when the attack occurred early the next morning, Bouquet executed a desperate feint. He pulled troops back in the center, creating the impression of an impending collapse. When the Indians surged forward to seize the apparent opportunity, the Highland troops flanked them, poured in devastating musket fire, then charged with their bayonets. The Indians broke before "the Irresistible Shock of our Men." With fifty men dead and sixty more wounded, Bouquet's little army limped the remaining twenty-six miles to Fort Pitt.[1] "The Highlanders are the bravest men I ever saw," wrote Bouquet, a Swiss career soldier who had seen plenty of action in both Europe and North America. "[T]heir behavior in that obstinate affair does them the highest honor."²

On one level, Bushy Run was a classic Indian-white conflict: Indians fighting on terrain of their choosing enjoyed initial success, but European discipline and firepower eventually took its toll. On another level, ironically, the Highland soldiers and Indian warriors who clashed in the Pennsylvania woods that August in a vicious struggle for and against empire had much in common. The battle pitched into conflict two groups who were at different stages in their dealings with the British Empire. Redcoats still garrisoned Fort William in the Scottish Highlands just as they now occupied Fort Pitt in Indian country. Highland warriors had battled against English colonial power on its northern frontier in the British Isles; now Highland soldiers were defending British colonial power on its western frontier in North America. Indians were now waging war against the British; in years to come they would go into battle with them against the Americans. Highland and Indian warriors engaged in combat separately against the British, fought each other, and eventually struggled together against the Americans.

In time, Highlanders and Indians both fought for the powers that colonized them. Employing allies from one region of the empire against enemies in another was standard imperial strategy, and employing tribal military culture against itself was common on the frontiers of Britain and America. To divide and conquer required enlisting Native allies, and fighting "savage" enemies justified using "savage" allies, as well as brutal tactics. People who were uprooted by or incorporated into new economic systems could be co-opted into enforcing and defending the new order. The government that tried to "civilize" the Highland clans also attempted to recruit them into imperial service after the Jacobite rising of 1745. Britain and the United States both condemned using Indian allies, yet each enlisted them when it suited their purposes. Once their "ferocity" was tamed, or at least harnessed, Highlanders and Indians made "excellent soldiers."³

Highlanders and Indians were reputed to be warlike by nature. Martial prowess and military tradition were key markers of masculine identity. "War rather than peace is their natural condition," John Major wrote of Highlanders in 1521.⁴ "As is the country, so are the inhabitants, a fierce fighting and furious kind of men," wrote Daniel Defoe two hundred years later.⁵ General Wade said they considered it a reproach to be seen without a "Musket, Broad Sword, Pistol and Durk," all of which were deemed part of their dress. When Wade first arrived in the Highlands, the inhabitants wore their weapons even to market and church, "which looked more like places of Parade for Soldiers, than Assemblies for Devotion or other meetings of Civil Societys."⁶ "Mountaineers are warlike," pronounced Doctor Johnson, "because by their feuds and competitions they consider themselves as surrounded by enemies, and are always prepared to repel incursions, or to make them. Like the Greeks in their unpolished state, described by Thucydides, the highlanders, till lately, went always armed, and carried their weapons to visits, and to church."[7] Highland men were well built and made fine warriors, noted another visitor, "and would choose to work in no other service than soldiering."[8] In Native North America, "warrior" and "man" were often synonymous terms. Europeans said war and hunting were the only things that Indian men esteemed. The "whole Business of their Lives is War and Hunting," said General Thomas Gage. John Stuart asserted exactly the same thing about Cherokee men: Their "whole business" was war and hunting. Among the Creeks, "to be a man was to be a hunter and warrior."[9]

Depictions of tribal peoples as inherently warlike and living in a state of perpetual violence said more about the agendas of colonial powers than about tribal realities. Highland men spent more time with crops and animals than with claymore and musket (the last clan battle in the Highlands occurred in 1688). The young men who turned out in the Jacobite risings and in Britain's imperial wars may have been accustomed to hard living, but they were more often raw recruits than seasoned fighters.[10] And although war was a regular and important event in Indian society, it was not a normal state of affairs: It was preceded by rituals of preparation and followed by rites of purification. It became endemic only after European contact generated new motives for fighting and new sources of international and intertribal competition. Compared with the warfare waged by disciplined armies of state societies, the wild charges and guerilla strikes that characterized tribal warfare seemed random and irrational; these were explosive acts of violence by people who were inherently warlike but inherently less effective than state warfare. In reality, non-state societies "waged war for different—but no less rational and no more savage—purposes than did the nation-states of Europe," who brought new levels of conflict to the frontiers of North Britain and North America.[11]

Nevertheless stories of bloody clan and tribal feuds allowed perpetrators of colonial violence to depict their own wars as a business as usual against people who lived in a state of perpetual warfare.

Warriors for the Crown

The Highlands certainly witnessed plenty of fighting over the years. Highland men rendered their chiefs military service—custom demanded it, the clan expected it, and, if necessary, the chief coerced it. Scots also had a long tradition of mercenary service abroad. They served in Ireland from the thirteenth to the sixteenth century: thirty-five thousand "redshanks" (many from the Hebrides) battled against the English conquest of Ireland in the late sixteenth century. They fought in the service of France against England in the Hundred Years' War, and the *Garde écossaise* served as the French king's bodyguard from 1419 until the eighteenth century.[12] A Scot named Tomás Blaque (Thomas Blake) accompanied Francisco de Coronado's army of Spaniards and Mexican Indians when it invaded New Mexico in 1541.[13] Scottish soldiers served in just about every army that fought in the Thirty Years' War (1618–1648). About five thousand served with the Dutch, eleven thousand with the French, twenty-five thousand with the Swedes, and almost fourteen thousand with the Danish-Norwegian army. The three hundred Scottish officers in the Danish-Norwegian army outnumbered Danish and Norwegian officers by a ratio of 3:1.[14] Patrick Gordon, who left Scotland at sixteen to seek his fortune as a soldier, fought in the armies of Sweden, Poland, and the Holy Roman Empire. He moved to Russia and rose in the tsar's service to become General Patrick Ivanovich Gordon. Gordon was buried in Moscow in 1699, but thousands more Scottish soldiers died anonymously in European wars.[15]

In Britain, long-standing English distaste for a large standing army meant that the government had to look elsewhere for the manpower to patrol the Highlands. In 1667 King Charles II issued a commission to the Earl of Atholl to raise independent companies to "keep watch along the Highland line." By the end of the century, Campbells, Frasers, Grants, Menzies, and Munros manned these companies. "The Watch," as it was known, failed to prevent the Jacobite rebellion of 1715 and was disbanded in 1717, but General Wade advised the king to restore it to help pacify the Highlands. Reestablished in 1725, it became known as *Am Freicadn Dubh,* the Black Watch, either from its uniform of dark green and blue tartan or from its service in keeping watch on "blackmailers." In 1739 a royal warrant increased its strength and made it a numbered regiment, meaning that it could be used for service overseas and not just to patrol the Highlands. (Initially the 43rd (Highland) Regiment, ten years later it became the 42nd Regiment after the disbanding of another regiment elevated it in seniority). Originally formed to patrol the northern frontier, the Black Watch would see more service on the western frontier of Britain's empire.[16]

Assuming that Highlanders came from a "warrior society," the army put Highland regiments into the field with minimal training. However, Highlanders were not always well suited for service with regular armies. A clan chief could raise the militia in his glen, but, noted economist Adam Smith, "they were less willing to follow him to any considerable distance, or to continue for any long time in the field. When they had acquired any booty they were eager to return home."[17] Regular officers made the same complaint about Indian allies. Tribal societies were not organized for the kind of wars nation-states waged. "Warriors" were part-time soldiers. Concern for crops, herds, families, and homes undermined their ability to sustain long campaigns and rendered them vulnerable to those waged by professional armies. The demands of planting and harvesting limited clan levies. As the Jacobite army retreated in the spring of 1746, many Highlanders slipped away home "as it was seed time." Crops and harvests often affected when and whether Highlanders enlisted.[18] Similarly, the timing of Green Corn ceremonies sometimes determined when and even whether Indians fought.[19]

On more than one occasion, Highland regiments mutinied against what they regarded as unacceptable conditions or a betrayal of trust. Like Indians who joined a war party, Highlanders who enlisted often expected to return home once the specific conflict was over. The Black Watch mutinied in 1743 when it learned it was to be dispatched overseas. Recalled from Flanders at the outbreak of the 1745 rebellion, it was stationed in the south of England and perhaps with good reason. (The government preferred to station Irish regiments in Scotland and Scottish regiments in Ireland.)[20] Nevertheless, after Culloden, when the government tried to stamp out cattle raiding and other lawlessness in the Highlands, "none of his Majesty's Forces [were] fit to be employed for remedying this insufferable evil, but Highlanders, who having their own Dress and language are the only people properest [sic] for the fatigue, of long and Night Marches through such rough and Uncouth Places, and can by their Intelligence (having the Irish Tongue) get these Thieves best ferreted out of their lurking holes."[21]

After the '45, service in the British army was the only way for a Highlander to legally bear arms and wear tartan. The Disarming Act of 1747 outlawed the carrying of weapons and established severe penalties (six months' imprisonment for a first offense, seven years' transportation for a second) for wearing "highland cloaths," except for those "as shall be employed as officers and soldiers in the King's forces."[22] The clan system collapsed, but the government maintained the military culture that had been associated with it to help fill the ranks, thereby encouraging the warrior tradition it had worked so hard to suppress. "To allure them into the army," said Doctor Johnson, "it was thought proper to indulge them in the continuance of their national dress." Clan loyalties were now channeled into allegiance to Highland regiments, whose dress, cultural background, and Gaelic language set them apart from other British regiments. Wearing "the Government's black tartan kept old ardours warm."[23]

Highland manpower became a major resource for the crown. Clan chiefs raised regiments for the king's wars abroad using the same techniques they had applied to rally their clans in the past: They appealed to their honor and loyalty and invoked the Celtic warrior tradition; they threatened them with higher rents or eviction; and they made promises and failed to keep them. Impressments, poverty, and hunger also helped fill the ranks of Highland regiments.[24] Scottish regiments regularly recruited from the slums of Glasgow and other Lowland industrial towns to which displaced Highlanders had migrated. Recruiting Highlanders into the British army established a tradition of military employment for Highland men and reinforced the association between the Highlands and militarism.[25] War shaped life in the Highlands after Culloden as much as it had before, but Highland militarism was now state sponsored rather than clan based. Highland regiments were as much a phenomenon of the post-Culloden age as sheep farming—and the sheep that drove men from their homes helped the government to fill the ranks.[26]

Estimates vary, but between the start of the Seven Years' War in 1756 and the end of the Napoleonic Wars in 1815, nearly fifty thousand men were recruited from the Highlands and islands to serve in twenty-three line regiments and twenty-six fencible regiments, not including the Black Watch. In the seven years after Britain declared war on revolutionary France in 1793, Scotland, with fifteen percent of the nation's population, provided sixty percent of its fencible foot soldiers and thirty percent of its horsemen. The Highlands produced twenty-three of the thirty-seven Scottish battalions. One commentator calculated that the Highlanders had sent virtually every other man of military age to fight in Britain's foreign wars. The figures reflect poverty and unemployment in the Highlands as much as valor and patriotism.[27]

Many Highlanders knew what the government was up to. Some former Jacobites fought with the French: For instance, James Johnstone, aide-de-camp to the Marquis de Montcalm at the siege of Quebec, had fought at Culloden. In 1759 Louis-Antoine de Bougainville recommended recruiting more—a "troupe d'Ecossais." Sixty Highlanders led by a MacLean, MacDonald, or some other chief of a respected clan would bolster the French war effort. The Highlanders understood very well that the government sent them to America to depopulate their lands and to have them die, said Bougainville.[28]

* * *

Highland Scots were first used as soldiers in America when the Georgia board of trustees sent Lieutenant Hugh McKay and Captain George Dunbar to the Highlands to recruit farmer-fighters who could serve as a buffer against the Spaniards to the south, the French to the west, and Indians in the back-country. Recruiting from Caithness and Sutherland and from Clan Chattan in Inverness-shire, McKay and Dunbar took the first batch of 177 emigrants in 1735, another group two years later, and the last in 1741. Led by John Mor Mackintosh, the emigrants settled on the Altamaha River. "The Highlandsmen have these three weeks had quiet possession of the Altamaha, and agree very well with the Indians," General James Oglethorpe reported in February 1736. At first they called their settlement New Inverness but renamed it Darien in defiant memory of the failed Scottish colony on the isthmus of Panama, which Spain had attacked at the end of the seventeenth century, and they declared their determination to defend it "to the Last Extremity." They "made a most manly appearance with their Plads, broad Swords, Target & Fire Arms." Oglethorpe was so impressed that he appeared among them in Highland dress himself. He formed an independent company of Highland rangers to police the contested frontier with Spanish Florida. He also used these "warlike colonists" to impress the Indians during negotiations. When war broke out between Britain and Spain, Oglethorpe's Highland rangers fought with English, Creek, Yuchee, and Chickasaw allies on the Florida frontier. They captured the Spanish forts at Picolata and San Diego in 1740 but were badly defeated by a vastly superior force of Spaniards and Yamassee Indians at Fort Mosa. Two years later they got their revenge when they ambushed a Spanish force. "The White people Indians and highlanders all had their Share in the Slaughter," wrote Oglethorpe. Thirty-eight members of the Black Watch joined Oglethorpe's settlement after being sent to Georgia as punishment for mutiny. Joint participation in military expeditions secured the colony of Georgia and consolidated the alliance of Highlanders and Indians.[29] "Until the eighteenth century was nearly gone," writes Roger Kennedy, "kilt-wearing, claymore-wielding Highlanders often went into battle beside cousins in blankets, breechclouts, and war-paint."[30]

After the Duke of Cumberland destroyed the Jacobite threat to Britain, he deployed new garrisons in other parts of the empire, as well as in Scotland. In the Mediterranean and North America, as well as in the Highlands, the garrisons were intended to keep the local inhabitants loyal and at the same time promote British civilization in frontier regions. General Edward Cornwallis, who had ravaged the Highlands with particular enthusiasm after Culloden, arrived in Nova Scotia as governor in 1749, with some twenty-five hundred settlers and soldiers. To rival the French fortress at Louisbourg, they built the town of Halifax in what was Mi'kmaq hunting territory. When Mi'kmaqs took up arms, Cornwallis described them in terms similar to those he had applied to the Jacobites—rebels and savages—and intended to treat them the same way: He had no qualms about offering bounties for the scalps of Mi'kmaq men, women, and children. His comrade-in-arms at Culloden, James Wolfe, who regarded Highlanders with disdain, recognized their potential for service in Nova Scotia. "I should imagine that two or three independent Highland companies might be of use," he said in 1751. "They are hardy, intrepid, accustomed to rough country and no great mischief if they fall."[31] Recently considered savages themselves, Highland soldiers were now fit instruments to root out savagery—and they were expendable.

At the start of the Seven Years' War, British forces experienced early set-backs and suffered disaster when French soldiers and Indians destroyed General Edward Braddock's army on the banks of the Monongahela River in 1755. British efforts to recruit Indian allies met with mixed results. Mohegans often supplied scouts to the English, and Sir William Johnson, the Irish superintendent of Indian affairs, generally managed to secure the support of the Mohawks and other tribes of the Iroquois confederacy. But most Algonquian tribes from the Saint Lawrence Valley to the Great Lakes sup-ported the French, to whom they were tied by trade, kinship, and a shared desire to curb British expansion. Britain had to look elsewhere for "savage allies" to fight in its American wars. It found them in the Highlands of Scotland.

The idea of recruiting Highlanders did not originate with Prime Minister William Pitt, but he took credit for it: "I there found a hardy race of men, able to do the country service, but labouring under a proscription: I called them forth to her aid and sent them forth to fight her battles. They did not disappoint my expectations, for their fidelity was equal to their valour."[32]

Britain's need for soldiers allowed some former Jacobite chiefs to redeem themselves in the eyes of the Hanoverian government by calling out their clansmen as they had in the old days. Simon Fraser of Lovat raised a regi-ment to serve the regime that beheaded his father for treason. Their services reaffirmed Lovat's own loyalty, and the forfeited estates were returned to the Fraser family in 1774.[33] The 77th, Montgomery's Highlanders, and Fraser's Highlanders, the 78th, were both raised in 1757 from Jacobite clans, particu-larly Camerons, Frasers, MacDonalds, MacLeans, and MacPhersons. Gaelic speakers from other regiments were reassigned as sergeants and corporals in the new regiments.[34] Fragments of Gaelic poetry composed in Scotland or by soldiers in British regiments suggest that the clan chiefs were not alone in seeing loyal military service in America as a way of atoning for a Jacobite past in Scotland.[35]

During the Seven Years' War "more Highlanders wore the King's red coat and the King's black tartan than ever followed the last Stuart prince."[36] In 1757 there were 3,867 Scots soldiers and NCOs and 207 Scots officers in America, representing 27.5 percent and 31.5 percent respectively of the total British force. They regularly found themselves in the thick of the fighting and bore the brunt of British losses.[37] In 1758, the Black Watch headed General Abercrombie's disastrous assault on Fort Ticonderoga and Major James Grant's Highland troops suffered heavy casualties in an abortive attack on Fort Duquesne. (Grant stole a march on the French and Indians at night, only to lose the element of surprise when he ordered drums beaten and bagpipes played at dawn—an action the Indians could only explain "by supposing that he had made too free with spirituous liquors during the night."[38]) Fraser's Highlanders were one of the first regiments to land at Louisbourg in 1758 and the next year helped win a stunning victory on the Plains of Abraham at Quebec while General Wolfe lay dying. Montgomery's Highlanders participated in invasions of Cherokee country in 1760 and 1761. In 1761 both battalions of the 42nd Regiment and nine companies of Montgomery's Highlanders—a total of 2,075 men—sailed to the West Indies, where they fell victim to malaria, yellow fever, and other diseases. By the time Martinique and Havana fell in 1762, only 795 men remained alive; the Black Watch could field only 480 soldiers. Battered and depleted, the remnants of the Highland regiments were sent back to mainland America. Encamped on Staten Island in the spring of 1763, they were recuperating from diseases variously described as "intermittent fever" and "ague" (malaria), "flux," and "bloody flux" (dysentery), as well as "bilious disorders," "venereal," coughs, chest pains, rheumatic pains, and various injuries and wounds. Because Donald McLean, regimental surgeon for Montgomery's Highlanders, was too sick to treat his own men, local physicians had to be brought in. Others, their constitutions broken beyond repair, requested leave to go home. When Pontiac's war broke out, the army scrambled to assemble an effective fighting force from the sick and wounded Highlanders. They were to be "ready to March at a Moment's Warning," but some of the men were listed as "fit to march if assisted by wagons." The broken regiments furnished the Highlanders who fought with Bouquet at Bushy Run. "By late August 1763, of more than 2,000 Highlanders who had sailed for the West Indies two years before, just 245 remained fit for duty." According to one account, of the twelve-hundred-strong Black Watch, "only seventy-six survived to see their country again."[39]

The casualty rate for Anglo-Americans in the Seven Years' War was nine percent; for Highland regiments it was thirty-two percent; "they might as well have been at Culloden," comments Murray Pittock. Touring the western Highlands some years later, Dr. Samuel Johnson said simply, "Those that went to the American war, went to their destruction."[40] In 1763 "the Nobility Gentry & Freeholders in

the Northern & Highland Counties of Scotland" sent a petition to the secretary
of war. Their regions had been so badly "drained of Men" by the war that they
were "put to great distress for want of hands to labour the ground." They requested
that "the few remains of these Gallant men be sent home to repeople the Country
and Breed a Race of Soldiers who may emulate the Actions of their Fathers in
another War."[41] Some of those who failed to return home remained in America
to build new lives on government land grants.

The sacrifices of the Highland regiments did not overcome prejudices in
England, where anti-Scots sentiment ran deep, fueled by the influence and patronage of the king's minister, the Earl of Bute, who, to make matters worse, bore the
surname Stuart. Two Highland officers, recently returned from Havana, were
hissed at and pelted with apples by the gallery mob when they attended a comic
opera at Covent Garden in December 1762. "Is this the thanks we get—to be
hussed when we come home?" they asked outraged fellow Scot James Boswell.[42]

Nonetheless, fighting as British soldiers helped heal some old wounds.
Campbells and MacDonalds now found common cause fighting for the
British Empire. During Pontiac's siege of Detroit in 1763, Captain Donald
Campbell was captured and killed by Indians. Overweight and nearsighted,
Campbell was an amiable fellow who had looked out for his junior officers
and was well liked. Lieutenant James MacDonald felt "pain beyond expres-
sion" at the murder. "I never had nor never shall have, a Friend or Acquaintance
that I valued more than him," he told Colonel Henry Bouquet.[43] Service in
the army helped reconcile members of rival clans and united English and
Scots in an officer elite in a process of state building.[44]

"Sauvages d'Écosse"

Not only did the English use Scottish regiments against Scots and Irish, but
they also pitted Indians against Indians and set Scots against Indians. "It is time
for the Scots to go hunting/After treacherous Frenchmen and Forest-folk," a
Gaelic song urged Highland soldiers.[45] The belief that Highlanders shared similar traits with Indians fostered the belief that they would make good "Indian
fighters."[46] Highlanders seem to have agreed. In 1753 Mungo Campbell took
over as government factor for the forfeited estate of Cameron Lochiel near Fort
William after his predecessor (his uncle) was murdered.[47] Four years of hard
service among disaffected tenants in the western Highlands led him to consider
a change of career and solicit a commission in the army: "I have lived long
enough in Lochaber to qualify me for fighting against Indians," he wrote.[48]

Their military experience and performance as light infantry seemed to suit Highlanders for American service: "For a campaign in the wastes of America, soldiers better qualified could not have been found."[49] Governor James Glen of South Carolina wrote to fellow Scot General John Forbes during the Seven Years' War: "The great superiority that the French have in Indians can hardly be compensated but by Colonel Montgomery's Scots Highlanders and Colonel Washington's American Highlanders."[50]

Fighting Highlanders and Indians was different from fighting the French: Tribal warriors fought in their own way, and English armies treated them differently. Highlanders and Indians made formidable enemies. Their "ways of war" were not "native" but a response to lethal new weapons and, for a time, proved effective against regular armies. Clansmen gave up the two-handed sword in favor of the single-handed claymore and adopted the mass charge as the most effective tactic against ranks of musket men, who were usually able to get off only one round before the Highland torrent fell upon them. Firearms, however cumbersome, unreliable, and inaccurate the early models, rendered obsolete the ritualized fights that had previously typified Indian warfare in much of North America. Indians turned to mobile guerilla tactics, in which fast-moving war parties fighting from cover sustained minimal casualties while picking off soldiers who fought in ranks.[51]

When Highlanders and Indians fought against "civilized" people, they were depicted as savage warriors who committed atrocities. Perpetrators of such actions could expect no mercy once the armies of civilization prevailed. Tales of bloodthirsty deeds preceded the Jacobite army as it advanced into England. Citing a report that the Jacobites had orders to give no quarter at Culloden, James Wolfe wrote after the battle: "We had the opportunity of avenging ourselves for that and many other things, and indeed we did not neglect it, as few Highlanders were made prisoners as possible." A dozen years later Wolfe applied similar justification to killing Mi'kmaqs during the siege of Louisbourg. "The Indians of this island gave us very little trouble," he wrote. "I take them to be the most contemptible *canaille* upon earth . . . a dastardly set of bloody rascals. We cut them to pieces whenever we found them, in return for a thousand acts of cruelty and barbarity."[52] Violent resistance by tribal peoples against colonial expansion reaffirmed their savagery in the eyes of the colonizers and reinforced the necessity for colonial programs of civilization. It also demonstrated their suitability for carrying out state-sponsored violence should the colonial project require it.

Contact and conflict with "savage" warriors could be an unsettling and terrifying experience for regular soldiers. Troops trained for conventional European combat sometimes became unnerved by the ferocity of a Highland charge or the guerrilla warfare of painted Indians notorious for torturing and scalping those who fell into their hands. British troops broke and ran under the impact of the Highland charge at Prestonpans in 1745, where the claymores inflicted horrendous wounds; ten years later they did so under sustained fire from concealed Indian enemies at the Monongahela River. In both cases, the officers blamed the "shameful" behavior of their men.[53] The slaughter of Braddock's men and of the English garrison at Fort William Henry in 1757 stood as stark reminders of the nightmarish possibilities of waging war against Indians, whose concepts of warfare seemed to differ markedly from those of "civilized" nations.[54] The report that, after Grant's failed attack on Fort Duquesne, Indians stuck the heads of Highland victims on stakes with their kilts hung underneath, flapping in the breeze seems to be an unsubstantiated later invention.[55] Nevertheless, Indians waged psychological warfare against their British enemies, and Indian warfare could be a transformative experience for British soldiers.[56]

British soldiers could match their tribal foes and allies atrocity for atrocity, of course, as Cumberland's men demonstrated after Culloden. Highlanders arrived in North America with a reputation for ferocity and sometimes built on it. At the beginning of the war the *Scots Magazine* carried a report of a Lieutenant Kennedy, who led Highlanders and Indians "to go a-scalping, in which he had some success." Quinton Kennedy, a Lowland Scot from Ayrshire, had come to America with Braddock in 1755 and survived the slaughter on the Monongahela. In 1756 he led "a motley contingent of some sixty Mohawks and Highlanders from the newly arrived Black Watch" on a daring raid into French territory. He painted himself like an Indian and headed a command of Stockbridge warriors known as the Indian Corps.[57] According to one newspaper report, when the Highlanders captured Mi'kmaqs during the campaign against Louisbourg, they chopped off their heads, "not being acquainted with the Method of Scalping." Evidently they were fast learners. Olaudah Equiano, a thirteen-year-old Ibo who had been kidnapped by slave traders in Africa and sold to a British naval officer, found himself at the attack. He vividly remembered the day he held in his hand the scalp of an Indian chief who had been killed in the fighting; "the scalp had been taken off by an Highlander," he recalled.[58] French prisoners who surrendered to the British during the siege of Louisbourg "told us they stood in the utmost awe of our Savages" (by which they meant the 78th [Fraser's] Regiment serving with Wolfe) and "feared lest our Highlanders should not give them quarter."[59] Two years later, routed by the charge of Fraser's Highlanders on the Plains of Abraham, the French called them "sauvages d'Écosse."[60]

Malcolm Fraser, a lieutenant in the 78th during the campaigns against Louisbourg and Quebec, made some telling observations on atrocities. Out with a scouting party, he came across several corpses lying in the road; "they were all scalped and mangled in a shocking manner. I dare say no human creature but an Indian or Canadian would be guilty of such inhumanity as to insult a dead body." It was an odd comment from a man whose father had been killed at Culloden. A week later Fraser reported that Goreham's Rangers killed a man and two boys they had taken prisoner, claiming they had no choice but boasting about it back in camp. Fraser now modified his opinion: "This barbarous action proceeded from that cowardice and barbarity which seems so natural to a native of America, whether of Indian or European extraction." In other words, vicious deeds were the product of an uncivilized environment. A couple of weeks later, he had to confront a heinous act among his own kind. Following a skirmish with a party of French and Indians, Captain Alexander Montgomery of the 43rd Regiment ordered several prisoners "butchered in a most inhuman and cruel manner." Fraser gave quarter to a couple of prisoners and handed them over to a sergeant, but the sergeant killed and scalped them both. There was, wrote Fraser, "no excuse for such an unparalleled piece of barbarity"—nor now any attempt by Fraser to attribute it to ethnicity or environment.[61]

An unfortunate incident in the Louisbourg campaign illustrated how close Highlanders and Indians stood in the minds of regular soldiers. A sentry, "seeing a man coming out of the wood, with his hair hanging loose, and wrapped up in a dark-coloured plaid," challenged him. Receiving no response from the Gaelic-speaking Highlander and mistaking him in the hazy weather for an Indian wearing a blanket, the sentry shot him dead.[62]

The discipline and determination of British troops could be as terrible for tribal peoples as Highland charges and Indian guerrilla warfare were for regulars. This, after all, was what the British military prided itself on: redcoats standing their ground and maintaining their calm under attack, pouring volleys of musket fire into the enemy, then advancing with measured tread to finish the job with cold steel. In the end, it was believed, the discipline and bayonets of British regulars would always prevail, as they did at Culloden and Bushy Run.

Friends and Foes in the French and Indian Wars

Highland officers and soldiers shared the prejudices of their class and compatriots. Their dealings with Indian people generally deviated little if at all from the policies and practices of the British government, the British military, and the British Indian department, in which Scots figured prominently. For instance, John Campbell, Earl of Loudon, who took over as commander in chief of the British forces in North America in 1756 had little use for Indians as allies, and Captain James Murray of the Black Watch wrote "Our Indians are an odd set of people." Nevertheless, Loudon believed that Indians had a special affinity with his Highland troops, and Murray said "they like the highlanders." Indians helped Murray and other wounded Highlanders off the field after the assault on Fort Ticonderoga. [63]

Since Highland regiments were regularly stationed in frontier outposts, Highland soldiers had regular contact with Indian people.[64] Officers and men cultivated relations with Indian women. Some learned their language, and a few even dressed and painted like Indians. Highland soldiers serving in Indian country often replaced shoes with moccasins, wore leggings under kilts, carried tomahawks in place of broadswords, and used powder horns, sometimes carried by a quillwork strap made by an Indian woman.[65] Close encounters meant that Highland soldiers were not always blind to their common humanity with Indian people or to some shared experiences.

Some officers in Highland regiments expressed sympathy (if not empathy) for the Indians. Highlanders and Cherokees served together in General Forbes's campaign against Fort Duquesne in the spring of 1758. (Born in Fife, Forbes had fought against the Jacobites at Culloden, where he narrowly escaped death when a musket ball struck a coin in his pocket.) When the Cherokees, "owing to their natural fickle disposition," showed signs of drifting away, Forbes hoped that seeing "their Cousins the Highlanders" would help keep them in line.[66] Two years

Figure 4.1. Highland soldier's engraved powder horn with a strap woven from moose hair by an Indian woman. The horn belonged to James Cameron of "the 42 Royall Heylanders." (National Museum of Scotland, Edinburgh.)

later the "cousins" were fighting each other. Fifteen years after Cumberland's vicious scorched-earth campaign in the Highlands, Highland troops under Colonel Archibald Montgomery and Major (breveted lieutenant colonel) James Grant conducted similar campaigns in Cherokee country. Montgomery was a Lowlander with Highland family ties and evidently spoke Gaelic; Grant, of Ballindalloch in Banffshire, had served with Cherokees in Forbes's campaign. The parallels between Cumberland's actions in the Highlands and their own in Cherokee country may not have been lost on them. In 1760 Montgomery, with Grant as second in command and twelve thousand Highland troops, burned the Lower Cherokee towns but turned back when he encountered almost impenetrable mountain terrain and stiff resistance at the Middle Cherokee towns. Grant returned the next year. With Captain Quinton Kennedy's corps of Mohawks and Stockbridges screening the army's advance from ambush, Grant burned fifteen towns, destroyed more than fourteen thousand acres of cornfields, and drove "about 5,000 Indians including Men, Women & Children" into the woods and mountains, where they faced a choice between starving and making peace. "I hope I shall not live to see such days again," said Cherokee chief Attakullakulla, or Little Carpenter: "You have destroyed our Towns & our Corn by which a great many of my people must die. I hope the dreadful warrior will have mercy now & spare us & do no more to destroy us."[67]

Montgomery and Grant both harbored doubts about the necessity for the war. Grant wondered why people who had formerly been allies had turned against the British. "These Indians are rogues, as they all are," he wrote commander in chief General Jeffery Amherst, "but I fancy they have sometimes been hardly dealt by and if they could tell their own story I doubt much if they are so much to blame as has been represented by the People of this Province." Grant hoped burning a couple of towns would bring them to peace terms. After destroying the town of Estatoe, in which his soldiers bayoneted and burned Cherokees, Montgomery felt the same way. "There can be no great advantage in continuing a war against those savages," he told Amherst. They had been "sufficiently corrected." Peace was the best thing.[68]

Amherst, along with many South Carolinians, wanted to see the Cherokees "hunted down & their throats cut." The Cherokees were "barbarian savages," guilty of "inhuman acts of cruelty," and must be "severely punished" before any peace was made.[69] But Montgomery and Grant did not share in the clamor for genocide. "I could not help pitying them a little," Grant wrote; "Their villages were agreeably situated; their houses neatly built; there were everywhere astonishing magazines of corn, which were all consumed." Grant fought to starve the Cherokees into making peace, not to destroy them. A "renegade" Highlander, Charles McLemore, an unlicensed trader, had acted as messenger

Figure 4.2. *Hugh Montgomerie, 12th Earl of Eglinton, 1739–1819,* by John Singleton Copley. A distant cousin of Archibald Montgomerie, Hugh served as a lieutenant in the 77th Regiment during the Cherokee War, an event commemorated in the background of this later portrait, where Highland soldiers are shown burning a village and killing Indians. (Scottish National Portrait Gallery, Edinburgh, PG 1516.)

from the Cherokees to Montgomery; now a "Baptiz'd Savage [Charles] McGunningham" prevented some Cherokees from coming by spreading "a most villainous report" among them. However, the Cherokees made peace at Charles Town in December 1761. When Grant and his Highlanders arrived in town, they were booed and hissed. Grant's campaign produced a bitter debate (between Henry Laurens and Christopher Gadsden) in the South Carolina press, and Grant fought a duel (nonlethal, it turned out) against Colonel Thomas Middleton of South Carolina. It seemed to many South Carolinians that Grant and Montgomery displayed a "preference for Cherokees over colonists."[70]

Hard on the heels of their thousand-mile campaign against the Cherokees, Montgomery's Highland battalion was dispatched to Halifax, Nova Scotia, for the winter. After the heat of South Carolina, Montgomery dreaded the consequences of the extreme cold on his troops and begged Amherst to change the order. Montgomery himself was given leave to return home, but his men went to Halifax.[71]

Several years later Montgomery's Highlanders again found themselves "on the side of" the Indians. In December 1763 Scotch-Irish settlers in western Pennsylvania, calling themselves the Paxton Boys, massacred innocent Christian Conestoga Indians near Lancaster. A detachment of the 77th Regiment, encamped outside Lancaster, was dispatched under Captain James Robertson to escort 140 surviving Indians to a safe haven in New York. When the Highlanders first arrived, according to one of the Indians, "they acted quite wild and particularly harassed our young women folk," but they seem to have carried out the escort without further incident, only to find that the governor of New York denied the Indians entry, and they had to return to Philadelphia. The Highlanders may have been grudging escorts, but Benjamin Franklin extolled their conduct, in sharp contrast to that of the Paxton Boys: "Highlanders have, in the Course of this War, suffered as much as any other Corps, and have frequently had their Ranks thinn'd by an Indian Enemy," he wrote, "yet they did not for this retain a brutal undistinguishing Resentment against all Indians, Friends as well as Foes."[72]

At the end of Pontiac's war, one hundred men of the Black Watch traveled through Indian country from Fort Pitt down the Ohio River to Fort Chartres, where they took possession of the Illinois country from the French commander. Lieutenant Alexander Fraser of the 78th Regiment had gone ahead with ten soldiers of the Black Watch, followed by Irish trader-agent George Croghan and a party of Shawnee, Iroquois, Delawares, and Wyandots, to make peace with the tribes of the region. When Fraser's party arrived at the Illinois, Kaskaskia Indians captured and beat them. Only Pontiac's intervention saved them from being burned. Kickapoos and Mascoutens attacked Croghan's party. Even so, both Croghan and Fraser made it through.[73]

The main Black Watch detachment left Fort Pitt in August 1765 in several boats. The party consisted of Captain Thomas Stirling, three lieutenants, four sergeants, two drummers, ninety-two privates, five artillery men, a couple of Indian interpreters, and a dozen Iroquois and Delaware warriors to serve as scouts and hunters. Shortly after departure, one man drowned, but the expedition suffered no other casualties. Like the Lewis and Clark expedition forty years later, the detachment met Indians of many different tribes, lived among them, and experienced a variety of relations with them. Their Indian scouts did most of the hunting, but soldiers sometimes accompanied them as they passed through country filled with "vast quantities of all kinds of game." They hunted buffalo regularly and occasionally killed bears. Stirling pronounced buffalo "as fine meat as ever England produced."[74]

Relations between the Black Watch soldiers and their Indian companions fluctuated. Stirling referred to the scouts as our "Copper Colored friends."[75] The officers complained that, since the Indians had no chiefs among them, they were "unsteady in their resolutions" and constantly threatened to abandon the expedition "if they were not indulged in every little whim they had." The officers placated them with gifts but showed little understanding of the cultural significance of gift giving, regarding it as a form of extortion they had to tolerate rather than an exchange to cement and sustain friendship. For their part, the Indians seem to have thought the British were not fulfilling their promises, hence the recurrent reminders of the need for gifts. They even "blacked their faces at us, which," said Stirling, "is the greatest sign of enmity they can show." When the expedition reached Fort Chartres the Indians became "very much dissatisfied." They complained "that now we had got within the four corners of a Fort, we don't mind them, and are worse than our words to them." Stirling had to buy goods at inflated prices from French traders to give to the Indians. A week after the Black Watch took over the fort, the Indians and the two interpreters left, "having each got a blanket, a pair of leggings, a knife, & a little paint." Nevertheless, they were still unhappy.[76]

There were moments, however, when things were different. Highlanders and Indians hunted together and "had excellent sport." They ate and smoked together. After they made it past the falls of the Ohio, they stopped to repair their boats, and the soldiers carved their names in the trunk of a tree. At night the Indians invited them to a feast to celebrate getting over the falls. They ate venison, turkey, and bear meat. The officers gave the Indians some rum, and the Indians "gave each of us Names, of some of their most famous Warriors, after which we had a War Dance, in which some of us joined them."[77] At times like this, Highlanders and Indians reached across the cultural chasm and met each other as humans engaged in a common enterprise;

on other occasions, and perhaps most of the time, prejudice and policy seem to have governed the soldiers' attitudes. The Indians in turn had little reason to see the Black Watch as tribal warriors rather than just British soldiers.

The expedition traveled deep into Indian country and passed numerous villages, occupied and empty. The soldiers received a crash course in Indian diversity. Their Iroquois companions included Senecas and a Kahnawake Mohawk. They met Mingos, Shawnees, Kaskaskias, Illinois, Chickasaws, and others, and each encounter differed from the others. Two days and about forty miles out of Fort Pitt they camped near a Seneca town on the bank of a river. The Senecas shared their best food with them, invited them to join in a feast and dance that night, and sent them on their way with good words. "The Friendly honest hospitality of those people, whom we are pleased to stile Savages, and that simplicity of manners which they had, pleased us all very much and in those Respects, might be a pattern to more Civilized People," noted an officer.[78] A week later they met a Seneca war party returning from Cherokee country. The soldiers gave them ammunition and some rum, which made some of them drunk and "troublesome."[79]

Passing the Scioto, Great Miami, and Miami rivers, they were deep in Shawnee country and sent out scouts to make contact with the Shawnees. When they did meet them, they got a cold reception. The Shawnee chief, Charlot, whom the English called Corn Cob, "accosted us in a very Cavalier manner, and in a stern voice, demanded who we were, what business we were going on, and what brought us into his Country as he called it, and order'd us to go immediately back." He showed them a calumet he had been given by the French governor of New Orleans, who warned him that the English were coming to take the Indians' lands, cheat them, and ultimately destroy them. Charlot's father had taught him to be an enemy to the English, he said, and he grew up hating them. "You are a greedy & encroaching People," he told the officers. Only after assurances from the Indians accompanying the detachment did the Shawnee chief let the expedition proceed "since he saw we were headstrong and mad enough to attempt what we would never succeed in."[80] Two days later, two young Shawnee warriors who had been with Croghan came and offered their services. They helped guide the soldiers to the Mississippi and mediated with other tribes.[81]

When the detachment reached Fort Chartres, the local Indians "could not believe that so small a party dared to have ventured 1500 Miles into a country full of enemies." Stirling thought that only his troop's sudden appearance had saved it from attack. Many Indians assumed it must be the advance guard of a larger force; even so, they became "insolent."[82] After the Black Watch formally took possession of the fort, about one hundred Illinois Indians—men, women, and children—came to talk. The Highlanders told them the British came in peace and backed up their reassurances with gifts. But many Indians, like the local French inhabitants, preferred to move across the Mississippi to Spanish territory.[83]

One of the officers who kept a journal of the expedition demonstrated a grasp of history, an interest in the geography, flora, and fauna along the way, and some knowledge of Indian peoples. He also displayed more sympathy for them than did Captain Stirling. At a time when many in the British high command denounced Pontiac as a treacherous savage, some Highland officers offered other views. Lieutenant Alexander Fraser, whose life Pontiac had saved, thought him "the most sensible man among all the Nations and the most humane Indian I ever saw."[84] The journal author, who, unlike Fraser, appears not to have met Pontiac, described him as a tall, well-built man, with "something very Bold and Majestick in his Countenance and deportment." He spoke French and English, as well as several Indian languages, and was noted for his oratory. Many anecdotes, from French, English, and Indians, testified "to the honor of this great man." He was clearly a chief of uncommon abilities and "a most Noble genius." The war he waged for the freedom of his country "would have done Honour to the most celebrated Greek or Roman." Formulaic and overblown in style, these were nevertheless remarkable comments from a British officer in 1765.[85]

Counterrevolutionary Allies

The Revolutionary era brought renewed conflict but also strengthened contacts between Highland soldiers and Indian warriors. When war broke out between the Shawnees and Virginians in 1774, many Highlanders fought in the Virginian ranks. In August, Colonel Angus McDonald of the Glengarry clan, who had migrated to America after participating in the Jacobite rebellion and had fought in the French and Indian War, led an expedition against the Shawnee towns on the Muskingum River in southern Ohio. He and his men burned Shawnee homes and cornfields, killed several people, and took three scalps.[86] Other men from the Highlands fought in the bloody battle between Virginians and Shawnees at Point Pleasant in October.

However, the outbreak of the American Revolution the next year produced more opportunities for Highland soldiers and Indian warriors to serve as comrades-in-arms, or at least as cautious allies. The Black Watch served during the war.[87] Highlanders living in America generally sided with the crown, for much the same reason they had served in the Seven Years' War, and local regiments of Highlanders clashed in bitter conflicts with patriot forces at Goose Creek and King's Mountain and on the New York frontier. Individual Highlanders became swept up in the war and served with the king's troops.[88]

Many Highlanders displaced from the Mohawk Valley by the Revolution joined Sir John Johnson's King's Royal Regiment of New York and continued the conflict from Canada. They fought alongside the Mohawks and Senecas at the bloody battle of Oriskany near Fort Stanwix in 1777, and Highland rangers and Indian warriors served together on scouting parties and guerilla raids. Patrick Campbell said they "went hand in hand" and formed a "band of brothers."[89]

Other Highlanders joined the Royal Highland Emigrants (which became the 84th Highland Regiment) that Allan Maclean raised in Nova Scotia, Prince Edward Island, and Quebec. Born at Torloisk on Mull, Maclean had escaped the slaughter of his clan at Culloden and fled to the Netherlands, where clan contacts procured him a commission in the Scots Brigade. After George II's amnesty, he joined the king's service and became a career officer in the British army, fighting during the Seven Years' War (he was wounded in the face at Ticonderoga). At the outbreak of the Revolution, recognizing "The Influence which Colonel Macleane is well known to have among the emigrants from the NorthWest parts of the No. Britain & the Zeal he has manifested upon all Occasions for the King's Service," the crown authorized grants of land in New York to the emigrants Maclean had recruited, on condition that they would "at the hazard of their Lives and fortunes, oppose all illegal Combinations and Insurrections whatsoever." Maclean's regiment served in the defense of Canada, and in 1777 Maclean was appointed military governor of Montreal.[90] Then he was appointed commander at Fort Niagara and thrust into contact with hundreds of Indian people who, like himself, had been displaced from their homelands.

Maclean had been to Fort Niagara before, when the British captured it from the French in 1759. Located in Seneca country, it was a trading post, supply depot, and key diplomatic hub in British-Indian affairs during the Revolution. A multiethnic society grew up around the fort, including Indians of various tribes, Loyalist refugees, British soldiers, and Indian Department personnel of English, Scots, Irish, French, Canadian, and Indian ancestry. After American expeditions ravaged Iroquois country in the fall of 1779, some three thousand Indians took refuge at Niagara, expecting their British father to honor his promises to provision and protect them. The British protested that they could not help until the supply fleet arrived. "Good God," fumed

Maclean, "why should the want of provision prevent our keeping faith with those poor People"? There were plenty of merchants at Niagara who could have provided supplies.[91] The logistical challenges and opportunities for profit in provisioning the Indians produced competition and contention between individual traders, between traders and the army, and between the army and the Indian Department.[92] When Maclean took command, the garrison was short of everything, and the Indian Department seemed to have plenty of everything. He conducted investigations that revealed abuses throughout the Indian Department.[93] Meanwhile, Indian refugees huddled around the fort, suffering from cold and disease, and war parties continued to strike the American frontier.

Frustrated in his efforts to clean things up, Maclean resented the Indians' dependence as much as the corruption within the system: "The People at the head of Indian department Seem to Vie with Each other who Shall Expend most Rum, and the great Chiefs are Striving who Shall Drink most Rum," he complained.[94] He considered Indian councils a waste of time and money.[95]

In 1783 the end of the war brought no improvement. Without consulting their Indian allies—the Indians were not even mentioned in the Peace of Paris—Britain ceded the Indians' homelands to the United States and agreed to give up Fort Niagara and other posts on the frontier between Canada and the new nation. The refugee Indians had lost everything and had nowhere to go. The prospect of dealing with the victorious Americans was too much for Maclean to contemplate. "I do not believe the World ever produced a more deceitful, or dangerous set of Men, than the Americans," he wrote, "and now they are become such Arch-Politicians by eight years practice, that were old Matchiavell [*sic*] alive, he might go to School to the Americans to learn Politicks more crooked than his own."[96] Maclean requested permission to return to Britain, but he was needed at Niagara.[97]

He was in a tough spot. Feeling betrayed by the peace treaty himself, Maclean had to bear the brunt of the Indians' outrage at their own betrayal. "You have repeatedly told us that you would remain with, and share the same fate with ourselves," said one Cayuga chief; but now "we have reason to fear we shall be left alone to defend our Women and Children, and a Country that has so long supported them, against a people who seem determined to over run it." In following British advice, the Indians had been ruined.[98] They told Maclean that "they never could believe that our king could pretend to Cede to America what was not his own to give, or that the Americans would accept from Him what he had no right to grant." They regarded Britain's conduct as "an Act of Cruelty and injustice that Christians only were capable of doing, that the Indians were incapable of acting so; to friends and Allies."

Maclean shared their anger and recognized "the miserable Situation in which we have left this unfortunate People." "I do from my Soul Pity these People," he wrote, "and should they Commit Outrages at giving up these Posts, it would by no means Surprise me."[99] Britain hung on to Fort Niagara and other posts for a dozen more years and provided lands for the Iroquois and other refugees on the Grand River in Ontario, the present Six Nations Reserve. But memories of British perfidy endured in Indian country.[100]

Those memories were reinforced when William Campbell barred the gates of Fort Miami and refused to shelter the surviving Indians after the battle of Fallen Timbers. But Highland soldiers and Indian warriors served together again in the War of 1812, when Canadian Scots, primarily Highlanders living on the banks of the Saint Lawrence, served in the militia.[101] Highlanders were encouraged to emigrate as soldier-farmers who would bolster Canada's defenses as Oglethorpe's recruits had done in Georgia.[102] Highland regiments remained in Upper Canada long after the War of 1812, pulling garrison duty against the possibility of renewed conflict with the United States and maintaining relations with Indians as potential allies in the event of such hostilities. Andrew Agnew, an officer in the 93rd (Sutherland) Highland Regiment (though he himself came from the Lowlands) participated in a two-month tour to Manitoulin Island, where approximately fifteen hundred Indians from the northern Great Lakes gathered for the annual gift-giving ceremony, a vital means of keeping the alliance alive. Agnew was fascinated by the Indians and attracted by some of the Métis and Indian women, who were "really beautiful," but he shared the prejudices of his time, society, and class. Indians wearing face paint "looked very like cannibals"; Indian dances were "as stupid and lame as possible," and Indian women were so in need of a bath "you might really think they had all an attack of hydrophobia."[103] Service in a Highland regiment and sharing a common interest in stemming American expansion did not ensure respect and empathy for Indian allies.

Serving the Empire at Home and Abroad

Highland soldiers grimly performed much of the dirty work as the colonial system used minority to suppress minority. They fought Indians in America and Indians in India. In the 1790s they quelled riots in the Highlands against eviction and sheep, though they had more in common with the rioters than with the lairds.[104] In 1792 the Black Watch was ordered to Ross-shire when the evicted people drove out the sheep. Since many of the regiment had been recruited from

Ross-shire, fortunately the disturbances were over by the time they arrived. Within the year, the regiment was quelling disorder in the Lowlands.[105] The 21st Regiment (the Royal Scots Fusiliers) was posted to Sutherland during the clearances. Though nominally a Scots regiment, the ranks of the 21st were filled mostly by Irish soldiers pressed into service by famine. They had bitter memories of 1798, when a fencible regiment from Sutherland had helped to suppress the rebellion in Ireland, and they had scores to settle.[106]

Despite their reputation as "natural warriors," Highlanders did not go blindly into war for Britain. Like Indian allies who had to be courted, Highland troops sometimes had to be coerced into service and convinced the cause was just. Even as they fought for the empire, however, the empire continued to ravage their homelands. Evictions produced rootless men eligible for enlistment, and landlords sometimes employed the threat of eviction or raised rent to fill the ranks; as Eric Richards describes it, "sons were traded for land."[107]

Veterans from foreign wars sometimes came home to empty glens, ruined houses, and dispersed families. Eventually, clearances and emigration deprived the crown of Highland manpower and, in Sutherland at least, of willing recruits.[108] During the potato famine in 1847, the Duke of Sutherland was asked to raise two hundred men from his estates for the 93rd Regiment. He got few takers. Although the duke provided some relief for his tenants during the famine and was willing to charter a vessel to carry emigrants to America, he adhered to the "difficult but essential rule" of withholding assistance from those capable of earning wages by finding employment elsewhere. He also sent out recruiters. Service in the 93rd Regiment offered "an excellent opportunity for any young man of spirit, none of proper age can have any pretence for complaining of want, if they prefer sitting in peat smoke at home to serving their country." He suggested publishing a list "of all fit & capable to serve, who have no fixed & regular occupation." Hunger and shame provided powerful incentives.[109]

The Duchess of Sutherland likewise "demanded her tenants' sons" for her regiment. Those who refused to enlist would "no longer be considered a credit to Sutherland, or any advantage over sheep or any other useful animal." In other words, they would be evicted. However, some veterans of the 93rd were active in mobilizing opposition to the clearances, and when the Crimean War broke out, many Sutherland men refused the call for recruits. Some imitated the bleating of sheep and suggested that the duke and duchess send their deer, dogs, sheep, shepherds, and gamekeepers to fight the Russians, "who have never done us any harm." One old man told the duke that, if the tsar took possession of the estates, "we could not expect worse treatment at his hands, than we have experienced at the hands of your family for the last fifty years."[110] Henry Mayhew met one veteran of the 93rd Regiment on the streets of

London in the 1850s, playing bagpipes while his daughter danced for pennies. He had been a corporal, served for ten years, and fought in the Indian mutiny, but ill health had forced him to leave the army. Since he had not served twenty-one years, however, he was not entitled to a pension. "I left the 93rd in 1852, and since that time I've been wandering about the different parts of England and Scotland, playing on the bagpipes," he told Mayhew.[111]

Yet when Highlanders served, they did so with constant gallantry—in the Napoleonic Wars, the Crimean War, the Indian mutiny, and the Boer War. Highland regiments maintaining their squares against the French cavalry at Waterloo in 1815 or holding the thin red line at Balaclava in 1854 won adulation. Major General David Stewart of Garth and others lionized and romanticized the Highland regiments and helped establish honor, courage, and loyalty as the characteristics of the soldiers who served in them. The heroic soldier serving the British Empire replaced the rebel warrior as the stereotypical figure of Highland manhood.[112] The increasingly positive image provided added incentive for enlistment into Highland regiments among Lowlanders and Highlanders alike. Highland regiments became important markers of Scottish identity within a broader British nationhood.[113]

Military service provided clan chiefs an opportunity to take their place as loyal members of the British ruling class.[114] It offered young men regimental community, identity, and a focus of loyalty in the wake of the shattering of the clan system. However, as in any army, soldiers had individual, localized, and complicated motives for joining up. Some enlisted to secure free passage across the Atlantic and access to land grants rather than out of patriotic duty. The poetry and songs of eighteenth-century Highland soldiers indicate that the attractions of military service included avoidance of farming and increased prospects of meeting women.[115]

By the time of the First World War, the service of Highland Scots was a long-established tradition in the British army. Approximately 560,000 Scots joined up. More than 128,000 died, a casualty rate exceeded only by Serbia and Turkey and in proportion the highest death toll of any Allied nation.[116] High casualty rates were also a long-established tradition.

Indian Soldiers

As did some Highland clans, several tribes found their own interests intersected with those of the colonizing nation. Judged from a modern perspective that would simplify history into racial or nationalist struggles and give people clear "them and us" choices, siding with the colonizing power constituted selling out, betrayal, collaboration at best. Nevertheless, many tribal peoples faced more immediate threats from other tribal groups than from a colonizing nation. In most of the so-called Indian wars, Indians fought Indians, as well as Europeans and Americans. Clans and tribes used colonizing powers as pawns in their own struggles, just as clan and tribal rivalries facilitated colonial divide-and-conquer strategies.[117]

English, French, and American officers who employed Indian allies pleaded necessity: They used them because they had no alternative.[118] Indians had their own reasons for serving with Europeans or Americans, but they too sometimes had no other option. Many Mohegans joined Connecticut's forces during the so-called French and Indian wars, and a Connecticut Indian, Samuel Ashpo, was the first Native American to be killed fighting in the American army, falling at the battle of Bunker Hill in 1775. The Mohegan preacher Samson Occom realized that, as in the Highlands, lack of economic opportunities propelled men into service: Many Indians joined the American army because they had "nothing else at hand to do," he said.[119] Like Highland clansmen who turned out for their chiefs and unlike British regulars, Indian warriors were part-time fighters who had families and communities to provide for and protect.

Military service, even on the "wrong side," sometimes offered opportunity rather than oppression. Serving with colonial or American armies often became the only avenue by which Indian males could achieve warrior status. The Shawnee Indians in the Ohio region are best known for their resistance to the United States, particularly the movement led by war chief Tecumseh. However, most Shawnees did not support Tecumseh, and many of them fought for the Americans in the War of 1812. Service with the American army provided younger Shawnee men with an opportunity to earn status at a time when traditional opportunities to do so as warriors and hunters were declining.[120]

Some twenty thousand Indians served in the American Civil War. Caught "between two fires," they fought on both sides but did so in their own interests and for their own survival as much as for the Union or Confederate cause. Daniel McIntosh and Chilly McIntosh, sons of the Scots-Creek chief William McIntosh, commanded Confederate Creek regiments and the last Confederate general to surrender was a Cherokee, Stand Watie, who commanded the Confederate Indian Cavalry Brigade.[121]

In the decades following the American Civil War, Indian scouts and allies participated in almost every campaign the United States launched against "hostile" Indians in the trans-Mississippi West. On the Great Plains, Crows, Pawnees, and Arikaras faced a greater threat from the Sioux than from the Americans. Major Frank North recruited Pawnee scouts for service against the Sioux, and Crows provided scouts for the U.S. army.[122] In addition to fighting tribal enemies, Indian scouts received pay, rations, clothing, and ammunition. The government hoped that military service would help promote the assimilation of Indian men, but for Indians it was actually a way to avoid the grueling transformation into a plow-pushing farmer the government had in store for them on the reservation and eventually the only way to carry on a military tradition. John Bourke, a U.S. Army officer, described how, just before the battle of the Rosebud against the Sioux in June 1876, a contingent of Shoshone allies galloped into General George Crook's camp: "a barbaric array of . . . fierce warriors . . . Resplendent in all the fantastic adornment of feathers, beads, brass buttons, bells, scarlet cloth, and flashing lances." The Crow allies were just as flamboyantly attired. After the battle, the Shoshones and Crows both held scalp dances.[123] On the reservations, this was exactly the kind of behavior the U.S. government was trying to stamp out. Nevertheless, the Americans' need for allies prompted them to invoke the Plains warrior tradition to attract recruits, just as the British government had invoked Highland military tradition to fill the ranks of Scottish regiments. Crows and Shoshones took the opportunity to fight old enemies, celebrate their warrior culture, and get paid for doing it.

To help win a war that was not going well, William Pitt had turned to Highlanders; General George Crook resorted to Apaches for the same reason. For fifteen years Apaches served the U.S. army as scouts on campaigns against other Apaches. Chiricahua Apache scouts helped track down Geronimo, only to be sent with their families from Arizona to Florida as prisoners of war after Geronimo surrendered in 1886. In the 1890s, Secretary of War Redfield Proctor introduced a "soldier program" that recruited Indians to serve with regular army units. Proctor saw his experiment as an instrument of social control and moral uplift that would instill good habits into Indian soldiers from "the war-like tribes." He was particularly gratified by its success among the Chiricahuas, forty-six of whom enlisted in Company I of the 12th Infantry. Proctor considered the Apaches "the least progressive and most dangerous of any we have to deal with" and hoped that army discipline would have beneficial and transformative effects. His soldier program was both "an important step toward their civilization, self-support, and control" and "the cheapest and best insurance against further Indian troubles." The plan lasted six years. The War Department ruled that Apaches who completed three years of service in the army would no longer be considered prisoners of war and would be free to return to Arizona. Their families, however, remained prisoners. All but two of the Apache soldiers opted for continued captivity.[124]

In some people's eyes, the First World War marked a significant point in the incorporation of American Indians into the American nation. Some Indians resisted the draft on the basis that they were not U.S. citizens or that it represented an infringement of their tribal sovereignty. Carlos Montezuma, a noted Yavapai physician and outspoken critic of the government's Indian policies, denounced the draft as another injustice against Indian people: How could a nation that would not grant Indians citizenship expect them to sacrifice their young men in its service?[125] The Iroquois Confederacy made a point of issuing its own declaration of war (as it did in World War II), as an independent nation, against Germany. But many Indians volunteered. About sixteen thousand served in the armed forces, and many more worked in war-related services on the home front.

Indian veterans cited their warrior traditions and the desire to demonstrate their loyalty to the United States as reasons for joining up, but many also said they hoped their efforts would help bring about belated justice for Indian people: "I will go and fight for a country that will not give me my rights," said Private John Whirlwind Horse, an Oglala Sioux. The American press interpreted their service as evidence of assimilation. "It may seem strange to see an Apache in a sailor's blue uniform," said one newspaper, "but it merely shows that he has become an American and has passed the tribal stage." Indians were now fighting for the United States, defending Western values and democracy. Their service offered "the ultimate vindication of U.S expansion" because "it proved that the vanquished were better off for having been conquered." Arthur C. Parker, Seneca president of the Society for American Indians, declared that the Indian had responded to the call "and shown himself a citizen of the world." Indians who served in World War I were granted U.S. citizenship, and in 1924 citizenship was extended to all Indians.[126] Like Highland Scots who pulled on red coats and created a new image and place for themselves in British society, Indians proved their loyalty to "their country" by shedding their blood in its service. They did it again in the Second World War, when twenty-five thousand served in the armed forces and another forty thousand took jobs in war-related industries, and they have responded similarly in every war the United States has waged since.[127]

In Canada, First Nations people, like Canadian Scots, went to war for the empire built on the service and sacrifice of numerous Highland Scots. The Canadian government expressed concern that the Germans might refuse to extend to Native soldiers "the privileges of civilized warfare," but more than four thousand status Indians (approximately thirty-five percent of those eligible for service) enlisted in World War I, as well as many nonstatus Indians. About half of the eligible Mi'kmaq and Maliseet men from New Brunswick and Nova Scotia joined up, as did some three hundred men from the Six Nations reserve at Grand River and high percentages from numerous smaller communities. More than three thousand Canadian Natives served in World War II. John McLeod, an Ojibwa from the Cape Croker agency in Ontario, served in the First World War and with the Veterans Guard of Canada in the Second World War. Six of his sons and one daughter enlisted during World War II; two sons died, and two more were wounded in action. Corporal Welby Lloyd Patterson, a Six Nations Indian from Ohsweken, won a Military Medal in 1944 while serving in Belgium with the Argyll and Sutherland Highlanders of Canada.[128] In 2001, in recognition of First Nations' services from the War of 1812 onward, Canada unveiled a National Aboriginal Veterans Monument in Ottawa.

Highlanders and Indians shared similar military statistics. In every war in which they fought for their country, they contributed a disproportionately high number of soldiers relative to their population and suffered a disproportionately high rate of casualties relative to total losses. Their shared reputation as peoples with a military tradition, as "natural warriors," frequently earned them assignments that placed them in the thick of danger; the belief that they were expendable no doubt played a role in some cases.

Socioeconomic factors more than inherent militarism or patriotism explain the overrepresentation of Highlanders and Indians in their countries' wars. Nevertheless, warrior traditions also provided motivation for military service and that service continues to be honored. At powwows and other important gatherings, a veteran carrying the Stars and Stripes accompanies an eagle staff bearer in leading the opening procession. The military tattoo held annually on the esplanade at Edinburgh Castle celebrates Scots' service in Britain's wars. In the war in Iraq, the deaths of young Black Watch soldiers and of Pfc. Lori Piestewa, a Hopi single mother, continued a long tradition of Native American and Highland sacrifice in the foreign wars of the nations their ancestors had fought against.

5

Highland Traders and Indian Hunters

The son of an Inverness merchant who had supported the Jacobite rebellion, John Stuart emigrated to Charles Town, South Carolina, in 1748. From 1761 until his death in 1779, he served as British superintendent of Indian affairs in the South. Stuart called trade "the Original great tye between the Indians and Europeans," an exchange that produced mutual benefits and mutual dependency.[1] Everywhere in North America the fur trade relied for its operation on Indians, and almost everywhere in the fur trade there were Highland Scots. From the middle of the eighteenth century to the middle of the nineteenth, Highland Scots and their sons by Indian women dominated the trade across large stretches of North America. It was an enterprise in which Highlanders and Indians participated jointly, although they engaged in it for different purposes, occupied diverse roles, and understood the exchange in dissimilar ways. It was also a way of life in which Highland traders and Indian people interacted, often on a daily basis. Indian peoples far removed from European settlements were pulled into the commercial systems of the Atlantic world; Scots from the northern fringes of Britain were drawn into the communal networks of the Indian world. Highland traders injected capitalist values and practices into the Indians' world even as capitalism transformed the tribal world in the Scottish Highlands.

When Jacques Cartier sailed into the Bay of Chaleur in the 1530s, Indians on the shore held up beaver pelts, signaling their willingness to trade, clear evidence that they had dealt with Europeans before. The exchange of pelts and hides harvested by Native hunters for goods manufactured in European factories was a key part of the economy of North America for hundreds of years. At one time or another Dutch, French, Swedes, Spaniards, Russians, British, and Americans all competed for Indian trade. Europeans provided capital, organization, equipment, and goods from the mills of Europe: steel knives and axes, firearms, kettles, cooking pots, and frying pans, woolen blankets and clothing, glass beads, mirrors, scissors, awls, spoons, linen shirts, hats, buckles, and a host of other items. Indians provided much of the labor force: They hunted the animals, guided the fur traders, and paddled the canoes that carried the pelts to market. Indian women prepared food and skins and often functioned as culture brokers. Water-repellant beaver pelts, especially ones that had been worn smooth, were much sought after in Europe and a mark of distinction for those who could afford them. Various groups of Indians secured and sustained a lucrative role as middlemen by conveying pelts and goods between European traders and more distant Indian tribes.

Canada attributes much of its national development to the fur trade, and rugged Highland fur traders figure prominently in the lore of Canadian history. For a time, Highlanders also dominated the deerskin trade in what is now the southeastern United States and influenced the emerging society of the Old South. The fur trade constituted a piece of Scottish history in North America, and Highlanders and Indians shaped societies that emerged out of the trade in both Canada and the United States.

A Cast of Characters

In the eighteenth century, Scots traders "settled into every port on the Atlantic coastline of North America from Nova Scotia to Key West, affecting a transition out of animal husbandry into commerce, from herd to ledger, from rainswept moors to palm-shaded patios along the Gulf."[2] They pushed deep into Indian country, where they fathered sons who also functioned on one side of the fur trade or the other, and sometimes both.

In what is now the southeastern region of the United States, Indian traders like Lachlan McGillivray made their fortunes and also acted as intermediaries between colonial governments and Indian leaders. They often were instrumental in negotiating the transfer of Indian lands. McGillivray was one of the original settlers at Darien but later entered the Indian trade through

Highland acquaintances. He learned to speak Muskogee, participated in the purgative black drink ritual, cultivated relationships with Creek chiefs, and mastered the subtle arts of intercultural diplomacy. He married well, taking as his wife Sehoy Marchand, the Creek daughter of a French officer; she was a member of the prestigious Wind Clan and sister of a Creek chief named Red Shoes. McGillivray spent a dozen years at Little Tallassee and became an influential figure in British-Indian relations and in colonial Georgia. John Stuart said the Creeks possessed "the most extensive hunting-ground of any nation to the southward," but in 1763, McGillivray sent his cousin John McGillivray to Mobile to extend the McGillivray trading network west to the Choctaws and Chickasaws. In 1764 Stuart estimated that the southeastern Indian trade was producing eight hundred thousand pounds of deerskins per year.[3]

The deerskin trade slowly declined after the American Revolution, but Scots continued to find opportunities in the southeastern Indian trade even as their political and economic influence waned in what had been the American colonies. In the aftermath of the Revolution, the firm of Panton, Leslie, and Company and its successor, John Forbes and Company, remained active in Indian affairs and the swirling international diplomacy of the region. The original partners, William Panton, John Leslie, Thomas Forbes, Charles McLatchy, and William Alexander, were all from northern Scotland. Panton, Leslie, and Forbes were born in the coastal area east of Inverness overlooking the Moray Firth; the birthplaces of McLatchy and Alexander are not known. As loyalist traders they took refuge in Saint Augustine during the Revolution. When Spain took over Florida by the terms of the Peace of Paris in 1783, it allowed the merchants to stay on. Although it did not grant Panton, Leslie, and Company a formal monopoly, Spain did business with no one else and permitted the Scots to sell British guns, goods, and cloth to help keep the Creeks and Seminoles in the Spanish interest. Working closely with the Creek chief, Alexander McGillivray, who was Lachlan McGillivray's son and who issued the licenses traders needed to operate in Creek towns, Panton, Leslie, and Company extended their operations from Florida to the Mississippi. Centering their business empire at Spanish Pensacola, they effectively controlled the whole southeastern trade, with trading posts and packhorse trains operating from the Bahamas to western Tennessee. Panton, Leslie, and Company and John Forbes and Company sent Scottish boys to live with Indian families and learn their languages and cultures. Panton and Leslie stymied the U.S. government's efforts to take over control of the Indian trade in the late eighteenth century, but by the time of the War of 1812, Forbes and Company had transferred its allegiance from Spain to the United States.[4]

In Canada, the Hudson's Bay Company originally recruited mainly from London but found that "if England can not furnish you with men, Scotland can, for that countrie is a hard country to live in, and poore-mens wages is cheap, they are hardy people, both to endure hunger, and cold, and are subject to obedience." They would need less pay and be more content with their spare diet than were Englishmen.[5] In the early eighteenth century, the company began recruiting from the Orkney Isles, where its vessels regularly stopped to take on water and supplies before heading out across the Atlantic. The young men of Orkney acquired basic literacy in their parish schools and were known to be hardy, but the islands offered few opportunities for employment. By the end of the century, Orkney men constituted almost eighty percent of the Hudson's Bay Company's rank-and-file employees. The Earl of Selkirk described them as "less alert and animated than the natives of some other parts of the kingdom" but "remarkably careful steady and sober"; trader Alexander Ross characterized them as "a quiet, honest, and plodding people, satisfied with little."[6]

However, it was men from the Highlands and western islands who came to dominate the fur trade. In the nineteenth century, the Hudson's Bay Company began recruiting from the Isle of Lewis. Governor George Simpson, never a man to mince words, acknowledged that the men from Lewis were "strong hearty active and fit to be immediately employed on laborious service" and "well behaved and generally of a serious turn of mind." On the other hand, he found them "exceedingly stubborn and difficult of management (read "independent") and so clannish that it is scarcely possible to deal with them singly," and he advocated recruiting no more. Highlanders, he added, "are equally objectionable from the same cause."[7] Peter Newman points out that all of the "great names" of the Hudson's Bay Company grew up in Scotland. Scottish trader Robert Ballantyne reckoned that "three fourths of the Company's servants are Scotch Highlanders and Orkneymen."[8]

Highlanders also became the dominant force in the Montreal-based fur business that challenged the Hudson's Bay Company's monopoly. After the fall of New France in 1763, traders from Montreal pushed west along the Saint Lawrence–Great Lakes–Lake Winnipeg water routes, picking up Indian customers who had formerly traded with the French and diverting Indian trade from the rivers leading down to Hudson Bay. Eventually, they formed the loosely organized North West Company. Aggressively searching out supplies of furs, they reduced to a shambles the Hudson's Bay Company's monopoly, granted by royal charter in 1670. The Hudson's Bay Company had no alternative then but to send traders out into Indian country to match the competition.

The core of the North West syndicate was "a group of related, originally Jacobite, families from the Great Glen," though many other Scots joined them.

Highlanders who entered the company as clerks could rise to become masters of trading posts and eventually attain the rank of wintering partner, which allowed them a voice in policy and a share of the profits. Many of the key figures in the North West Company lived before the Revolution as tenants on the Mohawk Valley estates of Sir William Johnson, where they had seen Indian trade and diplomacy firsthand and developed new ties of alliance and patronage. Forced north by the Revolution, they took their new skills and connections into the North West Company. Simon McTavish, who was born in Stratherrick, Invernesshire, around 1750, migrated to America at age thirteen. He got his start in the Indian trade in New York, then moved first to Detroit and later to Montreal after the Revolution. By 1787 he had become controlling partner of the North West Company, where he presided over a fur-trade empire that stretched from Montreal to the Rockies. The North West Company partners "behaved as though they were chiefs of a transcontinental clan." Their names have been likened to "a roll-call of the clans at Culloden." They included, at one time or another, "seven Simon Frasers, four Finlays, five Camerons, six McTavishes, seven MacLeods, eight McGillivrays, fourteen each of Grants and McKenzies and so many McDonalds that they had to differentiate themselves by including home towns in their surnames, as in John McDonald of Garth." Their families intermarried extensively, which more than compensated for the company's organizational instability.[9] Highland backgrounds, clan loyalties, kin ties, and self-interest bound Scots traders together in webs of loyalty that often transcended allegiance to king or company and frustrated non-Scots unable to break into the network. Scots merchants did business with Scots and employed Scots.

After the Hudson's Bay and North West companies merged in 1821, Scots occupied the higher echelons of the operation. George Simpson became governor of the huge Northern Department, which stretched from Hudson Bay to the Rockies and from the Arctic Ocean to the border of the United States and included the territories west of the Rockies. He then became governor in chief of all of the Hudson's Bay Company territories in North America. Simpson was born in Ross-shire in 1792 and had a meteoric rise through the company ranks. He traveled his fur-trade empire in the style of a Highland chieftain and even recruited a young piper, Colin Fraser, from the Highlands to accompany him on his canoe journeys and herald his arrival at the trading posts. Chief factor Archibald McDonald, who accompanied Simpson on one of these jaunts, said that the bagpipes and the sight of a Highland piper in full dress excited "emotions of admiration and wonder" in the Indians, but perhaps they were just bemused.[10] Simpson wrote in 1826 that, "although many years have elapsed

Figure 5.1.   Simon McTavish, by an unknown artist. (Library and Archives Canada, acc. no. 1956–6-1; C-000164.)

since I was an inhabitant of our beautiful glens and straths, nothing affords me so much delight as a communication with a brother highlander."[11]

Nevertheless, despite his Highland trappings and attachments, Simpson, in fur-trade historian Frederick Merk's estimation, was a "typical nineteenth-century captain of industry," with all of the characteristics of the hard-bitten, self-made man.[12] He was ruthless, relentless, and opinionated, whether laying off company employees to cut costs or venting his frustration with unco-operative Indians. John McLean, one of those who felt mistreated by Simpson, portrayed him as a fur-trade Ebenezer Scrooge. He was crafty and calculating, and "his cold and callous heart was incapable of sympathizing with the woes and pains of his fellow-men."[13]

In the winter of 1831–1832 Simpson wrote confidential comments about 25 chief factors, 25 chief traders, 88 clerks, and 19 postmasters of the Hudson's Bay Company. Most of them were Highland Scots or Scots Indians, the

Figure 5.2. Sir George Simpson. (Library and Archives Canada, acc. no. 1978–14–13; source: Manuscript Division, W. W. Campbell Collection [MG30 D]; C-023580.)

Métis sons of Highland fathers. Many of them had worked for the North West Company before the two enterprises merged. Simpson was living at Red River that winter, and things were not good. His new wife was unhappy and having a difficult pregnancy, and their infant son died the following spring. Simpson could be mean spirited at the best of times, and the comments he penned in his "character book" naturally reveal more about Simpson, his prejudices, suspicions, and state of mind than about the men he described. Nevertheless, they reflect the range of people and personalities, as well as the bewildering similarity of names, that comprised the Highland fur trade.[14]

Colin Robertson, son of a Perth weaver, had spent a quarter of a century and half his life in the fur trade but was now "a burden" to the business. Alexander

Stewart was slightly older but was "an easy, mild tempered, well disposed little man" who spoke Cree well "and acquires influence over Indians by his kind treatment and patient attention to them." William McIntosh, a "revengeful cold blooded black hearted Man," possessed "no abilities beyond such as qualify him to cheat an unfortunate Indian and to be guilty of a mean dirty trick." James McMillan was an energetic explorer and a good man, "provided he has no occasion to meddle with Pen & Ink in the use of which he is deficient his Education having been neglected." He was an excellent trader and spoke several Indian languages, but his "plain blunt manner" could not conceal "a vast deal of little highland Pride." Allen McDonnell had good sense, integrity, and a sense of humor, spoke Cree and Ojibwa well, and was "much liked by Indians." Duncan Finlayson was an honorable, well-educated man. "Firm Cool and decisive," he spoke Cree and had great influence with the Indians.

Simon McGillivray Jr., the Métis son of William McGillivray (and nephew of North West Company partner Simon McGillivray) was "Very Tyrannical among his people . . . and more feared than respected by Men & Indians who are constantly in terror either from his Club or his Dirk" (McGillivray assaulted an Indian at Fort Nez Perces about the time Simpson wrote his comments). Simpson said he had "a good deal of the Indian in disposition as well as in blood and appearance." He made almost identical comments about William McGillivray, a "half breed of the Cree Nation" who had been in the service for about eighteen years (William McGillivray drowned in the Fraser River just about the time Simpson was writing about him).

Alexander Roderick McLeod was a strong man, a good shot, and a skillful canoeist but an illiterate braggart. Aberdonian Samuel Black, formerly a fierce opponent of the Hudson's Bay Company, was "The strangest man I ever knew." (An Indian murdered him in 1841.) Colin Campbell from Glengarry, Ontario, was an excellent trader who spoke several Indian languages and had "the talent of conciliating the Friendship of Indians." His conduct was "highly correct and proper." By contrast, Alexander McTavish was "a sly, smirking plausible fellow who lies habitually." John Bell, a clerk in his thirties from the Isle of Mull, had been in the service about thirteen years and was "a quiet steady well behaved Man," but he lacked "the Manner address necessary to acquire influence over Indians." Thomas Fraser had been in the Indian country thirty years, "speaks Indian well," and "can live where an Indian would Starve." He was, said Simpson, "still as raw and unpolished as when he left his Father's Hut in the Highlands of Scotland."

Cuthbert Grant was the son of a North West Company officer from Speyside and a Cree mother.[15] Many people blamed him for the Seven Oaks massacre at Red River in 1816, but Simpson intended to use him to manage the Métis, among whom he enjoyed considerable influence. He declared him a "generous Warm Hearted Man who would not have been guilty of the Crimes laid to his charge had he not been drawn into them by designing Men." Like many of his contemporaries in the fur trade, Grant had a drinking problem that was taking its toll.

Charles McKenzie had spent twenty-nine of his fifty-six years in the service. Born in Easter Ross, he joined the North West Company in 1803 and worked as a clerk on the Assiniboine River. While trading with the Mandans, he met Lewis and Clark, and he published an account of the Indians of the Missouri.[16] He wore Indian clothing, married an Indian woman, and had several children. He joined the Hudson's Bay Company after the merger in 1821 but was critical of the company's policies and attitudes toward Indians. He retired to Red River in Manitoba, where he died in 1855. Simpson said he was "a queer prosing long Winded little highland body who traces his lineage back to Ossian." Twenty-seven-year-old Peter Mackenzie, with seven years in the service, was not well educated, rather dull, and in delicate health but "makes himself understood in Chippeway and is liked by the Natives." Clerks John McLeod and Donald McKenzie were both in their forties, "tolerably" educated with fourteen to sixteen years of service. McLeod spoke Cree, understood some Chipewyan, and was an excellent trader. McKenzie was "a trifling useless superficial fellow who can Drink & pilfer and rarely speaks the truth." Thirty-year-old John McKenzie had a good education and a good opinion of himself but "has not the talent of commanding respect either from Servants or Indians."

Thirty-four-year-old John McLean was a thirteen-year veteran and "a favorite with Indians." (Simpson ridiculed his writing style, but in 1849 McLean published a book, *Notes of a Twenty-five Years' Service in the Hudson's Bay Territory,* in which he roundly criticized Simpson's character and his regime.) William Nourse was also tolerably well educated and wrote a fair hand but lacked "Nerve among Indians." Charles Ross was a good classical scholar with a smattering of Indian languages but so painfully nervous that Simpson suspected he was "not quite of Sound Mind." George Ross was an active, good-looking young man "but not bright and exhibits a good deal of the vain silly puppy." He had the talent "of making himself agreeable to and acquiring an influence over Indians" but not the judgment for a difficult charge.

And then there was John McLoughlin. Born in Quebec, McLoughlin served first with the North West Company, but from 1824 to 1845 he was chief factor of the Hudson's Bay Company in the Columbia District, a territory larger than Great Britain. A giant of a man with a shock of white hair, he was known as White-headed Eagle. He made an impression on George Simpson when the latter met him in 1824:

He was such a figure as I should not like to meet in a dark Night in one of the bye lanes in the neighbourhood of London, dressed in Clothes that had once been fashionable, but now covered with a thousand patches of different Colors, his beard would do honor to the chin of a Grizzly bear, his face and hands evidently Shewing that he had not lost much time at his Toilette, loaded with Arms and his own herculean dimensions forming a tout ensemble that would convey a good idea of the high way men of former Days.[17]

Highlanders, like other traders, ran the gamut in their experience and expertise in dealing with Indian peoples. Even allowing for Simpson's prejudices, it is clear that Highland heritage provided no uniformity of character in the ranks of the Highland fur trade. Many factors besides Highland identity and cultural background influenced the way in which a trader got along with Indian people. Was he born in Scotland, the colonies, or Indian country? Was he interested in Indian cultures or only in Indian furs? Was he a veteran or a novice? What was his personality? To what extent did he "go native"? Did he have an Indian wife or family? Nevertheless, connected by networks of kinship and their own experiences of colonialism, Highlanders stood as a group apart as they entered the kinship networks of Native societies and dominated the colonial enterprise of the fur trade.

Highlanders across the Continent

Highlanders pushed far into the West and made contact with a vast array of Indian peoples from the Plains to the Pacific. They also encountered Indian peoples from the East: Iroquois, Abenaki, and Delaware trappers who, like the Highlanders, found employment in the western fur trade after the devastation of their economies at home.

The North West Company took the lead in reaching across the continent. Donald McKay was on the Saskatchewan River in the service of the North West Company in the 1780s before he joined the Hudson's Bay Company. Looking back from his retirement in Scotland, he recalled seeing "tribes of Indians that never saw any European before," including the Snakes or Shoshones, "whose Horses are very beautiful and swift; and who treated me with the utmost civility and hospitality."[18]

Alexander Mackenzie was the first European to cross the North American continent above the Rio Grande. Born in Stornaway on the Isle of Lewis around 1764, Mackenzie migrated with his father to New York at the age of

Map 3. The Highlanders' Fur-trading Country

ten and then, with the outbreak of the Revolution, moved to Montreal and entered the fur trade. In 1789, searching for a passage to the Pacific, he traveled the Mackenzie River from Fort Chipewyan to the Arctic Ocean and back, canoeing almost three thousand miles in three months. He returned to London to study navigation in 1791 and then embarked on another attempt to find the route to the Pacific. Following the Peace River to the Fraser, he and his companions finally abandoned their canoes and trekked to the Pacific on foot. Mixing vermilion in melted grease, Mackenzie inscribed on a rock a simple memorial to his momentous achievement: "Alexander Mackenzie, from Canada, by land, the twenty-second of July, one thousand seven hundred and ninety-three."[19] He reached the Pacific more than a decade before Lewis and Clark; in fact, the published account of his travels spurred Thomas Jefferson to launch the American expedition. Following Mackenzie's route, Simon Fraser, the American-born son of Highland parents, followed the Fraser River to its mouth in 1808.[20]

Like other explorers, Mackenzie and his small party relied on Indian guides, Indian knowledge and know-how, and Indian birch-bark canoes. On

Figure 5.3. Alexander Mackenzie. (Library and Archives Canada, C-001348.)

his voyage to the Arctic, Mackenzie employed an Indian he called the English Chief, who brought his two wives along on the expedition.[21] Mackenzie reckoned his French-Canadian paddlers were "the most expert canoe-men in the world" until he saw the Bella Coolas on the Pacific; even his own men acknowledged themselves "very inferior to these people" in handling their canoes.[22] (In a similar vein, after his Iroquois paddlers took him through "appalling" swells, Colin Robertson said that Canadians might be hardier and undergo more fatigue than the Iroquois, but for shooting rapids or crossing a lake, "give me the latter, from their calmness and presence of mind which never forsakes them in the greatest danger."[23])

Mackenzie acknowledged his debt to his Native guides and showed an interest in their language and culture. Having witnessed radical change in

Lewis, he expressed sympathy for the devastating changes wrought by disease, overhunting, and missionaries in Indian country. Nevertheless, he himself was not free of Eurocentric arrogance, as illustrated by a conversation with an Indian on the Fraser River. "What," the Indian demanded, "can be the reason that you are so particular and anxious in your inquiries of us respecting a knowledge of this country: do not you white men know everything in the world?" The question (and no doubt the tongue-in-cheek nature of it) took Mackenzie by surprise and "occasioned some hesitation before I could answer it." But he composed himself and replied "that we certainly were acquainted with the principal circumstances of every part of the world; that I knew where the sea is, and where I myself then was, but that I did not exactly understand what obstacles might interrupt me in getting to it; with which he and his relations must be well acquainted, as they had so frequently surmounted them. Thus I fortunately preserved the impression in their minds, of the superiority of white people over themselves."[24] Or so he thought.

Few traveled more widely than James Mackay. Born in Kildonan, Sutherland, in 1759, he emigrated to Canada around the time of the American Revolution and traveled "through the wild & unknown Deserts of this Continent." He journeyed across Canada to the foothills of the Rocky Mountains, ascended both the Red River of the north and the Missouri River, explored much of northeastern Nebraska, and visited the Mandan villages in North Dakota sixteen years before Lewis and Clark got there. Mackay transferred his allegiances, first from the North West Company to the Hudson's Bay Company and then to Spain. Relocating to Spanish Illinois, he became a Spanish citizen, one of a number of men from the Celtic fringes of Britain who joined the service of colonial Spain, and was appointed to manage the affairs of the Spanish Missouri Company on the upper Missouri. He spoke English, French, Spanish, Gaelic, and no doubt a smattering of Indian languages.

From 1795 to 1797, together with a twenty-five-year-old Welshman named John Evans (who was looking for Indians rumored to be descended from an eleventh-century Welsh prince called Madoc), he led an expedition from Saint Louis to the upper Missouri. Like the later Lewis and Clark expedition, its purpose was both to explore the country and assert dominion, specifically by driving out British traders. Mackay visited the Otos and Omahas and made a point of making friends with the powerful Omaha chief, Blackbird, "since he is the one to decide whether our communication [upriver] remains open and free." He talked with the Sioux and the Arikaras and issued a declaration in the name of the king of Spain prohibiting all foreigners "(especially all British subjects)" from operating on the Missouri. Mackay sent the document by John Evans. James Sutherland, the Hudson's Bay

Company factor at Brandon House, replied that he did not think this would be much of a problem for his company; John McDonnell of the North West Company was less accommodating: "British subjects are not to be tried by Spanish laws, nor do I look upon you as an officer commissioned to apprehend other people's servants." Thus did three Highland Scots, representing three companies and two crowns, communicate via a Welshman about who should control the Indian trade of the upper Missouri.

Later, petitioning for a position in the Spanish royal service, McKay claimed that he persuaded the Indian nations of the upper Missouri to make peace, made them understand that it was in their interest to trade and live in "the strictest alliance" with the Spanish, and drove the English out of Spain's territories. He did not do any of those things, but his contributions to geography and cartography were impressive, and his experience in Indian country was extensive.[25]

Other Highland traders covered vast amounts of Indian country and had wide-ranging contacts with different Indian peoples. Assuming command of an expedition to the Snake River country in 1823, Alexander Ross led a party of fifty-five hunters that included two Americans, seventeen Canadians, "five half breeds from the east sides of the mountains," a dozen Iroquois, two Abenakis, two Nipissings, an Ojibwa, two Crees, a Chinook, two Spokanes, two Kutenais, three Flatheads, two Kalispels, one Palouse, and a Shoshone slave. Twenty-five of the men were married and brought their wives with them, as well as sixty-four children. "The whole cavalcade, "stretched a mile or more in length" when they were on the move. Ross had plenty of experience with a mobile mixed community before he retired to a more sedentary mixed community at Red River.[26]

In the early years of the nineteenth century, Thomas Douglas, fifth Earl of Selkirk, and his family gained an interest in the Hudson's Bay Company and attempted to restore its monopoly and establish a settlement in the Hudson Bay region. In return for a nominal rent, the company granted Selkirk 116,000 square miles of land, about four times the size of Scotland, within its chartered territories. Selkirk envisioned the settlement at Red River as a community for retired company employees who preferred to stay in Indian country with their Native wives and children rather than return home. However, Selkirk also brought Highland emigrants to Red River. He promoted emigration to North America as a better option for displaced Highlanders than joining the ranks of the laboring poor in the slums of Glasgow. He had attempted previous settlements of Highlanders, first on Prince Edward Island and then in Upper Canada (Ontario), where he hoped to create a Gaelic-speaking barrier to American expansion.[27]

Unfortunately, Selkirk's Red River settlement aggravated the rivalry between the Hudson's Bay and North West companies. In Selkirk's view, the Hudson's Bay Company was a stabilizing and civilizing influence, with long-

Figure 5.4. Thomas Douglas, 5th Earl of Selkirk. (Library and Archives Canada, C-001346.)

term interests in the development of the country; the North West Company, in contrast, was "that unprincipled association," a dissolute, violent bunch motivated by immediate gain and short-term interest. They pressured Indians to run up debts, took their furs in payment, and "were not nice in discrimination between the Indians who had debts to pay, and those who had none," often seizing furs from any Indians who had them. The North West Company argued that Selkirk's Red River settlement blocked its supply routes and would interfere with the fur trade; Selkirk insisted that the real reason for its hostility was to keep law and order out of the area.[28]

A fur trade war ensued that pitted Scots against Scots.[29] In addition to company retirees, Canadians, and Métis, settlers at Red River included recent immigrants from Sutherland, recruited by Miles MacDonnell, from Glengarry, Ontario. Simon McGillivray of the North West Company tried to undermine MacDonnell's efforts to recruit in the Highlands, as did Alexander Mackenzie.[30] At Red River, Northwest Company agents tried to persuade the Sutherland settlers to abandon the settlement, warning of the dangers of Indian attacks if they stayed.[31] As a result, MacDonnell adopted a combative stance. Stressing that food produced in the district had to be used to feed his colonists, who had not yet been able to grow their crops, he issued a proclamation in January 1814 prohibiting the removal of food raised in Selkirk's territory. The announcement targeted especially pemmican—the high-calorie mixture of ground buffalo meat, melted fat, and berries, which was the mainstay of the fur brigades—and threatened the Red River Métis who had built an economy around provisioning the brigades. McDonnell actually seized a North West Company pemmican shipment.[32]

The North West Company responded by employing the sons of Highland traders to lead the Métis against the settlers. Cuthbert Grant was appointed "captain" of the Red River Métis. Grant had become a ward of William McGillivray when his own father died and had been educated in Edinburgh or Montreal before becoming a clerk in the North West Company.[33] He subjected the settlers to a campaign of intimidation and harassment. Some families gave up and left to take up residence farther south on the Red River at Pembina, but others rallied under Hudson's Bay Company officer Colin Robertson. The contest culminated in June 1816 in "the battle of Seven Oaks," when Grant and a band of Métis killed Governor Robert Semple and a score of settlers.[34]

When the Hudson's Bay Company retaliated, the confrontation escalated. Selkirk brought in a force of discharged soldiers from the Swiss de Meuron regiment to defend his settlement and seized the North West Company's headquarters at Fort William (Thunder Bay, Ontario). There were murders, fears that the conflict would escalate into an Indian war, charges and countercharges. In 1817 the prince regent issued a proclamation that called on both companies to desist.[35] The government then dispatched a commissioner from Lower Canada to investigate the affair. Complicated legal proceedings ensued, with suits and countersuits, legal and political maneuvers, trials postponed, moved from court to court, and even from Lower to Upper Canada. They produced little in the way of resolution, however. Beset by lawsuits and financial problems, Selkirk returned to Britain in 1818. In failing health, he moved to the south of France, where he died in 1820. The Hudson's Bay and North West companies amalgamated the next year.[36]

Service in a single company did nothing to limit the Highlanders' range of contacts with Indian peoples, however. For example, when Governor George Simpson moved regional headquarters to Fort Vancouver (now Vancouver, Washington) on the lower Columbia River, Highland Scots in the company's employ there rubbed shoulders with Indian traders, Indian laborers, and Indian slaves, with Chinooks, Métis from the prairies, and Iroquois and Delaware trappers from the East, as well as French Canadians. In addition to sending furs to London, the company on the Pacific diversified its operations by exporting salmon, timber, flour, and potatoes to Hawaii, Sitka (headquarters of the Russian American Fur company), and Yerba Buena (future San Francisco) in Mexican California.[37] Even Scots botanists helped promote the company's economic imperialism by extending knowledge about environmental patterns on the Pacific Coast: John Scouler and David Douglas (of "Douglas fir" fame) worked under company auspices "to advance the knowledge of those extensive regions which are within the sphere of their commercial exertions."[38]

Other Highland traders gravitated southward, tried their hands at the American fur trade, and transferred their allegiance to American companies and the United States. Born in Callendar, Perthshire, Robert Stuart first made his way to Canada and served as a clerk in the North West Company, but he soon joined and became a partner in John Jacob Astor's Pacific Fur Company, which was intent on keeping the British companies out of the fur-bearing regions of the Columbia River. Traveling from Astoria (on the Pacific coast) to Saint Louis from June 1812 to April 1813, Stuart recorded his observations of the Indians he met along the Columbia, Snake, Platte, and Missouri rivers. At the end of his journey, he learned that his former country and his adopted country had gone to war with one another the month he left.[39]

Artifacts, Interactions, and Attitudes

Highland Scots perhaps differed little from traders of other nationalities in displaying ignorance, greed, fear, arrogance, intolerance, sympathy, affection, bias, prejudice, and misunderstanding in their dealings with Indians. They shared with others of their time, society, and class similar notions about morality, gender, wealth and poverty, work and idleness.[40] They thought and acted as traders first and foremost—after all, that was why they were there. Indian hunters and customers in turn regarded them primarily as merchants. That Highland traders' attitudes and behaviors were typical of the fur business is not surprising; in many places and in many respects they *were* the fur business.

Some Highland traders maintained only dry records of their dealings, kept their comments on Indians to a minimum, and showed little or no interest in their welfare. Others wrote lengthy observations on Indian life and customs, compiled vocabularies of Indian languages, speculated about their origins, and pondered (and sometimes worried) about their future.[41] In many of their journals and letters, the Indians are nameless and faceless; in others, like the journal kept in 1800 and 1801 by Archibald Norman McLeod at Fort Alexandria on the upper Assiniboine River, Cree, Fall (Gros Ventre), Blood, and Assiniboine Indians are regularly identified by name as they come and go.[42]

For most Highland Scots, as for other Europeans, fur trading was a purely economic exchange, a business, an opportunity to accumulate wealth by buying and selling material objects. For Indian people, whose societies operated around both the practicality and the morality of sharing and reciprocity and whose networks of social and ethical responsibilities included animals, as well as humans, trading furs for manufactured goods had other purposes, meanings, and consequences. Exchange in Indian society was about cooperation rather than competition and was conducted to establish and reaffirm alliances and mutual obligations, not just to gain wealth. Highland traders who married into the extended kinship networks of Indian communities surely experienced misunderstandings and generated tensions as they tried to conduct business according to market demands and values with people who expected good relatives to share their material possessions with less fortunate kinsfolk. Meanwhile, Indians responded to new opportunities and necessities and made the shift from ritual exchange to commercial hunting.

Many objects made in Scotland and in Indian country acquired new meanings as they changed hands between Scots and Indians or traveled across the Atlantic. Sometimes Indians refashioned new items in traditional ways or attached their own values to them: Metal pots might be cut up for jewelry. Items cheaply produced in Europe, like blue glass beads, red cloth, and silver trade ornaments, possessed social and spiritual significances few Europeans understood.[43] Trade-silver ornaments were often more desirable for their protective powers than for their decorative appeal. Scottish double-heart brooches became so popular that they were sometimes called the "national badge" of the Iroquois but they had a different meaning from that in Scotland, where they were often heirlooms and love tokens. Native peoples often called crowned heart brooches owl brooches because they resembled owls, which were a good omen for some peoples and a bad one for others. Silver heart or owl brooches worn on clothing or fastened to a baby's blanket provided protection for the wearer. A deerskin bag embroidered with a thistle design (in the National Museum of Scotland) would likewise have held different meanings for its maker and its owner. John Rae from Orkney may have designed and commissioned the bag from a Cree craftswoman. Rae, who first brought word of the fate of Sir John Franklin's expedition, depended on Indian and Inuit knowledge and assistance during his trips to the Arctic. He generally thought highly of the Natives he knew, and he referred to many of them by name in his writings. He also became a collector of Native artifacts and admired the skill of Native craftswomen.[44]

Objects that were produced in the fur trade and wound up in museum collections in Glasgow, Perth, or Edinburgh have their own "biographies" that sometimes illuminate relationships between Indians and Scots. For example, a beadwork garter and three woven bands of glass seed beads donated to Glasgow Museums in 1998 are thought to have been made by a Cree woman named Christina Massan. Her Scottish husband, Henry Moir, worked for the Hudson's Bay Company. Moir, who died in 1920, seems to have wanted his sons sent to Scotland to be raised by their grand-parents. Christina did not go with them. Family tradition maintains that she gave her sons the beadwork to remind them of their Indian heritage because her Scottish relatives were unlikely to do so. Beaded moccasins and embroidered clothing that became curiosities in Europe could also be markers of cultural identity and bearers of complex family histories.[45]

Highlanders and Indians borrowed and adapted each other's clothing and styles of dress. Orkneymen and other sailors gave Indians around Hudson Bay "red coats for the Chiefs, adorned with tinsel lace."[46] The *Annual Register* for 1763 carried a report from Charles Town, South Carolina, that an Indian trader had sold the Cherokees "several garments of red baize, much in the nature of the Highlanders uniform, for which he had a valuable return of furs and deer-skins." Learning of their fondness for their new gar-ments, the governor ordered "a very magnificent suit of rich scarlet, in the same form, and trimmed with silver tassels to be presented to each of their chiefs; so that if this humour holds, they might soon see the whole Cherokee nation clad in regimentals, which may probably extend all over North America."[47]

Red cloth coats clearly meant something other than the king's service to their new wearers. Colors had meanings: White symbolized peace, good thoughts, and well-being; black signified death and negativity; red was the color of fire and emotion. Red was thus a potent symbol, and red cloth was often sought as an item of sacrifice and prayer. Ojibwas preferred red to other colors of wool clothing: It was a continuation of their earlier custom of paint-ing red ochre on leather garments and "expressed relationships with life-giving forces." A red coat, as Evan Haefeli points out, "was not a fashion statement," at least, not just a fashion statement; it was a political message. Scarlet coats were a common item in inventories of gifts given by traders and agents to influential Native leaders and came to symbolize a trading captain or ally. Donning an officer's coat gave the wearer status as he "dressed for success" on a cultural frontier, where effective leadership often involved mediating between European and Indian worlds.[48]

In the cross-cultural environment of the fur trade, hybrid types of clothing emerged. Scots Indian children combined styles derived from the cultures of both parents and often wore them to mark a distinct Métis identity. Alexander Ross said that Métis women "invariably attire themselves in gaudy prints and shawls, chiefly of the tartan kind." Tartan began to become a common article of dress among First Nations and Métis in the middle of the nineteenth century, about the same time it became fashionable in Britain. But as Sherry Farrell Racette points out, Native peoples probably identified tartan with the Hudson's Bay Company that provided it rather than with Scotland, which they had not seen, and wearing tartan rarely signified a connection with a particular clan. Tartan was used in making babies' mossbags, in ceremonies—even sometimes in sacred bundles—and in time became an expression of identity. In some Cree, Ojibwa, and Métis communities tartan shawls eventually came to signify tradition and cultural persistence. Letitia Hargrave, Scottish wife of the chief factor at York Factory, said that "Canadian half breeds . . . sometimes pay a whole year's wages for a cap, often a Highland bonnet covered with silver work." Although Mrs. Hargrave was "no admirer of indigenous fashion," even she wore Indian leggings.[49] Traveling in Saskatchewan and the Rocky mountains in 1859 and 1860, the Earl of Southesk saw Métis wearing "a dark-blue woolen, mushroom-topped, lowland Scotch bonnet, such as I remember common in Forfarshire in my boyhood."[50] In the nineteenth century Iroquois women began beading Glengarry-style caps like those worn by Highland soldiers stationed in Canada and sold them to tourists.

In the Southeast, Indian and Highland styles of clothing were sometimes not very different: Highland and Indian men eschewed trousers as unmanly, and traveler William Bartram described a breech cloth as a garment that "somewhat resembles . . . the kilt of the Highlanders."[51] Southeastern Indians adopted trade shirts, woolen and cotton cloth (sometimes in tartan), and silver jewelry. Creek and Seminole men's clothing displayed so much Highland influence and so many elements of Highland styles that, with each passing decade, their dress "seemed more like that of Highland lairds."[52]

If it was not uncommon to see Indians sporting red coats they had received as gifts or trophies, or Native women wearing tartan blankets, it was equally common to see Scots in Indian country wearing moccasins, leggings, and hunting shirts. Traders who lived and worked in Indian society adopted Indian ways and learned the protocols and obligations of exchange. Highlanders proved adaptable. In addition to being accustomed to difficult physical conditions, many were well educated and multilingual. Isaac Cowie said Highlanders

Figure 5.5. Portrait of Ambrose, a Salish warrior also known as Shilchelumela, or Five Crows, wearing a Scotch cap, by Gustavus Sohon, ca. 1855. (National Anthropological Archives, Smithsonian Institution, Washington, D.C., 37.416B.)

Figure 5.6. Glengarry-style Iroquois beaded cap, nineteenth century. (Bedford Collection, Royal Ontario Museum, Ontario, Toronto, 989.15.16. With permission of the Royal Ontario Museum, © ROM.)

quickly picked up Indian and French languages and that it was "pleasing to see how soon the Scottish mountaineers and the American Muskagoes [Swampy Cree] got on good terms with each other," each trying out words in Cree and Gaelic respectively. Highlanders not only learned Native languages but also introduced some aspects of Gaelic into the fur trade patois.[53]

Nevertheless, European and Indian values were always in tension. Similar experiences and kinship systems did not give Highland traders automatic insight into Indian culture or particular sympathy for Indian people. Whatever human relationships may have developed and however Indian ways may have influenced individual Scottish traders, they all, as Duncan McGillivray put it bluntly, divided Indians "into two classes; those who have furs and those who have none."[54] Highland traders shared the prejudices and attitudes of their English, Canadian, or American peers, and these were frequently negative.[55] Alexander Ross said Indians were like children.[56] He had little regard for Iroquois who worked in the western fur trade (they came mainly from the Mohawk community at Kahnawake near Montreal and composed about one third of the Hudson's Bay Company employees on the Columbia). He said they were "sullen, indolent, fickle, cowardly and treacherous."[57] Duncan Cameron called Indians "the greatest and most shameless beggars on earth." They were deceitful and notorious pilferers. "Being themselves unacquainted with honor and honesty, they are very distrustful of us, thinking us worse than themselves.[58] Joseph McGillivray, chief trader at the Hudson's Bay post at Fort Alexandria on the Columbia River, denounced the Carrier Indians as "Brutes." They were addicted to lying, thieving, and gambling, promiscuous, polygamous, vengeful, bloodthirsty, and unequalled in "filth, nastiness, and laziness." What was worse, perhaps, a Carrier was "the most selfish Animal in existence" (at least when it came to dealing with whites).[59]

The fur trade brought new items to Indian country, but the costs were enormous. New tools made life easier, but traditional craft skills declined. New weapons made warfare more lethal, and competition for them made it more common. Contagious diseases spread from tribe to tribe along trade networks that hummed with activity. Overhunting depleted animal populations to the point of extinction in some regions and undermined traditional hunting rituals and reciprocal relationships with the animal world. Balanced and diversified patterns of subsistence were disrupted as communities focused their energies on trapping to meet the apparently insatiable demands of the European fur markets. Indian bands moved to get access to trade routes, to keep ahead of advancing trade frontiers, and to secure and maintain middleman roles between trading posts and distant hunters. In some areas Indians sought out traders for what they wanted but resisted being pulled into a dependent relationship; others relied heavily on European goods and became vulnerable to European market forces.

In addition, traders brought alcohol into Indian country. Alcohol was a crucial commodity in the fur trade. It could be transported easily in concentrated form and diluted for sale at huge profits. It was quickly consumed and it was addictive. Traders used it to attract Indians to trade and to procure their furs on favorable terms. Not all Indians drank, and not all who did suffered from it, but alcohol wrought havoc in countless communities. Indian hunters who sold their catch for a bottle of rum often left their families in poverty. Drunken brawls disrupted social relations that traditionally stressed harmony and reciprocity. Like other people, Indians who drank to excess did so for a variety of social, cultural, genetic, and behavioral reasons. Some drank for the sensations alcohol produced, while some sought solace in times of wrenching change. Indian leaders throughout colonial America complained about the rum trade and asked that it be halted, but colonial governments could not or would not stem the tide of alcohol into Indian villages.[60]

Traders denounced the effects of alcohol and condemned Indians for drunkenness even as they dispensed it in vast quantities. Rival trading companies competing for customers flooded Indian country with alcohol. They knew better than to allow Indians to consume it within the trading post, however. Roderick McKenzie witnessed an Indian drinking binge that was so noisy and violent "that one might believe that all the Furies of Hell were let loose in our camp, but our gates were of course secured." The next morning he learned that five Indians had died.[61] References to alcohol and alcoholism occur repeatedly in Duncan McGillivray's journal of daily life at Fort George on the Saskatchewan in 1794 and 1795, and McGillivray had much to say about the alcohol trade. Indians were addicted to alcohol, would sacrifice a season of pelts and the chastity of their daughters for rum, and engaged in unrestrained and often violent bouts of binge drinking. Bands would arrive at the fort expecting to receive gifts of alcohol, then drink "24 hours and sometimes much longer for nothing—a privilege of which they take every advantage—for in the seat of an Opposition profusion is an absolute necessity to secure the trade of an Indian." (The Hudson's Bay Company had a rival trading post, Buckingham House, across the river.) Once the binge was over, they would start to trade, paying thirty beavers for a large keg of rum. "The love of rum is their first inducement to industry," McGillivray wrote. "When a nation becomes addicted to drinking, it affords a strong presumption that they will become excellent hunters." As the snow began to melt in April 1795, Indians began to come to the fort after their winter hunts "that they may once more pay their devotions at the shrine of Bacchus and drown all their cares with plentifull draughts of their favorite beverage, Rum." By mid-April, Indians from seven different nations had gathered at the fort. They spoke different languages, and many were mutual enemies, but, said McGillivray, "they seem all to agree in one measure which is to get heartily drunk." "Men, Women and children, promiscuously mingle together and join in one diabolical clamour of singing, crying, fighting &c and to such excess do they indulge their love of drinking that all regard to decency or decorum is forgotten."[62]

Yet the drunken behavior that McGillivray and most of his contemporaries denounced as an Indian trait was not unique to Indians. Hard drinking was a characteristic shared by all participants in the fur trade. French Canadian voyageurs joined the Scots partners and clerks in celebrating New Year's Day, and on Saint Andrew's Day "one bottle succeeded another so quick that scarcely a man in the Fort escaped a Black eye." On January 26, 1795, McGillivray recorded the following: "The Holidays were spent as usual in dissipation & enjoyment, intermixed with quarreling and fighting—the certain consequences of intoxication among the men."[63]

Moreover, Highland Scots were known for their fondness for whiskey, as well as beer and wine: "To speake truth without offence," wrote one observer in the early seventeenth century, "the excess of drinking was then far greater in generall among the Scots than the English." Distilling and distributing illicit whiskey was a small industry in the Highlands, and whiskey was "much too commonly used." In the late eighteenth century the *Scots Magazine* declared Scotland "the most drunken nation on the face of the earth."[64] Scots carried their capacity for consuming large quantities of whiskey to America. The bacchanalian orgies of the North West Company elite at the Beaver Club in Montreal were notorious and frequently ended with the participants in a drunken stupor. Consuming prodigious quantities of alcohol was almost a national pastime in the United States as well at this time.[65]

Traders' concerns about Indian drinking stemmed largely from the fact that Indians who were drunk were not hunting for furs. Neither were Indians who sat talking, smoking, or gambling or who were hunting or fishing for food. Those who were not actively contributing to the fur business were routinely described as idle. Salmon-fishing tribes in particular were considered "of a very indolent habit."[66] Indians were improvident if they did not lay aside ample stores of food. Trade employees recruited from the Highlands and islands of Scotland, where they "Seldom, if Ever, Eat Any thing better than Pease or Barley Bread with Salt Sellocks [fried fish] and Kale," had little reason to look askance at Native diets, but their superiors in the trade expected Indian men to supply regular and ample supplies of meat and furs. Writing to his sister, Dugald McTavish stated that the Indians around Moose Factory on James Bay "lead a curious life. . . . One day they are in the midst of plenty, the next they are starving—they have no care about them—when they have any thing to eat, they continue at it until it is finished altho' they have no immediate prospect of getting any thing more for a Month to come." His complaint was typical. Traders' ideas of hunger and starving, like their ideas about wealth and property, were derived from their own class and culture, expectations, and disappointments. They showed little tolerance for Native needs or for subsistence strategies that accommodated seasons of want and plenty and altered in response to changing ecological conditions. When traders said Indians were "starving," it sometimes meant only that they were hunting for food instead of furs.[67]

Reflections on the Trade

Most successful Highland fur traders were hard-headed businessmen who showed little concern for the Native people they exploited and worried little about what they were doing. But not all of them fit this mold. Donald Ross at Norway House, a well-read man who spiced his letters with discussions of literature and contemporary politics, thought that a trader bore some responsibilities to the people with whom he traded. At a time of falling fur prices, he refused to stop trading with them: "The muskrat trade is certainly unprofitable," he wrote his friend and chief factor, James Hargrave, in the winter of 1836, "but if we do not give the Indians strouds and Blankets for them, what are these unfortunates to do for clothing?" Ross had given it much thought and resolved never to be "a consenting party to any measure that may have the effect of reducing in any manner the few comforts which the native population of this country are allowed by our present system of Trading," even if it ate into profits. "Do not," he advised Hargrave, "get into the blues on account of money matters." People "gather, and gather and gather on but still the more they get the more they wish to have, until at last the old grim boy with the long scythe comes and without much ceremony, soon puts a final separation between a man and his dear money bags."[68]

John McLean, a twenty-five-year veteran who appears to have married Ross's Métis daughter, also denounced the calculating methods and motives of the fur business. He regarded greed and acquisitiveness as a European import. Whatever claims the Hudson's Company might make to the contrary, its sole object was gain. "In our intercourse with the natives of America no other object is discernible, no other object is thought of, no other object is allowed."⁶⁹ He made plenty of typically disparaging remarks about Indians but did not think "we have any right to blame a practice in them, which they have undoubtedly learned from us. What do they obtain from us without payment? Nothing." McLean recognized that, however Indians might deal with whites, between themselves they shared rather than accumulated wealth. "In fact, a community of goods seems almost established among them," he wrote, echoing William Penn; "the few articles they purchase from us shift from hand to hand and seldom remain more than two or three days in the hands of the original purchaser."⁷⁰

McLean dismissed claims that the Hudson's Bay Company showed any concern for the Indians' present or future well-being. Ridiculing one writer's statement that company posts served as hospitals, he pointed out that Europeans were more dependent on Indian medical knowledge than vice versa. He doubted that European examples and teachings had done anything to improve native morals and conditions. "What is to become of the natives when their lands can no longer furnish the means of subsistence?" he asked. Formerly independent, they were now dependent, unhappy, and decreasing "at an extraordinary rate." They appeared doomed to extinction, and the British government was doing nothing to prevent it. "Are they to be left to the tender mercies of the trader until famine and disease sweep them from the earth?" It is doubtful whether McLean's suggested alternative—abolish the Hudson's Bay Company charter, place the territory under government control, throw it "wide open to every individual of capital and enterprise," send in missionaries, and establish industrial training schools—would have done much to improve the Indians' situation; it did not in the United States. Nevertheless, McLean and some other Highland traders worried about what they and their kind were doing to the Indians.⁷¹

Highlanders who encountered Indians in the fur trade sometimes reflected on the collision of cultures they witnessed.⁷² Alexander Mackenzie (or at least his ghost writer, William Combe, sitting in debtor's prison) maintained that "experience proves that it requires much less time for a civilized people to deviate into the manners and customs of savage life, than for savages to rise into a state of civilization."⁷³ Alexander Ross said much the same thing. Ross migrated to Canada from Nairnshire when he was eighteen, taught school for several years, and then joined John Jacob Astor's Pacific Fur Company before transferring allegiance to the Hudson's Bay Company. After retiring with his family to Red River, he wrote an account of his life in the fur trade. "An Indian, accustomed to squat on the ground, and double himself up in the lodge, is long, long indeed before he can reconcile himself to sit in a chair," he said, "but the white man is at once at home in an Indian lodge, and becomes as easy and contented sitting, squatting, or lying amongst dirt and filth, dogs and fleas, as if in his armchair at home—showing how much more easy and natural it is for civilized man to degenerate than for the savage to elevate himself to the habits of civilized men." At the same time, Ross acknowledged that "progress" did not necessarily constitute improvement. Justice, humanity, and "forbearance" were as often found among Indians as among whites, and he reckoned there was less crime in an Indian village of five hundred people than in a "civilized" village half that size. The Indian was happy in his natural state, "but the moment he begins to walk in the path of the white man his happiness is at an end."[74]

Others were much less charitable in their descriptions of the process. Stationed on the lower Saint Lawrence River, James McKenzie, a trader with more than his share of prejudices against Canadian voyageurs, as well as Indians, had little good to say about the Naskapis. Like most "savages," they were lazy, treacherous, and great thieves, but at least they were isolated from European contact and retained their ancient habits "in all their savage purity." Not so the Montagnais. These Christianized Indians had "all the vices of the whites and Nascapees, without one of their virtuous qualities." They were indolent, ungrateful, malicious, stubborn, and given to lying, stealing, drinking, and trickery. They were, he said, "neither one thing nor the other, neither Nascapees nor whites, but, like the mule between the horse and the ass, a spurious breed between both, and a melancholy instance of the influence of European manners upon the morals of the wild inhabitants of the woods."[75]

Fur traders also had occasion to reflect on their own lot, and Highlanders may have done so more than most. John McLean said traders bid farewell to all of the comforts of civilized life "to vegetate at some desolate solitary post, hundreds of miles, perhaps, from any other human habitation, save the wigwam of the savage." Sometimes they became "semi-barbarians—so altered in habits and sentiments, that they not only become attached to savage life, but eventually lose all relish for any other."[76] Hearing that John McLeod was in poor health, Archibald McDonald wrote back from Fort Langley: "When decay & sickness overtake us, few mortals present a more dismal & forlorn situation than an Indian trader, in a manner abandoned by the world and by himself."[77] In a joint memorandum written after many years in the Canadian fur trade, Simon Fraser and John McDonald of Garth concisely summarized the experience of Highland Scots in the North West Company trade: "We have been feared, loved & respected by natives. We have kept our men under subordination. We have thus lived long lives."[78] Alexander Ross allowed that living for years "among savages in the far distant wilds of North America may appear in the light of banishment more than an appointment of choice," but he could think of few fur trade veterans who did not "look back with a mixture of fond remembrance and regret" on the independence, adventure, and scenes they had enjoyed.[79]

If other Highlanders showed sympathy for Indians and concern about the fur trade's impact on them, George Simpson did not. Taking over command of the Athabasca district in the wake of intense competition between Hudson's Bay and North West Company traders, Simpson found the Indians there "buoyed up with most extravagant notions" and weighed down with debts they had no hope of paying. He set about changing things. "I have paid them a great deal of personal attention, exhibited my finery, got the Interpreters to pass me off as a most extraordinary personage and by this time my fame has reached from one end of Athabasca to the other," he wrote. He studied the Indians and found them "a miserable abject race; covetous and selfish to an extreme, full of low cunning, and devoid of every good feeling." He drew distinctions between different groups of Indians—he much preferred the Beaver Indians of Peace River to the Chipewyans, whom he dismissed as "disgraceful to human nature"—but he based his assessments on their "worth" to his business.[80]

Simpson was also damning of company employees, whom he regularly described as indolent, incompetent rascals, and of company officers. He intended "to purge the Country of a few of them." In their place, he planned to engage a dozen young Scotsmen "of tolerable Education and moderate expectations" on five-year contracts. He would bring them to York Factory and send them out with bands of Indians the first winter, "which will inure them to the privations incident to the Country, give them a knowledge of the Cree Language which is understood throughout the Department, familiarise them to the habits and customs of the Natives and teach them the Rudiments of the Fur Trade."[81]

Several years later, having spent considerable time among the Chinooks, he felt qualified to write about their customs and way of life, including the practice of ornamentally flattening their heads (a couple of which he promised to send to the company's honorable committee "as a curiosity"). In his estimation, Chinooks were savvy traders, did not regard chastity as a virtue, and were "exceedingly filthy in their habits, their persons and habitation swarming with loathsome vermin which they do not take the trouble of hunting except for the purpose of conveying to their mouths."[82] Simpson took measures to curb the alcohol trade, although not primarily out of concern for its destructive effects on Native people. He regarded the use of alcohol as shortsighted and ultimately ruinous to the fur trade; far better, he said, "to encourage the Consumption of Woolens and other useful British Manufactures" as the basis for a stable commerce.[83]

"I have made it my study to examine the nature and character of the Indians," Simpson declared, "and however repugnant it may be to our feelings, I am convinced they must be ruled with a rod of iron." The best way to "keep them in a proper state of subordination" was to make them "feel their dependence upon us."[84] He had little use for Indians other than as hunters and traders. "I have always remarked that an enlightened Indian is good for nothing," he pronounced; "even the half Breeds of this Country who have been educated in Canada are blackguards of the very worst description, they not only pick up the vices of the Whites upon which they improve but retain those of the Indian in their utmost extent."[85]

In his study of fur trader's attitudes toward Indians, Lewis O. Saum concluded that "Judged by his views of the Indian, Simpson seems little more than an anthropomorphism of a giant, mindless economic concern."[86] Simpson's character and career demolish any notion that traders from the Highlands of Scotland necessarily enjoyed any special affinity with Indian people. Highland birth, background, or temperament was clearly no guarantee of positive relations with Indians.

Nevertheless, Simpson was not typical (and perhaps not even representative) of Highland fur traders who, time and again across North America, lived in Indian country, functioned as brokers between tribalism and capitalism, and introduced a distinctive Gaelic component to Indian communities. In Canada, as in other continents, Scots' trade-based relationships with Native peoples endured longer than in America, where such societies were swept aside by the flood of settlement that followed American independence.[87] Where and while the fur trade lasted, Highland traders and Native hunters, as customers and partners, operated in a Scots-Indian world.

6

Highland Men and Indian Families

At the Hudson's Bay post at Lake of Two Mountains (now called Oka), a mission village on the Saint Lawrence inhabited by Iroquois and Algonquins, John McLean and another young Highland trader (whom McLean not very imaginatively referred to as "Mac") struck up a conversation of sorts with two very pretty sisters: "We discoursed in Gaelic; they answered in Iroquois; and in a short time the best *understanding* imaginable was established between us." Nothing came of it, however, because the priest got wind of what was going on and gave the young men a talking-to. "I resolved from that moment to speak no more Gaelic to the Iroquois maidens," said McLean. At least that is what he wrote. "Mac," on the other hand, "continued his visits."[1] Other young men were not so easily dissuaded, either. Relations between Highland men and Native women ranged from casual sex to enduring monogamy and occurred often and everywhere in North America.

Highland men and Indian women produced Scots Indian children, Scots Indian families, and sometimes even Scots Indian communities. Their unions provide insights into (and exceptions to) changing marriage practices on the fur-trading frontier, where men took Native wives, then Métis wives, then dismissed both for white wives as part of the "domesticating" of the empire. Intermarriage between Highlanders and Indians, as well as between Highlanders and the daughters of other Highlanders and Indians, reached all across the continent and produced a population in both Canada and the United States that traced its descent from both Scottish clans and Indian tribes. Highland men and Indian women generated webs of allegiance and identity that persist to this day.

Sexual contact and intermarriage between Europeans and Indians produced what historian Albert Hurtado calls "intimate frontiers": social and cultural spaces where colonizers and colonized both defined and defied racial classifications and confirmed and confounded categories of dominance and power structures. Colonial relations shaped domestic relations. Power dynamics and economic factors governed the way in which relations played out, and European patriarchal concepts dominated. But human emotions, loves, and loyalties sometimes resisted or subverted colonial constraints.[2] European liaisons with Indian women were often violent, short term, and based on sexual need or economic self-interest, but sometimes they were consensual, stable, and romantic.[3]

Indian women were part of the lure of Indian country that troubled New England Puritans in the seventeenth century, as well as Benjamin Franklin and Hector St. Jean de Crèvecoeur in the eighteenth century. Despite John Rolfe's famous marriage to Pocahontas (notably a woman of high rank), Englishmen in the seventeenth century resisted intercourse and intermarriage with Indian women as a threat to their assumed cultural supremacy and their social order. However, in the eighteenth century they engaged in plenty of both on the frontiers, especially in the fur trade, where Indian partners brought commercial advantages, as well as sexual companionship.[4]

Sexual liaisons were a ubiquitous aspect of colonial encounter, and sexual violence against Native women was an integral part of the conquest and colonization of America.[5] Although it was something they were not often likely to admit in their writings, Highland Scotsmen were clearly not innocent of sexual predation. "I am really at a loss how to pass my time in this remote part of the Country if I dont take one of the Squaws into the Woods and play at all fours with her," one Highland soldier stationed at the Abenaki town of Saint Francis (now Odanak) near Montreal wrote to his brother in 1762.[6] Simon Fraser boasted of his sexual conquests with Indian women to Sir William Johnson (whose own sexual exploits with Iroquois women were legendary).[7]

Yet Highland Scots commonly encountered Indian women in situations where power relations were less imbalanced than gold-rush California, for instance, where a massive influx of young white males and the devastation of Native communities rendered women vulnerable to routine sexual violence. In the southeastern deerskin trade and the northern beaver trade, Highland men were a minority, depended on the goodwill of Indian communities, and often lacked the power to enforce their own will. Traders stayed in Indian country or returned regularly for long periods of their lives and lived with Indian women. Indian wives gave them kinship relations in the community where they did business. William Bartram, traveling in Florida in the late eighteenth century, said, "Seminole girls are by no means destitute of charms to please the rougher sex," while "the white traders are fully sensible how greatly it is to their advantage to gain their affections and friendship in matters of trade and commerce." Relations based on love, mutual interest, and reciprocity tended to last, he noted.[8]

European men and Indian women all across America produced children of mixed parentage, and Highland Scots probably had no more interactions with Indian women than did the French, who intermarried so commonly with Indian peoples of the Great Lakes and Canadian prairies that a "new" Métis population developed with a distinct ethnic identity.[9] Nonetheless, Scots took up with Indian women in large numbers, far more proportionately than did their English counterparts. An investigation of ethnic patterns of intermarriage with Indian people in the Pacific Northwest in the last two decades of the nineteenth century, for example, found that foreign-born settlers were far more likely than their American-born neighbors to marry Indians. Scottish setters accounted for only 1.4 percent of the total population but for 5.6 percent of marriage with Indians, a rate of intermarriage four times what would be predicted merely from their proportion of the region's total population.[10]

Scots may have adapted more easily than Englishmen to the marriage practices they encountered in Native America because marriage customs in Scotland were less rigid than those south of the border. In England, the Marriage Act of 1753 made a regularly conducted church wedding the sole proof of marriage; in Scotland, marriage was more often a civil contract entered into by mutual consent rather than a sacrament. By the law of Scotland, reported a correspondent in the *Annual Register,* "nothing more is required to make a marriage than the consent of the parties, declared in such a manner that it can be proved." Scottish law recognized "marriage by habit or repute."[11] Anglican Bishop George Hills described a white man and a Tsimshian woman in British Columbia in 1866 as "Married [;] that is not of course with [Christ]ian rites or in legal union but as Indians marry, & as I suppose would satisfy the essentials of marriage, as for instance in Scotland."[12]

Traders frequently complained—though they took advantage of it—that Indian men controlled and abused their women's bodies by offering their sexual services as commodities or as preludes to exchange. But for many

Indian societies, sexual intercourse and marriage were ways of incorporating outsiders as kin. In matrilineal societies all but the most temporary relationships had to involve women. By living and sleeping with European men, Indian women acted as cultural mediators and peacemakers, bringing potentially dangerous and disruptive strangers into the community. They might also tap their spiritual power. Highlanders who lived and married in Indian society, then, occupied a place in the Indians' social order as individuals, not just as representatives of a foreign power.[13] Marrying a European could enhance a woman's status by giving her family a patron, but at a cost: Among the matrilineal Cherokees, for instance, "the source of her own status and identity [now] came to derive from her husband rather than her mother, brother, lineage, or clan."[14]

Loneliness, love of a woman and/or the children she bore, the nature of doing business in Indian country, and a lack of social, sexual, and economic opportunities elsewhere doubtless all played a part in attaching individual Highlanders to Indian women. It is possible too that some Highlanders found in Indian communities an alternative to the society that was destroying their own. Highland Scots in Indian country would have had little tolerance for romantic notions about noble savages living lives of unspoiled primitivism; they saw firsthand that life could be as "nasty, brutish, and short" in Indian country as anywhere else. Yet they came from a country that was experiencing alienating social and economic changes, and while Indian communities may not have offered a substitute for Highland homes and ways of life, they did present a communal alternative to the capitalist world that was coming to dominate life on both sides of the Atlantic.

Scots Creeks and Scots Cherokees

In the Southeast, Highland traders and Indian agents frequently married Cherokee, Creek, Choctaw, and Chickasaw women. The tribes were matrilineal, and children who inherited membership in their mother's clan were fully accepted in Native society. Highland fathers who lacked membership in a Creek or Cherokee clan lacked a place in those tribes' social structure. The key relationship was that between the mother and the child: "The children were her relatives, not her husband's." The influential male figure in the child's life was not the father but the mother's brother, who had the responsibility of teaching and disciplining her children; if the father belonged to a different clan (or to no clan), he was a "legal stranger" to the child and might even invoke clan retaliation if he attempted to inflict punishment on his off-spring.[15] In most cases, sons and daughters of Highland fathers lived as Indians with their mother's people.

Nonetheless, some Highland fathers aspired to a closer and larger role in their children's lives. Highland clans were patrilineal, and children of Highland fathers and Creek or Cherokee mothers could claim clan inheritance through both parents and be simultaneously Scottish and Indian. In some cases they derived benefits of two clan networks: Their mother's gave them kinship relations in Indian society, and their father's gave them connections to a wider world of commerce and education. Being of dual clan descent was not always easy, however. Among the Creeks and Seminoles, wrote J. Letich Wright Jr., "Whenever a mestizo had to decide whether at heart he was a McGillivray, McIntosh, Perryman, or McQueen, or instead a Tiger, Wind, Panther, or Alligator, there was mental anguish and not infrequently bloodshed." Andrew Frank agrees: "As much as they pierced their ears and noses, shaved their hair according to Native custom, and plucked their beards, they could not and often did not want to cut their ties" to their father's society.[16] Some scholars maintain that the Cherokees had no concept of "half breed" or "mixed blood" and that paternity had no bearing on Cherokee identity. Others point out that models of kinship describe ideal rules of behavior in societies but that individual human practices often vary, making it likely that some "people with mixed parentage identified with both parents" and saw themselves (and were seen by others) as somehow distinct. Many children had little contact with their European fathers, whereas others grew up in their father's households and came to exert a profound influence on their mother's society.[17]

In the late 1750s and 1760s John Stuart formed a lasting friendship with the Cherokee chief Attakullakulla, or Little Carpenter. In 1756 John Stuart commanded the provincial forces at Fort Loudon in Cherokee country and Attakullakulla helped him escape death or captivity when the Cherokees captured the fort in 1760. Attakullakulla did not make friends with every Scot he met—General John Forbes called him a great "Rascal"[18]—but he and Stuart worked together to develop a British-Cherokee alliance as a basis for peace in place of bloodshed. In 1761 Attakullakulla urged Lieutenant Governor William Bull to appoint Stuart as agent to the Cherokees. "All the Indians love him," he said, "and there will never be any uneasiness if he is here." In 1763 Stuart was appointed British superintendent of Indian affairs in the South and he tried to implement a program of imperial regulation on the southern frontier. Stuart and many other Scots in the imperial administration saw British-Indian cooperation and alliance as the key to peace and order on the frontier. In their view colonists, more than Indians, must be controlled because whites, not Indians, constituted the main threat to peace. Stuart got Oconostota elected to the Saint Andrew's Society of Charles Town in 1773. That same year, as Attakullakulla embarked on a war party, he left Stuart a string of wampum "in Case he should fall, to remmember [sic] his two Children." Stuart called Attakullakulla his "old friend"; the Cherokees called the red-headed Stuart "bushy head." Stuart had a Scots wife, Sarah, but he also married Susannah Emory, a granddaughter of Highland trader Ludovic Grant. Born in the Highlands, Grant was captured as a Jacobite in 1716 and transported to America. He became a trader in Cherokee country and married Eughioote of the Long Hair clan. Their daughter married trader William Emory, and her daughter, Susannah (also of the Long Hair clan through her mother and grandmother), married Stuart. Stuart fathered Cherokee children and Bushyhead became a common Cherokee surname.[19]

Stuart appointed two fellow Highlanders, Alexander Cameron and John McDonald, as agents in Cherokee country. Alexander Cameron was a trader who lived with the Overhill Cherokees and married the daughter of Saloue, "The Young Warrior of Estatoe and Tugaloo," whom he apparently called Molly. They had three children: George, born in 1767; Susanna, born about 1770; and Jane, born about 1776.[20]

Cameron evidently had his son's education in mind from the time he was born. At the Treaty of Hard Labor in 1768 Cherokees gathered to negotiate the boundary line with Virginia and the Carolinas. On the British side stood superintendent Stuart, Cameron (his deputy), and an interpreter called David McDonald. Oconostota referred to Cameron as "Brother Scotchie," their "beloved brother," and asked that he be permitted to remain as the Cherokees' commissary. "He has long lived amongst us as a beloved Man. He has done us Justice and always told us the truth. We all regard him and love him and we hope he will not be taken away from us." Cameron and his Cherokee wife had a son, Oconostota continued, "and we are desirous that he may educate the Boy like the White People and cause him to be taught to read and write that he may resemble both red and White men and live amongst us when his father is dead." For that purpose, the Cherokees set aside a large tract of land in the Saluda River valley for Cameron's son to help provide for his education. Stuart assured the Cherokees that Cameron would continue as deputy among them but he could not include the gift of land in the treaty. It was Cherokee land on the Cherokee side of the boundary line. Cameron's son could "hold it of you as an Indian but not as a White man or one of his Majesty's white Subjects" because that would constitute a breach of the 1763 royal proclamation that prohibited any transfer of Indian land except to the crown. Presumably there were suspicions that Cameron had exerted his influence to get the Cherokees to make the offer since, years later, Cameron had to deny any such efforts on his part to Stuart, and Stuart had to explain things to Lord Hillsborough.[21]

With respect to Cameron, John Stuart said, "It will be next to impossible to find a Person so well Qualified in every respect to manage the Cherokee Indians." By the time of the Revolution Cameron had lived with the Cherokees so long that he "had almost become one of themselves." The war chief Tsi'yu-gûnsi'ni or Dragging Canoe adopted him as his brother. Hated by Americans who blamed him for instigating Cherokee attacks on the frontiers in 1775, Cameron was a marked man. Americans burned his plantation and he took refuge deep in Cherokee country. When Cherokees asked for peace terms from an invading American army in 1779, the American general demanded that they hand over Cameron; otherwise, he would burn their village. The Cherokees refused. "He was as good as his word," reported Cameron, "[and] burnt their houses and cut down their corn, and they are now living upon nuts and whatever they can get besides."[22] The British appointed Cameron superintendent of the Choctaws and Chickasaws, but he died in Savannah in December 1781. His Scots Cherokee children went to Britain: In 1787 George was living with Cameron's brother, Donald, and the two girls attended school in England under their uncle's guardianship.[23]

John McDonald was born in Inverness, emigrated to South Carolina at nineteen, and worked for a trading house before he became Stuart's deputy and commissary in Cherokee country. Like Cameron, he married a Cherokee woman, Annie Shorey, a daughter of Ghigooie of the Bird clan and interpreter William Shorey (who died at sea accompanying a Cherokee delegation to England in 1762). During the Revolution McDonald escaped to the villages of the Chickamaugas, who, rather than accept American peace terms, followed Dragging Canoe and seceded from the Cherokee Nation to continue the fight from new homes in western Tennessee. Trader William Panton, who was born on the Moray Firth, east of McDonald's birthplace, visited McDonald at his Chickamauga home in 1792 and enlisted him as a Spanish agent. Specifically, it seems Panton wanted Cameron to act as interpreter and mediator and accompany the Cherokee chief Little Turkey to Pensacola to meet the Spanish governor. McDonald wrote letters of recommendation for several Cherokee chiefs to help them get Spanish guns and ammunition to defend their lands.[24]

Two years later, Governor William Blount of Tennessee recommended that Secretary of War Henry Knox appoint McDonald U.S. agent to the Upper Creeks. McDonald by then was living among the Lower Cherokees and had more influence with them than any other white man residing among them. Blount felt he could help win over the hostile Creek towns and noted that his appointment would be pleasing to "several Scotch traders, heretofore adherents to the British Government." McDonald had apparently indicated his willingness to consider such an appointment.[25]

John Norton, himself of Scots and Cherokee parentage, met McDonald during his travels in Chickamauga country. McDonald, whose Cherokee name was Tekighwelliska, entertained Norton "with the hospitality of an ancient Caledonian or a modern Cherokee." He was, thought Norton, an honest and good man, who had served his king faithfully in the Revolution, but after the war was over "his affection for his wife and children induced him to remain, and share the fate of the Cherokees." By the time Norton met him, McDonald had lived forty years among the Cherokees and spoke their language "elegantly."[26] McDonald and Annie's daughter, Mary Molly, married Daniel Ross. Their son, McDonald's grandson, John Ross, became principal chief of the Cherokee Nation.[27]

John Norton met other Highland Cherokees when he traveled through Chickamauga country. John MacClamore or McLemore was one of several brothers who were "the Sons of a Scotch Highlander who married in the country" (one of whom was probably the "renegade trader" who acted as messenger during the Cherokee War in 1760). Having been raised to live like Cherokees and long exposed to the weather, they resembled other Cherokees, although one of them, said Norton, "has much of the Highland countenance." A Cherokee named McLemore, also known as Euskulacau, made his mark on treaties with the United States in 1794, 1804, 1805, and 1806.[28] There were several families named Campbell: One old Highlander of that name could not speak Cherokee and had not taught his family to speak English.[29] Another, named MacPherson, who had served with Sir John Johnson during the Revolution, had married a Cherokee woman and had raised eleven children.[30]

Scots operating in the southeastern deerskin trade strengthened their ties with each other by marriage and patronage, and they developed their ties in Indian country by marriage and trade.[31] Many children of Scots and Indian parentage grew to become leaders and culture brokers in the Indian Southeast, particularly those descended from Clan Chattan (the clan of the cat) on their father's side and from the Creek Wind clan on their mother's. James McQueen lived with the Upper Creeks in Alabama until his death in 1811, at the reputed age of 128. He married a Tallahassee woman of the Wind clan. U. S. Indian agent Benjamin Hawkins described him in 1797 as "the oldest white man in the [Creek] nation. . . . He is healthy and active; he has had a numerous family, but has outlived most of them."[32] His son, Peter McQueen, became a leading "Red Stick" in the Creek War, refused to attend the Treaty of Fort Jackson, and moved to Florida to continue the fight.

Trader Lachlan McGillivray married Sehoy Marchand of the Wind clan, named his first son Alexander (after the clan chief who fell at Culloden), and saw that he received a formal education in Charles Town, sending him to live with his cousin there, the Rev. Farquhar McGillivray. After the American Revolution, in which he supported the British cause, Alexander McGillivray emerged as the most prominent Creek chief in the nation's dealings with the United States and negotiated the Treaty of New York in 1790. He was also a silent partner in the firm of Panton, Leslie, and Company. He was perhaps the most influential Native figure in the Southeast, balancing Creek relations with the United States and Spain in an era and area of intense international competition. McGillivray married a Métis woman named McCrae, whom traveler John Pope described as "a Woman loveliest of the lovely Kind," and had two children, Alexander and Elizabeth.[33]

Although often viewed by historians as thoroughly Creek, McGillivray lived very differently from most Creeks. He was literate, and he studied Greek, Latin, English history, and literature. He owned and managed a large plantation and functioned effectively in the Atlantic commercial world. He and other Scots Indians brought far-reaching changes by accumulating unprecedented wealth, power, and property for themselves and reorienting Creek society toward a market economy.[34]

Having a Highland father and an Indian mother created a situation that required adjustment when it came to inheritance of property. Lachlan McGillivray married only one woman, Sehoy Marchand, yet his will divided his goods between his son, two cousins, his sisters, and his business friends. Sehoy and his two daughters were not included. "They would be taken care of by the Wind Clan."[35] When Alexander McGillivray died, his sisters, Sehoy McPherson Tait Weatherford and Sophia McGillivray Durant, laid claim to his estate. Under traditional systems of inheritance in matrilineal societies like the Creeks, a man's property went not to his sons but to his sisters and their children. McGillivray apparently refused to make a will, which would have meant that his sisters inherited, but just before he died "the Scots Indian embraced the European side of his ancestry" and said he wanted to leave most of his goods to his sons.[36] Creek law required that a white man who left the Creek nation and his Creek family must also leave all of his property to support his children.[37]

Like his father, Alexander McGillivray wanted his son to receive a formal education. William Panton honored his friend's wishes and sent the boy to Inverness, where he was reunited with his Highland grandfather and studied under a tutor. John Innerarity, Panton's brother-in-law and associate in London, reported in 1798 that Alexander Jr., nicknamed Aleck, "bids fair to make a good scholar and what is better a good man." Unfortunately, the young man never returned to Creek country: He died of pneumonia in 1802.[38]

In a world where prosperous Scots traders often owned plantations and slaves, Scots and Indian intermarriages sometimes became entwined with African intermarriage. Robert Grierson, a native of Scotland, lived for many years in Creek country as a deerskin trader, "spoke the language well, and had large possessions, negros [sic], cattle and horses," reported Benjamin Hawkins in 1796. He married a woman named Sinnugee who had fled or been captured from Spanish Florida "and was therefore," thinks historian Claudio Saunt, "probably part Spanish, Mesoamerican, and African." She was adopted by the Creeks into the Spanalgee or Spanish clan. Hawkins said Grierson was "much attached to this country and means to spend his days here with his Indian family and connexions." Grierson and Sinnugee had eight children and many descendants, including those of a daughter who had children with a man of African descent. But times changed and attitudes hardened. Over the course of the nineteenth century, in Saunt's words, "race drove a wedge between family members, separating those with African ancestry from those without, and driving the two sides apart until they denied their common origins." [39]

The Custom of the Country

Highlanders and Indians mated and married regularly in the Canadian fur trade. It was part of the "custom of the country." Traders established connections and kinship ties in the community where they traded, they acquired helpmates and "sleeping dictionaries," and, in many cases, they made a family that endured for years, at least until the trader returned home. Intermarriage and intercourse between Highland men and Indian women, as well as the multiplication of their offspring over time, gave the Canadian fur trade a distinctive social character.[40]

The Hudson's Bay Company at first tried to prevent intermarriage but soon turned a blind eye to it. By the mid-eighteenth century it was common for company governors to take an Indian wife. Andrew Graham, who wrote his "Observations on Hudson's Bay" after he retired to Edinburgh in 1775 (and donated his collection of "Indian curiosities" to the Edinburgh Royal Society), said the company refused to allow Indians into their posts except on business. An officer was allowed "to take in an Indian lady to his apartment, but by no means or on any account whatever to harbour her within the Fort at night." Factors, however, kept "a bedfellow within the Fort at all times." Graham concisely summed up the distinction between policy and practice: "The Company permits no European women to be brought within their territories, and forbid any natives to be harboured in the settlements. This latter has never been obeyed."[41] Graham knew what he was talking about: Although he married the daughter of an Edinburgh merchant during a furlough home after an absence of twenty-three years, he spent no more than four weeks with his new bride before returning to Hudson Bay and his Native wife, who bore him children.[42]

The company's Orkney employees regularly married Native women. In 2004 twenty-five members of the Saskatchewan First Nations, assisted by fund-raising on both sides of the Atlantic and a £10,000 grant from the Scottish Arts Council, visited Orkney. It was "a sort of pilgrimage . . . coming to see the home of their grandfathers." They treated their Orkney relatives to a sampling of dancing, drumming, singing, and storytelling. "These people are our cousins—direct descendants of the same forefathers," said Kim Foden, secretary of the Saskatchewan First Nations Coming Home Committee.[43]

The North West Company had few compunctions about intermarriage: All ranks took Indian partners, and the company accepted some responsibility for maintaining Native wives and families.[44] These wives and families served important functions in the company's operations in Indian country, as Patrick Campbell noted when he visited the home of Donald McKay en route from Quebec to Montreal. McKay's three sons were clerks in the North West Company:

> It is necessary for these clerks to acquire the Indian language as soon as they can; the more intelligent and expert they are at it, and the more of these languages they can speak, the fitter they are for their business; for these reasons they associate much with the Indians, and often have the squaws in keeping. It would seem McKay's sons were not wanting in that part of their duty, as there were three of their children then living in the house with their grandmother. When these children grow up, and are instructed in the French and English languages, they become very useful to the Company, as the Indians look upon all progeny of their women to be of the same tribe of which their mothers are; and whatever the father may be, the heritage goes always in the female line, of course they are looked upon as one of themselves and get preference in barter.

Prevailing opinion, especially by the nineteenth century, held that the offspring of Indian and European unions inherited the vices of both parents and the virtues of neither, but Campbell did not subscribe to that view. "Crossbreeding" was an advantage among the human species as with other species, he said; "I do not remember to have seen an instance where a white man and an Indian woman did not produce handsome and well looking children," even if they were a little "wild."[45]

Scots may have taken more easily than Englishmen to the "custom of the country," but living with Indian women was widespread, even standard, practice. By 1821, when the two companies merged, "practically all officers of the Hudson's Bay and North West Companies, and many lower-ranked employees as well, were allied with women born in the Indian country." Historian Jennifer S. H. Brown's research suggests that, overall, alliances contracted by Hudson's Bay Company traders had more staying power and exhibited more signs of mutual affection than those made by the more mobile and independent North Westers.[46]

As the offspring of white traders and Indian women proliferated, traders tended more often to marry Métis women, especially the daughters of colleagues or senior partners in the trade. Already closely connected by clan, kinship, and patronage, fur trade Highlanders became more closely interrelated through marriage.[47]

Malcolm Fraser, who served with General Wolfe at Louisbourg and Quebec, was granted land in Quebec and lived there until his death in 1815. He married a French Canadian woman, may have married a second time, and was reputed to have had "a Considerable number of illegitimate children." His eldest son, Alexander, became a clerk in the North West Company and rose to partner by 1799. He took up with an Indian woman known as Angélique Meadows, stayed with her throughout his fur trade career, and took his family with him when he retired to eastern Canada. In 1801 he and his father presented three of his children for baptism in Saint Andrew's Church in Quebec. However, he never formally married Angélique: When she died in 1833 her burial certificate recorded her as "Angélique, sauvage native du pays du Nord-Ouest." Like his father, Alexander had many children by several women. He married no one, apparently treated all of his children equally, and provided for them all in his will. Litigation over Fraser's estate dragged on until the 1880s. Alexander's sister, also called Angélique, married and had two sons. One of them, Dr. John McLoughlin, became Hudson's Bay Company's chief factor. McLoughlin married Marguerite Wadin, the Métis widow of trader Alexander McKay, and had four children with her. One son was killed by Indians.[48]

Highland networks persisted at some level within Métis society. Cuthbert Grant, the son of a Highland trader and a Cree French woman, married Elizabeth McKay, a woman of Highland and Indian parentage. After Elizabeth left him, taking their child with her, Cuthbert married another Métis, Madeleine Desmoins, of French Indian descent, for a time. In 1823 he married Marie McGillis, eldest daughter of a trader he knew who had retired to Red River with his family.[49]

Despite their important roles in fur trade society, Indian and Métis women were "at the mercy of a social structure devised primarily to meet the needs of European males."[50] When missionaries and white women arrived in the nineteenth century, changing social attitudes rendered the position of Native women even more vulnerable: They were no longer regarded as fit wives, only as objects of temporary sexual gratification.[51] Highland Scots had their own networks of clan and kinship that often trumped their ties to Indian or Métis mates. Even when they provided for their Native wives and children in their wills, their Scots relatives sometimes challenged the heirs' legitimacy.[52]

As men rose through the ranks of the fur trade or retired to "civilized" society, they sometimes severed their ties with women born in Indian country and married more "respectable" women. William McGillivray, who was born in Invernesshire in 1764, married a Cree or Métis woman named Susan, who bore him several children. In 1799 McGillivray became chief superintendent of the North West Company and the next year took up residence in Montreal, where he married Magdalen McDonald, sister of his fur trade colleague John McDonald of Garth. Magdalen died in 1810 or 1811; Susan died in 1819. Two of William and Susan's children, Simon and Joseph, became chief traders in the coalition of the companies in 1821.[53]

Some traders dissolved their alliances and abandoned their families with apparently little concern. Often men returning to eastern Canada or Britain handed their wives—and children—over to associates in the fur trade, a practice known as "turning off." Some, like Governor George Simpson, turned off wives and children even while he remained in Indian country. Simpson, himself an illegitimate son, fathered at least five children by four different women before he married an eighteen-year-old cousin in London in 1830. As governor, he encouraged traders to form "connubial alliances" as "the best security we can have of the good will of the natives"—and good business. He believed the policy of restricting "matrimonial alliances" was detrimental to the company's interests because it prohibited "forming a most important chain of connection" with the Indians and rendered the company dependent only on those "who have no other feelings than those which interest and mercenary views create towards us."[54] However, he regarded liaisons with Indian and Métis

Figure 6.1. *William McGillivray and His Family, 1805–1806*, by William von Moll Bercy. This was McGillivray's second family: He left his first wife and children in Indian country when he returned east and assumed the position of chief superintendent of the North West Company. He married Magdalen McDonald in 1800. Anne Marie, their first surviving child, was born in 1805. Magdalen died in 1810. (M18683, McCord Museum, Montreal.)

women as nonbinding and abandoned his partners without qualms when the relationship was no longer convenient to him. He rarely mentioned his women by name, referring to them instead as his "article" or "commodity." "If my Damsel is not gone pray send her to the Rock [the Company depot] at once as I do not want to be troubled with a Lady during the busy Season," he instructed his friend John George McTavish (then chief factor) in June 1822. "I suspect my name will become as notorious as the late Govr. in regard to plurality of wives," he said. Simpson often referred to Indian women in disparaging terms, calling them, for example, "bits of brown."[55]

Simpson married Margaret Taylor when she was sixteen. Margaret was the daughter of a Cree woman and a Hudson's Bay Company employee, one of at least eight children. In 1826, before he departed on a tour of company posts, Simpson left Margaret, who was pregnant, with McTavish at York Factory. "Pray keep an Eye on the commodity," he wrote. "If she bring forth anything in proper time & of the right colour let them be taken care of but if anything be amiss let the whole be bundled about their business." A few months later Margaret gave birth to their first child. Two years later, she accompanied Simpson on a grueling journey by canoe across the continent, through the Rockies, and down the turbulent Fraser River to the Pacific. "The commodity has been a great consolation to me," the governor wrote McTavish. Though pregnant with their second child, Margaret traveled with Simpson on the return trip, crossing the Rockies on snowshoes. She gave birth to their second child in August 1829. Six months later Simpson had a new wife.[56]

George Simpson, John George McTavish, and James McMillan at Fort Langley on the Lower Fraser River all found new wives in Britain in 1829 and 1830. McTavish had lived for seventeen years with Nancy or Matooskie, the Native-born daughter of Roderick McKenzie and niece of McTavish's colleague Donald McKenzie, and he had seven children with her. In 1830 McTavish married a new wife, from Aberdeenshire, and brought her to Moose Factory. McMillan, who had broken off relationships with his Clatsop wife, Kilakotah, married a "Scotch Lassie," who joined him a year later at York Factory, bringing their baby daughter with her. Simpson married his eighteen-year-old cousin Frances and brought her to Red River. Mrs. Simpson and Mrs. McTavish were the first British women to make the long canoe voyage from Montreal to interior Canada. Some of their colleagues in the fur trade were outraged by the callous indifference McTavish and Simpson displayed in casting off their Native wives and children, who had been waiting impatiently for their return, only to be summarily discarded. Simpson arranged for Margaret to marry a company employee, a voyageur and stonemason, who was hired to work on Simpson's new headquarters at Lower Fort Garry. "From her vantage point in the Métis labourers' camp just outside the walls," writes her great-great-great granddaughter, "Margaret would have been able to watch the Governor and his new bride take up residence in their magnificent new home." Margaret lived the rest of her life with the Métis on the Assiniboine River. She died in 1885. (Years later her son, ignoring or denying his Métis heritage, described her as "a sturdy Scotswoman.") McTavish arranged for his former wife Nancy to marry Pierre Le Blanc, a miller at Red River, in 1831. (Seven years later "the governor completed the house cleaning" by sending Le Blanc to the Columbia District. The five-year-old daughter of Nancy and LeBlanc died at the Athabaska portage, and then Le Blanc and three of the children drowned in a capsize on the Columbia. Nancy became a dependant at Fort Vancouver until she died at Cowlitz in 1851.) Simpson and McTavish did their best to keep their new wives ignorant of their former relationships, but the knowledge that they were not the first must have added to their wives' feelings of isolation and loneliness in the new country. After Frances Simpson lost her infant son in 1832, the governor took her back to England. She later returned to live at Lachine, near Montreal, but never again went back to Red River. McTavish's wife died in 1841; he married again, this time to the Scottish niece of his colleague Angus Cameron.[57]

Simpson was not just changing wives—he did that often enough. He was also changing, or reflecting changes in, the attitudes and expectations of the fur trade society. By the nineteenth century, notions of white racial superiority were becoming firmly established in Britain.[58] With the arrival of white women and increasing exposure to Victorian standards and double standards, fur trade society began to exhibit greater racial prejudice. Simpson embraced the new hypocrisy with the zeal of a convert. Fellow Scot and chief factor Colin Robertson married a Métis woman named Theresa Chalifoux and became known as a devoted husband and father. In 1825 he traveled to England to arrange an education for their five-year-old son, also called Colin. In 1831 Robertson and Theresa stopped off at Red River to visit their other children in school before going on to Canada. Robertson was past his prime as an effective figure in the business, and Simpson privately regarded him as "a frothy trifling conceited man, who would starve in any other Country and is perfectly useless here." Now he delivered a public snub. When Robertson attempted to introduce his wife to Mrs. Simpson, the governor refused in no uncertain terms. "Robertson brought his bit of Brown with him to the Settlement this Spring in hopes that She would pick up a few English manners before visiting the civilized World," wrote Simpson. "I told him distinctly that the thing was impossible which mortified him exceedingly."

Métis women were allowed in the governor's lady's presence only as servants. Nancy, the ex-wife of Simpson's friend McTavish, helped nurse Mrs. Simpson back to health after the birth of her first child. McTavish also snubbed the Métis wives and families of his fellow company officers after his marriage to a Scottish woman.[59]

However, many traders were far more attached to their Indian or Métis partners than Simpson was, and they felt separation and loss far more severely. William Sinclair, who left the Orkneys and became postmaster at Oxford House on Hudson Bay, married Nahovway, the daughter of a Cree woman and a British ex-soldier. Sinclair seems to have regarded their union as a lifetime obligation: They lived together for twenty-five years and had eleven children.[60] John McLean married his first wife, the Métis daughter of a company officer, probably chief trader Donald Ross, at Norway House in 1837. Within a year his "beloved wife" died, leaving McLean with a newborn son and "in a more wretched condition than words can express." Instead he reflected on what "was truly an eventful year for me—within that space I became a husband, a father, and a widower—I traversed the continent of America, performing a voyage of some 1,500 miles by sea, and a journey by land of fully 1,200 miles, on snow-shoes."[61] Such men did not need to be told to make provision for their families. Many left their wives reluctantly, and some refused to leave them, opting to remain in Indian country or retiring with their families to Red River. The Earl of Selkirk said he established that settlement in part because Hudson's Bay Company employees who grew too old for service were averse to leaving the country, "having formed connections with Indian women, and reared numerous families."[62]

In some cases, men took their wives back to Montreal or even back to Scotland when they retired, with the result that relationships between fur-trade Scots and Native women left their mark in places like Aberdeenshire, Lewis, and the Orkneys as well as in the Canadian Northwest. When George Keith retired as chief factor in 1844, he formally married his Métis wife, Nanette Sutherland, in order to legitimize their children. He then took his family, including a daughter with mental retardation, home. Nanette was seasick crossing the Atlantic and homesick living in Scotland but eventually became reconciled to her new home a few miles from Aberdeen. Alexander Christie, twice Hudson's Bay Company's governor of Assiniboine, also took his "country wife," Ann, home to the outskirts of Aberdeen.[63]

Others made provisions in their wills. John Macdonnell was born in Scotland in 1768, migrated first to New York and then to Canada, and entered the North West Company as a clerk in 1793. In Indian country he took an Indian girl (marriages to girls of twelve or fourteen years were not uncommon) as his wife.

Her name was Magdeleine, and she stayed with him the rest of his life. As he neared retirement in 1812, Macdonnell wrote to his brother, outlining his plans to educate his children and provide for his wife. "The mother has been my constant companion these eighteen years and under my protection since her twelfth year I find it cruel to turn her off in this country and to tear her Children from her—My intentions are to settle Something upon her to enable her to live in a comfortable obscure mediocrity."[64] Similarly, in 1833 Simon McGillivray provided well in his will for his country wife, Therese Roy, "who has lived with me 18 years on the most affectionate terms."[65]

Many Highland traders simply stayed where they were and lived their declining years with their families in Indian country. Trader George Sutherland apparently fathered twenty-seven children by three Cree wives and became head of his own band, all of whom were his descendants.[66]

Gaelinds

Although many Gaelinds—people with Highland fathers and Indian mothers—merged into Indian societies, they also formed a distinct group within a larger Métis population, and they exerted considerable influence in fur trade society. When James Carnegie, the Earl of Southesk, traveled through Saskatchewan and the Rockies in 1859 and 1860, Scots and Scots-Indian Métis were ubiquitous. When Lady Ishbel Aberdeen visited the Blackfeet in the 1860s, she saw "many faces reminding of Scottish character-istics." Treaty commissioners in Manitoba reported "a large population of French Metis and Scotch Halfbreeds." Although there was much general resemblance, the Earl of Southesk wrote, Scots-Indian Métis differed con-siderably from those of French Indian origin. They often had "the fair hair and other physical characteristics of a northern race, while in disposition they are more industrious and more actuated by a sense of duty."[67] The earl did not share the disdain for "half-breeds" commonly expressed by many of his nine-teenth-century contemporaries, but he clearly had his own prejudices.

Not unduly concerned about his own Métis children, George Simpson provided no assistance for those of other men. In Simpson's opinion, "half-breeds" possessed "all the savage ferocity of the Indians with all the cunning and knowledge of the whites."[68] Alexander Isbister, the son of a clerk from Orkney and a Métis Cree mother, resigned from the Hudson's Bay Company in protest over Simpson's reluctance to promote Métis employees. He even-tually moved to Britain, studied law at the University of Aberdeen, and had a career in England. Isbister criticized both the Hudson's Bay Company and the government for their treatment of Native and Métis people. In a memorial to the government, published as a pamphlet, he wrote: "We assert that they are steeped in ignorance, debased in mind, and crushed in spirit, that by the exercise of an illegal claim over the country of their forefathers, they are deprived of the natural rights and privileges of free born men, that they are virtually slaves." The government's "barbarous and selfish policy, founded on love of lucre" alienated their affections and shut them out from civilization. The "same heinous system" was "gradually effacing whole tribes from the soil on which they were born and nurtured." His words, Jenni Calder points out, "have echoes in some of the literature emerging in the nineteenth century concerning the plight of Highlanders."[69]

When the North West Company and Hudson's Bay Company merged in 1821, Simpson zealously took on the task of making the new company a leaner, more efficient, and more profitable operation. Many of the men who were cut from the company rolls had families, and there were also "numerous Halfbreed Children" whose parents had died or deserted them. Company policy dictated making some provision: "These people, form a burden which cannot be got rid of without expence," noted the Hudson's Bay Company committee. Left in their "uneducated and Savage Condition," they represented a threat to "the Peace of the Country and the Safety of the Trading Posts." The committee resolved that discharged employees should remove their dependants from the country or place them at Red River, where clergymen and school teachers would instruct them in Christianity, farming, and "other Works of Industry."[70]

Alexander Ross married an Okanagan woman around 1815, when he was working as a young clerk in the North West Company on the Columbia River. Several years later he took his wife, Sally, to live at Red River, where they raised a family of thirteen children. One of their daughters, Henrietta, married the Presbyterian minister at Red River, the Reverend John Black, in 1854, a marriage that raised the ire and eyebrows of Black's Scottish congregation. By then, at Red River as in the fur trade generally, attitudes toward mixed marriages were becoming increasingly Victorian and racist. In 1856, the year he died, Alexander Ross published a book on Red River but it made no mention of his Native family. At least one daughter, Jemima, was embarrassed to have an Indian mother. "What if Mama is an Indian!" her brother James chided her. "Remember the personal qualities that ought to endear mama to us. Who more tender-hearted? Who more attached to her children & more desirous of their happiness? Who more attentive to their wants—anxious about their welfare. None." Better to have a kind, affectionate and

Christian Indian mother, said James, than a "cold-hearted so-called lady" concerned with "etiquette & fussy nonsense."[71] Despite his loyalty to his Indian mother, James adopted fashionable European dress "to position himself in a social class suitable to his father and his Euro-Canadian wife, education and professional ambitions." The pressures on Scots Indians to find acceptance in their father's world caused considerable cultural ambivalence and sometimes psychological distress.[72]

In Indian societies, mothers normally took care of the children's upbringing, but in fur trade society European fathers exercised paternal authority and made the decisions regarding their offspring. Indian mothers may well have had different opinions, but European fathers rarely bothered to record them even if they considered them.[73] Highland fathers faced a choice between leaving their children to live as Indians with their mother's people and trying to provide them with enough of an education to make their way in the world. Many tried to place them in schools in Britain or Canada.[74] By the end of the 1770s so many Orkneymen had brought home Métis children "that a small college was founded at Saint Margaret's Hope in South Ronaldsay to school their offspring."[75] When Alexander McTavish, chief trader and a former North West Company clerk, died in 1832, he left two Native-born sons. His will stipulated that one of the sons, Donald, who was still in Indian country, "be sent to the Highlands of Scotland, and educated along with his Brother Duncan who is now there, both to live with their Grandmother till they arrive at an age capable of providing for themselves." McTavish's mother and cousin took their responsibility seriously and saw to it that both boys got a Scottish education and a start in a career, Duncan as a cabinetmaker, Donald as a clerk in Inverness. Like his father before him, Duncan thought of emigrating—but he had his eye on New South Wales, not Canada.[76] William Sinclair arranged for his son, James, to be educated in the Orkneys and then at Edinburgh University.[77] Nicol Finlayson took his Métis daughter with him when he retired from the Hudson's Bay Company and went home to Nairn. She married a young man who was a banker and a lawyer and, said Finlayson, was "very happy."[78]

Archibald McDonald of Glencoe led a group of emigrants to the Red River settlement in 1813 and joined the Hudson's Bay Company in 1820. He married Koale Koa (also known as Princess Sunday and Princess Raven), the youngest daughter of the Chinook chief, Concomly. Concomly was a key player in the maritime trade of the Northwest Coast and also had daughters married to traders Duncan MacDougall and Thomas McKay.[79] Koale Koa bore McDonald a son, Ranald, in 1824. She died soon after, and a year later

McDonald married Jane Klyne, daughter of a French Canadian father and a Métis mother. They raised Ranald, seven more sons, and a daughter. McDonald eventually rose to become a chief factor in charge of Fort Colville. Ranald, whom his father described as "a promising good natured-lad," attended school at Red River with his half-brothers. Like many parents in many places, McDonald worried about whether he was doing the right thing for his children. In a letter written at Fort Colville in 1836, when Ranald was twelve years old and attending the Red River academy, he declared he did not think he would stay much longer in Indian country:

> Taking us all together, we are men of extraordinary ideas; a set of selfish drones, incapable of entertaining liberal or correct notions of human life. Our great password is a *handsome provision for our children;* but behold the end of this mighty provision. While we are amassing it like exiled slaves, the offspring is let loose upon the wide world while young, without guide or protection (but always brimful of his own importance) to spend money & contract habits at his own free will & pleasure. The melancholy examples resulting from this blind practice are I am sorry to say but too common. Much better to dream of less, to set ourselves down with them in time & to endeavour to bring them up in habits of industry, economy & morality, than to aspire to all this visionary greatness for them. All the wealth of Rupert's Land will not make a half breed either a good Parson, a Shining Lawyer or an able physician if left to his own discretion while young.[80]

Ranald continued to be a worry to his father. He seemed to exemplify many of the "wild" traits attributed to "half-breeds" and hankered to exchange his job as a bank clerk for a more adventurous life. Believing the Japanese to be related to American Indians, in 1848, at age twenty-four he managed to get passage on a Yankee whaling ship that sailed via Hawaii and dropped him on the coast of northern Japan. Ranald first encountered the indigenous Ainu people, but Japan was still closed to foreigners, and he was arrested and imprisoned for seven months in Nagasaki. During his incarceration he managed to charm his guards and transcribe the Japanese language, and he wound up teaching English to Japanese interpreters, the first teacher of English at a time when Japan was coming under increasing pressure from the outside world. "I have broken the seal that made Japan a Sealed Empire to the West," he wrote. Commodore Perry arrived in 1853 to make the first commercial treaty. The world-traveling Chinook Scot later returned to the Northwest, where he registered himself as a member of the Lake tribe, one of the confederated tribes of the Colville Indian Reservation. Elizabeth Custer, widow of George Armstrong Custer, met him there during a trip to the far West in the summer of 1890 and described him as a "prince among paupers." When she inquired about the "dark-skinned children" (his nephew's) running about his home, "the old man waved his hand over them and said 'They are all McDonalds'; and no chief of the clan could have referred to his progeny in a more stately manner." He died in 1894. Today monuments to Ranald MacDonald (as he spelled his name) stand in Astoria, Oregon, in Toroda, Washington, and in Nagasaki and Rishiri in Japan.[81]

Angus McDonald, born in Craig in the Scottish Highlands in 1816, served as chief factor of Fort Colville, at the junction of the Colville and

Figure 6.2. Ranald MacDonald, Scots Chinook, in 1891. (K. Ross Toole Archives and Special Collections, Maureen and Mike Mansfield Library, University of Montana–Missoula, photo number Mss. 562.)

Columbia rivers, from 1854 until the post closed in 1871. In 1842 he married Catherine Baptiste, the daughter of a Nez Perce woman and "an Iroquois Frenchman" (presumably one of the many Mohawks from Kahnawake and other villages on the Saint Lawrence who worked for the Hudson's Bay Company). One of their sons, Joseph McDonald, recalled in 1941: "I have heard that my father and mother were first married by tribal custom, and that, after father became a convert to the church (R.C.), they were married by the fathers." Angus and Catherine lived together for about forty-seven years and had twelve children. New Englander Caroline Leighton, who visited Fort Colville in 1866, described McDonald as "an old Scotchman," an educated gentleman "of character and intelligence." It seemed to Leighton that Catherine, whom she identified as simply "an Indian woman," could not "live more than half the year in the house" as she spent the rest of the time "wandering about" with her friends and relatives. "It was interesting to see how this cultivated man, accustomed to the world as he had been, had adapted himself to life in this solitary spot on the frontier, with his Indian children for his only companions." Leighton could see Scottish traits in some of the children, "but in most the Indian blood was more apparent. The oldest son, a grown man, was a very dark Indian, decorated with wampum." The eldest daughter, Christine or Christina (who had almost drowned as "a toddling babe dressed in a Glengarry tartan frock"), most resembled her father and kept house for him "because, as she explained to us, her mother could not be much in-doors." Christina herself disliked being confined; she told Leighton she preferred being with the Blackfeet. McDonald spoke several Indian languages (as well as Gaelic and French), but Christina said he "was never weaned from his Scotch habits and ways." He founded the first school and hired a teacher for his own and other children in the area. McDonald sympathized with the Nez Perces in the war of 1877 and urged his son Duncan to interview Nez Perce fugitives on the Canadian side of the border and write newspaper articles on the war. After Fort Colville closed, McDonald moved his family to Montana and took up land on the Flathead reservation. He became a rancher and raised cattle until his death in 1889.

Christina married a Highland fur trader, James MacKenzie; after he died, she opened a trading post in Kamloops. Angus's son Duncan married a Salish woman named Red Sleep and lived as an Indian. Duncan McDonald became a prominent figure in late nineteenth-century and early twentieth-century Montana (McDonald Lake in Glacier National park is named after him; McDonald Peak is named after his father), and McDonald became a notable name on the Flathead reservation.[82]

Figure 6.3. Hudson's Bay Company fur trader Angus McDonald, undated. (K. Ross Toole Archives and Special Collections, Maureen and Mike Mansfield Library, University of Montana–Missoula, photo number 77–289.)

Archie McIntosh also seems to have had a family in the Pacific Northwest, although his travels brought him a family in Apache country. The son of a Scottish father and an Ojibwa mother, Archie worked for the Hudson's Bay Company but, when his father died, was educated in Edinburgh for two years. From the 1850s, he served the U.S. Army as a scout in both Oregon and Arizona. He was known, on occasion, to be too drunk for service, but when General Crook was organizing scouts for the campaign against the Chiricahua Apaches in 1883, "Archie McIntosh turned up again" and participated in Crook's last campaign against Geronimo. Afterward, he married an Apache woman, settled on the San Carlos reservation, and sent his Apache-Scot-Ojibwa son to Carlisle Boarding School.[83]

Within the fur trade society, children were usually identified by their parentage rather than by race. They were less likely to wander a cultural no-man's

Figure 6.4. Catherine Baptiste McDonald, wife of Angus McDonald, undated. Catherine's father was French Mohawk, her mother Nez Perce. (K. Ross Toole Archives and Special Collections, Maureen and Mike Mansfield Library, University of Montana–Missoula, photo number 83–96.)

land than to develop their own identities, create their own social spaces, and find their own niches in a world where so many were Scots Indians.[84] Scots Cree Cuthbert Grant became a leader among the Métis and a valuable ally of the Hudson's Bay Company and the Red River settlement that he had threatened in its infancy. His own settlement at Grantown protected Red River against possible attacks by the Sioux.[85] Joseph William McKay's parents were both children of Hudson's Bay Company traders and Native women. Born at Rupert's House in 1829, McKay was educated at the Red River Academy. He joined the company in 1844 and had a lengthy career in a variety of capacities. He then turned to business and politics. In the 1880s he became a federal Indian agent, serving first on the Northwest Coast and then at the Kamloops and Okanagan agencies. In addition to promoting stock raising and farming

Figure 6.5. Duncan McDonald, his wife, and friend Wuiuhachya, undated. Duncan is shown in the center, with headdress and moustache; his wife, Red Sleep (Louisa Quill), is on horseback. (K. Ross Toole Archives and Special Collections, Maureen and Mike Mansfield Library, University of Montana–Missoula, photo number 82–123.)

among Indian people, he defended their land rights against the Canadian Pacific Railway and settlers, started an industrial school near Kamloops, "and personally inoculated more than 1,300 Aboriginal people against smallpox."[86]

Usually it was from white society that Métis people experienced social stigma, but as ethnic tensions escalated they sometimes felt the precarious nature of their position as people "between." Simon McGillivray Jr., the son of senior North West Company partner Simon McGillivray and his Cree wife, was chief factor at Fort Nez Perce on the Columbia Plateau when malaria broke out in 1832. Indians suspected that Americans had caused the disease, and McGillivray feared that he and his Métis colleagues might be blamed as well, for "we are Whites equally."[87]

Not surprisingly, Highland names and individuals figure prominently in the Métis literature and sometimes in the oral traditions of North America. Author Maria Campbell's great-grandfather emigrated from Scotland and married a Cree woman. So did his brother. "They were both tough, hard men, and on the boat to Canada they got into a fight and disowned each other," she wrote in her autobiography. Nonetheless, they "settled in the same area, both married native women and raised families."[88] Lakota oral tradition recalls how the name Metcalf became part of the Brulé community. A "Scotch nobleman, Lord Metcalf," stopped at Fort Laramie in 1846 on his way to California and fell in love with an Indian girl. He "lived with her in the lodge," sleeping between buffalo robes and eating dried meat. After he left, the girl gave birth to a boy, who was enrolled at the agency under his father's name. He later married and fathered eight children, and Metcalf families proliferated.[89] Such stories were common.

In the eighteenth century, marriage between European men and Indian women had been a foundation of fur trade society. As their offspring multiplied, traders increasingly married Métis women, often the daughters of other traders. But during the nineteenth century, the position of Métis changed. The growing influx of white people and increasing categorizations of people according to assumed notions of race and color assigned fur trade children to the lower ranks in the emerging social order. As white women, Christian missionaries, and Victorian and racist attitudes reached fur trade communities like Red River, Indian and Métis women alike were relegated to an increasingly inferior status and an ever more vulnerable position. This was not an isolated phenomenon. Convinced that loose relations between the sexes and the races led to "degeneration" and threatened "the health and wealth of the male imperial body politic," Victorian reformers determined to police the boundaries and eradicate interracial unions. Elsewhere in the empire, men who had married Native women shifted to mixed-blood wives and then to wives from home. In the British Raj, wives were brought to India specifically to help limit familiarity between colonizing men and colonized women. In that sense, "white wives blighted racial harmony."[90]

In the new crown colony of British Columbia, established in 1858, the first governor was James Douglas, a former fur trader with a fur trade family. Born in British Guiana to a Scottish merchant father and a Creole mother, Douglas was educated in Scotland, apprenticed to the North West Company, and rose to become chief factor in the Hudson's Bay Company. He married Amelia Connelly, daughter of his immediate superior and a Cree mother, and they raised five children (others died in infancy). But the world that produced Governor and Lady Douglas and their family was changing rapidly. In the second half of the nineteenth century, reformers campaigned to replace Native companions with white wives who would make British Columbia "a respectable white settler colony."[91]

Wherever Highland Scots and Indians met in the deerskin and fur trades, they slept together, lived together, and produced families. In some places, the composition of the communities that resulted was so commonly Scots Indian that the inhabitants seem to have given little thought to it. "We were Cree and we were Scottish," says Albert MacLeod, a Winnipeg Métis whose Lewis-born ancestor joined the Hudson's Bay Company. "We were comfortable with that. We had our own way of living. We had a vision of how our future might be. But we could only have found our way to that future if we'd been left alone—and we weren't left alone."[92] In the biracial world constructed in nineteenth-century North America, people had to choose sides; more often the choice was made for them.

7

Clearances and Removals

People in Ross-shire in northwestern Scotland remembered 1792 as *Bliadna nan Caorach*, "the Year of the Sheep," when they faced and resisted eviction.[1] In the decades that followed many left and migrated across the Atlantic. In 1838 John Ross and his people were evicted from their homes and migrated. But John Ross was principal chief of the Cherokees, and his people moved across the Mississippi. Both events were episodes in larger historical processes and colonial projects that uprooted thousands of Highland Scots and thousands of American Indians. Highland clearances and Indian removal separated people from their homelands in the name of progress.

Migration lies at the heart of the American historical experience. Yet for many American Indians and American Scots the experience had a particularly bitter dimension, one that involved the heartbreak of expulsion from their native soil. Exile to distant lands is a prominent theme in the histories of many Highland clans and Indian tribes, as is attachment to homeland. "They are inseparable from their Highlands, and would never willingly leave them, even for the most beautiful place in the world," wrote one foreign visitor to Scotland. They would be much better off moving to England, but "a sort of patriotism holds them to these ungrateful lands."[2] Exile was equally traumatic whether they ended up in a Glasgow slum or a North American forest.[3]

Highlanders and Indians migrated long before the age of clearances and removals. Scots "had been on the move for centuries," and, long after the clearances were over, mass migration from Scotland continued until Scots became "a global people."[4] "In their far-flung wanderings, their diverse settlements, and their well-tended nostalgia," writes historian David Armitage, "the Scots are a diasporic people."[5] A character in *Dancing at the Rascal Fair,* Ivan Doig's novel about Scots in Montana, puts it another way: "The Scotch are wonderful at living anywhere but in Scotland."[6] Looking back over centuries of movement that carried Celtic peoples across northern Europe to the western edges of the British Isles, some commentators saw Atlantic migration as a natural next step: "The progress of the Gael has long been westward . . . ever westward," declared the Rev. D. Masson in 1873, until, in Canada, "the Gael of Caledonia has found, at last, a settled home."[7]

However, Highland Scots were not drawn to America by some inherent westering impulse, any more than "nomadism" propelled Indian peoples from the eastern woodlands to the western prairies. Highlanders and Indians were displaced as capitalism displaced tribalism. Colonial discourse identified different land uses with "civilization" and "savagery" and justified removing tribal peoples to make way for improvement.[8] Some Scots participated in expelling Indians from their lands, but many Cherokees, Creeks, and others who were driven west were descended from or related to people who had experienced similar expulsions from the Highlands. Many had the same names. For many exiled Scots and Cherokees, the Highland clearances and the Trail of Tears endured in the memory as defining experiences and became badges of identity.

Clearing the Highlands

Although the government sentenced many Jacobites to transportation, social and economic changes sent far more Highlanders to America than did political exile. The old economic systems in the Highlands could not accommodate population increases, the demand for food and wool was enormous, and the pressure on landlords to make their estates more productive and profitable was irresistible. The resulting transformation of rural Scotland produced workers for British factories, recruits for the British army, and emigrants for North America, although many "improvers" saw social and economic revolution as the only way to *prevent* large-scale migration.[9]

The '45 rising accelerated the state's efforts to subordinate and incorporate the Highlands and hastened the demise of the Highland clan system. The British government tried to convert clan chieftains into landlords and clans people into tenants. Most chiefs were content to comply with the changes and turn the Highlands into a client economy. After the defeat of the '45 and the abolition of heritable jurisdictions in 1747 "placed the Highland chieftains within the pale of the law, and placed them on the same footing as the other gentlemen of the land," wrote James Loch, a principal figure in the Sutherland clearances, "they began rapidly to acquire the same tastes." Clan chiefs sought to emulate English aristocratic lifestyle. To finance it, they did away with wadsets and tacks, raised rents, and turned their estates over to commercial sheep farming. "Luckily in this, as in every other instance in political economy," said Loch, "the interest of the individual, and the prosperity of the state went hand in hand."[10]

Southern sheep farmers introduced herds of Blackface and Cheviot sheep into Perthshire in the 1760s, and the herds spread steadily northward. Two thousand sheep were introduced to Callander in the 1770s; twenty years later, there were "18,000, all of the black-faced kind."[11] The invading flocks replaced black cattle, and, as lands they had inhabited from time immemorial were opened for grazing, people moved to seacoast crofts, to Lowland factory towns, or to emigrant ships.[12]

At first, many of the American emigrants went to the South. Many of the more than six hundred Jacobite prisoners exiled to America after the 1715 rebellion sailed to South Carolina. In North Carolina, Scots governor Gabriel Johnstone encouraged Highland immigration, and the colonial assembly remitted the taxes of Scottish immigrants for ten years. In 1739 Neil MacNeil led 350 people from Argyll and Islay, primarily tacksmen who left as the Duke of Argyll began "improving" his estates. They settled up the Cape Fear River, "not far from the *Indians,*" and sent home for more emigrants and a Presbyterian minister who could speak Gaelic. Their colony grew steadily over the next forty years as more and more Presbyterian Highlanders arrived from Argyll—Campbells, MacLeans, MacNeils, MacDougals and MacLachlans. They purchased land or took land grants from the crown and built new lives independent of clan and chief.[13]

Victory in the Seven Years' War opened up a new era of Scottish migration to North America. About 125,000 people left Britain for America between 1760 and 1775, at least 20,000 and perhaps as many as 40,000 of them Scots. Highlanders made up a substantial proportion, perhaps half to two-thirds, of the pre-Revolutionary Scottish immigration.[14] A second wave of emigration to North Carolina began around 1767 and continued through the early '70s, by which time "flattering accounts" of the good life to be expected there were circulating in Scotland. One said that Highlanders in North Carolina lived "as happy as princes." An anonymous author, writing under the pseudonym "Scotus Americanus," described the many attractions of North Carolina for "Highlanders of any degree." In Scotland, clan chiefs lived like absentee landlords and were interested only in the rents they could squeeze out of their tenants, but in North Carolina, Highlanders could "live in a state of health, ease, and independence."[15]

Many of the North Carolina emigrants came from the Isle of Skye. One report estimated that as many as 4,000 people—ten percent of the island's population—left Skye between 1769 and 1773. Certainly 2,000 left in the early 1770s: With tenants being pushed out "for not paying the great rents," 500 people left Skye and Islay for North Carolina in 1771; 450 followed the next year, and more than 800 left Skye and North Uist in 1773. "The only news on this Island is Emigration," Allan MacDonald wrote to John McKenzie of Delvine, "I believe the whole will go for America." Allan himself went, along with his wife, Flora, famous for having helped Prince Charles escape after Culloden. "It is melancholy to see the state of this miserable place," he said. They put their son under McKenzie's care and followed their friends to America, where, said Flora, they would "begin the world again, & newe, in a other Corner of it."[16] People were equally eager to leave the MacLeod estates on the Isle of Harris after the clan chief raised their rents to pay his debts.[17]

By the time Doctor Johnson visited the Highlands in 1773, emigration was in full swing. On a single day that June, for example, between seven and eight hundred people out of a population of about nine thousand left the island of Lewis, sailing from Stornaway for America.[18] Johnson described an "epidemick desire of wandering, which spreads its contagion from valley to valley." A new folk "dance called America" reflected the movement: More and more couples joined as the dance gathered momentum. The process of eviction, Johnson explained, severed ancient ties of kinship; as their rents increased, the chiefs' influence declined among the people. Creating a wilderness and calling it peace did not impress the doctor: "To hinder insurrection, by driving away the people, and to govern peaceably, by having no subjects is an expedient that argues no great profundity of politicks," he observed.[19]

Passenger lists of emigrants bound for America in 1774 revealed rents, cattle prices, unemployment, and "oppression" as motives for leaving. Emigrants from Caithness and Sutherland leaving Leith on the ship *Bachelor* for North Carolina said rents had gone up as much as two and three hundred percent while cattle prices had dropped by fifty percent. Encouraged to migrate by two sons already living in North Carolina, farmer William Gordon, "an old Man and lame so that it was indifferent to him in what Country he died," left with his whole family "for the greater benefit of his Children." Seventy-five-year-old Hector

McDonald and his three sons went: "Falling into reduced Circumstances he was assured by some of his Children already in America that his family might subsist more comfortably there, and in all events they can scarce be worse." Passengers bound for Philadelphia from Stornaway emigrated "in order to procure a Living abroad, as they were quite destitute of Bread at home." One hundred thirty-six people who left Glenurchy and embarked for North Carolina on the *Jupiter* "unanimously declare that they never would have thought of leaving their native Country, could they have supplied their Families in it." The farmers were compelled "to quit their Lands either on account of the advanced Rent or to make room for Shepherds," and the laborers could not support their families on the wages they earned. Only "the dread of want" forced them to "quit a Country which above all others they would wish to live in."[20]

Emigration continued up to the outbreak of the Revolution. "Not less than 700 Scotch People have been imported here within a few months," Governor Josiah Martin of North Carolina reported in March 1775.[21] Seven hundred more, mostly from the northern Highlands, sailed in four vessels from Glasgow and Greenock in May, and other ships sailed for North Carolina and Georgia. The emigrants said they would fight for the crown if necessary.[22] Caught up in the bitter warfare of the southern backcountry, some Loyalist Highlanders experienced further migration. Flora MacDonald and her husband were expelled from North Carolina to Nova Scotia and ultimately returned to Scotland. The Revolution interrupted the exodus, but it revived soon after, with most but not all Scots now heading for Canada rather than the United States.

Once clan chiefs had measured their social wealth and power by the number of their followers; now they counted sheep and cash. Alexander MacDonald's ninety-seven tenants on his Perthshire estate paid rents from 10 shillings to £5 each, "which had been very ill paid." Advised to remove them by degrees and "to let the estate in farms from £20 to £40," MacDonald had to choose between people and profits and in 1782 took steps to "improve" his lands.[23] "I have lived to see woful [*sic*] days," Sir Walter Scott reported an Argyll chief saying in 1788: "When I was young, the only question asked concerning a man's rank, was how many men lived on his estate—then it came to be how many black cattle it could keep—but now they only ask how many sheep the lands will carry."[24] As Highland landlords replaced the old "familial economy" with a commercial rent economy, tenants were left with little security and with rents they could not pay.[25] In Doctor Johnson's words, the chiefs "degenerate[d] from patriarchal rulers to rapacious landlords."[26] One Highland family told the Wordsworths that a neighboring laird "had gone, like the rest of them, to Edinburgh, left his lands and his own people, spending money where it brought him not any esteem, so that he was of no value, either at home or abroad."[27]

By the 1790s the minister of Lochbroom in Wester Ross reported "a general complaint in the Highlands" against the oppression of the landlords. "Whole districts have been already depopulated," he said: "Where formerly hundreds of people could be seen, no human faces are now to be met with, except a shepherd attended by his dog."[28] "Sheep must come on; and people must emigrate," concluded one reporter. Highlanders called the sheep "four-footed clansmen."[29] I'd rather bring up my sons to learn farming," Alexander McNab declared in 1793, "and send them at a proper Age to America where they may have plenty of good Lands, at a small expense where they and their Heirs need not be afraid of being tossed by the Avarice of Landlords." Others expressed similar sentiments: "They prefer to hide their Heads in the woods of America, rather than witness the degradation of their Offspring," said one report.[30]

Despite the mythology that all Highland emigration was a bitter leaving caused by greedy landlords and grinding oppression, migration involved pull as well as push. Historian J. M. Bumsted argues that the typical immigrant in the late eighteenth century "*chose* to come to America." With regional exceptions, clearing peasant communities to make way for sheep farms did not really fuel Highland migration until after 1815. Before then, it was not, at least not always, an exodus of desperate people fleeing hunger and poverty; most were tenants, the middle rank of Highland society. Tacksmen who formerly paid only nominal rent for their lands now paid higher rents themselves and were expected to extract higher rents from the clansmen. Many left not only in disgust but also in expectation of improving their prospects. They paid their own passage by selling cattle, sheep, and household goods. Numerous people followed friends and relatives. Whereas emigration from the Lowlands of Scotland tended to be individualistic and diffuse, Highland migration tended to be much more community based and channeled to particular regions where they already had kinship ties.[31]

Sometimes people left *despite* their landlords' efforts. Fearing the Highlands would be depopulated, British authorities tried to stem the tide. In 1784 members and agents of the landlord class formed the Highland and Agricultural Society (usually called the Highland Society). Its goal was to integrate the Highlands and islands with the rest of Britain by encouraging manufacturing, fisheries, and modern methods of commercial agriculture and at the same time pay "proper attention to the preservation of the Language, Poetry, and Music of the Highlands." With influential figures such as the Duke of Argyll among its members, the society lobbied hard to promote the work of "improvement." The landlord class preferred to redeploy rather than lose its workforce: Relocating Highlanders to the seacoasts to live in crofts and work in fishing or kelping would relieve the pressures of overpopulation and provide an alternative to emigration. Kelping required working long hours in miserable conditions cutting seaweed from the rocks and burning it to produce the calcined ashes—kelp—for alkali, which was used in the manufacture of soap and glass.[32] Some tenants may have invoked the threat of migrating and depriving landlords of their labor as a tactic to secure concessions.[33] Nevertheless, the authorities treated the threat as real.

For one thing, emigration would leave Britain without Highland troops. An observer commenting on emigration from Knoydart to Canada in 1786 ("already at least three hundred passengers engaged, and it is thought there will be many more") predicted that, once the emigrants settled in Canada, they would encourage others to leave, "as they are now encouraged by some friends before them." The cycle would continue, and after "our gallant Highlanders desert us, I fear that all the sheep that can be introduced and reared will form in their stead but a sorry defence against our enemies."[34] The fifth Duke of Argyll regarded the Highlands as "the best of all recruiting-grounds for the British Army" and did everything he could to stem the "perfect rage for migration."[35] Others feared that when "the hardy warlike peasantry of the highlands," who had served the country so often and so well, left to seek "asylum in the wilds of America," they might ultimately strengthen "our natural enemy" (France) in its efforts to rebuild an empire there.[36] Chiefs who were ingratiating themselves with the British aristocracy by raising troops did not want to drive their tenants into exile.[37] Ironically, many soldiers who went to America stayed there, effectively securing an assisted passage "courtesy of the British army."[38]

War with France after 1793 checked the flow of emigration, but it picked up after the Peace of Amiens in 1801. The Highland Society petitioned Parliament to promote public works, roads, canals, manufacturing, and fisheries in the Highlands to counteract the "spirit of emigration." So did the famous engineer Thomas Telford. Alarmed individuals and newspapers called for government intervention "to stem the torrent of depopulation." In 1803 reports warned that ten or twenty thousand people might emigrate in the next few years. One predicted that "the whole race of Highlanders will, in a very few years, be extinguished" as sheep engulfed the region. Rather than create inducements to stay, however, Parliament responded by making it more difficult for people to leave. The Passenger Vessels Act of 1803 limited the number of people a ship could carry. Ostensibly to prevent abuses, its intent and effect were to render emigration prohibitively expensive and keep the landlords' labor force at home.[39]

As one of the first to defend Highland emigration, Thomas Douglas, fifth Earl of Selkirk initiated several projects for settling Highlanders in British North America. After touring the Highlands in 1792, Selkirk became convinced that emigration offered the most effective cure for the region's ills during a period of necessary modernization and painful economic adjustment and the best hope of improvement for his northern compatriots. Attempts to keep people in the Highlands as a source of labor and military manpower were ineffective and shortsighted. The surplus population had to choose between migrating to factory towns in the Lowlands or crossing the Atlantic to reach America, where they could pursue an agricultural way of life and find prospects for advancement. In Selkirk's view, there was only one choice for a true Highlander. Born the seventh son of the fourth earl, he did not see much chance of promoting his plans, but all of his brothers predeceased him, and he inherited the family estate when his father died in 1799. In 1803 he organized the migration of some eight hundred settlers from Skye, Ross, Uist, and Argyll to Prince Edward Island. More emigrants followed in 1804 and in 1807 and 1808. Another Selkirk settlement at Baldoon near Lake St. Clair failed, but Selkirk toured Canada and the northeastern region of the United States, scouting out suitable sites for settling Highland communities. Such communities would recreate enclaves of Highland language and culture while simultaneously bolstering Canada's defenses against the United States. Like some advocates of Indian removal, Selkirk believed that migration offered tribal cultures the best chance of survival in a rapidly modernizing world.[40]

As long as Britain was at war with France, the government and most landowners saw the Highlands as recruiting grounds for continental carnage. However, the end of the Napoleonic Wars in 1815 brought an era of unaccustomed peace. Then hard times hit. Demobilization and the downturn in war-related industries produced a glut of workers. The high prices that kelp, cattle, and wool had brought in wartime plummeted. Renewed imports of Spanish barilla, the repeal of salt duties, and new developments in the chemical industry destroyed kelping in the western islands. Tenants could not pay their rents, and some landlords faced a choice between evicting them and going bankrupt. Landlords and politicians turned to emigration as a safety valve to alleviate social and economic problems caused by overpopulation. Now, writes James Hunter, "there was not the faintest echo of the humanitarian rhetoric of 1803." Government emigration policy became one of "expelling the unwanted." Parliament repealed the Passenger Vessels Act in 1817. After kelp prices collapsed in 1826 and 1827, the restrictions imposed by the 1803 act were completely removed.[41]

The migration that had seemed "epidemic" in the late eighteenth century paled compared with the flood that came in the nineteenth. More than ten thousand Highland Scots migrated to North America between 1770 and 1815; in the first half of the nineteenth century twenty thousand migrated to Cape Breton Island alone.[42] Emigration to Canada was now encouraged because it could bolster the colony's defenses and relieve the population stress at home.[43]

Sutherland

The removals were local upheavals in an agricultural revolution that was transforming the country but which hit the Highlands with particular force. No country in Europe changed as rapidly as Scotland, and no region of Scotland changed as rapidly as Sutherland. Patrick Sellar, an advocate and instrument of the change, described what he had seen in just a decade: roads built in every direction, a daily mail coach, new harbors, brickworks established, fields enclosed, new farming techniques and implements, crafts specialization, women wearing dresses made in Manchester, Glasgow, and Paisley, and English "made the language of the country." "We have jumped up at once to the level of our neighbours, with a velocity, I believe, quite unprecedented," he declared.[44] In Sutherland the human cost was the eviction of between five and ten thousand people in the first two decades of the nineteenth century, the largest of the Highland clearances.[45]

Elizabeth Gordon, Countess of Sutherland, "spoke no Gaelic and had inherited her family's contempt for the tongue, manners and customs of the Highland people."[46] She and her English husband, the wealthy Lord Stafford, employed two agricultural entrepreneurs from Morayshire—Patrick Sellar and William Young—and then James Loch, a lawyer trained at Edinburgh University, to mastermind the reorganization of their huge estate. As elsewhere in the Highlands, that meant consolidating small landholdings into large sheep farms, replacing the existing cattle economy, and moving people. Lists of tenants to be removed were drawn up, and those people were then relocated to the seacoasts, where they were offered small plots of land and encouraged to earn their living in the fishing and kelp industries or in coal mines around Brora.[47] Sheep were brought in to graze the now vacant glens and mountainsides. In 1811 there were about 15,000 sheep in Sutherland; by 1820 there were 130,000; and by 1855, 204,000.[48] Human population plummeted as the flocks of Cheviots grew. A group of families evicted from Strathnaver in 1806 and 1807 preferred to migrate to America rather than be resettled on the north coast. They died when their ship went down off Newfoundland.[49]

Patrick Sellar carried out evictions with the energy of a zealot.[50] He regarded the "new arrangement of this Country" as a humane measure. In his view, turning the interior over to shepherds and their flocks and relocating the people to the coast on lots of less than three acres—"sufficient for the maintenance of an industrious family, but pinched enough to cause them to turn their attention to fishing"—was "a benevolent action." It "put these barbarous hordes into a position, where they could better Associate together, apply to industry, educate their children, and advance in civilization."[51] Like Indian people in the United States, Highlanders were dispossessed and relocated "for their own good." Sellar routinely referred to the people he was evicting as "aborigines" and "savages." They were, he said, "the sad remnant of a people [the Celts] who once covered a great part of Europe, and who so long and so bravely withstood the invading strength of the Roman Empire." Their "obstinate adherence to the barbarous jargon of the times when Europe *was possessed by Savages*" isolated them from civilization and placed them:

> with relation to the enlightened nations of Europe in a position not very different from that betwixt the American Colonists and the Aborigines of that Country. The ones are the Aborigines of Britain shut out from the general stream of knowledge and cultivation, flowing in upon the Commonwealth of Europe from the remotest fountain of antiquity. The other are the Aborigines of America equally shut out from this stream; Both live in turf cabins in common with the brutes; Both are singular for patience, courage, cunning and address. Both are most virtuous where least in contact with men in a civilized State, and both are fast sinking under the baneful effects of ardent spirits.[52]

In Sellar's view, the tribal peoples of Scotland and North America merited similar treatment. He carried out evictions with such cruelty that he was brought to trial in 1816, when he was charged with culpable homicide, the equivalent of manslaughter, having allegedly caused the deaths of several people, including a woman in her nineties, when he burned their homes. He was acquitted.[53] However, in Gaelic memory and poetry he remained guilty, and for many people he personifies the evils of the clearances to this day.[54]

Taking for granted "the propriety" of the Sutherlands' improvement and removal policies, James Loch too described his "charges" in language that could have been used by any English missionary or American reformer frustrated by Native American cultural resilience. Under the old clan system, he wrote, Highlanders were tied to their chiefs by loyalty and kinship, held land in common, and had neither incentive nor opportunity to improve their lot. Unwilling to take on regular work, they left the heavy labor to their women. Like all mountaineers, they were accustomed to a wandering life. The men might help build a hut or cut peat for the fires, but, other than hunting or distilling illegal whiskey, they spent most of their time "in indolence and sloth." They lived in miserable of wood and turf, content with "the poorest and most simple fare." They deemed no new comfort worth possessing if it required hard work and no improvement worth adopting if it necessitated "sacrificing the customs or leaving the homes of their ancestors." In short, they "contributed nothing to the wealth of the empire." Bound to their old ways by ignorance, idleness, and tradition, they had to be made to embrace the new. Converting clan homeland to sheep pastures was "advantageous to the nation at large," said Loch, "even if it should unfortunately occasion emigration of some individuals."[55]

Evictions on the Sutherland estates were doubly hard in years of famine: The potato crop failed in 1808, bad weather in the spring produced a poor harvest in 1812, and a volcanic eruption at Krakatoa in the East Indies caused an unduly harsh winter and spring in 1816–1817.[56] Already drained of population by a decade of removals, Sutherland experienced further hemorrhaging. A listing of Sutherland families who moved in 1819 and 1820 amounted to 1,068 families out of a population of about 5,400. "In the space of twelve months more than a quarter of the entire population of the county was cleared," notes Eric Richards: "It was a social reorganization of staggering proportions in such a society." The parish of Kildonan had 1,574 people in 1811; ten years later it had 565, and only 257 remained in 1831.[57] Karl Marx singled out the Sutherland clearances in *Das Kapital* as a glaring example of capitalist landlords usurping communal property rights. In Marx's view, the duchess "hunted out" the people, drove them from the land "which from time immemorial belonged to the clan," and left them to become a rootless proletariat.[58]

The very people who should have protected the people perpetrated their evictions. Many Highlanders adhered to traditional clan values of *duthchas* long after the chiefs and landlords violated them. Churchmen collaborated with landlords by lending God's authority to pushing people off the land. "They literally prefer flocks of sheep to their human flocks," said one commentator.[59] The clearances caused cultural trauma and "enormous collective disorientation throughout the Gaelic world," which explains in part the relatively low level of resistance to the process.[60]

Not all Highlanders were silent, however.[61] The people of Kildonan rioted and resisted until the military was called in. William Young could not understand why they did not appreciate what had been done for them and was vexed "to see a banditti rise in open rebellion."[62] A letter to the duchess, signed by Donald Sutherland (which, in the northern Highlands, notes John Prebble, "was perhaps the equivalent of anonymity") was more direct: "You damned Bitch. You are a damned old Cat and deserve to be worried and burnt out for burning out the poor Highlanders."[63] Many of those who were removed from Kildonan to Helsmdale on the coast refused to take up their lots and either returned and rebuilt their homes or headed for the hills in Caithness and Ross-shire. Loch ordered the timbers of the houses destroyed if necessary to prevent the people from returning; "*a general and complete removal must be effected,*" he wrote, emphasizing his words; "*they shall not stay in the hills.*" He then expressed regret to hear that in carrying out their duty the constables had burned people's houses.[64] Donald Macleod, a stonemason from Strathnaver who emigrated to Canada, kept up a polemical assault against the Sutherland family thirty or forty years after the evictions.[65] In 1977 the Countess of Sutherland resigned from the presidency of the Mod, the national festival of Gaelic arts, following a press campaign against the office being held by someone whose ancestors had done so much to destroy Gaelic culture; in 1994 protesters mounted a public campaign to demolish a statue of the Duke of Sutherland that had been erected 160 years earlier on Ben Bragghie, overlooking majestic Dunrobin Castle on the east coast of Sutherland, in symbolic retribution for the long-dead duke's crimes.[66]

Like reformers determined to save Indians from themselves, "improvers" saw progress as a moral imperative, resistance as criminal. Loch and others published statements lauding the transformation of Sutherland from an isolated backwater to a prosperous region connected to the world by roads, bridges, and ferries, as well as a thriving economy. They attested that the inhabitants had received fair and decent treatment. Those who refused to take up crofting and hid out in the hills lived by the illicit distillation of whisky and smuggling, said Loch.[67] When Harriett Beecher Stowe visited Britain in 1851 and 1852 as part of her crusade against slavery, the Duchess of Sutherland lent her support. Stowe did not actually visit the Highlands, but she dismissed stories of oppression on the Sutherland estates as "ridiculous." The clearances were "the benevolent employment of superior wealth and power in shortening the struggles of advancing civilization."[68]

The Continuing Hemorrhage

And the sheep kept coming. By the 1840s the Mull of Kintyre had been "converted into an immense sheep-walk." Six thousand sheep occupied a country that half a century earlier had "supported thirty or forty families, whose ancestors had occupied that remote and extensive region for ages."[69] In 1800 there were only 50,000 sheep in Inverness. By 1855 their numbers had grown to 588,000, and by 1880 to 700,000. Some Highlanders became sheep farmers themselves.[70]

Most clearances were smaller and less sensational than in Sutherland. Some landlords tried to improve their estates without evicting their tenants; some did their best to assist their renters in making a transition they saw as inevitable; and some resisted the pressure to change and fell into bankruptcy. But the process of eroding the rural population and its accompanying human upheaval continued into the middle of the nineteenth century. MacLean chiefs shipped people from Coll and Rum to America. Removing people from the islands allowed them to charge higher rents to sheep farmers and help avert the worst ravages of famine.[71] Between 1838 and 1843, with his tenants unable to pay their rents now that the kelp industry had collapsed, Lord MacDonald helped thirteen hundred people emigrate from North Uist and converted their abandoned land into sheep farms.[72]

In 1843 Rev. John McLeod, parish minister of Morvern in Argyllshire, wrote a long account of the consequences of the "sheep system." People were living on small allotments in wretched villages and fell into poverty and idleness. "The evil effects of the allotment system are obvious," he concluded. In addition, Rev. N. McLean, minister for Tiree and Coll, reported that dividing the land into allotments had aggravated the population crisis. As tenants subdivided their lots among their families when they grew up, a croft originally designed for one family became divided between two or three, "and the whole are reduced to poverty."[73] The same problems would plague Native American families after the Allotment Act of 1887.

Colonel John Gordon of Cluny, a millionaire landowner who bought several islands in the Outer Hebrides and then cleared them in the late 1840s, earned a reputation to match that of Patrick Sellar for his cold-hearted evictions following the famine of 1847; he used any means necessary to push the inhabitants of Barra and South Uist on to emigrant ships bound for Canada.[74] A mass exodus from Lewis occurred in 1851. Newspaper reports of Macdonnell of Glengarry's clearance of Knoydart in 1853 and of a clash between police and women resisting evictions in Easter Ross in 1854 provided dramatic examples of avaricious landlords inflicting human suffering.[75]

Poverty and clearances produced chilling scenes. Traveling through Glengarry in 1841, Henry Cockburn "saw mud-hovels today, and beings with the outward forms of humanity within them, which I suspect the Esquimaux would shudder at."[76] A reporter from the *Times* who witnessed the evictions from Glen Calvie in 1845 captured an image of the clearances that could have been penned by a witness to the Cherokee Trail of Tears: "It was a most wretched spectacle to see these poor people march out of the glen in a body, with two or three carts filled with children, many of them mere infants, and other carts containing their bedding and other requisites."[77] Such images fueled "a long-running and passionate debate on the ethics of expelling the unwanted."[78]

In 1841 a Parliamentary committee concluded that mass emigration was the only way to relieve poverty in the overpopulated western Highlands.[79] George Douglas Campbell, eighth Duke of Argyll, agreed: Emigration was "the only real remedy for the poverty of the people." His grandfather, the fifth duke, had opposed it in the second half of the eighteenth century, but George Douglas Campbell, like James Loch, justified agricultural improvements—which meant clearances—with the kind of arguments and language used to justify carving up Indian reservations in the 1880s. In Campbell's view, the "disastrous old Highland system of communal holdings" was one "in which the superior intelligence of any one man was kept down under the stupidity of many others, and by the ruinous customs of an hereditary ignorance." Unaware of the basic principles of agricultural industry, the people did not practice crop rotation. "Their system of occupancy was communal, each man changing his wretched patch with his neighbours in the same village or township every year, by lot. The very idea of improvement was impossible. The individual mind, the source of all power, was kept down to the level of the stupidest, who had the right to object to any change." Under the new system, "every man could be sure of securing the advantages of his own industry and thrift, and of the landlord's help in capital."[80] Communal landholding and an economy of sharing stifled individual initiative and blocked progress.

When the potato crop failed between 1846 and 1855, the famine was not nearly so devastating in the Highlands and islands as it was in Ireland, in part because so many Highlanders had already left. Nevertheless, crofters who had been uprooted from their land by the clearances were dependent on potatoes and now faced malnutrition, starvation, and disease. The famine prompted a massive government and private relief effort, but for many, it was the last straw. A mass exodus took place. In historian Tom Devine's opinion, the Great Highland Famine finally severed people's emotional attachment to the land: Rather than stay and starve, they pulled up roots and departed, often with assistance from the government, their landlords, or public subscription. The famine clearances were "the last in the cycle of great evictions" that transformed Highland society from the last quarter of the eighteenth century.[81]

The famine also caused many Lowlanders and English to give up on the Highlanders. In the eighteenth century, many had subscribed to the philosophy that Highlanders were uncivilized but capable of improvement. Now more often people inclined to the view that they were incapable of making progress and that this latest tragedy stemmed from their inherently backward nature. Since they could not improve their lot in the Highlands, they had better leave.[82] Migration southward intensified. Henry Mayhew found Highlanders in rags on the streets of London in the 1850s, playing bagpipes for pennies.[83] Like Indian laborers on Canadian railroads, Highland men also went to work on railroad construction in Scotland. Thousands left for America. The potato famine prompted a major Hebridean emigration to Quebec and sent nearly five thousand Highlanders to Australia between 1852 and 1858.[84]

The owners and captains of the leaky ships used to transport timber from North America to Britain found a paying cargo with which to stuff their holds on the return journey. Thousands of Highlanders risked their lives traveling in steerage across the Atlantic. "The passage to Quebec was the cheapest transatlantic route and the vilest: thirty percent of passengers died on the voyage or just after landing."[85] In the early 1830s, with cholera rampant in Britain, the Canadian authorities established a quarantine station at Grosse Isle in the St. Lawrence River for disembarking immigrants. Catherine Parr Traill, an English woman who emigrated to Canada with her Scottish husband, an officer on half pay, crossed the Atlantic in relative luxury in 1832, but her ship was detained at Grosse Isle for three days while another ship flew a yellow flag, "the melancholy symbol of disease." Passengers from such ships were conveyed to the cholera hospital, a wooden building on the shore surrounded with palisades and guarded by soldiers. There, victims of smallpox, typhus, and cholera were separated from their families. Few of the immigrants who passed through Grosse Isle forgot the scenes as children were separated from parents, wives from husbands. Many did not make it. One inlet at Grosse Isle became known as Cholera Bay, and small mounds on the island mark mass graves. Cape Breton was inundated by thousands of Highlanders from disease-ridden timber ships.[86]

On the island of Tiree at one time, half the adult population worked in kelping, but by 1837 production had ceased entirely.[87] In 1849 the Duke of Argyll shipped almost six hundred people from Tiree to Canada. Cholera broke out during the Atlantic crossing. When they reached Quebec, no shelter was available because the immigrant sheds were already "crammed with the human debris of the Irish famine." Unable to work or move, the Tiree immigrants huddled on Quebec's wharves, where many of them perished of exposure and disease.[88] Opponents of emigration, oral tradition, and popular memory may have exaggerated its horrors, but for thousands of Highlanders the Atlantic passage was a nightmare.

Returning Highlanders felt bitterly the emptiness of the glens. Trader John McLean returned home to Mull for a six-week visit after twenty-three years in Hudson's Bay Territory. "The meeting of a mother with an only son, after so long an absence, need not be described, nor the feelings the well-known scenes of youthful sports and youthful joys gave rise to. These scenes were still the same, as far as the hand of Nature was concerned," he wrote, but where were the human inhabitants? "Far distant from their much-loved native lands in the wilds of America, or toiling for a miserable existence in the crowded cities of the Lowlands." Gaelic poet William Livingston (1808–1870) wrote the following:

> *The houses once owned by those who have left us*
> *lie in cold heaps throughout the land;*
> *the Gaels have gone, and they will never return.*
> *Foreigners and taxes have triumphed.*[89]

Large-scale clearances ended in the Highlands after the 1850s, but a new round of evictions threatened in the 1880s. As Australian competition rendered sheep farming less profitable, landowners rented their estates for sport hunting. By 1885 1.7 million acres, one-sixth of the Highlands had been converted to deer forests.[90] This time, opposition was so widespread that the government had to take action. Beginning with protests on Skye, crofters challenged the social and economic order they had so far endured. The Napier Commission produced a detailed report on the economic problems of the Highlands and the conflicts between landlords and crofters. In 1886 Parliament passed the Crofters' Act, which outlawed further clearances and inserted the government into relations between landlord and tenant. It guaranteed security of tenure to crofters, enabled them to bequeath their crofts to family members, and set up a commission to fix fair rents and oversee administration of the act. Landlord classes considered the new legislation radical, but it did not restore or redistribute land or solve the problems of regional underdevelopment, and it actually bound many crofters more firmly to their small and unproductive plots of land. Agitation for land reform in the Highlands thus continued.[91] Uprooted from their homes, relocated to small and hardscrabble plots of land, and burdened with debts, crofters had little hope of improving their situation.[92]

In the twentieth century, poet Sorley MacLean described Mull as an island so scarred by "the terrible imprint of the clearances" as to be "heartbreaking."[93] When novelist Hugh McLennan, a Canadian of Highland ancestry, visited Kintail in the 1950s, he felt the emptiness of the Highlands, so close to overcrowded England, to be very different from that of Canada's Northwest Territories: "Above the sixtieth parallel in Canada you feel that nobody but God has ever been there before you, but in a deserted Highland glen you feel that everyone who ever mattered is dead and gone."[94]

In the mid-nineteenth century Rev. Thomas Grierson, minister of Kirkbean and a regular traveler to the Highlands, wrote the following: "Like the Irish, the Highlanders are indolent and inactive at home but in almost all cases are industrious and excellent workers abroad."[95] In America there was plenty of opportunity and plenty of land for hard-working Highland exiles—once the land was cleared of its Native inhabitants.

Removing the Indians

By the 1820s and '30s, as the Highland clearances were in full swing pushing people across the Atlantic, Indian removals in the United States impelled people across the Mississippi. The roots of the Indian removal policy lay in earlier efforts to solve the "problem" of what to do with Indians and, one could argue, in the writings of Scottish philosophical historian William Robertson.[96]

Building on the assumptions that peoples who existed at an earlier stage of societal development must progress or perish, Thomas Jefferson and others solved the dilemma of how to take Indian lands and still deal honorably with them by determining that having too much land was an obstacle to Indians becoming "civilized." Ignoring the role of agriculture in eastern woodland societies, they argued that as long as Indians had plenty of land they would continue to hunt rather than settle down as farmers. Taking their surplus lands forced Indians into an agricultural and "civilized" way of life and therefore was good for them in the long run. Jefferson encouraged Indians to run up credit at government trading houses, knowing they would have to sell land to pay off their accumulated debts. In Jefferson's view, this policy simply accelerated a natural and inevitable process of dispossession. As Indians took up farming, he wrote to William Henry Harrison, governor of the Indiana Territory, "they will perceive how useless to them are their extensive forests, and will be willing to pare them off from time to time in exchange for necessaries for their farms and families." To promote this process "we shall push our trading houses, and be glad to see the good and influential individuals run into debt, because we observe that when these debts get beyond what the individuals can pay, they become willing to lop them off by a cession of lands." American settlements would gradually surround the Indians, and they would "in time either incorporate with us as citizens of the United States, or remove beyond the Mississippi."[97]

In 1803 American emissaries in Paris purchased the Louisiana Territory—some 827,000 square miles of territory between the Mississippi and the Rocky Mountains for a mere $15 million—and the United States doubled its size overnight. Many Americans saw the West as barren and virtually empty, useless for American farmers but good enough for Indian hunters. Removing Indians from the East was now a practical possibility.

Some moved west voluntarily, whereas others determined never to abandon their ancestral lands. But the pressure to move mounted steadily. By the 1830s, the American South was producing about half the cotton consumed in the world. Like wool from the Highlands of Scotland, Southern cotton fed the mills of northern England, as well as those in New England. Southeastern lands were too valuable to be left in Indian hands. As American pressures and capitalist market forces undermined traditional social and economic structures, many Indians faced a choice between destitution and removal.

As early as 1820, Andrew Jackson, a renowned Indian fighter and staunch advocate of removal, bullied and threatened Choctaw chiefs into making a treaty at Doak's Stand, ceding lands in Mississippi to the United States and accepting territories in the West in return. Ten years later, the Choctaws signed the Treaty of Dancing Rabbit Creek. Although some Choctaws remained in Mississippi, most headed west, an ominous move for a people whose migration legends described coming *from* the West as an escape from a land of death.[98]

Americans who hated Indians and wanted their lands favored removal as a means of opening up territory; others advocated displacement as the only way to protect Indians from rapacious white neighbors. Pro-removal forces received a boost when Andrew Jackson was elected president in 1828. Jackson knew the settled and agriculturally based Creeks and Cherokees firsthand, but, like other advocates of relocation, he depicted them as wandering hunters who could not be allowed to impede progress. Indians did not put the land to good use and could not be allowed to deny that land to American farmers. "Civilization" and "progress" demanded they go.

Ironically, many of the southern tribes displayed more of the attributes of supposedly "civilized" society than did the American frontiersmen—many of Scotch-Irish descent—who were so eager to occupy their lands. However, this did not save them. As in the Highlands, there were those who argued (or convinced themselves) that relegation to more distant lands was inevitable and ultimately beneficial for the people who would be leaving. William Wirt, the former attorney general of the United States who took up the Cherokee defense, stated that "there are many well meaning men who think it the interest of the Cherokees to remove."[99] In 1825 President James Monroe told Congress that relocating the tribes would "not only shield them from impending ruin, but promote their welfare and happiness." In "their present state," it was impossible to incorporate them "into our system." If something were not done soon, "their degradation and extermination will be inevitable."[100]

As in the Highlands, some chiefs (a number of whom were of Scots ancestry) collaborated in dispossessing their own people. A petition from Cherokee women in June 1818 stated that "there are some white men among us who have been raised in this country from their youth, are connected with us by marriage, & have considerable families, who are very active in encouraging the emigration of our nation. These ought to be our truest friends but prove our worst enemies."[101] Scots Indians Alexander McGillivray and William Weatherford had both resisted land cessions and American expansion, but William McIntosh helped the Americans—and himself—in transferring Indian lands. McIntosh, whose Creek name was Tustunnuggee Hutkee or White Warrior, was born around 1778 in the Lower Creek town of Coweta. His grandfather had emigrated from Inverness to Georgia in 1736, married a Scotswoman, Margaret McGillivray, and later established a trading post on the Tombigbee River. His father, who fought as a Loyalist officer in the Revolution, married a Creek woman called Senoya, who was a member of the Wind Clan. Like Alexander McGillivray, McIntosh was of both Clan Chattan and the Wind Clan. He sat on the Creek National Council and also had relatives who were prominent in Georgia affairs. During the Creek War of 1812–1814 he led the pro-American faction of the Lower Creeks against the Nativist "Red Stick" Upper Creeks and fought with Andrew Jackson at the battle of Horseshoe Bend, only to see the victorious Jackson confiscate two-thirds of *all* Creek land at the Treaty of Fort Jackson in 1814. He built and operated a thirty-four-room inn at Indian Springs, grew wealthy through a series of shady land deals, and engineered further cessions of Creek lands into American hands. In addition to the treaty of Fort Jackson, he signed treaties with the Americans in 1805, 1818, and twice in 1821 (when a John McIntosh was one of the three commissioners from Georgia). He offered bribes to John Ross and other Cherokee chiefs to try to buy their support for land cessions and was exposed for doing so by Ross before the Cherokee National Council. In 1825 McIntosh and a handful of minor chiefs (including his half-brother, Artus Mico, also known as Roley McIntosh, and son, Chilly McIntosh) signed the Treaty of Indian Springs, giving up all remaining Creek lands in Georgia between the Flint and Chattahoochee rivers. In return the United States paid $400,000 to "the emigrating nation" and an additional $200,000 directly to McIntosh and the treaty signers. The agreement blatantly flouted a recent tribal law that made selling tribal lands a capital offense. Creek warriors acting on the instructions of the Creek National Council assassinated McIntosh for treason soon after.[102]

In Scotland, in east Invernesshire, the Mackintosh clan chief was also head chief of Clan Chattan, a confederation of several clans that included the McGillivrays. In the early seventeenth century, as the central government attempted to extend its control over the Highlands, the Mackintoshes and

MC INTOSH,

A CREEK CHIEF

Figure 7.1. William McIntosh, Creek chief and son of a Highland trader, was assassinated for selling tribal lands. From Thomas L. McKenney and James Hall, *History of the Indian tribes of North America, with biographical sketches and anecdotes of the principal chiefs. Embellished with one hundred and twenty portraits, from the Indian gallery in the Department of War, at Washington* (Philadelphia: Edward C. Biddle, 1836–1844). McKenney described McIntosh as a "handsome Creek chief who looks like a swarthy-skinned Scots Highland chief." (Courtesy of the Rauner Library, Dartmouth College.)

Clan Chattan had tried allying with the earls of Argyll, cooperating with the crown, and assimilating into Lowland society as their best strategy for survival in tumultuous times.[103] Though he likely did not know it, William McIntosh was following a strategy his Clan Chattan ancestors would have recognized.

As the Sutherland clearances came to epitomize those in the Highlands, so the Cherokee Trail of Tears came to epitomize Indian removal. Cherokee territory originally extended into five southeastern states, but by the 1820s most Cherokees were confined to Georgia. After gold was discovered in 1827, prospectors flooded into Cherokee country. In December of that year the Georgia legislature passed a resolution asserting its sovereignty over Cherokee lands within the state's borders. Georgia demanded that the federal government begin negotiations to compel the Cherokees to cede their land and carried out a systematic campaign of harassment and intimidation, which culminated in an assault on the Cherokee government. In 1830 Georgia created a police force—the Georgia Guard—to patrol Cherokee country. Over the next few years the guard harassed Cherokee people, arrested principal chief John Ross and seized his papers, and confiscated the printing press of the tribal newspaper, the *Cherokee Phoenix*.

Opponents of relocation attacked it on moral and humanitarian grounds. Faced with the dilemma of how to dispossess Indians whom the United States judged "civilized," removal advocates like President Jackson and Governor Lewis Cass of Michigan Territory denied that the Cherokees were civilized after all. A few had become wealthy, Cass allowed, but the majority remained mired in poverty. Despite every effort to civilize them, "their habits were stationary and unbending; never changing with the change of circumstances." Jefferson, like the Scottish Enlightenment thinkers, had regarded Indians as culturally inferior but capable of improvement; Cass and Jackson, like nineteenth-century Lowlanders who portrayed famine-stricken Highlanders as inherently backward, portrayed them as racially inferior. Incapable of bettering themselves or their lands, Indians must make way for civilized white people, who would put their land to good use.[104] Like "improvers" who had no patience for Highlanders who clung to outdated ways, Cass dismissed Cherokees as unfit for the modern world. They would be better off displaced from it. As in Scotland, the way tribal peoples used the land justified ousting them from it. In 1831, Jackson appointed Cass Secretary of War, the department responsible for Indian affairs.

In May 1830 Congress passed the Indian Removal Act, which authorized the president to negotiate treaties of relocation with all Indian tribes living east of the Mississippi. The bill sparked extensive debate and passed after a close vote in both houses. Jackson defended the act in his State of the Union Address: He claimed that it gave the Indians a fair exchange and moved them out of the way at government expense. "What good man," Jackson asked, "would prefer a country covered with forests and ranged by a few thousand savages to our extensive Republic, studded with cities, towns and prosperous farms, embellished with all the improvements that art can devise or industry execute, occupied by more than 12,000,000 happy people and filled with all the blessings of civilization, liberty and religion?" The removal policy was only "progressive change by a milder process." It moved the Indians to new homes where they would be better off and could live undisturbed. "Doubtless it will be painful to leave the graves of their fathers," Jackson acknowledged, but it was no more than others had done before them. "To better their condition in an unknown land our forefathers left all that was dear in earthly objects," he said, invoking the experiences of his parents, Scotch-Irish immigrants who had arrived in Pennsylvania in 1765 and then migrated southwest through Virginia and the Appalachian foothills.[105]

Despite the Supreme Court ruling in *Worcester v. Georgia* in 1832, which declared that the Cherokee Nation was a distinct community with its own territory in which state laws had no force, Georgia continued to harass the Cherokees in order to drive them to the treaty table. In 1835 U.S. commissioners signed the Treaty of New Echota with a minority of Cherokees who agreed to move west voluntarily. This "treaty party" included Elias Boudinot, Major Ridge, John Ridge, and others who now saw no alternative but to migrate. "In another country, and under other circumstances, there is a better prospect," sighed Boudinot. He could have been a MacLean or a MacDonald stepping aboard an emigrant ship.[106]

Although John Ross and the majority of Cherokees denounced the Treaty of New Echota, in 1838, citing the treaty, federal troops moved in and forced the Cherokees out. Thousands died on the journey west, aptly named the "Trail of Tears." For most Cherokees, the march to Indian Territory was the beginning of a new era in which they would have to adjust to life in a strange land and rebuild their societies. Throughout the East, other Indians experienced similar relocations—Choctaws in 1830, Creeks, Chickasaws, Seminoles, and Shawnees in 1832, and Potawatomis between 1833 and 1838. Some managed to stay in their traditional lands. Many Seminoles withdrew to the Florida Everglades, and some Cherokees evaded the evictions and survived in North Carolina as the Eastern Band of Cherokees. North Carolina was home to Highland Scots who were among the first to emigrate and Cherokees who refused to leave their country.

Critics of the removals on both sides of the Atlantic said they constituted acts of betrayal. Highland Scots had demonstrated their loyalty by service to the crown, only to be evicted from their homes.[107] Moreover, southeastern Indians had made great strides along the path to "civilization," only to be expelled from their homelands in the name of progress. Commentators pointed to the government's hypocrisy and even raised the specter of divine retribution. "Can we as a nation be guiltless, and allow so many of our fellow creatures to be treated in such a manner, and not exert ourselves to put a stop to it and punish the perpetrators?" asked opponents of the Highland clearances. Would not God hold the nation accountable?[108] Opponents of Indian removal asked the same question. Jeremiah Evarts of the American Board of Commissioners for Foreign Missions prayed: "May a gracious Providence avert from this country the awful calamity of exposing ourselves to the wrath of heaven, as a consequence of disregarding the cries of the poor and defenceless, and perverting to purposes of cruelty and oppression, that power which was given us to promote the happiness of our fellow men."[109]

Nonetheless, such voices were insufficient and sometimes empty. Whigs found it expedient to denounce the Jacksonian relocation policy when they were in opposition "but equally expedient to continue that policy when they themselves were in power." The pressure from a market economy dominated by "expectant capitalists" swept aside the voices of protest. Indian lands were national resources that must be made available for purchase and settlement; thus, Indian presence and title to the lands could not hinder progress. Equating displacement with the preservation and civilization of Indians made it palatable and acceptable to the majority of Americans, especially as they could see no viable alternative policy. "Apathy, barbarism, and heathenism must give way to energy, civilization, and Christianity," wrote Indian commissioner William Medill in his annual report to Congress in 1848. Clinging to old ways and resistant to change, Indians were bound to suffer in the clash with a dynamic, expanding society. "Hence, it is to natural and unavoidable causes ... rather than to willful neglect, or to deliberate oppression and wrong, that we must in great measure attribute the rapid decline and disappearance of our Indian population." As long as hunting territory was plentiful, nothing could induce an Indian to labor, but when "compelled to face the stern necessities of life and to resort to labor for a maintenance, he in a very short time becomes a changed being" who is willing to receive "instruction in all that may aid him in improving his condition." Like the Highland clearances, Indian removal seemed "a logical and even enlightened policy" when presented in humanitarian terms.[110]

* * *

The clearances and removals are sometimes depicted as parallel examples of ethnic cleansing. Evicted Highlanders perished on cramped and disease-ridden emigrant ships; Indians died of hunger and exposure on the trails west. Writer James Hunter calls the north coast settlements to which Highlanders were relocated "nineteenth-century Sutherland's equivalent of Indian reservations." Tom Cunningham agrees: "Herded on to a narrow and barely productive croft, many a Highlander came to know the misery of the reservations." Indians were told to take up farming; Highlanders were told to take up fishing.[111] The parallels can be overdrawn—removing Highlanders to America involved none of the complex issues of states' rights, treaty-making power, and constitutional authority raised by Indian relocations in the United States, and none of the kind of military force employed to expel Indian people. Nevertheless, the assault on communal land produced similar effects in North Britain and North America.

Capitalism and empire building first demanded the removal of tribal peoples where they stood in the way of progress and then romanticized their

Figure 7.2. *The Last of the Clan,* by Thomas Faed, 1865. (Glasgow Museums 3366; courtesy of the Glasgow City Council.)

Figure 7.3. *Last of Their Race,* 1857, by John Mix Stanley. (Buffalo Bill Historical Center, Cody, Wyoming; 5.75.)

tragic dispossession. Cunningham points out "the eerie similarity" of John Mix Stanley's *Last of Their Race* (1857) and Thomas Faed's *Last of the Clan* (1865).[112] In both paintings, the dispossessed have been pushed to the western coasts of their land, indicating the end of their way of life. The Highlanders wait to embark on a voyage that will take them to a new world; the Indians have nowhere to go and stand on the verge of extinction.

Many Highland Scots and American Indians shared the experience of relocation. The children of Highlanders walked the Trail of Tears as Cherokees. The Highland-Cherokee connection survived removal, and that shared experience reinforced it. In April 1847, after the potato crop failed in the Western Highlands and islands, Cherokee chief John Ross wrote to the editor of the *Cherokee Advocate:* "It is said that there are not less than 300,000 Scotch on the Highlands and Islands, who must through charity, be fed during the ensuing summer or die of famine." He urged Cherokees to do something for this "benevolent and Christian cause." "Have the Scotch no claim upon the Cherokees?" Ross asked. "Have they

Figure 7.4. John Neagle, John Ross, 1848. The principal chief of the Cherokees as he appeared around the time of the Great Highland Famine. (Philbrook Museum of Art, Tulsa, Oklahoma, Museum purchase, 1942.12.1, © 2007.)

not a very especial claim? They have." Ross recommended that a meeting of the Cherokee people be held at Tahlequah to take steps to raise money. The meeting appointed a "relief committee." Nine days later, in mid-May, Ross sent a bank draft for $190 "for the relief of those who are suffering by the famine in Scotland."[113] It was more than many Lowland Scots were willing to do for their Highland compatriots.[114]

8

Highland Settlers and Indian Lands

Duncan MacDonald, a Scots Indian living on the Flathead reservation in Montana, said Indian tribes and Highland clans were alike in their ties to the land. Both regarded land as a source of their collective identity.[1] But migration to America separated thousands of Scots from their own homeland and put them in a new relationship with other peoples' land. Highland Scots dominated the fur trade, which was in many ways antithetical to settlement— fur traders sought to preserve Indian country as hunting territory, whereas settlers attempted to remake it into a world of farms, fields, and fences—but many more Highlanders made the trek to America to settle Indian lands. People with Highland surnames walked the Trail of Tears, but more people with Highland surnames benefited from the Indians' expulsion. Tribal people who had been dispossessed in Scotland joined the vast colonial onslaught that drove out tribal peoples in America. It was part of the "great land rush" that opened communal domains to capitalist ownership and shaped the modern world.[2]

Highlanders migrated to America at a time when attitudes toward land at home were undergoing fundamental changes. Agricultural reorganizations altered the social as well as the physical landscape of the Highlands, thereby undermining the concept of *duthchas* and killing the runrig system of communal farming.[3] Reformers expressed "unanimous abhorrence . . . for anything but individual and permanent tenure of land."[4] Land was to be managed as property for profit rather than maintained to support a population; the clan homeland's economic value far outweighed its social worth. The commoditization of land "disinherited people from a fundamental relationship with a landscape that, with its previous system of communal tenure, was inscribed with human experience and could be read as a map of social relations." Once clan estates became real estate, it was not long before English and Lowland buyers began to purchase them piecemeal.[5] In America, Indian lands were converted into American real estate by deed, treaty, and allotment, which broke up the communal land base of reservations. On both sides of the Atlantic, tribal lands fractured under the insistence of outsiders that individual land ownership was essential to progress.

Highlanders often tried to recreate in America the kind of communal and kinship-based societies they had known at home. However, they could not recreate relationships with the land that had developed over generations. In America they were newcomers, not natives, and, as historian Richard White points out, landscapes do not speak to strangers.[6] In Europe, like Indians, they saw land as a repository of history and identity. Still, in America, with no historical attachment, they could describe land only in terms of its economic potential.[7] Highlanders settled on land that, as yet, had no deeper meaning for them. Calling their new homes Perth, Inverness, or Glengarry, they inscribed on the landscape names that had meaning to them, not to the Native inhabitants. Like other settler societies, they erased the Native past and presence by naming and claiming Native homelands as their own. These names reflected uprooting, not deep roots. The new lands were not yet their homeland.

Joining the stream of emigration to America relatively late and seeking land for agriculture, Highlanders tended to gravitate to frontier regions. They were not motivated by abstract notions of liberty or seeking freedom from king and parliament; they wanted "freedom from the tyranny of their landlords, freedom to own land, and freedom to be their own masters."[8] After Norman MacLeod of MacLeod increased rents on the Isle of Harris to help pay his debts, many of the people looked to new lands across the Atlantic: "A Spirit of Emigration has now got in among them which in a few years will carry the Inhabitants of the Highlands and Islands of Scotland into North America," an observer reported in 1772:

Disdaining to become Possessors of farms in the low Countries and follow the Customs of its Inhabitants which they held in Contempt they launched out into a new world breathing a Spirit of Liberty and a Desire of every individual becoming a Proprietor, where they imagine they can still obtain Land for themselves, and their flocks of Cattle, at a trifling Rent, or of conquering it from the Indians with the sword, the most desireable [sic] holding of any for a Highlander.[9]

Highland Scots did not figure as prominently as the Scotch-Irish in settling the trans-Appalachian frontier.[10] Eventually, however, they made their way into every corner of North America. The pervasive image of European settlement on the frontier depicts individual families hacking plots of land out of the forest and living independently of their neighbors. The promise of independence through landownership was a powerful incentive for Highlanders, too, but preserving, joining, or recreating a Highland community was often equally important. Highlanders tended to emigrate in family groups and to settle in Highland communities. According to a prospective recruiter of emigrants to Georgia, Highlanders "would go in Shoals to any Colony in America, provided there was a Sufficient Detachment of their own people planted before 'em." Once the first group was settled, others would follow, and, he predicted, "We should have in a very few years as many trussed up Plaids in Georgia as in the Highlands of Scotland."[11] "When Highlanders are removed from their native Glen, or Tribe," said a report on emigration at the beginning of the nineteenth century, "it becomes very immaterial to them, whether they move across a mountain, to a strange Glen, or across the Atlantic, to a foreign Clime. If their Tribe or kindred are in the latter, their decision will be for it."[12]

The Southeast

The Highlanders recruited in the 1730s as fighting farmers on the Georgia frontier received grants of twenty acres on the Altamaha River. It was an attractive inducement for people accustomed to subsistence farming on leased lands. Their leader, John Mohr Mackintosh, had lost his inheritance in the forfeitures following the 1715 Jacobite rebellion. They cleared lands, planted crops, and impressed Oglethorpe with their industry and diligence.[13] Mackintosh's eldest son, Lachlan, who was eight or nine when the family emigrated, remembered that "All fears of hostility from the Indian tribes round New Inverness soon vanished & the MacKintoshes, McBains & McKays & McGillivrays soon gained their friendship. The feathered caps, swinging kilts, naked knees & barthen [sic] shoes appealed to the Indians & they patronized & traded with New Inverness. . . . The best of terms existed between the Indian chiefs and the young men of New Inverness. They emulated each other in sports and hunting."[14]

Amicable relations with the Indians did not always endure after the colony was secure and Georgia reverted to royal control. The Highland regiment was disbanded, and many of the Highlanders left Darien. They and their descendants pursued diverse roles in regard to Indian lands. Lachlan McIntosh (as he spelled the name) moved to Charles Town, South Carolina, for eight years but returned to the Altamaha Valley in the 1750s and became a prosperous rice planter, investing in land, slaves, and commerce. Like most planters, says his biographer, McIntosh had "a nearly insatiable desire for land." By the time of the Revolution he was one of the richest planters in southern Georgia, having amassed more than fourteen thousand acres by royal grants and purchases. Most of it was land formerly occupied by his father's Creek Indian allies. When the Revolution broke out, McIntosh took the Patriot side and served as a brigadier general in the Western Department. He signed the Treaty of Fort Pitt with the Delawares in 1778 (the United States' first treaty with an Indian nation) and led an abortive expedition through Ohio Indian country against Detroit. After the war, while trying to rebuild his fortunes, McIntosh served as a federal Indian commissioner, representing the United States at the Treaty of Hopewell with the Cherokees, Choctaws, and Chickasaws in 1785 and 1786 and negotiating the transfer of Creek lands.[15]

McIntosh's interest in Indian lands placed him squarely in opposition to another descendant of Clan Chattan and son of a Darien settler. Alexander McGillivray's father, Lachlan, had emigrated with the first batch of Darien settlers when he was sixteen, spent a dozen years in the Indian trade, married a Creek wife, and built a plantation, which he lost during the Revolution. Lachlan returned to Scotland, but Alexander emerged as a leader among his mother's people. He opposed selling the Creek lands between the Ogeechee and Oconee rivers until he signed the Treaty of New York in 1790, when the boundary was fixed on the Oconee.[16] At the same time, McGillivray inculcated new values regarding land and property in Creek society.[17] Another descendant of a Darien settler, Lower Creek chief William McIntosh, lined his pockets and was assassinated for selling Creek lands. (See page 193.)

Many Scots traders in the Southeast speculated in real estate as well as dealing in deerskins, and some amassed huge amounts of land. Anticipating Jeffersonian Indian policy, Lachlan McGillivray, William Panton, and John Forbes used Indian debts to leverage sales of tribal land. Although Panton and Forbes encouraged Indians to hold on to their lands in the face of American encroachment, both collaborated with the United States to obtain Indian holdings. They bought at discount the debts individual hunters owed small traders and then aggregated them into one lump sum. By 1803 the southeastern tribes owed John Forbes and Company $192,526; the Creeks alone were in arrears for $113,000. The United States compelled the Creeks to cede millions of acres, in exchange for which it paid off some of their debts. In 1805 the traders exerted their influence among the Choctaws, Chickasaws, Cherokees, and Upper Creeks to help secure the cession of almost eight million acres. The United States paid the tribes a total of $380,000 in money and goods, of which more than $77,000 went to Forbes and Company to settle the Indians' debts. Eventually the company recouped all but a little less than $7,000 of the original debt. In this way, "thousands of small, face-to-face exchanges between traders and hunters were transmuted by a multinational company and an expanding nation-state into massive land cessions that affected an entire people." In west Florida, the Spanish government allowed Indians to extinguish their debts by ceding lands directly to the company, making it the largest landowner in the Floridas during the second Spanish era. Company members consistently put profit above national loyalty by switching allegiance from Britain to Spain to the United States. Recognizing that American efforts to turn Indian hunters into farmers spelled the demise of the deerskin trade, they devoted more effort to persuading Indians to sell land than trading with them.[18] By collaborating in the vast transfer of lands from Indian hunting and farming to cotton production, the Scots traders unwittingly helped return the South to dependence on British money, mills, and markets and thereby promoted reliance on a single crop, which had terrible consequences for the South and the land.[19]

New York and Ontario

In the 1730s the British government advertised for "Protestants of all Nations and Denominations" to help settle New York. At the same time, the Campbell estates were being reorganized. Lauchlin Campbell visited New York in 1737 and returned soon after with thirty-five families from Islay. By 1740 ninety-three Highland families had settled in his "Argyll Colony" near Fort Ann.[20]

Victory over France in the Seven Years' War opened New York to settlement, and "sundry Scotch people" took advantage of it.[21] Soldiers wrote home describing the fertility of the lands they had seen and encouraged friends and relatives to join them. Lands were rich and plentiful, and America was a good country, one in which poor men could make a decent living, they said. Emigrants from the Highlands gravitated to regions where Highland soldiers had campaigned: the Hudson, Champlain, and Saint Lawrence valleys, the Maritime provinces, and the Carolinas.[22]

With gloomy prospects awaiting them in Scotland, many soldiers opted to remain in America when their regiments disbanded and take up government land grants. Officers and men from the Black Watch, the 77th and 78th regiments, as well as Highlanders who had served in other regiments, petitioned for grants of lands on both sides of the Hudson River, between Lake George and Lake Champlain, and west of the Green Mountains. Captains were entitled to three thousand acres, lieutenants to two thousand, sergeants two hundred, corporals one hundred, and privates fifty acres. Most petitioned as individuals, but many former comrades-in-arms did so in groups and sought lands adjacent to one another.[23] Men from Montgomery's Highlanders took up land grants near Fort Edward. Soldiers from the Black Watch settled on Otter Creek east of Lake Champlain.[24]

On February 28, 1764, for example, Allen Cameron, three other sergeants, and seven privates, formerly in the 77th regiment, filed a petition "praying their quota of the lands to be granted to non-commissioned officers and privates who served during the late war, pursuant to his majesty's proclamation."[25] On May 31, 1766, Neal McLean (formerly a lieutenant in the 77th Regiment), Donald McLean (a surgeon in the regiment), and Malachy Treat (surgeon's mate) petitioned "for a grant of 2,000 acres to each, within a certain tract of land, purchased of the Catts Kill Indians in the county of Albany, on the west side of Hudson's River."[26] Long after the initial avalanche of postwar petitions, Highlanders' names figured prominently in New York land grants.

Many veterans claimed lands east of Lake Champlain, in what is now Vermont but which was then part of New York.[27] The Abenaki people who lived there had allied with the French during the war and had not relinquished their land, but they now felt severely the northward press of settlers from the English colonies.[28] Other colonists came direct from Scotland. The Scots American Company of Farmers purchased lands at Ryegate, Vermont, in the early 1770s as a refuge for farmers and artisans from the west Lowlands; another "Company of Farmers" from Perthshire and Stirlingshire bought lands in Barnet, Vermont, in 1774.[29]

In the Mohawk Valley, Sir William Johnson had lands to rent. Johnson, an Irishman, was the British superintendent of Indian affairs in the North. He began his career as a trader, but when military service brought him honors, he used his connections in Indian country to establish himself as a kind of marcher lord and a key player in British-Indian relations. As the richest landowner in the Mohawk Valley, he had a keen eye for developing his investment. He considered Highland Scots industrious people and settled them on lands he had obtained from the Mohawks.

About twenty veterans mustered out of Fraser's Highlanders and their families settled on Johnson's estate, and he helped others secure bounty lands

in northern New York. Hugh Fraser, who had been a lieutenant in the regiment, went to the Mohawk Valley in 1764, then returned to Scotland and
came back with his wife and a number of Highland tenants. Successive parties
of Highland migrants followed. Some three hundred emigrants from
Glengarry in western Inverness-shire migrated to New York in 1773; many of
them headed for the Mohawk Valley. Six hundred people from Lochaber,
recruited by their local parish priest, boarded the *Pearl* and sailed from Fort
William. Most settled on the Kingsborough patent, about fifty thousand acres
of Johnson's property lying four miles north of the Mohawk River and com-
prising most of the present township of Johnstown in Fulton County. Most of
the people listed on the rent rolls were Macdonnells, along with Camerons,
Chisholms, Frasers, Grants, McGregors, McKays, McPhersons, and other
clans.[30]

Johnson complained that the large number of Highlanders settling on his
estates placed him under "a verry heavy burthen," but he had great hopes for
his tenants: "Nothing upon Earth delights me more than to see the rude
woods made cultivable and afford Sustenance to the poor & distressed," he
said. "Johnson Bush," as it became known, had a distinctly Highland character.[31] In attracting Gaelic-speaking and predominantly Catholic Highlanders
to his estates, Johnson may have being "re-creating a kind of nostalgic Gaelic
chieftaincy in the Mohawk Valley" in his declining years.[32] At a time when
traditional ties of patronage and loyalty were unraveling in Scotland, the settlers developed similar ties in the New World with and through Sir William
and his family. They lived near Indians, and some learned the business of the
Indian trade. Norman MacLeod, a captain in the British army, became
friends with Johnson, settled on land Johnson provided after the war, and
brought his kinfolk from Scotland to become Johnson's tenants in 1772. He
later became a trader around Detroit and in the North West Company. Other
Mohawk Valley Highlanders took their trading skills to Canada and the
North West Company after the Revolution.[33]

Most Mohawk Valley Macdonnells were former Jacobites, but during the
Revolution they supported the crown, as did most of their Mohawk neighbors. Ordered to raise as many men as possible, Captain Alexander McDonald
trekked "through frost snow & Ice" to the Mohawk Valley, "where there was
two hundred Men of my own Name, who had fled from the Severity of their
Landlords in the Highlands of Scotland." He engaged "every one of them."[34]
When American troops invaded the Johnson estate in 1775, Sir John Johnson
and a party of Highland Scots and Palatine German tenants escaped through
the Adirondack Mountains to the Mohawk village at Saint Regis (Akwesasne)
and took refuge in Canada. Mohawks who had lost their lands and Highlanders

who had settled and then lost Mohawk lands made common cause against the Americans who seized and settled those same lands.[35]

After the Revolution, Highland and Mohawk Loyalists were scattered across northern New York and Ontario. Patrick Campbell spent several days with Highlanders at New Johnston (now Cornwall, Ontario). Some still wore "their Highland plaids and bonnets," but, hearing of the rent increases in their mother country, they "blessed their stars that they had left Scotland while they had something to pay their way." One, whom Campbell had known in his youth in Inverness, now owned a 150-acre farm, "all his own property" with tools, cattle, and grain. The only thing he missed was "the Highland hills of his youth." In general, they owned their own lands and lived "comfortably and happy."[36] In Canada, the British government set aside land for the Mohawks and their allies at the Grand River in Ontario, now known as the Six Nations Reserve. It set aside further lands for the Highlanders at Glengarry.[37] In both cases, the territories originally belonged to other Indians.

After the Revolution, emigration from the Highlands to America slowed— but not to Canada. In the next decade about twelve hundred people went to Glengarry County. War with France and the high costs of an Atlantic passage curbed emigration in the first decade of the nineteenth century, but the War of 1812 prompted the British government to encourage and assist the emigration of Highlanders to bolster Canada's defenses against the United States. Almost three hundred more emigrated to Glengarry in 1815, and they kept coming, migrating as communities rather than as individuals. Glengarry County took on "the character of a Highland preserve," with people from the same regions sharing the same language and culture and even the same names.[38] As ties to homelands frayed in western Inverness, Glengarry offered Highlanders a new community in North America with land they could own.[39]

Nova Scotia

Nova Scotia was the site of failed Scottish colonial enterprise in the seventeenth century,[40] but in the eighteenth, Scots returned. In 1772 John MacDonald of Glenaladale established a Highland community of some 250 people on Prince Edward Island. The next year two hundred Highlanders from Wester Ross sailed to Nova Scotia on board the *Hector.* The horrors of their ten-week voyage are recalled in oral tradition and in the waterfront museum displays at Pictou. Like the Mayflower in New England, the *Hector* became a part of a "foundation myth."[41] Appalling hardship became almost a rite of passage for early Highland emigrants in Nova Scotia.[42] Winter was "of a severity dreadful to newcomers," wrote John McAlpine; there the extreme cold "benumbs the very faculties of the mind." Rory Steel at St. John's Island (later named Prince Edward Island) wrote a friend in Scotland: "This Province is terrible Cold[;] we have here Seven Months of Snow and frost and sometimes Eight." A man who wet his hand or foot half a mile from his house could lose it to frostbite. The price of potatoes was exorbitant, and people were starving. Tell Scots to stay home, he warned: "Their Constitution will not answer to the Climate here."[43]

Traveling through New Brunswick about the same time, Patrick Campbell painted a much rosier picture. Everywhere he met Highlanders who had left home to escape "the inhumanity and oppression of their landlords." Few regretted their decision. In one area the Highlanders "were in many respects not a whit better than the real Indians" in that they would go out hunting in the forests for weeks on end in dead of winter and return with sleds loaded with venison and moose, "yet they were acknowledged to be the most industrious farmers in all this province of New Brunswick, and lived most easy and independent." He found settlers from disbanded Highland regiments "happily situated, each on his own property . . . on beautiful spacious flats on each side of the river." Their greatest shortage was wives for their young men. One woman said, "They had every necessary of life in abundance on their own property." The only thing she missed was heather.[44]

In 1803 the Earl of Selkirk established a Highland community of about eight hundred emigrants on Prince Edward Island. At least forty thousand Scots migrated to Nova Scotia and Cape Breton in the eighty years after the *Hector*. Despite the horrendous conditions aboard leaky timber ships, Nova Scotia's rapidly expanding timber trade with Britain proved a magnet for Highlanders, many of whom got their start working as lumberjacks in an industry developed with Scottish capital by Scottish merchants. Highlanders settled first on the east side of the province near the bays and rivers most favorably located for harvesting and collecting timber. More arrived as Loyalist refugees from New York, New Jersey, and North Carolina. Veterans from the disbanded 82nd Regiment, which had been on garrison duty at Halifax, and the 84th Royal Highland Regiment, which had been stationed at Quebec and Halifax, took allotments in the Cobequid Bay region or around Pictou Harbour. After colonizing Pictou County, Highlanders pushed southwest into Colchester and Cumberland counties and northeast into Cape Breton, seeking choice locations along the waterways. Opened to settlement after 1784, Cape Breton by the 1820s surpassed Nova Scotia as the preferred destination for emigrants from the Highlands and Hebrides. About twenty-four thousand Scots migrated to Nova Scotia and Cape Breton between 1815 and 1838, eating up the supply of cheap land.[45]

In 1843 R. C. MacDonald, chief of the Highland Society of Nova Scotia, compiled a promotional text that contained advice to prospective immigrants. They should make their living in Nova Scotia, New Brunswick, and Prince Edward Island, not the United States, it counseled. The climate was healthy, the land abundant, the rivers were full of fish, and the forests rich in game. A Highlander could do well there. "He must cut down the trees and cultivate the soil—he must go to work with a cheerful heart, and success will crown his labours."[46] Reality was somewhat different, of course. Many Highlanders arrived destitute, and many remained so. Petitions for government relief from starvation were common in Cape Breton. After the potato blight struck in 1846 and 1848, emigrants who fled famine in the Highlands met similar scarcity of food again in Cape Breton. Some migrated again, this time to Australia and New Zealand.[47]

Nonetheless, most stayed, and they did not always live in self-sufficient rural enclaves. They participated in commercialized agriculture by supplying food for the West Indies trade, Newfoundland fisheries, and local industrializing communities and engaged as well in seasonal wage labor in New England.[48] By 1871 two out of three people in Cape Breton were of Scottish descent, and Cape Breton came to have the largest Gaelic-speaking population in the world outside of Scotland.[49]

When settlers were successful, it was often at the expense of the Native inhabitants. In the seventeenth century, the Mi'kmaqs occupied an intermediary role in the fur trade and spoke with a confident voice, rejecting European claims to cultural superiority and asserting the value of their own way of life.[50] Things were very different by the time Highland Scots settled in Mi'kmaq country, however. European diseases and European conflicts had ravaged the area. After Britain took Nova Scotia from France, colonial officials maintained that the indigenous Mi'kmaq people had lost their lands by right of conquest. The Mi'kmaqs consequently had to petition the government for grants to occupy lands where they had always lived. Incoming Europeans coveted the same areas, squatted on lands the government had granted the Mi'kmaqs, and made claims to lands that were not properly surveyed. Disease, land loss, environmental changes, depleted fish and wildlife, and starvation reduced the Mi'kmaqs to desperate straits. The lieutenant governor of Nova Scotia, Sir Colin Campbell, ignored requests from London for information on the condition of the Native peoples (information Parliament was gathering from throughout the empire). In the 1830s and '40s, however, in petitions bearing their totems to the colonial government, the Mi'kmaqs complained about the destruction of game and requested relief. In 1841 chief Pemmeenauweet sent a petition and a belt of white wampum to Queen Victoria herself. "All these Woods [were] once ours," he said. "Our Fathers possessed them all. Now we cannot cut a Tree to warm our wigwams in Winter unless the white Man please." White men had taken everything they had. "Let us not perish," he begged the queen. The next year, Nova Scotia passed an Act to Provide for the Instruction and Permanent Settlement of the Indians. The act created the post of Indian commissioner, who was to supervise the Indian reserves, promote agriculture, and eject squatters, but the position was unpaid. The first commissioner, Joseph Howe, frustrated by lack of support and anti-Indian sentiment, lasted little more than a year.[51]

Reports on crown lands and Indian affairs submitted to the Nova Scotia assembly regularly addressed the problem of Scottish trespassers. There were six Indian reserves on Cape Breton: Eskasoni, Whykokomagh, Wagamatcook, Malagawaatchk, Chapel Island, and the tiny Marguerite, totaling slightly more than twelve thousand acres. By 1845 the Mi'kmaqs were reduced to some six hundred people. Encroaching settlement circumscribed their former mobile lifestyle of hunting and trapping. Sooner or later they would have to rely on farming their reserved land, even though much of it was "hilly, broken land, only serviceable for providing fuel." And even those lands were "eagerly coveted by the Scotch Presbyterian settlers," said one report:

> That the Micmacs' fathers were sole possessors of these regions is a matter of no weight with the Scottish emigrants. They are by no means disposed to leave the aborigines a resting place in the Island of Cape Breton; and it will not be easy for any Commissioner holding a seat in the Provincial Assembly, either for Cape Breton or Inverness, to do justice to the Indians to retain the good will of his constituents.

In the 1820s and '30s Scots settled the fertile Wagamatcook Valley and Whykokomagh, the inlandmost point on the interior waters of Cape Breton. Some claimed to have rented fields from local chiefs; some claimed the lands they occupied were "empty"; and others took parts of the Indian reserves by force. Many regarded squatting on Indian land "as a right that cannot be questioned or taken away." At Wagamatcook, one of the largest reserves, Scots squatters defied the government's repeated orders to leave and ignored writs served by the sheriff. "Their impunity will no doubt encourage similar invasions on the other reserves. They have been complained of also by the Indians of Whykokomagh and Malagawaatchkt, and it is understood that the Indians have been driven off altogether from the Marguerite Reserves. No lenient measures will make impression on these people." Scots settlers cut down timber, destroyed the Indians' hay and crops, and knocked down fences to let their cattle graze. Afraid to resist, Indians complained to the authorities, but the commissioner of Indian affairs stated that "It would be vain to seek a verdict from any jury in this Island against the trespassers on the reserve" and difficult to find a lawyer to argue the Indians' case.[52] Highland squatters in the Wagamatcook Valley persuaded the government to sanction their rights to the land by arguing that the Indians were not using it.[53]

In 1859 the Act concerning Indian Reserves allowed squatters who were already established on Indian land to buy it, the money to be placed in a fund for Indian relief. Future squatters were to be ejected. Surveys were regularized, the boundaries of the reserves clarified, and plots of land allocated to individual Indians. However, "few of the squatters paid anything and none paid in full." The Indian fund provided destitute Mi'kmaqs with little more than blankets and clothing.[54]

Like European settler societies everywhere, Highlanders ignored indigenous rights and justified their own occupation of the land by arguing that the Natives did not put it to good use. Displaced from their homelands in

Figure 8.1. Nova Scotian Scots and Mi'kmaqs pose at the "150th Anniversary Landing of the Scottish Pioneers," in Pictou, Nova Scotia, 1923. (History Collection, Nova Scotia Museum, Halifax, P81/88.27.6/N-12170.)

Scotland, Highlanders had no compunctions about ousting Indian people from their homelands in Nova Scotia and Cape Breton.

Red River

Located at the junction of the Red and Assiniboine rivers, the Red River colony was planned by the Earl of Selkirk as a place for Highland emigrants, as well as retired Hudson's Bay Company employees and their families. Although remote, it offered fertile land in what seemed to be an ideal location. "As fine a tract of land as the world possesses," thought John McLean; a wooded "oasis" in an otherwise "vast treeless prairie," said Robert Ballantyne. Colin Robertson felt no better country could have been chosen: "In every other part of America the emigrant must pass his life, in clearing lands to procure a subsistence for himself and family, but in Red River the land is already cleared, and only requires the plough to yield crops."[55]

Red River was a multiethnic social experiment, an embryonic community in which the Highland settlers would provide Indians with models of agriculture and industry.[56] The newcomers were the first Europeans the Plains Ojibwas had seen who were not traders.[57] They may not have been impressed. John Tanner, an American captive who lived for thirty years in Indian country, married an Ojibwa, and became culturally Ojibwa, worked for four months for the Hudson's Bay Company, hunting buffalo to help feed "the Scots people in great distress for want of provisions." He was accompanied by company clerks and laborers who carted the meat to Red River. "Those Scots labourers who were with me, were much more rough and brutal in their manners than any people I had seen before," he recalled. "Even when they had plenty, they ate like starved dogs, and never failed to quarrel over their meat."[58]

Many of the Highland settlers came from Kildonan, although the Duchess of Sutherland refused to encourage Selkirk's recruitment efforts, insisting that her people were better off where they were "than sent by him God knows where." William Young, who kept the duchess informed of Selkirk's recruitment efforts (which included an advertisement in the *Inverness Journal*), thought it "extreme folly" and "a wild idea."[59] Miles MacDonnell, who recruited and led the emigrants, was the son of a Glengarry Macdonell who had taken land in the Mohawk Valley at the invitation of Sir William Johnson. He fought in the King's Royal Regiment of New York during the Revolution and then moved to Canada. His personal life was marred with tragedy: Three wives and one daughter predeceased him. In 1811, through Selkirk's offices, he was named first governor of Assiniboia, an appointment that would bring him further trial and tribulation.[60]

Although the Highland immigrants must have felt Red River was in the middle of nowhere, it was in fact the heart of a bitterly contested region. The Plains Cree who formerly inhabited the area were moving south in response to declining fur and game resources and to continue their role as provisioners for the trading companies. As the Cree withdrew, the Plains Ojibwa or Saulteaux moved in behind them. However, they faced growing competition for dwindling resources from rival Indian groups, Métis, and free traders.[61] The North West Company viewed Selkirk's settlers as agents of the rival Hudson's Bay Company, placed there to disrupt its supply routes and stores of pemmican, which the local Métis produced for the fur trade brigades. The Métis, some of whom descended from Highland traders, as well as from French and English, saw the colonists as a threat to their economic role. Intertribal raids added to the volatility: Trader John McDonnell said the Red River Valley was "very little frequented except by war parties, it being a warlike route between the Sauteux [sic] and their enemies the Sioux, who are ever at variance."[62]

Miles MacDonnell and his colonists initially feared the Indians but evidently developed relatively amicable relations with those in the region, approximately forty-five hundred people by MacDonnell's best guess.[63] MacDonnell felt himself a novice in Indian affairs: "In all these matters I stand alone, there being no person to advise with," he wrote to Selkirk in 1813. He found himself "at a loss how to purchase land from the Indians." It had originally belonged to the Crees, but the Assiniboines, whom MacDonnell correctly identified as a branch of the Sioux, had driven them off. The Ojibwas "do not call themselves owners of the soil, although long in possession." Alexander Ross described the Saulteaux as "a turbulent and revengeful people" with "no claim at all to the lands of Red River." MacDonnell believed a small annual present would satisfy them. He held conferences with the principal chiefs and was as generous to them "as the state of our stores can afford." The threats the Indians had previously made blew over, he reported to Selkirk. "They are now favorably disposed towards the colony."[64]

Selkirk told MacDonnell not to worry about making a formal purchase. "I was indeed mistaken in thinking that a purchase from the Indians would strengthen our rights either of property or jurisdiction," he wrote. All that was necessary to maintain peace was to give each of the bands an annual present, stipulating nevertheless that they were not to hunt within specified boundaries in the immediate neighborhood of the settlement. Keep expenses down, but keep the Indians in good humor.[65]

Figure 8.2. *A family from the tribe of wild Sautaux [sic] Indians on the Red River, Manitoba, c. 1821*, by Peter Rindisbacher. (Library and Archives Canada, acc. no. 1988–250–28; C-001929.)

MacDonnell did his best. He was aided by Peguis or Pegowis (also known as Cutnose, after he was disfigured in a fight), whom MacDonnell called the "Premier or supreme hereditary chief of the Saulteaux tribe." Peguis befriended the settlers, apparently taught them how to hunt buffalo, and encouraged the Indians of Lac la Pluie to move toward the Red River, settle there, and plant corn. MacDonnell cultivated his friendship, and the chief liked the attention. When Peguis agreed to join the Crees and Assiniboines in a war against the Sioux, he asked MacDonnell for permission and some supplies. The former was surely only a courtesy to help him obtain the latter—Peguis hardly needed MacDonnell's approval. MacDonnell would rather have seen the Sioux and Ojibwas at peace, but he consented since Peguis was "much bent on the war."[66] Like Selkirk, MacDonnell hoped the Red River settlement would serve as a buffer against American expansion: With a small force of regulars joined to the colonists and the local Indians, "we could defend ourselves"; if the Sioux and Ojibwas could be united in defending the country, "we could bid defiance to the Yankees."[67] Peguis and his people felt they had made "something like an alliance" and likely expected the settlers to reciprocate by assisting them against the Sioux.[68]

The North West Company played on fears of Indian hostilities. Simon McGillivray told Lord Bathurst in 1815 that he always feared Selkirk's colony would lead to "fatal quarrels" between the settlers and the Indians. As "a humble individual," he did everything in his power to prevent "my country-men in the Highlands of Scotland . . . from being misled by his Lordship's illusive advertisements." He placed an article in the *Inverness Journal* that warned people against the folly of Selkirk's scheme. The settlement was two thousand miles from civilization and surrounded by "warlike savage nations" who would consider the settlers "as intruders come to spoil their hunting ground, to drive away the wild animals, and to destroy the Indians, as the white men have already done in Canada and the United States." But placing a warning, McGillivray hastened to remind Bathurst, was not the same thing as instigating the Indians to massacre fellow Highlanders.[69]

When settlers from Sutherland arrived at Red River, Duncan Cameron (son of a Loyalist who had emigrated from Scotland and settled in the Mohawk Valley and a bitter opponent of the Hudson's Bay Company and Selkirk), along with other North West Company agents, tried to win their confidence. They spoke to them in Gaelic and treated them to Highland hospitality with bag-pipes and "a dram." They also regaled them with tales of Indian atrocities and told them the Indians would cut their throats. Moreover, they offered them safer lands in Upper Canada, with cattle and implements provided. Some of the newcomers accepted the offer.[70] MacDonnell and Selkirk insisted that, despite attempts to stir them up, no Indians did any violence: "The untutored savage remained uncorruptible," wrote MacDonnell, "while those calling themselves civilized committed every outrage against their fellow subject, in violation of the laws of the country and of every honest feeling."[71]

Selkirk, whom the Indians called the Silver Chief,[72] paid far less attention to the Métis, and his settlers paid the price. He failed to recognize that the Métis were important stakeholders in the contest. In fact, the conflict seems to have acted as a catalyst for an incipient Métis nationhood—they displayed their own flag during the fighting around Red River and, "for the first time," Selkirk wrote in retrospect, "consider[ed] themselves a separate tribe of men, and distinguished by a separate name."[73] The "massacre" at Seven Oaks was attributed to "a parcel of the North West Company's clerks, and men, half breeds and Indians," but the majority were Métis.[74] As the bloodshed made clear, the fur trade and settlement were often at odds.

According to some accounts, Indians warned Governor Semple that an attack was coming and helped bury the dead.[75] In the turbulent aftermath of Seven Oaks, Peguis and his band provided the settlers with meat, hauling it to the fort on sledges and accepting credit notes in payment. Peguis had more than one hundred warriors to defend the settlers. "The Indians are staunch friends," Selkirk assured his wife, Jane, "notwithstanding our store being entirely out of rum, tobacco, and almost every other supply." Amid reports of escalating violence at Red River, Lady Selkirk, in Montreal with the children and a new baby her husband had not yet seen, no doubt needed the reassurance.[76]

The Red River settlers hardly acted as the Ojibwas expected allies should. In July 1817 Selkirk and his officers made a treaty with Peguis and four other Ojibwa and Cree chiefs. The Indians "agreed to all that was asked of land . . . giving us the two banks of the river and two miles broad on each side" and a swath of territory extending to Pembina. In return Selkirk promised the Indians who had fed and protected his colony one hundred pounds of tobacco a year and gave Peguis a medal. It was, he admitted to his wife, "a trifling quit rent." The Ojibwas likely saw the treaty as reaffirming their relationship with the colony, but it evidently caused some ill feeling among the Crees, who regarded this as their land and resented the inclusion of the Ojibwas as inter-lopers. The issue of aboriginal title at Red River—and just what Peguis ceded in the treaty—remained unresolved half a century later. Peguis and his band took up farming on Netley Creek as a way of coping with diminishing game. The settlers evidently liked him but nonetheless occupied lands that had not been ceded by the treaty, and relations became strained. Peguis continued to press for the Ojibwas' rights under the 1817 treaty until his death in 1864.[77]

Nevertheless, Peguis remained firm in his commitment to the settlement even after Selkirk's death and identified himself "as a colony chief, not a trader chief." He complained about inadequate gifts ("We are poor and piti-ful, it is time to change") and about Governor Alexander McDonnell *("truth never comes out of his mouth")*. Still, he had promised Selkirk he would take the colony under his care, he said, "and I shall hold it as the eagle keeps its prey in its talons."[78]

John West, an Anglican missionary at Red River from 1820 to 1823, left his impressions of Peguis and the colony. Both were colored by West's conviction that he was in a wilderness of heathenism and human depravity. Instead of an orderly farming community in a cluster of cottages, he found huts scattered along the river and little evidence of agriculture. Almost every inhabitant he met carried a gun on his shoulder, and "all appeared in a wild and hunter-like state." Indians came in to trade and then returned "to roam through the for-ests, like animals, without any fixed residence." Those from the plains wore buffalo skins "wrapped round them, or worn tastefully over the shoulder like the Highland plaid." Peguis and his band provided food when the colonists were hungry and asked for provisions when *they* were hungry. Indians, many

of whom had relatives in the settlement, also came for seasonal farm employment during the spring, summer, and fall when extra hands were needed.
West performed marriage ceremonies for many of the men who were living
with Indian women and baptized many of their children. It was a multiethnic
community—Canadians, retired Hudson's Bay Company employees,
Highland settlers, Indian wives, Métis families, and German, Swiss, French,
Polish, and Italian mercenaries from the de Meuron Regiment discharged
after the War of 1812. West eventually distributed Bibles in English, Gaelic,
German, Danish, Italian, and French. Highlanders and Ojibwas must have
adjusted and accommodated their native languages as they communicated in
Gaelic and Algonquian.[79] The Bungee dialect of English spoken in the Red
River Valley by the late nineteenth century originated in the intermingling of
Cree, Saulteaux, Gaelic, Scots, Orkney, English, and French people in the
region. Bungee contains Cree, Scots, Gaelic, and French words and expres-
sions and is described as having a Scottish "lilt."[80]

Selkirk may have planned to establish a school for Indians at Red River.[81]
West wanted to build a mission school that would stand as "a Protestant
land-mark in a vast field of heathenism." Like many missionaries he found
the Natives did not share his enthusiasm. Presbyterian Scots attended his
Anglican services somewhat reluctantly and he was disappointed by their
"prejudices against the English liturgy." One evening when Peguis and his
son came and drank tea with him, West told the chief about the school and
how well-intentioned people in England would help provide food and clothing for the children while they were being educated. Peguis said that was
good, but he was in no hurry to part with his sons: "Indians like to have time
to consider about these matters," he said. They smoked the calumet pipe for
a while, and then Peguis "shrewdly asked me what I would do with the children after they were taught what I wished them to know." West replied that
the boys would see the advantages of farming over hunting, the girls would
learn to knit, and all would learn to read the Bible. And by the way, he added,
it was God's will that a man should have only one wife. Peguis smiled and
said he thought there was no more harm in Indians having two wives than in
the settlers having them. West "grieved for the depravity of the Europeans."
Peguis impressed West with his "penetration and mental ability," even though,
as an Indian, he was concerned only with present needs, not with his future
state. West left Red River in 1833.[82]

His replacement, Welsh-born David Jones, also tried to get Peguis to send
boys to the mission school. Peguis promised to talk it over with his people:
"We want our people to become like white people," he said, "to get plenty of
Indian corn, wheat and potatoes, for since you white people have got our

lands we are very poor. Before that we had plenty—our rivers were full of fish, and we always conquered our enemies, but now the white people promise much and give nothing. And now you come and want our children, but I do not know what to say." Peguis continued to stall.[83] He finally had his first son baptized in 1837. By then, with buffalo becoming scarce and a shrinking land base, living as Christian farmers offered an alternative to starvation, but the Ojibwas held on to their culture.[84]

Peguis and the Ojibwas were vital to the survival of Red River. Governor George Simpson called it an "ill-fated colony."[85] Plagues of grasshoppers ate the crops, a prairie fire rendered buffalo scarce on the plains, and the settlers faced starvation. Goods were expensive, and many of the Highlanders were deep in debt.[86] Robert Dickson, a Lowland Scottish trader prominent in the British Indian Department and influential among the Sioux, planned to drive cattle to the colony but the enterprise failed.[87] Plans to establish a Buffalo Wool Company and other projects were also unsuccessful. Moreover, according to a hostile North West Company source, the colonists "imported with them the measles and chincough [whooping cough], which have been so fatal among the natives, that one fifth of the population of this country is said to have been destroyed all the way from Lac La Pluie to Athabasca."[88] The Sioux were a recurrent threat, and sometimes it seemed the colonists might get caught up in the Ojibwas' conflicts with them.[89] Fortunately, Cuthbert Grant's Métis settlement on the Assiniboine afforded a buffer against potential Sioux attacks.

Simpson had no great hopes for Red River. The inhabitants were a lawless bunch of "malcontents and renegades." Governor Alexander McDonnell was drunk and dishonest, "despised and held in contempt by every person connected with the place." His affairs were "in a labyrinth of confusion," and he was not up to the challenge of leading the colony in times of crisis. Among other things, he carried on "a very disgraceful traffic in horses," buying them from the Indians and the Hudson's Bay Company and selling them to settlers at inflated prices. "There is not a man in the settlement I have such a bad opinion of as McDonnell." Simpson insisted Red River could not flourish without a code of laws and a military presence to back up the civil authorities.[90]

In Simpson's mind, part of the problem was the human composition of the colony. The Métis, the Canadians, and the Swiss were worthless; they were poor settlers and troublemakers who lacked proper respect for authority. Fond of showy dress and liquor, the Canadians and Métis were accustomed to "an erratic life" and reluctant to take up farming. Not so his Highland compatriots. "The Scotch are steady and well disposed, and consider Red River as much their home as the land of their nativity formerly was, they never will think of leaving the colony, unless some evil which is not to be anticipated should arise." Admittedly, they had unreasonable expectations as to what the company should provide them, "but grumbling is the characteristic of Highlanders, and neither a change of country nor of circumstance will alter their nature." The Highlanders spoke nothing but Gaelic, did not mix with the other settlers, and, said Simpson, were honest in their dealings with everyone except the Hudson's Bay Company.[91]

Despite his assertions that the Highlanders would never leave, Simpson occasionally had trouble keeping them there. A settler named Campbell, who had taken up one hundred acres and married one of Selkirk's Highland emigrés, wanted to sell out and move to Canada. Simpson was dead against it, as it might encourage others to desert. "[T]he object of the Company in giving these grants gratis," he sputtered, "was with a view to the settling for life, improving the lots, and raising a numerous white population . . . not merely for the purpose of their favouring us with their company for one or two years."[92] David Tully, the Scottish blacksmith at Fort Douglas, decided to try his fortunes in the United States despite Simpson's efforts to dissuade him. The Sioux caught the Tully family on the prairie and captured the two children. The children were later recovered, but the event served as a warning to others who might have contemplated leaving. "I do not believe many of them will venture in that direction again," commented Simpson.[93]

Many of Peguis's band had to beg for food at Red River in the winter of 1825–1826, but the settlers were no better off than they were.[94] Despite his inclination to blame the victims, especially if they were not Scots, Simpson felt "there seems to be a strange fatality attending the unfortunate colony, as no sooner is one evil got rid of, than another presents itself." Others agreed: "Misfortune seems to attend R. R. Settlement."[95] The settlers seemed to have put the worst behind them, however. Their crops had recovered, there were buffalo to hunt again, and Donald McKenzie had replaced the hapless Alexander McDonnell as governor. Simpson had every confidence in McKenzie as a popular and effective leader (although his opinion would later change).[96] "Honest Donald" (as John McLean called the Highland settler) "was beginning to find himself at his ease, when, lo! all his dreams of future wealth and happiness vanished in a moment."[97] In 1826 a rapid spring thaw after a heavy winter caused the Red River to overflow its banks, producing massive flooding, not an uncommon occurrence (the same thing happened again in 1852 and 1861). "Lake Winnipeg now extends to Pembina," said Simpson. The floodwaters wiped out crops, carried away buildings, sent settlers scurrying to high ground, and brought misery and the threat of starvation. For some it was the last straw. Simpson "held out no encouragement to remain" to those he deemed "the useless and disaffected" (Swiss, Canadians, and Métis), and some left for the United States and Canada. To "the Scotch and other well disposed settlers," he "held out every inducement" he could.[98]

Simpson might have changed his tune a few years later. In 1830 he took his new wife to live at Red River. They both suffered from ill health, and in six months Simpson had had enough of the place. By January 1832, soured by "Vindictive & Malicious intrigue," he was "sick and tired of Red River and would be off tomorrow if I currently could." Simpson was never one to mince words in criticizing a fellow human, but his frame of mind surely explains some of the biting comments in the "character book" he wrote that winter. His infant son died in the spring.[99]

The Red River colony had more than its share of infighting. In December 1830 James McMillan complained to his friend James Hargrave that "the Scotch Settlers were at cross purposes all the fall" over debts and land, and "they grumble confoundedly." Three years later things seemed quiet except for "a few squabbles down amongst the Scotch." In the spring of 1834, when it came time for McMillan to leave, he was "ready to be off." He would not miss Red River, he told a friend: "I believe the world cannot produce such a set of ungrateful wretches. Their whole Soul seems Bent on Back-biting [sic] and Slander."[100] John McLean claimed that the "frugal and industrious habits" of his Highland countrymen earned them a superior material standard of living that made them "objects of envy and hatred to their hybrid neighbors."[101]

But Red River survived its plagues and petty jealousies. In 1834 the school was "doing wonders in the improvement of our Half Breeds," a new church was built that was "superior to nine tenths of the Scotch country churches," and a Catholic cathedral was under construction.[102] Whooping cough "thinned the swarm of children not a little" in 1834 and spread among the Indians, who "suffered dreadfully." Influenza hit the next year, again causing devastation in Indian country.[103] However, by December 1835 severe winter weather had ended the flu epidemic, and the settlement was "quiet & healthy." The harvest had been good, and there was plenty to eat. The Red River community was alive and well, as was the culture of its Highland settlers. "Plenty and gaiety are the order of the day, and the young folks are splicing at double quick time," wrote Thomas Simpson (the governor's brother). "I was the other week at a genuine highland wedding, where we danced, kissed, and talked Gaelic, till midnight."[104]

In 1851, the Scots Presbyterian settlers finally got their own minister when the Presbyterian Church of Scotland in Canada sent Rev. John Black, a Lowland Scot, as missionary to Red River. The congregation began building Kildonan Presbyterian Church, modeled after the kirk in Helmsdale, Sutherland, from where many of them had emigrated. Long before, the

Spaniards had superimposed Christian edifices on Native sacred spaces in New Spain and the Red River Highlanders followed suit. They built their new kirk on what Rev. Black described as "a piece of land long desecrated by the idolatrous revels of the Indians"; in other words, "a site where they had encamped every year and held their annual Dog Feast before they separated for the winter."[105] In 1817, between 100 and 150 families lived at Red River. In the summer of 1818 there were 224 people—153 Highland Scots, 45 De Meurons, and 26 Canadians—living in fifty-seven houses. In 1834 the population had increased to 2,982. In 1835 the Selkirk family sold Red River to the Hudson's Bay Company. In 1843 the population was "upwards of 5,000 souls" and rising. Despite a flu epidemic in 1846 that killed more than 300 people, most of them children, the population reached 6,522 in 1856. Eventually, Red River grew into the city of Winnipeg.[106]

Selkirk had hoped his colony would serve as a model of agricultural civilization that would benefit the Indians. Peguis's band did take up farming, and Robert Ballantyne said, "The Scotch and Indian settlers cultivate wheat, barley, and Indian corn in abundance."[107] The Ojibwas brought furs, hides, moccasins, bark containers, meat, fish, and ducks to trade at Red River and were exposed to the languages, material culture, and customs of the Scots, Irish, French-Canadian, Swiss, and English settlers, as well as to new objects and practices such as potato-growing, mosquito nets, beer-brewing, and knitting. They also got a taste of first-footing at Hogmanay: on New Year's Day 1844, the settlers gave the Indians currant buns.[108] Nevertheless, in 1856 Alexander Ross declared that "forty years' experience" proved Selkirk's experiment "a complete failure." Like many of his contemporaries, Ross believed "civilized" people could easily adjust to Indian ways but that it was almost a hopeless task "to accustom the children of the wilderness to the use of the hoe, the spade, or the plough; even after they have been made to taste of the fruits arising from industry." "Civilized habits are altogether out of the question with people habituated to Indian habits," Ross concluded.[109] Highlanders were more likely to live like Indians than Indians were to live like them.

Preserving Communities and Changing the Land

The words of the song ("We've turned into Indians, sure enough") reflected a fear shared by many immigrants that the new environment might strip away their civilized veneer. If people could ascend the ladder of societal progress, they could also, presumably, descend. Adopting Indian ways and subsistence practices was often a necessity, especially in the early years. Governor Martin worried that many of the Highland emigrants who had arrived in North Carolina in the early months of 1775 and squatted on "the King's vacant Lands in spite of every effort to prevent them" would die "before they can learn to live."[110] Selkirk's emigrants on Prince Edward Island in 1803 struggled to adjust to the forest and the climate. At first they "lodged themselves in temporary wigwams, constructed after the fashion of the Indians."[111] According to Alexander Ross, during times of food shortages, Red River settlers "became good hunters; they could kill buffalo; walk on snow-shoes; had trains of dogs trimmed with ribbons, bells and feathers, in the true Indian style; and in other respects were making rapid strides towards a savage life."[112] Highland settlers grew Indian corn using Indian techniques, made maple sugar, and wore Indian moccasins. The emigrant "will not do well without them in winter in America," warned Robert MacDougall. "I wore a beautiful pair all last winter," wrote Catherine Parr Traill, "worked with porcupine-quills and bound with scarlet ribbon."[113]

But Highland settlers did not come to America to become Indians. They came to make a new world for themselves—as Highlanders. To do that they had to preserve their Gaelic communities and transform the Indians' land. Many Highlanders, especially those from treeless Hebridean environments, found the deep forests of North America disorienting. From Georgia to Nova Scotia, they viewed the "immense woods" with apprehension.[114] One Gaelic poem described Canada as simply "the land of the trees."[115] They set about cutting them down, clearing the forests to make way for fields. "Many of these very farms you see in so thriving a condition were wild land thirty years ago, nothing but Indian hunting-grounds," a tavern landlady in Upper Canada told Catherine Parr Traill in 1832. "The industry of men, and many of them poor men, that had not a rood of land of their own in their own country, has effected this change."[116] Traill's *Canadian Settler's Guide* described how the forest had disappeared "before the axe of the industrious emigrant" and towns and villages had sprung up "where the bear and the wolf had their lair."[117] In the nineteenth and twentieth centuries Canadian lumbermen of Highland ancestry "felled millions of the soaring pines, spruces and oaks which constituted the Atlantic timber trade's raw material."[118]

The Rev. D. Masson, who visited the Gaelic-speaking settlements in the Saugeen Valley near Lake Huron in the 1870s, said that in just seventeen years the Highlanders had transformed the "forest solitudes" into "an unbroken succession of 200 acre lots, all closely adjoining, each with its comfortable homestead, and more than half cleared." To hear Masson talk, thriving communities of industrious Highlanders were producing grain for market and building homes, schools, and churches "side by side with the still surviving wigwam of the Indian."[119] Many Highland settlers (or at least their parents) had witnessed such things before in Scotland when economic transformation had produced new roads, bridges, mills, and "fields laid off and substantially enclosed."[120] History repeated itself, and Highlanders were now the agents of change.

Like the domesticated animals of European settlers elsewhere, Highlanders' cows and pigs trampled and ate Indian cornfields, competed with deer for browse, destroyed vegetation, and caused disputes. They contributed to the environmental degradation and transformation of the landscape that Indians had inhabited and cultivated for centuries.[121]

Land-hungry emigrants were likely to value economic factors over kinship ties, and Highlanders in North America participated in a market-oriented farming economy quite different from what they had known at home. Still, maintaining clan allegiances remained important in their landholding practices: Emigrants tended to settle near relatives and held lands in

Figure 8.3. An Indian boatman takes Patrick Campbell (and his dog) past a changing landscape (from Patrick Campbell, *Travels in the Interior Inhabited Parts of North America*). (Courtesy of the Champlain Society.)

common as they had in the Highlands.[122] Unlike Americans who dispersed their settlements over large areas, Selkirk's Highlanders on Prince Edward Isle built their homes close together in clusters, each "inhabited by persons nearly related." Selkirk recommended the lots be laid out with intervals between them, which could be filled in by friends and relatives who came later; "in taking several hundred acres, an individual does not imagine he shall cultivate or need it all himself," he said, "but he must have room to spread, & room for his brother or his cousin that is to follow him." The "social clannish disposition of the Highlanders" meant they refused to go anywhere without their friends and family.[123] Indians responded in much the same manner when the Allotment Act in 1887 began dividing reservations into family plots. Many were given no choice, but those who were often made decisions based on noneconomic reasoning, selecting land close to relatives in preference to more fertile land farther away.

Settling in their own ethnic colonies helped Highlanders to preserve their distinct culture. When Lady Liston, wife of British diplomat Robert Liston, visited North Carolina in 1797, she found a settlement of Highlanders that extended thirty miles. The inhabitants had suffered severely for their loyalism during the Revolution. The neighboring Catawba Indians, huddled on a small fifteen-square-mile reservation and surrounded by whites, were "obliged to adopt some of their customs and vices," but the Highlanders kept their Highland ways: "The Gallic language is still prevalent amongst them, their Negros [sic] speak it, & they have a Clergyman who Preaches in it." Highlanders in North Carolina's Cape Fear region sent to Scotland for kilt-wearing, pipe-playing, Gaelic-speaking ministers, and some continued to speak Gaelic into the twentieth century.[124] In Nova Scotia, John McGregor observed that wherever Highlanders formed "distinct settlements," their habits, farming methods, "ancient hospitable customs," and language changed very little. They spent their evenings reciting traditional poems in Gaelic, kept alive the old music and dances, held on to ancient superstitions, relived old battles and lost causes, and recalled the glens of home with affection.[125] In Cape Breton, Highland emigrants seem to have settled around religious as well as cultural cores, with Protestant settlements predominantly on the eastern seaboard, Catholic communities on the western shores of the island.[126]

The Rev. Masson said that in eight months he "heard more Gaelic, and met more Gaelic men in Canada than in the previous twenty years at home." Traveling from Cape Breton to the Great Lakes and preaching most days of the week, he was never without a Gaelic congregation. He also heard of more remote communities he had no time to visit, including descendents of Fraser's Highlanders, "who spoke Gaelic, French, and Indian, but not a word of

English." In Montreal and Ottawa large congregations worshipped with him "in the mother tongue," while in Cape Breton he found "people to this day, even in dress, very much the same as they were in the Highlands when I was a child."[127]

The pattern held in the American West. Neil Calder left Sutherland in 1888 to seek his fortune in America and traveled widely in the West, where he saw the diversity of Indian life. Finally realizing he could not make money "running around the country," he settled at Granite, Montana. "Most of the people around here is Scotch Canadians," he wrote his brother, "and you will here [sic] as much Gaelic spoken as you will in Bonar Bridge. I was speaking to the descendants of Sutherlandshire people here and you would think they just came across from Assynt or some other place."[128]

Sticking together and clinging to their own ways attracted criticism: Highlanders failed to learn from the experiences or the new agricultural techniques of non-Highland neighbors; they were "land hungry," but their drive to acquire land was not matched by a determination to improve it or their own standard of living; they lacked ambition and were too willing to "make do."[129] Selkirk complained that once they achieved the level of comfort they had known in the old country, some Highland settlers preferred to indulge "old habits of indolence" rather than accumulate property "by a continuance of active industry."[130]

In Nova Scotia many of Highlanders scrimped and saved to buy more land rather than improving what they already had. Joseph Howe explained this as a function of having lived in a country where property was at a premium and few could aspire to escape tenant status.[131] Captain William Moorsom also noted the Nova Scotian Highlanders' willingness to make do with the roughest fare. Emigrants from Perthshire, Inverness-shire, and Sutherland established settlements along the St. Mary's River, an area noted for "magnificent timber, extensive intervals, rivers teeming with fish and the abundance of game in the forest." However, they made "indifferent farmers; accustomed to a hard and penurious mode of life, they are too easily satisfied with the bare existence that even indolence can procure in this country, and care little for raising themselves and their families to a state of comfort and abundance."[132]

Most Euro-Americans could not understand a people who made do with the minimum in the midst of abundance. In 1889 A. M. Burgess (himself a Scot) of the Canadian Department of the Interior complained: "The Crofters and the Highland people generally are excellent settlers when they emigrate of their own accord, and are placed alongside of people of other nationalities, but when settled in compact body they are like the Indians in that they spend a great deal of time talking over their grievances, real or fancied . . . they are content to make very little progress when left to themselves."[133]

No one leveled such complaints against Highlanders who dominated the upper echelons of the fur trade or individuals who thrived in the capitalist economy. Like complaints leveled against Indians reservation communities, comments about Highlanders' limited ambitions indicate the persistence of communal values within the new capitalist order, a moral economy of sharing and reciprocity rather than of individual advancement and endless accumulation.[134] Such values survived among twentieth-century crofters ("Time is not money in the Gaelic value-system, and money is anyway not necessarily the most desirable acquisition") and among twentieth-century Native Americans ("We are a sharing people and our tribal traits are still with us," said an Ojibwa woman living in Chicago in the 1950s).[135]

By the nineteenth century, prospective emigrants to the United States and Canada had access to a host of guidebooks. In 1841 Robert MacDougall published one in Gaelic. MacDougall had migrated from Perthshire to Canada, spent three years there, and then returned home before migrating again, this time for good, to Australia. Dismissing books written by English authors as misleading in their claims and inappropriate for Gaels, MacDougall wrote his book "solely to meet the needs of the inhabitants of the Highlands."[136] He provided information on preparations, fares, domestic and wild animals, selecting and clearing land, crops, and Indians. He tried to depict the Indians of Upper Canada for people who had never been outside Scotland: He described their dress and subsistence activities, compared their skin tone to cloth that had been immersed three times in a tub of lichen dye, claimed that their chiefs were "just like the clan chiefs who were once among the Gaels," and noted the care and attention they devoted to raising their children.[137] His main focus, of course, was land and the future prospects it held for Highland emigrants. Canada was not for everyone, he said, and described the kind of people who should and should not go.[138] Winter was brutal—so cold he could not find words in Gaelic to describe it. And his readers should not believe the inflated claims other writers made. Nevertheless, Upper Canada offered the best land in British North America and was the finest place for a man with a family to make a permanent home. Clearing and planting were hard work, but a Highlander working his own land would be motivated by "the memory of working on other people's land . . . as well as the sum he paid them per year in order to receive permission to work on it."[139]

Once Highlanders were forced "to expatriate themselves from the beloved tho' sterile possessions of their ancestors," the prospect of owning their own property "on the simple condition of transporting themselves across the

Atlantic" was compelling.[140] The Scottish press regularly publicized the benefits of landownership in Canada, and land companies targeted Scots as prospective settlers. The Canada Company, founded in 1824, secured one million acres of government land on the shores of Lake Huron and Ontario on the condition that the area be improved and settled. It sold half its territories within the first decade. Despite his concerns about the Canada Company's false claims in advertising, MacDougall acknowledged it was doing everything it could to develop the Upper Huron tract, "cutting out roads, constructing bridges, building mills."[141] Modeled on the Canada Company and founded a decade later, the British American Land Company purchased almost one million acres of crown lands in Quebec's eastern townships on the borders of Vermont and New Hampshire, attracting families from Lewis and other Outer Hebridean islands in particular. Land could also be bought at auction. In 1841 a land act set prices low enough to attract farmers but high enough to deter speculators. The Dominion Lands Act of 1872 offered 160 acres in the new western prairie territories to heads of families or anyone over twenty-one and promised full legal title after three years' occupancy and evidence of cultivation.[142]

Like the Red River settlers, emigrants on the western prairies made a great effort to survive during their early years in a region that had once belonged to Indians and was still, in many ways, Indian country. The Indians struggled even more. The Natives of Canada, wrote a Scottish minister there in 1867, melted away before the advance of civilization. Fragments of tribes were settled here and there "on portions of land made over to them and their children."[143] The fundamental economic change from traditional common land usage to exclusive private property that had hit Highlanders hard in Scotland was disastrous for Indian and Métis peoples on the prairies of western Canada. Growing population and commerce increased the pressures on the region's resources, game was depleted, and wood lots were cut out. "Such dwindling riches as remained might not now be used except by the owner of a homestead, a railway right of way, a grazing lease, or a timber-cutting license." The prairies were surveyed, fenced in, cut across by railroads, and policed by red-coated Mounties who protected the rights of private owners. Meanwhile, treaties confined Indians to reserves, where they were caught in "an uneasy limbo" between their old common-property system of shared resources and the new private system that was transforming their world.[144] Highland emigrants played a major role in bounding the prairies and reducing the Indians to such a state. Having seen or escaped similar transformations in Scotland, they came to Canada to build new lives and a new country on the lands Indians lost. The Canadian government sponsored Scots migration on to the western prairies in the 1880s and was still sending Gaelic-speaking recruiting agents to the Highlands and islands in the early twentieth century.[145]

The westward-moving Gael had finally found a home in Canada, said the Rev. Masson, where "the land is his own." Nonetheless, transforming the land into a homeland required more than simply occupying it. Lakota author Luther Standing Bear, writing in the 1930s, said that the European was still an alien in America: "Men must be born and reborn to belong. Their bodies must be formed of the dust of their forefathers' bones." Uprooted from the land where his forefathers were buried, the Highland settler had to begin anew the long process of belonging. And so, in Canada, said Masson, "in token of perpetual possession, in his own land he has buried his dead."[146]

9

Empires, Myths, and New Traditions

In 1730 Sir Alexander Cuming made a dramatic appearance in Cherokee country. Acting as unofficial envoy for George II, he stood before Cherokee leaders armed with pistols, a gun, and a sword and demanded their allegiance. Highland trader Ludovic Grant who witnessed the event said it was "pretty Extraordinary" and that Cuming's strange speech did not create "a very favorable impression." Whether the Cherokees were intimidated or thought him mentally unstable and therefore possessing special powers, they nonetheless pursued the option of alliance with Britain. That same year seven Cherokees accompanied Cuming to London.[1] Cuming was from Aberdeenshire and, according to some accounts, he donned full Highland dress on his embassy to the Cherokee towns. If so, his use of Highland—tribal—garb to enlist tribal allies is interesting. Highland symbols would be enlisted regularly in the service of the British Empire.

Although Highlanders and Indians shared some parallel experiences in their dealings with empire, in time those experiences diverged dramatically. Scots not only found a place in the British Empire but also played a large role in running it.[2] The growth of a "British" identity, a common language, and shared political institutions helped Scots unite with English in pursuit of similar economic goals and imperial aspirations. Highland Scots confronted (and sometimes preserved) cultural differences, but most eventually joined the common endeavor.[3] In time, they participated in American empire building, too. Many Native Americans participated in European and American

230

colonization as partners in trade and allies in war, but their identities, languages, cultures, and aspirations, coupled with increasingly racial Euro-American attitudes, kept them forever separate. Indians were excluded from the empire the United States built on their lands, an empire that demanded their dispossession and ultimately their disappearance.

As tribal threats receded, imperial powers constructed myths about tribal peoples. With the people gone and silent, those who took over the land were free to create romantic images about those who had lived there. They distorted tribal histories to fit their own version of the past. Tribal peoples were doomed to defeat and relegated to irrelevance. Their histories were over; their stories absorbed or ignored as the dominant society included or excluded them; and their languages bound to disappear as vestiges of an outdated way of life. Once tribal homelands became romantic wilderness there was no place in them for real Natives, only for abstract and idealized Natives acting out prescribed roles: loyal yet still courageous Highlanders serving the British Empire; Indians fading away into the sunset.[4] Rayna Green argues that for non-Indians to be able to play Indian, "real Indians" must be absent—either physically removed or removed from consciousness.[5] It was true for Highlanders, too: "The emptier the Highlands became the more romantic they appeared."[6]

Edward Said, Homi Bhabha, and others have argued that colonialism requires the *partial* assimilation of colonized groups: Colonized people must adopt the colonizers' ways to demonstrate the supremacy of colonial rule and "civilization," but they cannot be fully assimilated since that would imply they were the equal of the colonizers. So colonialism creates and perpetuates images that keep the colonized separate and unequal.[7] However, images have their own power, and Highlanders and Indians shaped and used them for their own purposes. As Scotland was brought more firmly into the British orbit and Scottish history became subordinated to Britain's, myths about Scotland's past became important components of a separate Scottish identity. Scots found ways to remain Scots, retaining (and sometimes developing) a distinctive Highland identity within a larger "British" allegiance. American Indians likewise found ways to remain Indians within the American nation state.

Empires, Scots, and Indians

After the Act of Union in 1707, Scots became incorporated into a greater Britain and gained access to its overseas empire. Highlanders complained "that no town but Glasgow had advantage of trade by it."[8] However, it marked a new era in Scots participation in the British Empire and a new era in the growth of Scottish nationhood.[9] Scots imperial participation increased again after 1745 and contributed significantly to victories in the Seven Years' War and the Napoleonic wars.

Scots lived on imperial frontiers and fought in imperial conflicts long before they served the British Empire. They had served as governors as well as military commanders in frontier zones in Scandinavia in the seventeenth century; they now assumed similar roles in Britain's empire.[10] As the East India Company emerged as rulers of India, Scots rose through the ranks and were appointed governors of Madras and Bombay. Scots constituted little more than ten percent of Britain's population in the mid-eighteenth century but at least fifty percent of the East India Company employees.[11] They held key posts in governing the empire their soldiers had helped to win, although there was plenty of Scotophobia in England and fears that the clannish Scots were taking over. As many as thirty Scots served as governors and lieutenant governors in the American colonies in the eighteenth century. In 1763 John Stuart, Earl of Bute and first lord of the treasury, appointed a fellow Scot as governor of each of the new provinces Britain acquired at the end of the Seven Years' War: James Murray in Quebec, James Grant in east Florida, George Johnstone in west Florida, and Robert Melville in the islands of Domingo, Grenada, Saint Vincent, and Tobago.

By the nineteenth century Scots seemed to be everywhere in the empire. Building their own networks, they acquired and dispensed the patronage that was key to advancement in the imperial administration.[12] Scottish universities produced more graduates than Scotland could provide professional employment for; Scots dominated the medical, scientific, engineering, and maritime professions, and thousands of Scots went abroad. Anti-Scottish sentiments followed them, but "they knew their bread was buttered on the British side."[13]

By raising clansmen to fight Britain's imperial wars and placing themselves in the imperial bureaucracy, many leading Highland families managed to do what the Campbells had been doing since the seventeenth century: In James Hunter's words, they "merged into the United Kingdom's ruling order" and "got themselves on to history's winning side." Class conflict replaced clan conflicts in the Highlands.[14] Ordinary Highland folk did not take so easily to empire or benefit much from it. Lowland Scots tended to pursue commercial and civilian opportunities; Highlanders favored, or were restricted, to military service.[15] Some Scots invested money in the empire and made it theirs; others invested their sweat and blood. The empire rested on the backs of workers in Lanarkshire collieries and Clydesdale shipyards and depended for its defense on regiments recruited from displaced Highlanders. As they did throughout Britain, the lower classes provided cheap labor and cheap lives.

Historians have often portrayed the experiences of Scots, Welsh, and Irish as parts of a single national endeavor that culminated in the British Empire.[16] Indeed, it has been argued that nineteenth-century Scots abandoned the Scottish past, with its negative associations with feudalism, as a "meaningful history" and adopted instead an Anglo-British interpretation of history.[17] However, despite efforts at the metropolitan center to promote it, there was not a single vision of empire. "British" was not and is not the same as "English." Many eighteenth-century Englishmen resented Scottish influence on "their" empire, and Scots retained a distinctive identity and sometimes a distinctive Highland, regional, and clan identity within a larger "British" allegiance. The ties that bound them to Scotland and to one another in the imperial diaspora "prevented them from wholly assimilating to Anglo-British norms, and fostered that attachment to a homeland that is so characteristic of diasporic peoples," explains David Armitage. At a time when British national identity was still evolving, instead of "succumbing helplessly to an alien identity imposed by others," writes Linda Colley, Scots "helped construct what being British was all about."[18]

In retaining a distinct identity while asserting its allegiance to the crown and its partnership in the imperial project, argues Peter Womack, "the indigenous ruling class" needed to be sure that that identity did not represent a threat to the crown or the imperial partnership. That which might pose a threat, the Highlanders' militarism, was put at the service of the empire. Nonthreatening elements could be celebrated, so Highland romance became a core piece of Scottish identity. "Highlandism" allowed Scots to celebrate their distinctive culture without jeopardizing their political and economic union with England. The Highlands and islands were not assimilated in the same way the Lowlands were, and their continuing peripheral status and imagined community served an important role by "representing Scotland for the English." Scots absorption into a larger British society "left them with all the differentiae of nationality and none of those of statehood."[19]

Highland Scots who emigrated to the United States and Canada made places for themselves in the empires being built there, too. The "contributions-of-notable-Scots" approach implies that neither the United States nor Canada would have become what they are had it not been for Scots and their descendants. That is true for other groups as well, but English and Scottish immigrants adapted to life in nineteenth-century America more easily than did people from other parts of Europe. More than Polish, German, Italian, or Irish immigrants, Scots possessed the educational and technical skills and the social, political, and religious attitudes to take advantage of opportunities denied them at home and to embrace a social order with a confident belief in progress. Highland communities might preserve communal economies, but individual Scottish emigrants who embraced the capitalist values and work ethic of nineteenth-century America often seemed to thrive. "The Scotch," wrote Hector St. Jean de Crèvecoeur in the early 1780s, "are all industrious and saving; they want nothing more than a field to exert themselves in, and they are commonly sure of succeeding." He illustrated the point with the story of Andrew the Hebridean, "a simple Scotchman" who showed what could be achieved in America when "sobriety and industry . . . united with good land and freedom."[20] Scottish success stories in America are commonplace. Traditions of self-help equipped Scots to do well in a nation where individuals helped themselves. "In celebrating their ethnic success Scots were celebrating America. They were constructing and identifying with American nationality. . . . The United States was Scotland realized beyond the seas."[21]

As Matthew Frye Jacobson points out, it was *whiteness* that "opened the Golden Door" to America's opportunities. For non-Anglo-Saxon immigrants, whiteness was something to attain. *White* was a constructed and fluid category that could include and exclude people depending upon their perceived "fitness for government," hard work, thrift, and other characteristics deemed necessary in "free white persons." Like the Irish, Highland Scots had to earn the privileges that came with membership in the white race in America, but they faced fewer obstacles to admission. It was easier for them to become "white."[22] By the late nineteenth century the decline of Gaelic removed another obstacle to the Americanization of Highland Scots who, lamented one Gaelic poet who migrated to Illinois, "like the Gentiles around them/Grow cold-hearted with their wealth."[23]

Scots participated in the conquest and colonization of the trans-Mississippi West as they had in that of the trans-Appalachian West. Scots traders and explorers contributed to mapping the land, a prelude to surveying and bounding it. They reached to the Pacific. Hugo Reid, originally from Cardross (north of the Clyde), came to America as a sailor and jumped ship at Los Angeles in 1832. He married a Gabrielino Indian woman named Victoria and adopted her children, who took his surname and evidently also took to wearing kilts. Reid wrote a series of letters on the Indians of Los Angeles County.[24] More Scots arrived in California during the gold rush, an economic, demographic, and environmental disaster for the Indian inhabitants. Scots also participated in the Black Hills gold rush in the 1870s; one of them, Scotty Philip, who had emigrated from Banffshire to Kansas, married a Sioux woman.[25]

Settlers and soldiers of Scottish birth and parentage pushed into Indian country as the industrializing United States extended its dominion over the West. For
example, Civil War veteran Colonel Ranald Mackenzie—a New Yorker born to
Highland parents—attacked a village of Comanches, Kiowas, and Southern
Cheyennes at the battle of Palo Duro Canyon in 1874, burned four hundred
lodges, and slaughtered a thousand ponies. The attack had much the same effect
as James Grant's campaign against the Cherokees, and starving Indians drifted
in to the reservations. Scots fought in the campaign to take the Black Hills. In
violation of treaty guarantees, the United States first pressured the Sioux to sell
the hills and then pushed them into war. As the British government had done
with recalcitrant Highland clans in 1692, the army issued a wintertime ultimatum
that ordered all Sioux bands on to the reservations by January 31, 1876. It then
launched a three-pronged campaign "to pacify" the "hostiles" who failed or
refused to come in. Lieutenant Donald MacIntosh, a Scots Iroquois from
Canada, and John Stuart Stuart Forbes (a plaque to whose memory can be
found in Saint John's Church, Edinburgh) both died when the Sioux and
Cheyennes annihilated Custer's command at the Little Bighorn that summer.[26]

As Highlanders and their cattle had to make way for sheep to feed the
growing populations of industrial Britain, Indians and buffalo on the Great
Plains made way for ranchers, cattle, and farmers who would feed the industrial workers in eastern cities. Between 1867 and 1883 American hunters sys-
tematically slaughtered the once-vast buffalo herds.[27] Despite exaggerated
claims that traditions of cattle raising (and cattle thieving) spread from the
Scottish borders and Highlands through the Carolinas to Texas, Scots figured prominently in the cattle industry, which replaced the Plains Indian
buffalo economy.[28] Jesse Chisholm, part Scot, part Cherokee, blazed a cattle
trail from Texas to Indian Territory. Scotsmen and Scottish capital, primarily
from the Lowlands, helped build the western cattle-ranching industry, just as
they had the Highland sheep-farming business. Scottish shepherds, Scottish
sheep, and Scottish border collies established themselves on newly emptied
grazing lands in Oregon, Washington, and Wyoming. Archie, Peter, and
John McGregor, whose parents migrated from Mull to Canada in the 1850s,
took up sheep farming and built the successful and long-lasting McGregor
Corporation in Washington State. Scots invested in mining and timber companies and in the railroads that cut across Indian lands, brought more settlers,
and traversed the continent in both Canada and the United States.[29] Like
Highlanders in Scotland and Indians in the East, western Indians were
relocated to make way for a new economic order; they were confined to reservations and in many cases removed to Indian Territory in what became the
state of Oklahoma.

Settling the western prairies of Canada required extinguishing Indian claims, instituting a survey system, and imposing law and order. Governments headed by two Scottish-born prime ministers, John A. Macdonald and Alexander Mackenzie, initiated these policies, and Scots were at the forefront implementing them. Macdonald, Canada's first prime minister, was committed to building a nation that stretched from the Atlantic to the Pacific and linking it with a railroad. That involved bringing order to the vast prairies and keeping the Canadian West out of American hands. In 1873 the North West Mounted Police was formed to do both.

In 1876 James MacLeod, who had migrated from Skye with his family in 1845, became the North West Mounted Police commissioner. MacLeod earned a reputation for honesty and integrity in dealing with Indians. He promised them fair treatment and one law for all of the queen's subjects, developed a relationship of trust with Blackfoot chief Crowfoot, and employed an interpreter the Blackfoot liked, Jerry Potts, son of a Scottish trader and a Piegan woman. In 1877 Sitting Bull and his followers sought refuge from the U.S. cavalry after the Little Bighorn by crossing the "medicine line" into Canada. At a conference between Sitting Bull and American general Alfred Terry, MacLeod acted as mediator. "We like you and the police very much," Sitting Bull told MacLeod, but he did not like or trust Terry. The Sioux refused to return to the United States. However, although MacLeod earned the Indians' trust, he was first and foremost an agent of Canadian expansion, and he made treaties that opened large stretches of Alberta to white settlement.[30]

In the fall of 1877, MacLeod and David Laird, lieutenant-governor of the North West Territories, negotiated Treaty Number 7 with the Blackfoot confederacy—the Siksika or northern Blackfoot, the Bloods, and the Piegans, along with the Sarcees and Stonies (Rev. John McDougall, a Weslyan missionary, acted as interpreter for the Stonies). Laird said MacLeod was "indefatigable in his exertions to bring the negotiations to a successful conclusion." Although they suspected the Mounted Police had come to their country to protect white people from Indians rather than to protect Indians from whiskey peddlers, the Blackfoot regarded MacLeod as "their great benefactor." They called him Staximotokan. Red Crow, head chief of the southern Bloods, said that since MacLeod and the police first came to their country he had made many promises and kept them all. "I entirely trust Staximotokan, and will leave everything to him. I will sign with Crowfoot," said Red Crow. One by one, the assembled chiefs followed Crowfoot's lead and gave their agreement. The treaty assigned the Blackfoot to reserves and took from them fifty thousand square miles between the Cypress Hills and the Rockies.[31]

Lieutenant governor Alexander Morris of Manitoba and the North West Territories was born in Perth, Upper Canada, and educated in Canada and Scotland. He was the principal commissioner in negotiating five Indian treaties; in the three treaties that covered "virtually all of what became the settled areas of Alberta and Saskatchewan," all of the commissioners were Scots. Scottish capital fueled land development, as well as the building of the Canadian Northern transcontinental railroad, an enterprise of William Mackenzie and Donald Mann, which opened up additional land to settlement.[32]

In Canada, "the Gael everywhere takes his place in the first rank of professions and of public life," Rev. D. Masson observed in the 1870s.[33] At home, Highlanders might still be regarded as "an inferior race"; abroad, serving the British Empire and building empires in North America at a time when the United States was developing an increasingly biracial society, they shed the "nonwhite" status men like James Oglethorpe and Patrick Sellar had assigned them.[34]

* * *

The kind of empire that American Indians confronted was different from the type that Highland Scots had fought against and helped to build, and they had very dissimilar experiences in the nineteenth-century West. After winning independence from the British Empire, Americans turned westward and proceeded to build an empire of their own on Indian lands.[35] Instead of struggling to hold expansive forces in check as the British had done, the United States involved—and sometimes followed—its citizens in the process of empire building. Americans enjoyed the fruits of empire in a way few peoples had been able to under older imperial systems. It was, in Jefferson's words, "an empire of liberty." But because it was an empire that excluded rather than incorporated people, not everyone could participate. The British Empire, as Anthony Wallace observes, was hierarchical and authoritarian but "ethnically inclusive." The Jeffersonian state was "egalitarian, democratic, and ethnically exclusive." Linda Colley agrees. Empire, "so often assumed to be necessarily racist in operation and ethos, could sometimes be conspicuously poly-ethnic in quality and policy, because it had to be." The United States offered unprecedented egalitarianism and opportunity but was also "firmly exclusionist and aggressively expansionist." Ideally, citizenship was reserved to "free white persons."[36]

Highlanders, once coupled with Indians as nonwhites, now qualified as free white persons. African Americans were regarded as forever excluded. Indians were eligible for inclusion if they gave up the things that made them

Indian and adopted white American ways of living and thinking. The first step in that process was to relinquish most of their land and live as farmers on their remaining plots. In Jefferson's vision of the future, Indians who adopted civilized ways of living might take their place as citizens of the new republic, but as the Cherokees and other "civilized tribes" found out, a republic that wanted their land required their absence, not their presence. The empire of liberty that America was building ultimately had no place for Indians.

As the empire pushed beyond the Mississippi, the western tribes, like tribal peoples in the East and in the Highlands, succumbed to superior power, internal divisions, divide-and-rule strategies, and the destruction of their food supplies. For some western tribes as for some western clans, the expansion of the nation-state offered opportunities to acquire new allies and strike back at old enemies. The migration of the powerful Lakota Sioux in the late eighteenth and early nineteenth centuries sent ripple effects across the northern and central plains. Crows, Arikaras, Omahas, Pawnees, Shoshones, and others who bore the brunt of Sioux expansion aligned themselves with the Lakotas' new American enemies.[37] But whether they fought for or against the United States, Indians had to cope with a new order imposed from outside.

The campaign to change them and their world accelerated throughout the nineteenth century. With their food supply gone, Indians faced a choice between starvation and the reservation. As in the Highlands, some leaders opted for accommodation and attempted to control the pace of change. Red Cloud and Spotted Tail of the Sioux, Washakie of the Shoshones, Plenty Coups of the Crow, Ouray of the Utes, and others realized that survival required dealing with the reality of American power and presence. They tried to cooperate with the government in the hope of retaining some of their tribal homelands or sometimes just to secure food, clothing, and shelter for their people. Men whose traditional roles as warriors and hunters had been taken away occasionally joined the Indian police as a way to attain status and help their people through hard times.

The adversity lasted a long time. Once-prosperous tribes were reduced to poverty and rendered dependent on government assistance. Once free and mobile, they were confined to arid reservations, where they endured poor health and diet, high mortality rates, and low life expectancy. Reservations were supposed to be crucibles of change, where government agents, teachers, and farmers instructed Indians in the arts of civilization and prepared them to take their place in American society. When Indians did not embrace the new ways, it seemed instead that reservations were functioning as bastions of traditional life and communal landholding that hindered the march of progress. Reformers, like those who sought to improve Highlanders or remove Cherokees, grew impatient. Indians would have to be pushed into mainstream culture and forced to become hard-working Americans motivated by the acquisition of private property.

In 1887 Congress passed the Dawes Allotment Act. Reservations were to be surveyed and divided into 160-acre sections that would be allotted to individual families. "Surplus lands" would be offered for sale to non-Indians. Allotment would terminate communal ownership and, its supporters believed, liberate Indians from the stifling hold of tribe and community. "There is no selfishness, which is at the bottom of civilization," said Senator Henry Dawes of Massachusetts, who introduced the legislation. Citizenship and allotment, said Commissioner Thomas A. Morgan, "necessarily looks toward the entire destruction of the tribal relation; the Indians are to be looked upon as individuals and not en masse; they are to stand on their own personal rights and be freed absolutely from the trammels of the tribe and the limitations of chieftaincy." Theodore Roosevelt praised allotment as "a vast pulverizing engine to break up the tribal mass."[38]

In many cases Indians maintained old tribal connections and social bonds even as they adjusted to the new system. In some cases they continued to use the land as families and communities rather than as individual property owners.[39] Nevertheless, designed purportedly to lift Indians from backwardness and dependency, allotment stripped Indian tribes of two-thirds of their remaining lands and brought increased poverty and suffering. Sounding like a critic of crofting allotments in the Highlands, Commissioner of Indian Affairs John Collier in 1934 acknowledged that allotment "merely deprived vast numbers of them of their land, turned them into paupers, and imposed an ever-growing relief problem on the Government."[40]

While the government sustained a systematic assault on reservation lands and cultures, Indian children were shipped off to schools where they were subjected to military-style discipline and a rigid regimen and stripped of their Native clothing, hairstyles, and languages. Boarding schools—and the punishments they inflicted on students caught speaking their Native tongue—sent many tribal languages into decline. The schools taught an Anglo-American curriculum that ignored or dismissed Native American history and culture and offered instruction in reading, writing, and math. Boys received training in mechanical arts, girls in domestic service; they were being educated to occupy the lower echelons of American economy and society. By the early twentieth century, reformers had developed increasingly pessimistic views of Indians' abilities and more limited objectives for themselves: Indians would be incorporated, but they could never become fully "civilized" citizens. As far as the reformers were concerned, the campaign to assimilate the Indians was over.[41]

Many reformers on the other side of the Atlantic thought their work was complete, too. After all, the Crofters Act of 1886 provided some security of land tenure. But in the western Highlands as in western America, people who once shared homelands were confined on tiny plots of land. Those who were removed from their homes and families and deprived of their language and cultural groundings struggled to make their way in a society that now regarded them as left behind.

Imperial Myths, Imagined Peoples, and Imagined Lands

Although Highland Scots and American Indians had divergent backgrounds within the British and American empires, they shared experiences as subjects for imperial myth making. Nations with an imperial past need to explain themselves and make palatable the experiences of the peoples they colonized. Even as Britain and the United States worked to destroy tribal ways of life, they created romantic images of the people and distorted their history. Images of Highland Scots and American Indians were constructed and transformed to suit changing needs and tastes; historical experiences were reconstructed and reremembered. When British and American colonizers and beneficiaries of colonialism looked again at the peoples, cultures, and environments they had assaulted, altered, or destroyed, they viewed them with a kind of "imperialist nostalgia." Mourning "the passing of what they themselves ha[d] transformed," they incorporated them into an imagined past.[42] The presence of Highland Scots in a triumphant British Empire convinced imperialists of the essential rightness of a project that united all Britons. Highland culture, once a marker of savagery and Jacobitism, was reinvented and made fashionable and gradually came to represent Scotland as a whole, and Scotland's history of resisting British dominion now became a noble tradition. The presence of American Indians in the American empire proved more troublesome. Images of stereotypical Indian warriors conveyed memories of a heroic foe, defeated by a great nation, but more often they were relegated to an imagined past that took them out of the nation's history.

Romantic poets and painters recoiled from the ugly and soulless urban and industrial landscape they saw and lamented the world that was being lost. Jean Jacques Rousseau and other writers depicted American Indians and other tribal peoples before contact as living unspoiled lives close to nature and free from the corruptions and vices of eighteenth-century European society. "All that was tribal and primeval—whether it was to be found among eighteenth-century North America's native peoples or among Europe's own much earlier inhabitants—was thus in vogue, by the 1760s, as it had never been before." In Scotland James Macpherson, who claimed to have found and translated the Gaelic poems of Ossian, invoked an older, purer, and more heroic past. Macpherson romanticized ancient Highlanders by portraying them like contemporary American Indians, as representatives of a shared tribal life. In the process he helped create what James Hunter calls "the slightly bizarre self-image which the country has kept polished ever since."[43]

According to English historian Hugh Trevor-Roper, "the whole concept of a distinct Highland culture and tradition is a retrospective invention." Before the mid-seventeenth century, the Highlanders of Scotland were not even a distinct people; they were "simply the overflow of Ireland," and their Gaelic language and culture were essentially Irish. "Being a cultural dependency of Ireland under the 'foreign,' and somewhat ineffective, rule of the Scottish crown, the Highlands and Islands of Scotland were culturally depressed." Not until the eighteenth century did an independent Highland tradition emerge, and in the nineteenth century it was foisted on the whole of Scotland as its national tradition. Before 1745 Highlanders were seen as a barbaric threat; after 1746, as their society crumbled, said Trevor-Roper, "they combined the romance of a primitive people with the charm of an endangered species."[44] Hugh Trevor-Roper was arguably one of Britain's "great" historians, but he was not gifted with cultural sensibilities to balance his Anglo-centrism (he once dismissed the history of Africa and other regions before European colonization as "the unrewarding gyrations of barbarous tribes in picturesque but irrelevant corners of the globe"[45]). Nevertheless, he raised important questions about the links between cultural survival and cultural change.

Kilts and tartans offer a case in point. In the 1720s Edmund Burt saw "quelts," but the kilt in its modern form seems to have developed in the middle of the eighteenth century. An English Quaker, Thomas Rawlinson, adapted the plaid to make it more convenient for the Highland workers in his iron furnace near Inverness. Rawlinson's tailor separated the skirt from the plaid and made it a distinct garment, the philibeg, or "small kilt." The kilt is thus, according to Trevor-Roper, "a purely modern costume" designed by an English industrialist who gave it to Highlanders "not to preserve their traditional way of life but to ease its transformation: to bring them out of the heather and into the factory."[46] Rawlinson no doubt encouraged its use, but Scots have taken pleasure in finding earlier images and descriptions of the philibeg that refute Trevor-Roper's assertions.

Today tartans are badges of clan identity, but this was not always the case.[47] The plaids Burt described were "of chequered Tartan," but the colors were muted hues, and the various patterns were regional, produced by local weavers, rather than clan designations. There were no specific clan tartans at the time of the '45, but tartan underwent a transformation in the second half of the eighteenth century. After Culloden, Parliament outlawed "Highland costume," and people were arrested for wearing it.[48] Visitors saw Highlanders wearing kilts in defiance of the law, although generally "their attire is such as produces, in a sufficient degree, the effect intended by the law, of abolishing the dissimilitude of appearance between the highlanders and the other inhabitants of Britain."[49] However, kilted Highland regiments earned glory, and the ban on tartan was lifted in 1782. Tartan kilts became fashionable attire among clan chiefs, regimental officers, "Anglicized Scottish peers, improving gentry, well-educated Edinburgh lawyers and prudent merchants of Aberdeen." The Prince of Wales (later George IV) and his brothers were given complete sets of Highland dress in 1789, coincidentally the year Charles Stuart died in Rome.[50]

Once the political and military threat of the Jacobite rebellions had been removed, the "wildness" of the Highlanders' language, culture, and clan system exerted a strange attraction on people who had formerly despised them.[51] Clan gentry and others resident in the capitals formed Highland societies in Edinburgh (1784) and London (1788), whose purpose was to preserve the dress, music, language, poetry, and "martial spirit" of the Highlands, as well as improve conditions by promoting agricultural and other reforms.[52] They held forth about preserving Highland traditions and the Gaelic language while the inhabitants were being ousted from their homelands.[53]

By the end of the eighteenth century Scotland was becoming known as North Britain, a region of a greater England, not a distinct nation. Scottish identity was being subordinated to an emerging British identity and nationhood.[54] Then a lawyer who found the practice of law "sheer drudgery" began to find escape in writing poetry and prose that not only reinvented Scotland but made it immensely popular. Sir Walter Scott took a brutal past of religious strife and civil conflict and turned it into historical romance and best sellers. Robert Clyde describes Scott as "a Tory and a social climber [who] believed that everything good and distinctive about Gaeldom was embodied in the chiefs and clan gentry. The fact that they might be Eton educated and permanently resident in London was immaterial to him."[55] A prolific writer, Scott, in historical novels like *Waverley* (1814) and *Rob Roy* (1818), rehabilitated the Highlander as a chivalric and romantic figure, albeit, tragically, one doomed to disappear as surely as Patrick Sellar's "aborigines" or Thomas Jefferson's Indians.[56] Scott's version of Scotland's history and culture was one that never existed, but it caught on and became a national obsession.

Colonel Alasdair Ranaldson Macdonnell of Glengarry seemed to fit Scott's mold. A combative and controversial figure, he posed as a traditional Highland chief; some called him "the last of the chiefs." In 1815 he formed the Society of True Highlanders at Inverlochy near Fort William. At the same time, he embraced the new system of estate management that eradicated the old way of life he celebrated and promoted. He raised rents, cleared his glens to make room for sheep, and sold land and timber to the Caledonian Canal.[57] Colonel David Stewart of Garth did much to create the image of Highland Scots as loyal soldiers of empire. An army officer on half pay after the end of the Napoleonic wars, he devoted his time to studying Highland regiments and traditions. In 1820 he founded the Celtic Society of Edinburgh "to promote the general use of the ancient Highland dress in the Highlands," and in 1822 he published *Sketches of the Character, Manners, and Present State of the Highlanders of Scotland,* which presented kilts and clan-distinct tartans as part of that ancient dress, celebrated the virtues of ancient Highland society, and denounced agricultural improvements and clearances. Yet Stewart supported his Perthshire estate with income from inherited slave plantations in the West Indies. When that failed to suffice, he was compelled to raise rents and persuade his tenants to emigrate.[58]

The president of the Celtic Society of Edinburgh was Sir Walter Scott. So influential did Scott become that he was able to arrange a royal visit to Scotland in 1822—quite an achievement, for no English monarch had been north of the border in two hundred years. Scott stage-managed the whole affair and summoned the clans to Edinburgh to receive His Majesty George IV. They were to line the Royal Mile between Edinburgh Castle and Holyrood Palace, and, as Scott instructed them in the program he wrote for the event (and sold for a shilling), gentlemen were not permitted to wear anything but "the ancient Highland costume." Scott's assistant in matters of ceremony and dress was David Stewart of Garth.[59]

Scott and Garth prescribed tartans for each clan. Weavers, brought in for the event, worked day and night to turn out the new tartans, and clan chiefs scurried around Edinburgh, trying, like modern-day American tourists, to find their "official" tartan. Fat and sixty, the king pulled on a pair of flesh-colored tights and staggered down the Royal Mile in procession wearing the regalia of a Highland chieftain between ranks of Scotsmen wearing "clan tartans" they had never seen before.[60] George IV's visit made the new Highland regalia fashionable and made kilts Scotland's national dress. Macdonnell of Glengarry was there. So too were many non-Highlanders, eager to attend. Men who had never dreamed of wearing tartan or kilt now donned both for Scott's orchestrated display of Scottish heritage and loyalty to the Hanoverian regime. George IV was evidently impressed: Several years later he assumed Highland dress again for his official portrait (artist David Wilkie said it took three hours to get him trussed up and to accommodate all of the bulges and that His Majesty resembled nothing so much as an over-stuffed sausage).[61]

Once outlawed as a symbol of treason, Highland dress became a symbol of Scottish military prowess and Scottish identity. In the late nineteenth century the British military required all Scottish regiments, whether Highland or Lowland, to wear tartan. In 1843 James Logan, an Aberdonian living in London and president of the Highland Society, published *Clans of the Scottish Highlands,* illustrated with seventy-two paintings by R. R. MacIan. Prints of MacIan's clansmen in their distinctive, "ancient" tartans sell everywhere in Scotland.[62] "Having first been an ethnic peculiarity, then a proscribed symbol, and then a military uniform," Highland kilts and tartan became at last, in Peter Womack's words, "a form of fancy dress."[63]

Highland "culture" had arrived and it was here to stay. It came to represent Scotland as a whole both to the rest of the world and to Scotland itself. The tartan industry was born. The displays of tartan on sale in Edinburgh, Inverness, and even in Heathrow Airport, as well as most everything else that sells Scotland, are largely attributable to the imagination of a nineteenth-century attorney with a romantic view of the past and a gift for churning out historical novels. The monolithic Scottish culture he foisted on the world said that Scotland was Highlanders, chivalry, and romance. "This development," argues Robert Clyde, "would not have been possible without the conscious co-operation of the chiefs and clan gentry eager to deflect criticism of their treatment of their erstwhile clans."[64]

Scottish history—a bloody and troubled past pockmarked by clan feuds, murder, and treachery—became a romantic pageant. Stuart kings and pretenders came to represent a Scottish past that had been lost and to personify "Scottish" values. Scotland became reimagined as a Celtic nation, unified by a long history of resistance to England. The 1745 Jacobite rebellion, a brutal little war with reluctant Highlanders pressed into service by clan chiefs on both sides, became a rallying of loyal clansmen to the banner of Bonnie Prince Charlie in a war to preserve the Highland way of life, which it never was.[65] Gaelic songs of the '45 lack the sentimentality, romanticism, and defeatism that became common in English-language songs of the uprising. Lady Caroline Nairne, whose ancestors fought for the Jacobites, became, in John Prebble's words, a "sweet songstress of the lost cause." Drawing on bits of traditional verse and mixing romantic longings and family history, she wrote Jacobite songs "so beguiling that many take them for the true voices of men and women long dead before she was born."[66] Fighting for a lost cause became a prelude to fighting for the imperial cause. Soldiers in Highland regiments enjoyed improved status, even as increasing numbers of recruits came from the urbanizing Lowlands rather than the depleted Highlands.[67]

Highland games, clubs, and societies proliferated as formal expressions of Scottish heritage and identity. The first Highland games took place at Saint Fillans on Loch Earn in 1819. The Braemar Highland Society also staged one of the first (and subsequently the most famous) Highland gatherings with contests to preserve the music, dress, and games of the Highlands. Queen Victoria regularly attended the Braemar games and "indulged her taste for romantic Highland fantasy" at Balmoral, which she bought in 1842. English society, in John Prebble's words, went "à l'Ecosse" until her death in 1901.[68]

Highland societies that sought to "rescue" the "traditions" of the Gaels often made themselves "authorities" on what was or was not "authentic." They controlled bagpipe competitions, introduced standardized settings, and tried make pipe music conform to "a set of cultural expectations which were largely mistaken."[69] *Comunn an Fheilidh* [the Kilt Society], founded in Inverness around 1902 and dedicated to encouraging and perpetuating the wearing of Highland dress, provided information on how it should be worn and thereby helped to confirm "a created history of tartan."[70]

The new imagery ignored and obscured urban Scotland, industrial Scotland, lowland Scotland, universities, medicine, coal mines, textile mills, and slums. Perhaps it offered escape from the harsh new industrial world by sentimentalizing the rural world that had been lost. Meanwhile, a way of life was unraveling in the Highlands and islands.

* * *

Like the people who lived there, the Scottish Highlands and the American West were reimagined as they had never been. In the Highlands, notes Simon Schaama, the English found mountain ranges that "invited subjugation, survey, and appreciation, very much in that order." Paul Sandby was sent to Scotland in 1747 as part of an official survey of the country. He sketched as he surveyed. In his drawings, rugged Highland terrain appeared rather gentle, even English, in character: "His vision reflects the obedient topography of pacification." But changing tastes soon permitted and expected more dramatic and picturesque depictions of Highland scenery, and Sandby obliged. In his pen drawing of Strathtay in 1747 the mountains are gently sloping hills; in his engraving of the same scene in 1780, the mountains are towering peaks under a threatening sky. Sandby increased their altitude, ruggedness, and for-estation, refashioning the landscape to match the expectations of the time.[71] Dorothy and William Wordsworth and Samuel Taylor Coleridge toured the Highlands in 1803, looking for romantic scenes, and found them in the beauty and bareness of the landscape. Loch Lomond presented "an outlandish scene—we might have believed ourselves in North America," wrote Dorothy. On the way to Glencoe their boatman's calling to a group of tinkers in Gaelic seemed "a savage cry to our ears, in that lonely and romantic place." Sir Walter Scott's poem "The Lady of the Lake" (1810) turned Loch Katrine and the Trossachs into tourist attractions. Eighteenth-century visitors had seen the landscape as desolate; nineteenth-century visitors went looking for romance and fulfillment.[72]

The barren landscapes romanticized in imagery were also being created in reality. The "romance" of the Highland landscape is in the eye of the beholder from outside, argues Peter Womack: "The historical encounter which is encoded in scenic awe is ultimately a colonial one." As the Highlands were emptied of people, the introduction of potatoes, commercial exploitation of forestland, and proliferation of sheep grazing altered the environment and reinforced the notion of the glens as bleak and empty wasteland. The romance and solitude of the Highlands depended on associations with a dead or dying culture and a people who had gone elsewhere. The mythologizing of emptiness was apparent as early as 1803, in William Wordsworth's "The Solitary Reaper," in which a Highland lass "sings a melancholy strain," distantly in a language the poet could not understand, the tune lingering in his heart. The Highland text in the poem was eloquent and evocative, says Womack, "precisely because it had been erased."[73]

The myth of emptiness became lethal. Like Indian country in the wake of epidemics, the Highlands were characterized as unpopulated, not depopu-lated, always empty, not recently emptied. In a passage that could have been written about American attitudes toward Indians in the nineteenth century, Womack explains how the myth of aboriginal emptiness justified leading Highlanders out of their unchanging past:

Within the myth . . . the Highlands are devoid of indigenous conflict or innovation: the land has no history but exhibits the aspect it wore at creation; the people, wise but not intelligent, don't reflect on their situation but merely remain true to the traditions of their ancestors. Highlanders are either children who *must,* or non-rational creatures who *cannot,* follow the developmental path of the rest of the nation.[74]

Like Indians, the imagined Highlander of the past was a spiritual being who had inhabited a romantic landscape and lived close to nature at a more primitive stage.[75]

As the Highlands were being evacuated, they were also being made more accessible to outsiders. After the 1860s, as imports from Australia and elsewhere drove down wool and mutton prices, large tracts of the Highlands were converted to deer forests and, farther south and east in Perthshire and Aberdeenshire, grouse moors for hunting. In T. C. Smout's words, "a landscape of use" changed to "a landscape of delight, kept empty of people." Maintaining game populations and having them "available on demand for the few weeks in the year when the Victorian and Edwardian gentlemen took time to shoot them" required extensive land management and ruthless control of predators, which resulted in plummeting wildlife populations.[76] Tourists and sportsmen came to see the grand wilderness scenery to hunt or to enjoy temporary escape from their own worlds, which were becoming increasingly urban and industrial. Seagoing paddle steamers from the Clyde brought visitors to the west coast and the Inner Hebrides. Cook's travel company began tours of the Highlands using steamers and railways in 1846, ironically the year the potato famine hit.[77] The Highlands gradually became "a playground for the rich." Millionaires and industrial magnates bought estates and sojourned there for pleasure. Lowland Scot–turned–American steel baron Andrew Carnegie bought Cluny and Skibo castles in Sutherland, where he claimed to be "home at last." In the twentieth century the Highlands became "a sort of national Park for the nation at large."[78]

However, the Highland wilderness celebrated by modern conservationists and enjoyed by fresh-air tourists is not as natural as they assume; it is in reality the result of nineteenth-century landlords and sheep having stripped it of its people and vegetation.[79] "Yes," says a character in John McGrath's play *The Cheviot, the Stag, and the Black, Black Oil,* "the tragedy of the Highlands has become a saleable commodity."[80]

Sir Walter Scott has much to answer for.

* * *

As Scott lay dying on the banks of the Tweed in 1832, similar developments were taking place in the United States. Scott had helped create a Scottish national literature by writing about landscape, history, traditions, and legends. "The message for America was obvious," notes Andrew Hook. James Fenimore Cooper led the way in producing a distinctly American romantic literature that dealt with American history, land, legend, and, of course,

Indians. Cooper was apparently chagrined to be nicknamed "the American Scott," but, says Hook, "the Scottishness of Scott has much in common with the Americanness of Cooper." Like Scott, Cooper depicted the clash of old and new ways of life, primitivism versus civilization, natives and newcomers. "The Highland line becomes Cooper's frontier." What Scott did with Highland Scots, Cooper did with American Indians by portraying noble savages who embodied heroic traditions that were fading away before the relentless advance of a modern civilization. Even in "his handling of the language of the Native American and particularly in the exalted rhetorical eloquence attributed to the chieftains, Cooper was once again deeply indebted to the example of Scot," Hook notes: "Scottish Highlander and American chief often declaim in a remarkably similar sonorous style."[81] James Hunter sees Ossian as Cooper's inspiration: "Not only do Cooper's Indians talk like Ossianic Highlanders. They similarly invest landscape . . . with a tragic, but nevertheless romantic, ambience which stems ultimately from their own extinction."[82] Macpherson had drawn on images of Indians to create the Celtic heroes of Ossian in the first place; "a cumulative cycle of literary import/export" existed in which "ancient Celts and contemporary Native Americans were imagined in terms of each other over and over again."[83]

Cooper's *Last of the Mohicans* (1826) established Indians as a tragic race, inevitably disappearing before the relentless tide of European contact: "The palefaces are masters of the earth," pronounces Tamenund as Hawkeye and Chingachgook bow their heads together and shed "scalding tears" over the fallen Uncas. "My day has been too long. In the morning I saw the sons of Unamis happy and strong; and yet, before the night has come, have I lived to see the last warrior of the wise race of the Mohicans."[84] Like Jacobite clan chiefs, once Indian chiefs ceased to be enemies, they became tragic heroes.[85]

The stereotype of the disappearing Indian had some disastrous consequences for Indian people, especially in some areas of the East where they were written out of history.[86] Eighteenth- and nineteenth-century writers portrayed Indians as fading from sight as they were edged off their lands, "doomed to recede and disappear," said Hector St. Jean de Crèvecoeur. Most Americans seem to have shared the assumption.[87] Nowhere did Indian extinction seem more assured than in New England. John Adams recalled Indian friends and neighbors from his boyhood, "but the Girls went out to Service and the Boys to Sea, till not a Soul is left," he wrote in 1812. "We scarcely see an Indian in a year."[88] Jedediah Morse in his *Report on Indian Affairs* submitted to the Secretary of War in 1822 portrayed the Indian communities in New England as a "few feeble remnants" teetering on the brink of extinction.[89] A decade later Alexis de Tocqueville concluded that the tribes

ASSEOLA.
A SEMINOLE LEADER.

PUBLISHED BY DANIEL RICE & JAMES G. CLARK, PHILAD.

Fig 9.1. In the pose of warrior chiefs: *Asseola, a Seminole Leader,* from *History of the Indian Tribes of North America,* ca. 1842. Copy after Charles Bird King. A leader of Seminole resistance to removal, Osceola was captured under a flag of truce and died in an American prison. (Smithsonian American Art Museum, Washington, D.C./Art Resource, New York.)

who had once inhabited New England now lived "only in men's memories."[90] Wordsworth's solitary reaper could have been an Algonquian woman on a New England hillside.

As New England went into economic decline, the region adopted the image of white buildings surrounding village greens as a romantic symbol of community. Like Scott's vision of Highland glens inhabited by loyal clansmen, it was a nineteenth-century invention of an imagined past.[91] It bore little resemblance to mill towns on the Connecticut and Merrimack rivers. Moreover, it ignored the continuing presence of Indian communities in New England and that of Indian people in New England communities.

Like their non-Indian neighbors, many Indian people changed their ways of living and working in areas that were becoming increasingly industrial and urban. Many young women left home to find work in textile mills in Lowell and Worcester, Massachusetts, or in Manchester, New Hampshire. Many men moved to Boston or New York City. A mobile Indian labor force developed as people shifted from job to job, city to city, and home community to urban slum.[92] Others preferred occupations that more closely resembled traditional patterns of life, work, and movement. Men found employment as seasonal laborers, loggers, trappers, and guides. Women wove baskets, peddled them door-to-door in white settlements, and sold them to Victorian-era tourists at summer resorts, as Seneca women sold beaded Glengarry bonnets at Niagara Falls.[93] Indian people who experienced poverty and dislocation in the new economic climate sometimes found themselves persecuted as paupers and "delinquents." Indians who maintained more traditional lifestyles sometimes found themselves harassed as "vagrants" and "transients."

The disappearance of New England Indians was confirmed in the eye of the beholder because they did not look like Indians were supposed to look. As the Highlander represented all Scots, the Plains Indian came to represent all Indians. George Catlin's paintings in the 1830s suggested that the surviving Indians were Plains Indians. However, the idea that real Indians were dead or dying applied in the West, as well as the East. Artists like Carl Wimar and John Mix Stanley depicted their Indian subjects against heavy sunsets, clearly people on the way out.

But they never quite left. It has been argued that narratives of nation building and empire need reminders of defeated peoples to sustain them. As the American nation grew, American Indians were removed from their lands and excluded from the nation; instead, Renée Bergland and Philip J. Deloria argue, they were placed within the American imagination as ghosts. They haunted the national narrative and shared in the national story as historical curiosities.[94]

Figure 9.2. In the pose of warrior chiefs: Colonel Alasdair Macdonnell of Glengarry, by Sir Henry Raeburn. Even as he raised rents, relocated his people, and embraced the technology of the industrial revolution, Macdonell posed and paraded in the regalia of a Highland chief and cultivated a reputation as the "last of the chiefs." (National Gallery of Scotland, NU420.)

While the Highlands of Scotland were being romanticized in art and literature and turned into an aristocrats' sport-hunting preserve, similar things
were happening in the American West. George Catlin, Karl Bodmer, Alfred
Jacob Miller, Alfred Bierstadt, and others depicted Western scenery, as well
as Western Indians, in a heavily romantic vein. As did Paul Sandby in
Scotland, in the 1830s Swiss artist Karl Bodmer increased the elevation of
mountains and rendered geographical features on the upper Missouri more
dramatic to suit contemporary romantic tastes. Miller, who read and admired
Scott's novels, depicted his patron, Scotsman Sir William Drummond
Stewart, as a wandering knight errant in the Rocky Mountain West.

Stewart, whose ancestral home was Murthly Castle in Perthshire, traveled
the West in the 1830s and again in 1843, hunting, joining fur-trade rendezvous
in the shadows of the Rockies, and sleeping with Indian women, yet maintaining the trappings of a Scottish gentleman with his own cook and ample supplies of wine and brandy. When he returned to Scotland in 1839, he took home
Indian artifacts, specimens of western wildlife, and bison for a "buffalo park" at
Murthly Castle. He had the buffalo and other specimens of western fauna and
flora transported across the Plains, floated down the Mississippi to New
Orleans, and shipped to Liverpool by boat and then by train to Perth. He also
brought home his Cree French hunter, Clement, and two Indians as "gamekeepers." Not much is known of the Indians' experiences, although one story
has Clement and his two companions hitching a pair of buffalo to a makeshift
cart and driving drunk through the streets of Dunkeld one evening. Stewart
shipped a collection of Miller's paintings and sketches, and the artist himself
lived and worked at Murthly Castle for two years, where he painted ten more
oil-on-canvas works, including his famous paintings *Attack by Crows* (1840) and
The Trapper's Bride (1841). It has been suggested that Stewart, drawing on long-
standing beliefs in the similarities between Highland and Indian ways of life,
collected western and Indian artifacts as a way to reaffirm the values of tribal
life and reinvigorate his Scottish identity at a time of growing nostalgia for a
Highland way life that was fast disappearing. Like other European aristocrats
who traveled to Indian country in the first half of the nineteenth century, he
felt a kinship with American Indians and saw a "peculiar affinity between the
destiny of warrior elites from two worlds."[95]

Like Stewart, the Earl of Southesk dressed in buckskins but traveled in
style when he visited western Canada in 1859, accompanied by a retinue that
included an Iroquois cook and a gamekeeper from his Angus estate. Like
Stewart, he took home Indian artifacts and clothing. (The collection lay in a
trunk in the attic in Kinnaird Castle near Brechin for almost 150 years before
most of it "returned home" to the Royal Alberta Museum.[96])

Figure 9.3. Alfred Jacob Miller, *The Rendezvous near Green River . . . Final Destination of the American Fur Company Caravan,* shows William Drummond Stewart accepting a pipe at the annual summer fur-trade gathering at Green River in present-day Wyoming. (Library and Archives Canada, acc. no. 1946–146–1; gift of Mrs. J. B. Jardine; C-000439.)

Well-to-do sportsmen from the East and from Europe continued to stage extravagant hunting trips that contributed to the slaughter of animal life in the West. The dramatic scenery and empty landscapes of the West came to represent America as much as the Highlands represented Scotland. Artistic representations of the West as a vast wilderness and a land of romance served the ideological and political purposes of an expanding nation and helped create a national identity.[97]

By the turn of the century Buffalo Bill Cody's Wild West shows had fixed the Plains Indian stereotype, and Hollywood confirmed it. Feather headdresses and buckskins became the things most non-Indians identified as distinctively "Indian." The Wild West show brought Sioux Indians to Scotland as it did to other parts of the world. Most of Cody's performers were Lakotas who were escaping poverty and oppression on the reservations. The end of the nineteenth century was a dark era for Native Americans: invisible in the East, confined in the West, and everywhere predicted to be on the brink of extinction. Government boarding schools took their children, allotment took more of their lands, and assimilationist policies sought to take away their cultures. In 1890 the U.S. Census Bureau declared that the American frontier no longer existed. In December 1890, after the Ghost Dance religion spread to Sioux country and as if to emphasize the end of an era, Indian police assassinated Sitting Bull in his home, and the Seventh Cavalry slaughtered more than two hundred Lakota men, women, and children in the snow at Wounded Knee. The next year some Lakota Ghost Dancers recently released from prison, notably Kicking Bear and Short Bull, joined Cody's show for its second tour of Britain. In Glasgow, the troupe's interpreter, George C. Crager, sold a collection of Indian items, including a ghost shirt, to Glasgow's Kelvingrove Museum. (In 1995 and 1998 Lakota representatives visited Glasgow to request the shirt be returned. In 1999, at a ceremony held at the site of the massacre, with bagpipes playing, Glasgow city delegates returned the ghost shirt to the Sioux.[98])

As in Britain, so in America the image of tribal peoples changed after they ceased to be perceived as a threat. As had happened in the East, the stereotype of the savage warrior gave way to that of the disappearing red man. In the paintings of Catlin and Bierstadt and the photographs of Edward Curtis, Western Indians moved from the realm of history "to natural history and ethnography, and finally to extinction and elegy."[99] Curtis purported to capture images of Indians as they faded into history, but he catered to a national need by dissolving the threat of savagery and portraying the "vanishing race" in ways that were "beautiful and reassuring." He claimed to record the real thing, but in many cases he fabricated what he photographed by stage-managing his shots and dressing his subjects in "traditional costume," just as Sir Walter Scott had bedecked his Highlanders. In Alan Tracthenberg's words, "the shadows this great 'shadow catcher' caught were of his own culture's construction of itself."[100] In an age when most Indian people were rendered silent, the selected oratory of some (like Chief Joseph's famous surrender speech, "From where the sun now stands, I will fight no more forever,") satisfied American needs by conveying the nobility, pathos, and tragedy of people who had given up the fight and were dying away.[101]

Once again the Indians were Jefferson's tragic figures, doomed to disappearance as modern America engulfed their world. Conquest and colonization as causative factors were relegated to the background as Indians slid quietly into darkness. Defeated and gone, they left behind an impression that could in some ways stand for America itself, as had the conception of the Indian in pre-Revolutionary times. Some among the ruling elite began to fear "that change had occurred too rapidly, that the past slipped away too swiftly, the frontier gone, the cities filled with strange new peoples and voices." Commemorating Indians as a vanishing race "answered several needs at once—for a historical narrative of legitimacy, for mourning the passing of old ways, and for absolution of guilt."[102]

Nevertheless, despite erosion of land and language and changes in dress and appearance—the things outsiders saw as markers of identity and culture—many Indian people maintained their ties of community, family, and kinship, and some spoke up time and again in defense of their lands and rights. In the late nineteenth and early twentieth centuries, Indian intellectuals took on some of the performative roles expected of Indians as a way of getting a public hearing for their cause and advancing their own agendas.[103] Many Indian people in New England avoided attracting attention to themselves, and many families suppressed and denied knowledge of Indian ancestry, but in the early twentieth century more people began to display their Indian identity in public events and ceremonies. Often they adopted popular symbols of "Indianness" for these occasions.

Plains Indian dress and stereotypes had little historic connection to New England, where, by this time, Indian people were urban dwellers, factory laborers, tradespeople, domestic servants, ministers, soldiers, sailors, and whaling ship captains. But in 1923 the New England Indian Council formed, adopting for its motto "I still live," and council members posed for photographs in buckskins and feather headdresses.[104] New England Indians, no less than Highland Scots, rebuilt communities during and after the dark ages initiated by English colonialism. Like the Scots, they adopted and recrafted new symbols as markers of their survival and identity.

Sir Walter Scott does have much to answer for. Nevertheless, he achieved something important. He gave Scotland a new vision of itself and its history. "Invented traditions" helped Scotland to halt the decline into being just "North Britain" and revive its individuality. Together with Robert Burns, Scott provided a country formerly dismissed as a cultural backwater with a national literature that appealed to readers on both sides of the Atlantic. After the devastation of the First World War and the Great Depression, Scotland seemed poised once more to "disappear." Its population declined more precipitously in the first half of the twentieth century than it had during the clearances.[105] Instead, like Indian nations in the United States,[106] Scotland came back in the late twentieth century, with the symbolism of Highlandism prominently displayed. The clan tartans and paraphernalia worn by Scots to proclaim their uniqueness may have few ancient roots, but that does not mean that the people who have accepted them as markers of their allegiance are any less Scottish. They have gone beyond being badges of identity to become banners of a resurgent Scottish nationhood.

In 1964 Waldo McIntosh attended the annual gathering of his clan in the Highlands. On the face of it, this was not remarkable. But McIntosh was also called Tustunugee Micco. Descended from eighteenth-century emigrants who had married Indian women, he was principal chief of the Creek Nation of Oklahoma and appeared wearing the regalia of a Plains Indian, with a full headdress and elaborately embroidered buckskins.[107] Resplendent in their respective regalia, the Creek chief and the Mackintosh clan chief wore clothing their ancestors would hardly have been seen dead in three hundred years earlier. On both sides of the Atlantic, Native people took stereotypes and used them for their own purposes. Highland Scots and American Indians revitalized their nations and cultures in ways that both confounded and incorporated images generated by imperial nostalgia. They found new ways of declaring who they were.

Epilogue

History, Heritage, and Identity

Edward Said wrote that imperialism and resistance to imperialism are inextricably linked; subordinate peoples produce cultures of resistance, and identities are born out of opposition.[1] For American Indians and Highland Scots, identities were forged in part by their responses to the power and policies of outsiders. In some cases they still are.

In the 1940s the U.S. Air Force took possession of 341,726 acres on the Pine Ridge reservation in South Dakota for use as an aerial gunnery and bombing range, leaving unexploded ordnance and shrapnel scattered across the area, still a problem for the Oglala Sioux residents; in the early 1950s the British government considered testing Britain's first atomic bomb in the Highlands (in the end the plan was dropped, not the bomb).[2] In the twentieth century, outsiders looked to Indian country and the Highlands for energy rather than land. Indian people continued to be relocated—to make way for dams that flooded their homelands, as part of the government's program of moving families from the reservations to the cities, or to provide access to mineral and energy resources.[3] In John McGrath's 1970s' play, *The Cheviot, the Stag, and the Black, Black Oil,* the discovery and exploitation of North Sea oil by outside interests represented just one more phase in "the savage progress of capitalism" in the Highlands.[4] Critics charged Prime Minister Margaret Thatcher's government in the 1980s with treating Scotland as "a Conservative colony."[5] The list of problems that, despite repeated reform efforts, Eric Richards identified as plaguing the Highlands in the late twentieth century reads like a report on conditions on Indian reservations: "the shortage of arable land, the deficiency of internally generated capital, the lack of self-sustaining secondary industry, underemployment, resource deficiencies and cultural decline."[6]

Some parts of the Highlands that were depopulated by the clearances are now being repopulated, as affluent people from England and the Lowlands try to find a better quality of life away from the rat race. The newcomers drive up house prices, and some locals worry that these outsiders will undermine their "traditional" culture and usurp their identity. They call them "white settlers."[7] In Indian country and the Highlands of Scotland there are communities that bear the marks of past policies of removal and relocation, protest the continued exploitation and export of their resources, resent decisions being made for them by a distant government, and struggle to maintain their community, culture, language, and identity amid the pressures of the modern world. The argument that Highlanders need to put the past behind them, step out from dependence on outside sources, and "take their place on the same footing as everyone else" will sound awfully familiar to many Native Americans and students of United States policy.[8]

Highland Scots and American Indians confront enduring challenges as they try to preserve a distinctiveness within a larger national identity. In a world of endangered languages, where English is becoming overwhelmingly the global language, speaking or learning Gaelic or an Indian language today is often as much about identity as communication.[9] As in Indian country, so in the Highlands it is primarily older people who speak Gaelic as a first language. The Education Act of 1872 introduced compulsory schooling but made no mention of Gaelic since English was assumed to be the language of education. A student at Tobermory remembered his headmaster, as late as 1914, threatening to whip anyone who spoke Gaelic within the precincts of the school.[10] The Education Act of 1918 included a clause that there should be "adequate provision" for teaching Gaelic in Gaelic-speaking areas, but it was too little to halt the decline produced by more than three centuries of governmental attempts to eradicate the language. Gaelic had become firmly identified as a "backward" language of diminishing relevance. People who wanted to get on in the world spoke English.[11]

Former students of Indian boarding schools recalled being beaten and having their knuckles rapped or their mouths washed out with lye for speaking their Native tongue. Nevertheless, some students found ways to keep their language alive in private: Like Highlanders for whom Gaelic remained the language of prayer, one Ojibwa woman recalled that she always prayed in

Ojibwa so she could speak it when she returned home.[12] Other graduates spared their children pain by not passing on the language. A crofter from Port Henderson recalled similar experiences in Scotland:

I grew up speaking Gaelic and only started to learn English when I went to school. Children had their knuckles smacked if the teacher found them speaking Gaelic in the classroom or in the playground. Many children lost the Gaelic and I live in an area where there are few Gaelic speakers. Parents didn't think it was important for their children to speak Gaelic anymore, because, I suppose, they had to get by in English. What was the use of Gaelic?[13]

In the mid-nineteenth century my great-grandfather, James McLean, moved as a boy with his family from Argyll to the parish of Clunie in Perthshire. When he grew up he made a living as a small farmer on a *pendicle*, a small holding or property that is a subsidiary part of a larger estate. He wanted to return to Argyll but he "was treated as an outsider because he had lost his Gaelic."[14] Many Indian students experienced similar distancing from their home community when they returned from boarding schools that had deprived them of their Native language.

On the other hand, Highlanders who emigrated often held on to their native tongue even as they adapted it and added to it. Catholic Highlanders in particular (more so than Presbyterians) held on to their Gaelic language. "Gaelic was easily the third most commonly spoken European language (after English and French) in British North America in 1815." Even after it was no longer spoken, it still influenced speech patterns in Canada.[15] Gaelic was spoken in the Cape Fear region of North Carolina into the early twentieth century. In Nova Scotia, children who spoke Gaelic rather than English at school "were either scolded by the gentle teachers or beaten by the impatient."[16] The language persisted, and there have been programs of language revitalization, but the number of Gaelic speakers continues to decline, and, as with Native languages, preserving knowledge of a language is not the same as the language surviving as a spoken vernacular.[17]

Scotland within the United Kingdom and Indian tribes within the United States and Canada constitute nations within a larger nation, although the nature of their nationhood and the conditions of their inclusion vary considerably and spark debate. Scotland is no longer a junior partner in British imperialism. The empire is gone, Britain as a national concept seems increasingly precarious, and Scotland has its own parliament again and its own identity.[18] In recent years Scotland and the Indian nations have reasserted their sovereignty, but that reassertion has prompted questions: What are the criteria for membership in these nations? What makes a Scot a Scot and an Indian an Indian? Great Britain does not recognize any of its peoples as indigenous in the way the United States and Canada accord that recognition to Native Americans and First Nations respectively, and Gaelic claims to "aboriginality" rest on historical occupation and injustice rather than distinct ethnicity.[19] Being Scottish, like being Indian, can involve "concentric rings" of identity. Within the United Kingdom, Scots enjoy a kind of dual citizenship; they are Scottish, but they are also British. American Indians are citizens of the United States and of the individual state in which they live as well as citizens of their own tribes.

Identities are constructed and are not static. They are often complex and fluid and sometimes rooted in histories and memories that reach to other places. How people define themselves may involve personal, family, regional, national, class, and other issues and allegiances that exert greater or lesser influence at one time or another; how others define them may change as they are incorporated into or stand apart from the dominant culture. Membership, bloodlines, and descent all play a role, but the criteria are rarely fixed. Some stake their identity on history and heritage rather than on current cultural or political affiliation. At a conference several years ago I was speaking about this book with a woman who identified herself as having some Cherokee ancestry but quickly qualified it with an apologetic shrug and a look, saying, "you know." In the course of our conversation about the Highland clearances and the Cherokee Trail of Tears, she announced, "They treated you just like us." Her use of pronouns was odd. I suppose "they" embraced the usual cast of suspects and powers that be. By "you" she clearly meant my Scottish ancestors and me. By "us," this woman included herself as a victim of removal, as she regarded me as a victim of the clearances. Clearly uncomfortable claiming a contemporary Cherokee identity, she had no hesitation claiming a historic Cherokee identity or assigning me a historic Highland one.

Changing political situations and social climates, cultural and ethnic revitalizations, and renewed pride in diverse heritages have produced complicated and sometimes contested issues surrounding identity in the Highlands of Scotland, as well as in Indian America.[20] In 1900 the U.S. Census counted 237,000 Indian people, which was a gross undercount: The census takers decided who was or was not Indian and often recorded Indian people as "black." Moreover, at a time when it was not healthy to be Indian in the United States, many Indian people preferred to pass as something else. In 2000 people self-identified, and, for the first time, the census made provision for those who wished to identify as part Indian: Of census respondents, 2.5 million people identified as Indian only, while 1.6 million more identified as part Indian. For a variety of reasons, who is an Indian remains a contentious issue. Indian people routinely joke about a whole new tribe of Wannabees— people who are not Indian but "wanna be."[21] At the same time, many Indians have Scottish surnames and trace or claim descent from Highland clans. Many Americans apply for membership in Highland clan societies. Many have a clear line of descent; others may be "MacWannabees."

More radical groups denounce the repopulating of some areas of the Highlands and islands by wealthy outsiders as an instance of continuing English colonialism. Others see people, wherever they come from, as crucial to the region's healthy development; after all, they say, Highlanders themselves originally migrated there from somewhere else. The population of Skye increased about forty percent in the last quarter of the twentieth century, and in the 1990s the population of the Highlands began to grow for the first time since 1850. The increases are far less dramatic than those reported for Native Americans in the U.S. censuses, but they raise similar questions. What will they mean for Highland identity? "Can we define the term 'Highlander' in such a way that the issue of a person's ancestry becomes of much less importance than the fact that a person lives in, works in, is committed to, this quite amazing territory?" asks James Hunter.[22] None of the present-day inhabitants of Knoydart are descended from people who lived there in the eighteenth century. Nevertheless, they took over the 17,500-acre Knoydart Estate in 1999, giving the residents, as the plaque commemorating the event says, "custody of the land on which they live." And custody, as one Knoydart farmer explained and most American Indians would agree, means care rather than ownership. "We don't really own the land—nobody does. We are only stewards of it for as long as we are here."[23]

Highlanders historically considered themselves the "ancient Scots," distinct from Lowlanders, who were a mix of Scots, Picts, English, French, and other peoples. But like American Indians, Highlanders have a history of intermarrying with and incorporating outsiders in ways that have made their communities and cultures stronger and more vibrant. "Sane Scots know that we were always mongrels," writes Angus Calder, "and we are exogamous with it. A typical present-day Scot will have one Highland granny and one English one, with two Lowland granddads and a lot of Canadian cousins." Identity has little to do with pedigree. "We define ourselves by what we are not. We are not English."[24]

Benedict Anderson argues that all communities bigger than face-to-face villages or small tribes are in many ways "imagined communities," and so all broader identities, whether national or ethnic, are constructed, as well as inherited by biological descent.[25] Looking back to ancient times to find the origins of Scottish national identity is nothing new—historians have been doing it since the Middle Ages.[26] Like the history of the Scottish nation, that national identity "has been neither coherent nor progressive. It ebbs, it flows, it breaks up, it muddles along."[27] Today people look to history for personal, as well as national, identity.

Romantic images of Highlanders and Indians created in the nineteenth century feed a modern-day hunger for a connection with an earlier, better, preindustrial, noncapitalist society. Scottish and Native American political aspirations and cultural revivals have been accompanied by a growing interest, indeed fascination, among broader segments of society who attribute to historic Celtic and Native American cultures a spirituality and a morality lacking in our own. For some people, identifying with these ways of life represents taking a stand against the flattening effects of globalization. Increasing numbers of people have traced, discovered, or invented roots in Gaelic and Indian societies. Shifting identity (or maintaining fluid ones) to take advantage of new opportunities or in response to changing political and economic circumstances is neither new nor unique to Highland Scots or American Indians.[28] Yet, more than most people, American Scots and Indians confront—and sometimes play upon—entrenched images of what it means to be Scottish or Indian. Moreover, a tribal past and experience of colonialism provide no immunity to perpetuating stereotypes and colonial caricatures of others, of Indians and Scots by Scots and Indians.[29]

The romantic yet tragic image of the Highlands had great appeal for Scots in North America who constructed an identity and cultivated a memory that rested heavily on a sense of exile. James Loch, who had little patience for such sentiments, acknowledged that the loss of old ways and customs produced feelings of regret but suggested that such regret "has been always felt and expressed more strongly, by those who had themselves long abandoned their paternal homes and national habits, than by those who continued to reside among their native hills."[30] Highland games were as much a Canadian as a Scottish creation. In 1819, the same year the first Highland games were held in Scotland, Bishop Alexander Macdonnell and fur traders William McGillivray and John McDonald of Garth established a Highland Society in Glengarry County for organizing games in Canada. In 1829 *Blackwoods Edinburgh Magazine* published the "Canadian Boat Song," ostensibly a translation of a Gaelic rowing song sung by Highlanders on the Saint Lawrence, which became famous as an evocative longing for a lost homeland that spoke to all Highlanders "in exile." In reality, it was probably an English, not a

Gaelic, production, composed by a couple of journalists in the magazine's offices.[31] Lowlanders and Ulster Scots distanced themselves from Highland Scots in eighteenth-century America; in the mid-nineteenth century many were happy to be included under the new romantic umbrella image of Highlander.[32] In one's imagined history as well as one's invented traditions, being Scottish meant to be a Highlander.

A sense of homeland is vital to the identity of diasporic peoples. Every year, thousands of American Scots "go back" to Scotland; many thousands more talk about doing so. As James Hunter notes, it is an interesting choice of words by people, many of whom "cannot, as a matter of literal fact, go back to Scotland—because they have never been there." What they wish to do is renew their ancestral connection to the place.[33] A growing heritage tourism industry caters to and fuels this longing. This "roots tourism" emphasizes the heritage of place and, by making the homeland the focus for rerembering and imagining the past, provides important sources of identity for those rediscovering their roots.[34] Thousands more Americans and Canadians who do not cross the Atlantic join clan societies, participate in Highland games, and indulge in Celtic nostalgia.

In his essay "Imaginary Homelands," Salman Rushdie, an Indian writer living in north London in the 1980s, wrote that exiles, emigrants, and expatriates "are haunted by some sense of loss, some urge to reclaim, to look back." However, if they do look back, they must recognize that they "will not be capable of reclaiming precisely the thing that was lost; that we will, in short, create fictions . . . imaginary homelands, Indias of the mind." In a sense, "the past is a country from which we have all emigrated, [and] its loss is part of our common humanity," but people who are "out of country" often "experience this loss in an intensified form."[35]

People these days identify more comfortably with victims of empire than with imperialists, and victims as well as victors create their own histories. Emigrants in all times and places have tended "to construct and freeze their own chosen image of the homeland as they left, an image which became more indelible and unalterable as time went by." Emigrants who returned home to Scotland—and there were many—tended to emphasize the positive aspects of their emigrant experience, but successful emigrants and their descendants often "nurture a culture of victimhood." Despite the facts that Scots participated in—and even ran—the British Empire, that most came from urban and Lowland origins, and that most migrated voluntarily, the image of Highlanders brutally evicted and forced onto disease-ridden emigrant ships remains powerful and pervasive. Many American and Canadian Scots depict themselves as "children of the clearances," invoke a "genealogical victimhood," and indulge in the "moral rhetoric of exile."[36]

How and when people left their homeland are often key components of identity. Experiences, memories, and retellings of removal played a significant role in the construction of identity for American Scots, as well as for many American Indians, and the clearances and removals thus became layered with myth and meaning. Clearances were a Highland rather than a Lowland phenomenon, and not all Highland emigrants were forced out by sheep. However, popular imagination often conflated all Scottish emigrations into one tragic series of removals, and many American Scots cultivated a remembered history of cultural and community survival in the face of repression and adversity.[37] Claiming a connection with the clearances or the removals offers identification with homelands, ways of life, and causes that have been lost.

Collective identities are often linked to—and sometimes form around—cultural traumas, and cultural traumas involve imagining and reremembering past events as much as the events themselves. Sociologists tell us that it is not necessary to have experienced something first-hand to share in its cultural trauma and to connect with it as a source of group identity. Collective identity thus becomes "a perception of shared status or relation, which may be imagined rather than experienced directly."[38] I remember as a child hearing the clearances spoken about as if they had happened yesterday.[39] Scots understand that Scots bear a large share of the blame for the Highland clearances, but, being Scots, they know in their bones that the English must have been behind it somehow. The clearances became not only a part of Scottish political identity but also "a narrative of betrayal which shines a torch on the virtues of the betrayed."[40]

In the same way, Cherokees recite stories of the Trail of Tears, and Navajos recall tales of their "Long Walk" from Arizona to Bosque Redondo in New Mexico in 1864 and their four-year incarceration near Fort Sumner. Anthropologists in the mid-twentieth century had no difficulty finding older Navajos to talk it. "Those who were not there themselves heard so many poignant tales from their parents that they speak as if they themselves had experienced all the horror of the 'Long Walk.'"[41] Forced removals—the clearances, the Trail of Tears, the Long Walk—left an indelible mark on group consciousness and collective identity, on those who were there and on many who were not. Those who did not suffer, even those who were not yet born, often internalize the suffering of those who did. Moreover, identifying with the suffering of ancestors places one in opposition to those who perpetrated the acts, even if one has ancestors on both sides.[42]

Migration from the Highlands resulted in the creation of new Highland communities, whether in Glasgow or Glengarry. Highlanders in Lowland towns maintained their cultures and identities by forming Highland chapels and clubs, speaking Gaelic to one another, following their own patterns of work and residence, and operating within their own networks of support, just as Indians who moved to towns and cities maintained their Native American identity, followed Native patterns of work and residence, and relied on Native support networks.[43] Nevertheless, ties to the homeland weakened and sometimes broke. Such separations were better attributed to merciless landlords in cahoots with the English than to personal choice or the search for economic advantage. Expulsion of ancestors became an explanation of location and more of a marker of identity than did Gaelic language. Nostalgic longing for a homeland they had left—or never seen—confirmed the notion that all Scots in America were victims of the clearances; why else would they have left Scotland? As Celeste Ray explains, "Being exiled for political or religious beliefs and thereby deprived of one's native land and heritage seems more noble than to have voluntary deserted the same for economic reasons (though these were undeniably compelling for many Highlanders)."[44]

Not all North American Scots subscribed (or subscribe) to memories of victimization. David Craig did not find them when he went to Canada to collect popular memories of the clearances. Instead, he found Canadian Scots proud that their ancestors had decided to migrate, make new lives, and build a new country. In Glengarry, Cape Breton, and Cape Fear, America was "from a Highland perspective, a land of liberation."[45] Gaelic folklore lamented the forced exile of Highlanders, but many of the songs and poems that powerfully convey the despair and longing of emigrants may in fact have been penned by men from the middle and upper echelons of Highland society who bitterly resented the economic transformation of the Highlands and blamed the commercialization of agriculture for the decline from traditional values. Historians and tourist boards later amplified their words. In Nova Scotia, for example, Gaelic folklore contained many songs celebrating emigration as an opportunity for a new life and an escape from hardship and misery in the Highlands. The mythology that all Highlanders were driven from their homelands to make way for sheep and took to their new homes with deep longing for their old appears to be more prominent in narratives written in English than in memories preserved in Gaelic.[46] The displaced Highlander and associated displays of tartan became symbols of Nova Scotia's Scottishness, but Ian McKay maintains that Nova Scotia discovered and constructed its Highland heritage during and after the Great Depression, reaching back in time and across the Atlantic to find its roots in a more romantic, preindustrial society.[47]

The Scots, argues Edward Cowan, "have perhaps the greatest capacity for self-mythologization of any nation on the planet, outside the United States."[48] Yet, is there more to it all than self-delusion and tourism? For one middle-aged businesswoman, born and raised in Vancouver, visiting the Highlands of Scotland represented a homecoming with profound implications for descendants of settler societies in North America: "If you live in North America you understand that you have only a very tenuous hold on the geography. There has to be a place to which you have a stronger connection, that tells the myths and legends of your ancestors, not someone else's. In this country we will always be immigrants, not really belonging in that very primal way." She had Irish and Lowland Scots ancestors as well, but for this woman the Highlands of her paternal grandparents constituted homeland. And even though her grandparents migrated to Canada early in the twentieth century, long after the clearances were over, she described herself as "a child of the outcasts." She "really didn't see that much difference between what happened in the Highlands to Gaels and what happened in North America to the Native Indian population. Except that the Indians were not actually expelled from the continent." As Paul Basu notes, depicting themselves as children of the clearances links the expatriate population to a traumatic event and provides "a folk memory—albeit an 'acquired' one—of the great historic injustice which binds the group together as a diaspora."[49]

The Trail of Tears binds Cherokees in similar ways. Today the Cherokee Nation of Oklahoma has more than 175,000 enrolled members, but what it means to be Cherokee is often a controversial and contested issue. Cherokee identity is a complex social and political process that involves notions about blood, race, and color. In 2007 the Cherokees voted to amend to the tribal constitution and limit citizenship to descendants of "by blood" tribal members listed on the federal Dawes Commission rolls more than one hundred years ago, thereby revoking tribal membership of some 2,800 descendants of people Cherokees once held as slaves. However, many Cherokees include criteria other than blood ancestry, such as cultural behavior, language, and community commitment. For some at least, descent from ancestors who trekked the Trail of Tears, whether they were Indian, white, or black, transcends other criteria and unites Cherokees as survivors of a shared past of oppression and removal: "Their ancestors came over on the Trail of Tears just the same as mine did," said one.[50] At the same time, Eastern Cherokees, whose ancestors escaped removal, also claim the Trail of Tears as part of their history. So do many self-identified Cherokees, who are not recognized by the Cherokee Nation of Oklahoma, by the Eastern Band of Cherokees, or by the federal government as members of an Indian tribe. For some people—"racial shifters," anthropologist Circe Sturm calls them—laying claim to the defining event in Cherokee history can be tantamount to claiming a new identity.[51]

Most Oklahoma Cherokees consider Oklahoma to be their home, "but almost all look back to the South, to their original homeland" and long to return to their roots. Some make pilgrimages, save money to buy land, or ask to be buried there. "Many never get a chance to go back, but those geographic, historical, and cultural origins continually visit their imaginations and shape their identities in complex ways."[52] Circe Sturm could be describing the sentiments of thousands of North American Scots, who every year make pilgrimages to the old country. They visit the romantic haunts already embedded in their imagination, buy their clan tartan, and pay good money to visit the ancestral castles of the clan chiefs whose ancestors sold out their ancestors. The Highland clearances have thus become as much a badge of identity for Scots in America as the Trail of Tears for Cherokees in Oklahoma.[53]

Some people claim both events as part of their heritage and participate in both Scottish festivals and Indian powwows. Native American Scots sometimes send their children to compete in dance competitions at Highland games *and* at powwows, and clan tents and sales booths at Scottish festivals occasionally display a mixture of Highland and Indian artifacts and articles of dress.[54]

When I attend Scottish festivals and Highland games in the United States, I am reminded of my grandmother Jessie McLean (who, when I knew her, wore nothing but gray with perhaps a purple scarf when she was "going out") saying something to the effect that one's degree of Scottish ancestry was usually in inverse proportion to the amount of tartan one wore. At powwows I have heard similar comments about feathers and beads and the ancestry of some of the participants. Some people simply enjoy displaying their Scottish or Indian ancestry, connection, or interest. Some feel (and announce) that their Highland regalia demonstrates their connection with an ancient clan nobility; others wear it in defiant demonstration of their association with a tribal past and with people who were always at odds with power and privilege. At Scottish gatherings in the South, which are often huge, it is not uncommon to see people wearing Scottish tartan and Confederate garb—a kind of Bonnie Prince Charlie meets Robert E. Lee lost-cause combo. Such displays of pride in one's heritage often have less to do with history than with invoking emotions about an imagined past and making a statement about the present. Highland games and powwows provide a forum for people of Celtic and Native American heritage to "assert a non-WASP identity."[55] Some of these assertions are temporary and restricted to these events, and some of those who make them then happily reassume a WASP identity that serves them well in the rest of their lives.

The dress, music, competitions, and paraphernalia of Highland festivals are often regarded as unbroken traditions, "authentic" representations of a way of life that predated the birth of the United States and are, therefore, by American standards, "ancient." The cultures, homelands, histories, and lost causes they represent offer imagined alternatives to the mundanity, modernity, and globalization of real life. Life there and then was simpler, more virtuous, more in tune with nature; it is the way we think we would have lived had it not been for the forces of imperialism, capitalism, and commercialism. The myth of Highland romance has universal appeal, says Peter Womack, "because it encodes a paradoxical nostalgia for a homeland which no one ever had, but which everyone has been promised." Utopianism wrapped in tartan, it offers "a *rapprochement* between naïve ethnicity and sentimental universality which is ultimately fraudulent."[56]

The same could be said for the popular appeal of an imagined Native American culture, wrapped in beads and feathers. Philip Deloria argues that generations of white Americans have imagined Indians and played Indians in a variety of ways and attached various meanings to them while struggling with their country's treatment of Native peoples and with their own not-very-secure identities.[57] Some people who self-identify as Native and play Indians at powwows and other public occasions may be doing much the same thing.

Yet, while critics can ridicule the tartans, feathers, and new traditions on display at powwows and Highland games (and some participants no doubt just like to pose), these gatherings serve important functions. For people who feel they have always been on the wrong side of history they are a marker of identity, an expression of group solidarity, and a celebration, despite all the odds, of cultural survival. American Scots participate in Highland festivals "not because they want to play at being Scots but because they want to celebrate the fact of their being North American Scottish Highlanders." Scottish games and gatherings in North America provide an emotional link to Scotland, but they are better understood as aspects of North American Scottish culture rather than judged against supposedly "more authentic" events in the old country.[58] Scots in Scotland may raise their eyebrows at American Scots' tartan parades, clan societies, and deference to clan chiefs, but, points out James Hunter, "this is to overlook the extent to which our diaspora possesses its own agenda."[59] Native Americans too have experienced diaspora—within North America. Powwow participants celebrate the fact of their survival as North American Indians, and, with more than two-thirds of the population now living in cities and not on reservations, returning home for powwows and other social and ceremonial occasions serves as an important opportunity for participating in the culture and community, sharing tribal values, and reinforcing identity.[60]

"The Gaels never die!" wrote poet Hugh MacDiarmid. "They either 'change' or 'travel.'"[61] Many did both. It is said that Scots have a transportable nationality; they do not stop being Scots just because they live in Canada, the United States, Australia, or even England. They may even become more Scottish the farther from home they find themselves. Contrary to popular expectations that other peoples' cultures are "real" or "authentic" only if they have survived without change, cultures survive only if they do change. People do not pass their culture from generation to generation as a complete package; they select, rearrange, and reemphasize different pieces of it as time and circumstances change. Highland and Native American cultures provide plenty of evidence of change, adaptation, redefinition, and reinvention. Yet they also possess a core of continuity and survived the best efforts of colonial governments to destroy them. Even if they had tried, the English government and its agents in the eighteenth century were no more able to arrest every lone piper who played a pibroch in a symbolic act of Gaelic defiance than the U.S. government and its agents in the nineteenth century were able to stamp out every American Indian ritual. Cultural cores survived, and later generations undertook, in James Hunter's words, "the task of reassembling a Highland identity from the wreckage left by the clearances."[62]

American Scots measure, maintain, and celebrate their Scottish identities in their own ways and create an American Scottish culture that, like all cultures, mixes old and new elements. Traditional Highland pipes and piping persisted in Gaelic Cape Breton until late in the twentieth century, and many American and Canadian pipers today play with a dedication to old ways.[63] Highland and Indian cultures continue to mix, even in bagpiping. In the mid-twentieth century Jim Forbes, who migrated from Dumbarton to Canada, began teaching bagpipes to nine Indian girls at a Catholic Mission School at Williams Lake, northwest of Kamloops. The mission raised money to buy the girls pipes, and the nuns made tartan uniforms. "Jim found himself in charge of the world's first Red Indian Pipe Band— and a girls' Band at that," reported the Glasgow College of Piping's *Pipe Band Magazine*.[64]

What matters about identity, writes J. M. Bumsted, "is not whether it is real or mythological, whether it is based on historical record or the imagination of its inhabitants, but whether it exists and whether a large number of inhabitants subscribe to it."[65] In Jenni Calder's words, "in the U.S., a Scotland survives that many Scots may not recognize, but which has a powerful reality for those who subscribe to its blend of heightened images." In other words, traditions and symbols may be "phony but full of meaning."[66] People draw strength from their heritage and from a remembered past of courage in the face of adversity. How much of that past is imaginary is difficult to say; ancestral loyalties rest on fancy as much as fact.

So, most Scots identify with the battle of Culloden and Indians with the battle of the Little Bighorn, no matter what side their ancestors took in those conflicts. Both assume "last battle status." They mark the final effort to preserve tribal independence by armed resistance and herald the rapid dismantling of the tribal way of life. Scots composed about half of the Duke of Cumberland's Hanoverian army and committed their share of the atrocities. Yet Culloden is remembered as a Scottish defeat. Arikaras, Crows, Shoshones, and others fought with the U.S. cavalry against the Lakotas and Cheyennes, but today the battle of the Little Bighorn stands as a last great victory for Indian people of all tribes. These conflicts symbolize more today than what was at issue on the day of the battle. They have become icons of how we feel about our past, how we imagine ourselves lining up in past and present conflicts, who we are, and what we have lost in the world we have made.

Mel Gibson's 1995 movie *Braveheart* outdid even Sir Walter Scott in distorting history. It took an internally complex struggle and turned it into a medieval war of national independence from arrogant English, many of whom, for some reason, spoke like Prince Charles, the current Prince of Wales (they would have spoken Middle English). It turned a historic Lowland figure, William Wallace, first into a Highlander and then, painted, into a Pict, or into an Indian for Hollywood purposes. Despite its historical distortions (or perhaps because of them), the film made an impact in Scotland and in the United States. Different groups of people found appeal in its heroism, its violence, and its "congenial ideology" of "freedom."[67] Applications for membership in Scottish clan societies rose dramatically after the release of the film, and at least one seasoned observer of Scottish politics credited *Braveheart*'s impact on the young as a factor in the growing majority favoring devolution and the reconvening of a Scottish parliament in 1999.[68] William Wallace figurines that resemble Mel Gibson in paint and plaid now accompany tartan and shortbread as standard fare in Edinburgh gift shops; a new statue that looks remarkably like Mel Gibson stands at the base of the Wallace monument in Stirling.

The manufacture and commercialization of a romanticized Highland past leads some authors to lament that Scotland suffers from "too much heritage"—Bonnie Prince Charlie shortbread tins, Mary Queen of Scots dolls, *Braveheart* figures, and tartan everything. In North America it ultimately produces "a tartan travesty in which Scottish identity has become little more than a series of unconnected marketable goods."[69] The American Scotland, in Michael Fry's opinion, is a caricature, "an exercise in make-believe" that shows little understanding of Scotland or Scottish realities. "It displays rather a desire to assimilate Scotland and the Scots into an American construction of the world and into the American requirements for multiculturalism."[70]

In 1998 U.S. Senate Resolution 155 declared the Declaration of Arbroath, signed April 6, 1320, the model for the Declaration of Independence, and Americans now celebrate April 6 as Tartan Day. The events caused raised eyebrows and chuckles on the other side of the Atlantic, but that did not stop Scottish notables from flying over to take part. After all, it is just another invention, as were Burns Night and Saint Andrew's Day at one time.[71] People can celebrate what they want as they remind themselves who they are—or want to be.

History is still mostly written by the winners, but heritage, according to David Lowenthal, "increasingly belongs to the losers. Even victors now aspire to a legacy of defeat," he says. "History tells all who will listen what has happened and how things came to be as they are. Heritage passes on exclusive myths of origin and continuance, endowing a select group with prestige and common purpose." "We ask of heritage an imagined past, not an actual one."[72] Hugh Trevor-Roper argued that Scots had no real culture. Like-minded critics might argue that Scots and Indians have no real history either, just a heritage for history's losers to take comfort in.

However, it is not that tidy. Heritage, myth, and memory may not be the same as history, but they are not easily separated from it, and they shape it as well. They are interwoven and they interact. To steal a phrase from George W. Bush, history, like math, can get fuzzy. The histories that underdogs construct are no more or less fanciful than those created and perpetuated by power and privilege.

My ancestors who fought at Culloden would have been bemused by Sir Walter Scott's tartan pageants; Sir Walter would be deeply disturbed by the commercially defiant tribalism of a modern band like *Allbanach* (formerly *Clann n Drumma*), who invoke *Braveheart*-influenced images of Highlandism. None of it is "authentic," or is it? People find new ways of expressing who they are just as they find new ways of understanding their histories. There are few better statements on authenticity, change, and continuity than that quoted by Scottish journalist Neal Acherson: "This is my grandfather's axe. My father gave it a new handle. I gave it a new head."[73]

* * *

For Highland Scots and American Indians, identities were forged in part by their experiences with colonialism, and they continue to be shaped by memories—real or imagined—of those experiences. Those who were uprooted from the homelands that held so much of their identity carried core pieces of their culture with them, as if carefully wrapped for transportation, to be preserved in another place and revitalized in another era. Despite centuries of dispossession and dislocation, Indian country survives, a mixture of old and new, a network of relationships as much as a place, reaching into everyday walks of life, as well as across reservations. In similar ways, diasporic Scots created a new *Gàidhealtachd* in North America, a network of relationships and interests deriving its core values and cultures from the Highlands of Scotland but adapted to a new world. Revived symbols and reinvented traditions may reveal or conceal assumed identities and a fabricated heritage, but they also stand for cultural endurance, histories of resistance, and community reconstruction in the face of adversity. They represent the capacity of humans to survive man's inhumanity to man. And that, ultimately, is about the best we can draw from the past, real or imagined.

Notes

NOTES TO PREFACE

1. Allen D. Candler et al., eds., *The Colonial Records of the State of Georgia*. 32 vols. (Atlanta: State Printer, 1904–1989; vol. 27: Athens: University of Georgia Press), 4; also quoted in Anthony W. Parker, *Scottish Highlanders in Colonial Georgia: The Recruitment, Emigration, and Settlement at Darien, 1735–1748* (Athens: University of Georgia Press, 1997), 91.

2. Jenni Calder, *Scots in the USA* (Edinburgh: Luath, 2006); Michael Fry, *How the Scots Made America* (New York: St. Martin's, 2003); Arthur Herman, *How the Scots Invented the Modern World* (New York: Crown, 2001), ch. 14; Jim Hewitson, *Tam Blake and Co.: The Story of the Scots in America* (Edinburgh: Canongate, 1993); Ferenc Morton Szasz, *Scots in the North American West, 1790–1917* (Norman: University of Oklahoma Press, 2000); Tom Bryan, *Rich Man, Beggar Man, Indian Chief: Fascinating Scots in Canada and America* (Insch, Aberdeenshire: Thistle, 1997); William R. Brock, *Scotus Americanus: A Survey of the Sources for Links between Scotland and America in the Eighteenth Century* (Edinburgh: Edinburgh University Press, 1982); Bruce Le Roy, *Lairds, Bards, and Mariners: The Scot in Northwest America* (Tacoma: Washington State American Revolution Bicentennial Commission, 1976). Michael Newton, *We're Indians Sure Enough: The Legacy of the Scottish Highlanders in the United States* (Richmond, Va.: Saorsa Media, 2001) uncovers the cultural legacies left in Gaelic poetry and oral tradition in North America. For Canada see Jenni

Calder, *Scots in Canada* (Edinburgh: Luath, 2003); W. J. Rattray, *The Scot in British North America*. 4 vols. (Toronto: Maclear, 1880); W. Stanford Reid, ed., *The Scottish Tradition in Canada* (Toronto: McClelland and Stewart, 1976). On Celtic influences see Rowland Berthoff, "Celtic Mist over the South," *Journal of Southern History* 52 (1986): 523–46, and the response by Forrest McDonald and Grady McWhinney in *ibid.*, 547–48. Claims for Scots-Irish contributions in America include James Webb, *Born Fighting: How the Scots-Irish Shaped America* (New York: Broadway, 2004), and Charles A. Hanna, *The Scotch-Irish, or The Scot in North Britain, North Ireland, and North America*. 2 vols. (New York: G. P. Putnam's Sons, 1902).

3. Gary E. Moulton, ed., *The Journals of the Lewis and Clark Expedition*. 13 vols. (Lincoln: University of Nebraska Press, 1986–2001), 4: 10.

4. Celeste Ray, ed., *Transatlantic Scots* (Tuscaloosa: University of Alabama Press, 2005), 38, 81.

NOTES TO INTRODUCTION

1. *A Collection of Voyages and Travels . . . from the curious and valuable Library of the late Earl of Oxford*, 2 vols. (London: Thomas Osborne, 1745); Roxann Wheeler, *The Complexion of Race: Categories of Difference in Eighteenth-century British Culture* (Philadelphia: University of Pennsylvania Press, 2000), 18.

2. Tom F. Cunningham, *The Diamond's Ace: Scotland and the Native Americans* (Edinburgh: Mainstream, 2001), 48.

3. *Scots Magazine* 18 (Oct. 1756), 520. Similar accounts of the event are in J. P. MacLean, *An Historical Account of the Settlements of Scotch Highlanders in America prior to the Peace of 1783, Together with Notices of Highland Regiments and Biographical Sketches* (1900; reprinted Bowie, Md.: Heritage, 2001), 256, and James Browne, *History of the Highlands and the Highland Clans* (Glasgow, 1838), iv, 155; quoted in Robert Clyde, *From Rebel to Hero: The Image of the Highlander, 1745–1830* (East Linton, Scotland: Tuckwell, 1995), 154.

4. Loudon to Cumberland (1756) in *Military Affairs in North America, 1748–1765: Selected Papers from the Cumberland Papers in Windsor Castle*, ed. Stanley Pargellis (New York: Appleton-Century, 1936), 264; Alfred Proctor James, ed., *Writings of General John Forbes relating to His Services in North America* (Menasha, Wis.: Collegiate Press, 1938), 117.

5. Papers of the Continental Congress, 1774–1789, National Archives Microfilm, no. M247, reel 85, item 71, vol. 2, 205.

6. Quoted in Charles W. Dunn, *Highland Settler: A Portrait of the Scottish Gael in Nova Scotia* (Toronto: University of Toronto Press, 1953), 27–28. The song is often but evidently erroneously attributed to John Macrae, who emigrated to North Carolina in the 1770s; Michael Newton, *We're Indians Sure Enough: The*

Legacy of the Scottish Highlanders in the United States (Richmond, Va.: Saorsa Media, 2001), 121, 178, 239; Michael Newton, "In Their Own Words: Gaelic Literature in North Carolina," *Scotia* 25 (2001), 1–28, esp. 19–20.

7. Mae Atwood, ed., *In Rupert's Land: Memoirs of Walter Traill* (Toronto: McClelland and Stewart, 1970), 61.

8. Elizabeth Thompson, ed., *The Emigrant's Guide to North America (Ceann-iùil an Fhir-imrich Do Dh'America Mu-Thuath)*, 1841; translated (Toronto: Natural Heritage Books, 1998), 39, 140, 143.

9. Archibald McDonald said that bagpipe music "pleased them to admiration." Malcolm McLeod, ed., *Peace River; a Canoe Voyage from Hudson's Bay to the Pacific by the late Sir George Simpson in 1828. Journal of the late chief factor, Archibald McDonald, who accompanied him* (Ottawa: J. Durie and Son, 1872), 24. James Sutherland, in charge of the Hudson's Bay post at Brandon House in 1793, wrote that the Indians "were very fond of" his men "dancing to the Bag Pipes." Allan I. Macinnes, Marjory-Ann D. Harper, and Linda G. Fryer, eds., *Scotland and the Americas, c. 1650–c.1939: A Documentary Source Book* (Edinburgh: Scottish History Society, 2002), 146.

10. Quoted in James Hunter, *Scottish Exodus: Travels among a Worldwide Clan* (Edinburgh: Mainstream, 2005), 84.

11. Canasatego, "Speech at the Treaty of Lancaster," in *The World Turned Upside Down: Indian Voices from Early America.* ed. Colin G. Calloway (Boston: Bedford/St. Martin's, 1994), 101.

12. "State of Emigration from the Highlands of Scotland, its extent, causes, & proposed remedy," Mar. 21, 1803, NLS, Adv. Ms. 35.6.18: 5–6, 18–19.

13. Michael Newton, *A Handbook of the Scottish Gaelic World* (Dublin: Four Courts Press, 2000), chs. 6–7; Charles Jedrej and Mark Nutall, *White Settlers: The Impact of Rural Repopulation in Scotland* (Luxembourg: Harwood Academic Publishers, 1996), quote at 122.

14. Keith Basso, *Wisdom Sits in Places: Landscape and Language among the Western Apache* (Albuquerque: University of New Mexico Press, 1996), 34; Jeanette Armstrong, "Land Speaking," in *Speaking for the Generations: Native Writers on Writing,* ed. Simon J. Ortiz (Tucson: University of Arizona Press, 1998), 174–94, quote at 175–76. I am grateful to Hartmut Lutz for bringing Armstrong's statement to my attention.

15. Colin G. Calloway, *One Vast Winter Count: The Native American West before Lewis and Clark* (Lincoln: University of Nebraska Press, 2004), ch. 1; cf. Jedrej and Nutall, *White Settlers,* 125.

16. Raymond J. DeMallie, ed., *The Sixth Grandfather: Black Elk's Teachings Given to John G. Neihardt* (Lincoln: University of Nebraska Press, 1984), 69.

17. Robin Ridington, "Northern Hunters," in *America in 1492: The World of the Indian Peoples before the Arrival of Columbus,* ed. Alvin M. Josephy Jr. (New York: Knopf, 1992), 32.

18. Craig Howe, "Keep Your Thoughts above the Trees: Ideas on Developing and Presenting Tribal Histories," in *Clearing a Path: Theorizing the Past in Native American Studies,* ed. Nancy Shoemaker (New York: Routledge, 2002), 165.

19. Rory Stewart, *The Places In Between* (London: Picador, 2004), 180.

20. On the prevalence of such beliefs and practices in the seventeenth-century Highlands and islands see Donald J. Macleod, ed., *A Description of the Western Islands of Scotland circa 1695 and a Late Voyage to St. Kilda by Martin Martin, Gent.* (Edinburgh: Birlinn, 1999); and Newton, *Handbook of the Scottish Gaelic World;* in Indian New England, see William S. Simmons, *Spirit of the New England Tribes: Indian History and Folklore, 1620–1984* (Hanover, N.H.: University Press of New England, 1986); more generally, Peter Nabokov, *Where the Lightning Strikes: The Lives of American Indian Sacred Places* (New York: Viking, 2006).

21. Newton, *Handbook of the Scottish Gaelic World,* 209; James Hunter, *The Last of the Free: A Millennial History of the Highlands and Islands of Scotland* (Edinburgh: Mainstream, 1999), 172.

22. Eric Richards, *A History of the Highland Clearances.* Vol. 1, *Agrarian Transformation and the Evictions, 1746–1886* (London: Croom Helm, 1982), 76–80, 123; Jedrej and Nutall, *White Settlers,* 119–21; Robert A. Dodgshon, *From Chiefs to Landlords: Social and Economic Change in the Western Highlands and Islands, c. 1493–1820* (Edinburgh: Edinburgh University Press, 198), 151–53. Dodgshon rejects the idea that runrig arrangements represented a form of primitive communism and sees them rather as a kind of temporary or revolving private property.

23. T. M. Devine, *Clanship to Crofters' War: The Social Transformation of the Scottish Highlands* (Manchester, UK: Manchester University Press, 1994), 8; Raymond J. DeMallie, "Kinship and Biology in Sioux Culture," in *North American Indian Anthropology: Essays on Society and Culture,* ed. Raymond J. DeMallie and Alfonso Ortiz (Norman: University of Oklahoma Press, 1994), 125–46.

24. Laura Peers, *The Ojibwa of Western Canada, 1780–1870* (St. Paul: Minnesota Historical Society Press, 1994), 22.

25. Theda Perdue, *Cherokee Women* (Lincoln: University of Nebraska Press, 1998), 41–42, 46–47; John Phillip Reid, *A Law of Blood: The Primitive Law of the Cherokee Nation* (New York: New York University Press, 1970), ch. 5.

26. Christopher Duffy, *The '45: Bonnie Prince Charlie and the Untold Story of the Jacobite Rising* (London: Cassell, 2003), 89; Allan I. Macinnes, *Clanship, Commerce, and the House of Stuart, 1603–1788* (East Linton, Scotland: Tuckwell, 1996), ch. 1; Bruce Lenman, *The Jacobite Clans of the Great Glen, 1650–1784* (London: Methuen, 1984), ch. 1, esp. 5–7.

27. "Some Thoughts concerning the State of the Highlands of Scotland," *Culloden Papers . . . from the Originals in possession of Duncan George Forbes of Culloden* (London: T. Cadell and W. Davies, 1815), 298; Sir Walter Scott, *Manners, Customs, and History of the Highlanders of Scotland* (1816; repr., New York: Barnes and Noble, 2004), 28–29.

28. Thomas Douglas, Earl of Selkirk, *Observations on the Present State of the Highlands of Scotland, with a View of the Causes and Probable Consequences of Emigration* (London: Longman, Hurst, Rees, and Orme, 1805), 18.

29. Rosemary E. Ommer, "Primitive Accumulation and the Scottish *Clann* in the Old World and the New," *Journal of Historical Geography* 12 (1986), 121–41, quote at 128.

30. Robert S. Neighbors, "The Na-ü-ni, or Comanches of Texas," in *The Indian Papers of Texas and the Southwest, 1825–1916*, ed. Dorman H. Winfrey and James M. Day, 5 vols. (Austin: Texas State Library, 1959–1961), vol. 3, 357; Robert M. Utley, *The Lance and the Shield: The Life and Times of Sitting Bull* (New York: Ballantine, 1993), 11–12 ("disgraceful").

31. Newton, *Handbook of the Scottish Gaelic World*, 133; Eric R. Wolf, *Europe and the People without History* (Berkeley: University of California Press, 1982), 91–92, 96–99.

32. Nairne's place of birth in Scotland is unknown, although his surname suggests family connections to the northeast. Alexander Moore, ed., *Nairne's Muskhogean Journals: The 1708 Expedition to the Mississippi River* (Jackson: University Press of Mississippi, 1988), 7, 32; Rev. David Jones, *A Journal of Two Visits made to some Nations of Indians on the West Side of the River Ohio, in the Years 1772 and 1773* (Burlington, Vt.: Isaac Collins, printer, 1774), 54; Neighbors, "The Na-ü-ni, or Comanches of Texas," 353.

33. Tim Fulford, *Romantic Indians: Native Americans, British Literature, and Transatlantic Culture* (New York: Oxford University Press, 2006), 7–8, 196; Hugh Blair, *A Critical Dissertation on the Poems of Ossian, the Son of Fingal* (London: Becket and De Hendt, 1763), 2.

34. MacLean, *An Historical Account of the Settlements of Scotch Highlanders in America*, 20–21; Norman Scarfe, ed., *To the Highlands in 1786: The Inquisitive Journey of a Young French Aristocrat* (Woodbridge, UK: Boydell, 2001), xix, 172, 223; General Wade, "Report, &, Relating to the Highlands, 1724," in *Historical Papers relating to the Jacobite Period, 1699–1750*, ed. Col. James Allardyce, 2 vols. (Aberdeen: New Spalding Club, 1895–1896), vol. 1, 137; "Some Thoughts concerning the State of the Highlands," *Culloden Papers*, 298.

35. Anne Grant, *Memoirs of an American Lady*, 2 vols. (London: Longman, Hurst, Rees, and Orme, 1809), vol. 1, 126; J. P. Grant, ed., *Letters from the Mountains; being the Correspondence with her friends, between the year 1773 and 1803, of Mrs. Grant of Laggan*, 6th ed., 2 vols. (London: Longman, Brown, Green, and Longmans, 1845), vol. 1, 48, 53.

36. Anne MacVicar Grant, *Essays on the Superstitions of the Highlanders of Scotland*, 2 vols. (London: Hurst, Rees, Orme, and Brown, 1811), vol. 1, 51.

37. Celeste Ray, ed., *Transatlantic Scots* (Tuscaloosa: University of Alabama Press, 2005), 38–39, n.4 (quoting R. Cohen).

38. Quoted in Jane H. Olmeyer, "'Civilizinge of those Rude Partes': Colonization within Britain and Ireland, 1580s–1640s," in *The Oxford History of the British Empire*. Vol. 1, *The Origins of Empire*, ed. Nicholas Canny (New York: Oxford University Press, 1998), 126.

39. Quoted in Charles M. Segal and David C. Stinebeck, *Puritans, Indians, and Manifest Destiny* (New York: Putnam's, 1977), 113.

40. Macinnes, *Clanship, Commerce, and the House of Stuart, 1603–1788.*
41. Michael Fry, *How the Scots Made America* (New York: St. Martin's, 2003), 134–35.
42. Wolf, *Europe and the People without History,* ch. 3.
43. Allan I. Macinnes, "Scottish Gaeldom: The First Phase of Clearance," in *People and Society in Scotland.* Vol. 1, *1760–1830,* ed. T. M. Devine and Rosalind Mitcheson (Edinburgh: John Donald, 1988), 70; John C. Weaver, *The Great Land Rush: Making the Modern World, 1650–1900* (Montreal: McGill-Queens, 2003).
44. A. Mackillop and Steve Murdoch, eds., *Military Governors and Imperial Frontiers, c. 1600–1800: A Study of Scotland and Empires* (Leiden, the Netherlands: Brill, 2003), xiii.
45. See, for example, James O. Gump, *The Dust Rose like Smoke: The Subjugation of the Zulu and the Sioux* (Lincoln: University of Nebraska Press, 1994).
46. John Clive and Bernard Bailyn, "England's Cultural Provinces: Scotland and America," *William and Mary Quarterly,* 3d ser., 11 (1954): 200–13.
47. T. C. Smout, N. C. Landsman, and T. M. Devine, "Scottish Emigration in the Seventeenth and Eighteenth Centuries," in *Europeans on the Move: Studies on European Migration, 1500–1800,* ed. Nicholas Canny (New York: Clarendon, 1994), 99; Arthur Herman, *How the Scots Invented the Modern World* (New York: Crown, 2001).
48. Neil Davidson, *The Origins of Scottish Nationhood* (London: Pluto, 2000), ch. 5; Angus Calder, *Scotlands of the Mind* (Edinburgh: Luath, 2002), 21–25, 163, 191.
49. Amy Kaplan, "Left Alone with America: The Absence of Empire in the Study of American Culture," in *Cultures of United States Imperialism,* ed. Amy Kaplan and Donald E. Pease (Durham, N.C.: Duke University Press, 1993), 3–21.
50. Linda Tuhiwai Smith, *Decolonizing Methodologies: Research and Indigenous Peoples* (New York: Zed, 1999), 21–23.
51. Edward Said, *Culture and Imperialism* (New York: Vintage, 1994), quote at 9.
52. Taiaiake Alfred, "Warrior Scholarship: Seeing the University as a Ground of Contention," in *Indigenizing the Academy: Transforming Scholarship and Empowering Communities,* ed. Devon Abbott Mihesuah and Angela Cavendar Wilson (Lincoln: University of Nebraska Press, 2004), 89.
53. Cynthia Radding, *Wandering Peoples: Colonialism, Ethnic Spaces, and Ecological Frontiers in Northwestern Mexico, 1700–1850* (Durham, N.C.: Duke University Press, 1997), xvii.
54. Michael Hechter, *Internal Colonialism: The Celtic Fringe in British National Development, 1536–1966* (Berkeley: University of California Press, 1975). For criticism of Hechter's attempt to apply an explicit Wallersteinian, world-systems model to Britain see, for example, David McCrone, *Understanding Scotland: The Sociology of a Nation,* 2d ed. (New York: Routledge, 2001), 64–67.
55. Smith, *Decolonizing Methodologies,* 27.
56. Francis Jennings, *The Ambiguous Iroquois Empire: The Covenant Chain Confederation of Indian Tribes with English Colonies from Its Beginnings to*

the Lancaster Treaty of 1744 (New York: Norton, 1984); Gilbert C. Din and Abraham P. Nasatir, *The Imperial Osages: Spanish-Indian Diplomacy in the Mississippi Valley* (Norman: University of Oklahoma Press, 1983); Willard H. Rollings, *The Osage: An Ethnohistorical Study of Hegemony on the Prairie-Plains* (Columbia: University of Missouri Press, 1992); Pekka Hämäläinen, *The Comanche Empire* (New Haven: Yale University Press, 2008); Richard White, "The Winning of the West: The Expansion of the Western Sioux in the Eighteenth and Nineteenth Centuries," *Journal of American History* 65 (1978): 319–43; Kathleen DuVal, *The Native Ground: Indians and Colonists in the Heart of the Continent* (Philadelphia: University of Pennsylvania Press, 2006); Ned Blackhawk, *Violence over the Land: Indians and Empires in the Early American West* (Cambridge, Mass.: Harvard University Press, 2006).

57. Smith, *Decolonizing Methodologies*, ch. 1; Amy E. Den Ouden, *Beyond Conquest: Native Peoples and the Struggle for History in New England* (Lincoln: University of Nebraska Press, 2005), 37; Michael C. Coleman, *American Indians, the Irish, and Government Schooling: A Comparative Study* (Lincoln: University of Nebraska Press, 2007).

58. On the importance to the imperial project of "the power to narrate, or to block other narratives from forming and emerging," see Said, *Culture and Imperialism*, esp. xiii.

59. McIlvanney in the *Herald*, Mar. 6, 1999, quoted in McCrone, *Understanding Scotland*, 128.

60. Scott, *Manners, Customs, and History of the Highlanders of Scotland*, 2.

61. *SAS* 9: 584, 596, 601–602; NSAS 10, 499.

62. Murray G. H. Pittock, *The Invention of Scotland: The Stuart Myth and the Scottish Identity, 1638 to the Present* (New York: Routledge, 1991), 87; Colin Kidd, *British Identities before Nationalism: Ethnicity and Nationhood in the Atlantic World, 1600–1800* (New York: Cambridge University Press, 1999), 124, 279.

63. P. Hume Brown, ed., *Scotland before 1700 from Contemporary Documents* (Edinburgh: David Douglas, 1893), 12; G. W. S. Barrow, "The Lost Gàidhealtachd of Medieval Scotland," in *Gaelic and Scotland*, ed. William Gillies (Edinburgh: Edinburgh University Press, 1989), ch. 5, qualifies Fordun's stark contrasts.

64. Brown, ed., *Scotland before 1700*, 60.

65. R. Jamieson, ed., *Burt's Letters from the North of Scotland*, 2 vols. (Edinburgh: John Donald, 1974), vol. 2, 24; Scarfe, ed., *To the Highlands in 1786*, 173.

66. Tobias Smollett, *The Expedition of Humphrey Clinker* (Athens: University of Georgia Press, 1990), 245.

67. "The Present Situation of the Highlands" [1724], NLS, ms. 2200: 60–60a; reprinted as General Wade, "Report, &, Relating to the Highlands, 1724," 133.

68. Samuel Johnson and James Boswell, *A Journey to the Western Islands of Scotland and the Journal of a Tour to the Hebrides*, ed. Peter Levi (New York: Penguin, 1984), 57.

69. "The Voyage of Don Manoel Gonzales," in *A Collection of Voyages and Travels . . . from the curious and valuable Library of the late Earl of Oxford*, 1: 201; Scarfe, ed., *To the Highlands in 1786*, 223.

70. David Hackett Fischer, *Albion's Seed: Four British Folkways in America* (New York: Oxford University Press, 1989).

71. Quoted in Robbie Ethridge, *Creek Country: The Creek Indians and Their World* (Chapel Hill: University of North Carolina Press, 2003), 111.

72. Richard White, *The Middle Ground: Indians, Empires, and Republics, 1650–1815* (New York: Cambridge University Press, 1991).

73. Colin G. Calloway, Gerd Gemünden, and Susanne Zantop, eds., *Germans and Indians: Fantasies, Encounters, Projections* (Lincoln: University of Nebraska Press, 2002), 77; David Blackbourn, *The Conquest of Nature: Water, Landscape, and the Making of Modern Germany* (New York: Norton, 2006), 303–306 (Hitler quoted at 303). I am grateful to my colleague Michael Ermarth for bringing to my attention this source and the Nazi equating of Poles with Indians.

74. Colin G. Calloway, *Crown and Calumet: British-Indian Relations, 1783–1815* (Norman: University of Oklahoma Press, 1987).

75. Herman, *How the Scots Invented the Modern World*, 323; James Buchan, *Crowded with Genius: The Scottish Enlightenment: Edinburgh's Moment of the Mind* (New York: Harper Collins, 2003).

76. Niall Ferguson, *Empire: The Rise and Demise of the British World Order and the Lessons for Global Power* (New York: Basic Books, 2003), 34; Simon Schama, *A History of Britain*. Vol. 3, *The Fate of Empire, 1776–2000* (New York: Hyperion, 2002), 275.

77. Fry, *How the Scots Made America*, 145.

78. David Armitage, "The Scottish Diaspora," in *Scotland: A History*, ed. Jenny Wormald (New York: Oxford University Press, 2005), quote at 299, photograph at 300.

79. Wheeler, *The Complexion of Race*.

80. Fry, *How the Scots Made America*, 145–46; Sylvia Van Kirk, *Many Tender Ties: Women in Fur-trade Society, 1670–1870* (Norman: University of Oklahoma Press, 1983), 240–41.

NOTES TO CHAPTER 1

1. J. P. Grant, ed., *Letters from the Mountains, being the correspondence with her friends between the years 1773 and 1803, of Mrs. Grant of Laggan*, 6th ed., 2 vols. (London: Longman, Brown, Green, and Longmans, 1845), vol. 1, 56.

2. "The Aspinall Papers," *Collections of the Massachusetts Historical Society*, 4th series (1871), vol. 9, 488.

3. Eric Richards, "Leaving the Highlands: Colonial Destinations in Canada and Australia," in *Myth, Migration, and the Making of Memory*, ed. Marjory Harper and Michael E. Vance, 105–26 (Edinburgh: John Donald, 1999), quote at 107.

4. Thomas Pennant, *A Tour in Scotland, 1772* (London, 1776; Edinburgh: Birlinn, 2000), 89–90.

5. Tacitus, *The Agricola and the Germania*, ed. and trans. H. Mattingly (Harmondsworth, U.K.: Penguin, 1970), 80–81. James Hunter takes the words Tacitus attributed to Calgacus as the title and theme of his comprehensive narrative of this thousand-year struggle, *Last of the Free: A Millennial History of the Highlands and Islands of Scotland* (Edinburgh: Mainstream, 1999).

6. Jenny Wormald, ed., *Scotland: A History* (New York: Oxford University Press, 2005), 5–6.

7. Anthony Kamm, *The Last Frontier: The Roman Invasions of Scotland* (Stroud, U.K.: Tempus, 2004).

8. Anthony Pagden, *Lords of All the World: Ideologies of Empire in Spain, Britain, and France, c. 1500–c. 1800* (New Haven, Conn.: Yale University Press, 1995), 23.

9. William Ferguson, *The Identity of the Scottish Nation: An Historic Quest* (Edinburgh: Edinburgh University Press, 1998); Colin Kidd, *British Identities before Nationalism: Ethnicity and Nationhood in the Atlantic World, 1600–1800* (New York: Cambridge University Press, 1999).

10. Alistair Moffat, *Before Scotland: The Story of Scotland before History* (London: Thames and Hudson, 2005), 285.

11. Wormald, *Scotland*, 53–61.

12. Ibid., 39.

13. Hunter, *Last of the Free*, 107–11.

14. Wormald, *Scotland*, 73–76; T. C. Smout, *A History of the Scottish People, 1560–1830* (London: Collins, 1969), 27, 33, 39.

15. Robert A. Dodgshon, *From Chiefs to Landlords: Social and Economic Change in the Western Highlands and Islands, c. 1493–1820* (Edinburgh: Edinburgh University Press, 1998). James Hunter sees the Scottish crown's destruction of the lordship of the isles as "a prominent landmark on the road that was to culminate in Culloden and the Highland Clearances." James Hunter, *On the Other Side of Sorrow: Nature and People in the Scottish Highlands* (Edinburgh: Mainstream, 1995), 74.

16. Smout, *History of the Scottish People*, 43.

17. George MacDonald Fraser, *The Steel Bonnets: The Story of the Anglo-Scottish Border Reivers* (1971; repr., London: HarperCollins, 1995); P. Hume Brown, ed., *Scotland before 1700 from Contemporary Documents* (Edinburgh: David Douglas, 1893), 68, 167, 169.

18. Allan I. Macinnes, *Clanship, Commerce, and the House of Stuart, 1603–1788* (East Linton, Scotland: Tuckwell, 1996), ch. 2; John L. Roberts, *Clan, King, and Covenant: History of the Highland Clans from the Civil War to the Glencoe Massacre* (Edinburgh: Edinburgh University Press, 2000); General Wade, "Report, &, Relating to the Highlands, 1724," in *Historical Papers relating to the Jacobite Period, 1699–1750*, ed. Col. James Allardyce, 2 vols. (Aberdeen: New

Spalding Club, 1895–1896), vol. 1, 134–36. Dodgshon, *From Chiefs to Landlords*, 87 (capacity to feast, etc.). Clan histories in this period often are a litany of conflicts; see, for example, Nicholas Maclean-Bristol, *Warriors and Priests: The History of the Clan Maclean, 1300–1570* (East Linton, Scotland: Tuckwell, 1995).

19. A. H. Williamson, "Scots, Indians, and Empire: The Scottish Politics of Civilization, 1519–1609," *Past and Present* 150 (Feb. 1996): 46–83.

20. David Armitage, "Making the Empire British: Scotland in the Atlantic World, 1542–1707," *Past and Present* 155 (May 1997): 34–63, quotes at 39–40.

21. Hunter, *Last of the Free*, 164–65.

22. Bruce Lenman, *The Jacobite Clans of the Great Glen, 1650–1784* (London: Methuen, 1984); Dodgshon, *From Chiefs to Landlords*, chs. 2–4; J. R. N. MacPhail, ed., *Highland Papers*, 4 vols. (Edinburgh: Scottish History Society, 1914–1934), vol. 1, 53 ("treason").

23. Michael Fry, *Wild Scots: Four Hundred Years of Highland History* (London: John Murray, 2005), half kingdom quote at 2; Armitage, "Making the Empire British," 44; M. Perceval-Maxwell, *The Scottish Migration to Ulster in the Reign of James I* (London: Routledge and Kegan Paul, 1973).

24. Alison Cathcart, "Crisis of Identity? Clan Chattan's Response to Government Policy in the Scottish Highlands, c. 1580–1609," in *Fighting for Identity: Scottish Military Experience, c. 1550–1900*, ed. Steve Murdoch and A. Mackillop (Leiden, the Netherlands: Brill, 2002), 163–84, quote at 176; Julian Goodare, "The Statutes of Iona in Context," *Scottish Historical Review* 77 (Apr. 1998): 31–57; Macinnes, *Clanship, Commerce, and the House of Stuart*, 56.

25. Aonghas MacCoinnich, "'His Spirit was Given only to Warre': Conflict and Identity in the Scottish Gàidhealtachd c. 1580–c. 1630," in *Fighting for Identity*, 161.

26. Macinnes, *Clanship, Commerce, and the House of Stuart*, 61; MacCoinnich, "'His Spirit was Given Only to Warre,'" 152–53; Roberts, *Clan, King, and Covenant*, 10; Pennant, *Tour in Scotland, 1769*, 150–51; Thomas Garnett, *Observations on a Tour through the Highlands and Part of the Western Isles of Scotland*, 2 vols. (London: Cadell and Davies, 1800), vol. 1, 33–34, 63–66; Sir Walter Scott, "Life and Exploits of Rob Roy and Historical Account of the Clan MacGregor," 1829, repr. in *Manners, Customs, and History of the Highlanders of Scotland* (New York: Barnes and Noble, 2004), quote at 77. David Stevenson, *The Hunt for Rob Roy: The Man and the Myths* (Edinburgh: John Donald, 2004), offers a more realistic portrayal of the Scottish hero.

27. Macinnes, *Clanship, Commerce, and the House of Stuart*, 109.

28. Samuel Johnson and James Boswell, *A Journey to the Western Islands of Scotland and the Journal of a Tour to the Hebrides*, ed. Peter Levi (New York: Penguin, 1984), 51; Daniel Defoe, *A Tour through the Whole Island of Great Britain*, ed. Pat Rogers (Exeter, UK: Webb and Bower, 1989; Promotional Reprint, 1992),

234; Garnett, *Observations on a Tour,* vol. 1, 315; Hunter, *Last of the Free,* 146–47 (Inverness as a trade center).

29. Christopher Duffy, *The '45: Bonnie Prince Charlie and the Untold Story of the Jacobite Rising* (London: Cassell, 2003), 149.

30. J. G. Fyfe, ed., *Scottish Diaries and Memoirs, 1746–1843* (Stirling, Scotland: Eneas Mackay, 1942), 574.

31. Roberts, *Clan, King, and Covenant,* 9; Dodgshon, *From Chiefs to Landlords.*

32. Oliver Thomson, *The Great Feud: The Campbells and the MacDonalds* (Thrupp, Stroud, Gloucestershire: Sutton, 2000), xvi.

33. Roberts, *Clan, King, and Covenant,* 5–6, 9, 32–33; Dodgshon, *From Chiefs to Landlords,* 34–40; T. M. Devine, *Clanship to Crofter's War: The Social Transformation of the Scottish Highlands* (Manchester, UK: Manchester University Press, 1994), 25 ("rampant imperialism"); Hunter, *Last of the Free,* 186. Garnett, *Observations on a Tour,* vol. 1, 204–15, presents a lengthy account of the MacLean-MacDonald feud. Paul Hopkins, *Glencoe and the End of the Highland War* (Edinburgh: John Donald, 1986), provides a detailed account of the wars.

34. John Prebble, *Glencoe* (Harmondsworth, UK: Penguin, 1968); Hopkins, *Glencoe and the End of the Highland War,* 488.

35. Christopher A. Whatly, *Bought and Sold for English Gold?: Explaining the Union of 1707,* 2d ed. (Edinburgh: Tuckwell, 2001).

36. Daniel Szechi, *1715: The Great Jacobite Rebellion* (New Haven, Conn.: Yale University Press, 2006), 125–26, 208.

37. Cathcart, "Crisis of Identity?" 181–83.

38. Defoe, *A Tour through the Whole Island of Great Britain,* 238.

39. "The Present Situation of the Highlands" (1724), NLS, ms. 2200, 60; Wade, "Report, &, Relating to the Highlands, 1724," *Historical Papers relating to the Jacobite Period,. vol. 1,* 132, 144; "Memoriall Anent the True State of the Highlands," ibid., vol. 1, 167–74.

40. Duffy, *The '45,* 153–61.

41. Wade, "Report, &, Relating to the Highlands, 1724," and "Report, &, Relating to the Highlands, 1727," both in *Historical Papers relating to the Jacobite Period,* vol. 1, 140–42, 147–49, 162–65; Garnett, *Observations on a Tour,* vol. 1, 313–14.

42. Grant, ed., *Letters from the Mountains,* vol. 1, 58.

43. Duffy, *The '45,* 88; Murray G. H. Pittock, *The Myth of the Jacobite Clans* (Edinburgh: Edinburgh University Press, 1995).

44. Wade, "Report, &, Relating to the Highlands, 1724," 136, 146; "Some Thoughts concerning the State of the Highlands of Scotland," in *Culloden Papers . . . from the Originals in possession of Duncan George Forbes, of Culloden* (London: T. Cadell and W. Davies, 1815), 299.

45. Lord Elcho, a member of the prince's council, provided an account of the dissension within the army and the dispersal for food on the eve of Culloden in Fyfe, ed., *Scottish Diaries and Memoirs,* 418–35.

46. Jeremy Black, *Culloden and the '45* (New York: St. Martin's, 1990), 165–74; The Duke of Cumberland's account of the battle, published April 26 at Westminster, in "The 1745 Rebellion Papers," PRO, TS/20/2: (reel 1; quotes at 2); *Historical Papers relating to the Jacobite Period*, 2: 608 ("beat back with bayonets"), 610 ("lay in heaps").

47. Geoffrey Plank, *Rebellion and Savagery: The Jacobite Rising of 1745 and the British Empire* (Philadelphia: University of Pennsylvania Press, 2006).

48. Duffy, *The '45*, 547.

49. John Prebble, *Culloden* (Harmondsworth, UK: Penguin, 1967), 182.

50. The papers relating to the prosecution, trials, and sentencing of captured rebels are in "The 1745 Rebellion Papers," PRO, TS/20 (8 reels); Annette M. Smith, *Jacobite Estates of the Forty-five* (Edinburgh: John Donald, 1982).

51. Plank, *Rebellion and Savagery*, 79, 99.

52. Ibid., 93.

53. Black, *Culloden and the '45*, 68; Lenman, *Jacobite Clans of the Great Glen* (Chisholm example at 24).

54. M. M. McKay, ed., "A Highland Minister's Diary," *Cornhill Magazine* 152 (July–Dec. 1935), 579–80.

55. Plank, *Rebellion and Savagery*, 65–66.

56. Ibid., 59, 75–76.

57. Robert Clyde, *From Rebel to Hero: The Image of the Highlander, 1745–1830* (East Linton, Scotland: Tuckwell, 1995), 6; Wormald, *Scotland*, 186–89.

58. "Some Considerations by way of Essay, upon the means of Civilizing the Highlands & extinguishing Jacobitism in Scotland" (1748), NLS, ms. 5201, 40.

59. Devine, *Clanship to Crofter's War*, 29.

60. Alex Murdoch, "James Glen and the Indians," in *Military Governors and Imperial Frontiers, c. 1600–1800: A Study of Scotland and Empires*, ed. A. Mackillop and Steve Murdoch (Leiden, the Netherlands: Brill, 2003), 141–60.

61. D. B. Quinn, *The Elizabethans and the Irish* (Ithaca, N.Y.: Cornell University Press, 1966), quotes at 119, 122.

62. Nicholas Canny, *The Elizabethan Conquest of Ireland: A Pattern Established, 1565–1576* (New York: Barnes and Noble, 1976); K. R. Andrews, N. P. Cannny, and P. E. H. Hair, eds., *The Westward Enterprise: English Activities in Ireland, the Atlantic, and America, 1480–1650* (Detroit: Wayne State University Press, 1979); Nicholas Canny, *Kingdom and Colony: Ireland in the Atlantic World, 1560–1800* (Baltimore: Johns Hopkins University Press, 1988); Nicholas Canny, *Making Ireland British, 1580–1650* (New York: Oxford University Press, 2001); James Muldoon, "The Indian as Irishman," *Essex Institute Historical Collections* 111(4) (1975): 267–89; William Christie MacLeod, "Celt and Indian: Britain's Old Frontier in Relation to the New," in *Beyond the Frontier: Social Process and Cultural Change*, ed. Paul Bohannan and Fred Plog, 25–41 (Garden City, N.Y.: Natural History Press, 1967); first reservations, 33–36.

63. Nicholas P. Canny, "The Ideology of English Colonization: From Ireland to America," *William and Mary Quarterly*, 3d ser., 30 (1973): 575–98; Katie Kane, "Nits Make Lice: Drogheda, Sand Creek, and the Poetics of Colonial Extermination," *Cultural Critique* 42 (1999): 81–103.

64. Nicholas Canny, "England's New World and the Old, 1480s–1630s," in *The Oxford History of the British Empire*. Vol. 1: *The Origins of Empire*, ed. Canny (New York: Oxford University Press, 1998), 156–57; Michael Leroy Oberg, *Dominion and Civility: English Imperialism and Native America, 1585–1685* (Ithaca, N.Y.: Cornell University Press, 1999); Frederic W. Gleach, *Powhatan's World and Colonial Virginia: A Conflict of Cultures* (Lincoln: University of Nebraska Press, 1997), ch. 4.

65. Alfred A. Cave, *The Pequot War* (Amherst: University of Massachusetts Press, 1996), 178; Richard Drinnon, *Facing West: The Metaphysics of Indian-hating and Empire-building* (New York: New American Library, 1980), ch. 5.

66. William Bradford, *Of Plymouth Plantation*, ed. Harvey Wish (New York: Capricorn, 1962), 184.

67. MacLeod, "Celt and Indian," 25–26.

68. William Douglass, *A Summary, Historical and Political, of the First Planting, Progressive Improvements, and Present State of the British Settlements in North America*, 2 vols. (Boston, 1749, 1787), vol. 1, 193–94. According to Hopkins, *Glencoe and the End of the Highland War*, 19, the MacGregors were forbidden to use their name just five years before, in 1633.

69. Michael Leroy Oberg, *Uncas, First of the Mohegans* (Ithaca, N.Y.: Cornell University Press, 2003); Eric Johnson, "Uncas and the Politics of Contact," in *Northeastern Indian Lives, 1632–1816*, ed. Robert S. Grumet, 29–47 (Amherst: University of Massachusetts Press, 1996).

70. James Drake, *King Philip's War: Civil War in New England, 1675–1676* (Amherst: University of Massachusetts Press, 1999); Jenny Hale Pulsifer, *Subjects unto the Same King: Indians, English, and the Contest for Authority in Colonial New England* (Philadelphia: University of Pennsylvania Press, 2005).

71. Logan's concerns in Richard F. Hofstadter, *America at 1750: A Social Portrait* (New York: Vintage, 1973), 28–29.

72. David Hackett Fischer, *Albion's Seed: Four British Folkways in America* (New York: Oxford University Press, 1989), 634.

73. Fischer, *Albion's Seed*, 618, 639, 642–50; James G. Leyburn, *The Scotch-Irish: A Social History* (Chapel Hill: University of North Carolina Press, 1962), 191–92; Grady McWhiney, *Cracker Culture: Celtic Ways in the Old South* (Tuscaloosa: University of Alabama Press, 1998); ch. 6; James Webb, *Born Fighting: How the Scots-Irish Shaped America* (New York: Broadway, 2004).

74. Oberg, *Dominion and Civility*.

75. Peter E. Russell, "Redcoats in the Wilderness: British Officers and Irregular Warfare in Europe and America, 1740–1760," *William and Mary Quarterly*, 3d ser., 35 (1978): 629–52, quote at 645.

76. *Journals of Major Robert Rogers* (Dublin: J. Milliken, 1769); Stephen Brumwell, *White Devil* (London: Weidenfield and Nicholson, 2004), 51–52.

77. Merchant James Parker, quoted in Woody Holton, *Forced Founders: Indians, Debtors, Slaves, and the Making of the American Revolution in Virginia* (Chapel Hill: University of North Carolina Press, 1999), 144.

78. Colin G. Calloway, *The American Revolution in Indian Country: Crisis and Diversity in Native American Communities* (New York: Cambridge University Press, 1995).

79. David Armitage, "The Scottish Diaspora," in Wormald, ed., *Scotland*, 294.

80. Joseph Waterman, *With Sword and Lancet: The Life of General Hugh Mercer* (Richmond, Va.: Garret and Massie, 1941).

81. Claudio Saunt, *A New Order of Things: Property, Power, and the Transformation of the Creek Indians, 1733–1816* (New York: Cambridge University Press, 1999).

82. Quoted in Fred Anderson and Andrew Cayton, *The Dominion of War: Empire and Liberty in North America, 1500–2000* (New York: Penguin, 2005), 232.

83. NLS, Cochrane Papers, ms. 2348: 32–34; 2346: 2–3.

NOTES TO CHAPTER 2

1. A. J. Youngson, *After the Forty-five: The Economic Impact on the Scottish Highlands* (Edinburgh: Edinburgh University Press, 1973).

2. Simon Schama, *A History of Britain*. Vol. 2, *The Wars of the British, 1603–1776* (New York: Hyperion, 2001), 330.

3. Cf. Claudio Saunt, *A New Order of Things: Property, Power, and the Transformation of the Creek Indians, 1733–1816* (New York: Cambridge University Press, 1999), 82.

4. NSAS 7: 93; Charles W. J. Withers, *Gaelic Scotland: The Transformation of a Culture Region* (London: Routledge, 1988), 253.

5. Quoted in P. J. Marshall and Glyndwr Williams, *The Great Map of Mankind: Perceptions of New Worlds in the Age of Enlightenment* (Cambridge, Mass.: Harvard University Press, 1982), 190.

6. P. Hume Brown, ed., *Scotland before 1700 from Contemporary Documents* (Edinburgh: David Douglas, 1893), 67.

7. Ned C. Landsman, *Scotland and Its First American Colony, 1683–1765* (Princeton, N.J.: Princeton University Press, 1985).

8. Alan L. Karras, *Sojourners in the Sun: Scottish Migrants in Jamaica and the Chesapeake, 1740–1800* (Ithaca, N.Y.: Cornell University Press, 1992).

9. Allan I. Macinnes, "Scottish Gaeldom: The First Phase of Clearance," in *People and Society in Scotland*. Vol. 1, *1760–1830*, ed. T. M. Devine and Rosalind Mitchison (Edinburgh: John Donald, 1988), 77.

10. Thomas Pennant, *A Tour in Scotland, 1769* (1771; repr., Edinburgh: Birlinn, 2000), xvii.

11. David Miles, *The Tribes of Britain* (London: Phoenix, 2006), 362, 364.
12. A. R. B. Haldane, *New Ways through the Glens: Highland Road, Bridge, and Canal Makers of the Early Nineteenth Century* (Isle of Colonsay, Argyll, Scotland: House of Lochaber, 1962), quotes at 137–38; Robert Southey, *Journal of a Tour in Scotland in 1819,* ed. C. H. Herford (London: John Murray, 1929), 185.
13. Eric Richards, *A History of the Highland Clearances.* Vol. 1, *Agrarian Transformation and the Evictions, 1746–1886* (London: Croom Helm, 1982), 85–88 (cattle and meal trade), 88–96 (famines).
14. Southey, *Journal of a Tour,* 141.
15. T. M. Devine, *The Transformation of Rural Scotland: Social Change and the Agrarian Economy, 1660–1815* (Edinburgh: John Donald, 1994).
16. Eric Richards, *A History of the Highland Clearances.* Vol. 2, *Emigration, Protest, Reasons* (London: Croom Helm, 1985), 14–19; Adam Smith, *An Inquiry into the Nature and Causes of the Wealth of Nations,* ed. R. H. Campbell, A. S. Skinner, and W. B. Todd; 2 vols. (Oxford, UK: Clarendon, 1976).
17. Devine, *Transformation of Rural Scotland,* population figures at 35–36; Youngson, *After the Forty-five,* ch. 7, population figures at 161; Macinnes, *Clanship, Commerce, and the House of Stuart,* 142–43, 221 (Highland population increase); Richards, *History of the Highland Clearances,* vol. 2, 181, 237 (percentages of Highland-born people in Greenock and Glasgow). On population growth see also T. C. Smout, *A History of the Scottish People, 1560–1830* (London: Collins, 1969), ch. 11; R. A. Houston, "The Demographic Regime," in *People and Society in Scotland,* vol. 1, ed. Devine and Mitichison, ch. 1, and Withers, *Gaelic Scotland,* ch. 4; Richards, *Highland Clearances,* 45–49, quote at 45; James Hunter, *The Making of the Crofting Community,* new ed. (Edinburgh: John Donald/Birlinn, 2000), quote at 9.
18. Jenny Wormald, ed., *Scotland: A History* (New York: Oxford University Press, 2005), 217.
19. For ongoing changes in the landscapes of North Britain see T. C. Smout, *Nature Contested: Environmental History in Scotland and Northern England since 1600* (Edinburgh: Edinburgh University Press, 2000), 57–58, 125–31, for sheep grazing.
20. William L. McDowell, ed., *Colonial Records of South Carolina: Documents relating to Indian Affairs,* Vol. 1, *1750–1754* (Columbia: South Carolina Archives Department, 1958), 453.
21. Robert S. Grumet, *National Historic Landmark Theme Study: Historic Contact: Early Relations between Indian People and Colonists in Northeastern North America, 1524–1783* (National Park Service, 1992), 183.
22. Timothy Pickering Papers, Massachusetts Historical Society, Boston, reel 62: 157–74; Colin G. Calloway, *The American Revolution in Indian Country* (New York: Cambridge University Press, 1995), 2, 12.
23. Patrick C. T. White, ed., *Lord Selkirk's Diary 1803–1804: A Journal of His Travels in British North America and the Northeastern United States* (Toronto: Champlain Society, 1958), 196.

288 NOTES TO PAGES 48–50

24. James Axtell, "The First Consumer Revolution," in James Axtell, *Beyond 1492: Encounters in Colonial America* (New York: Oxford University Press, 1992), ch. 5; Timothy H. Breen, "An Empire of Goods: The Anglicization of Early America, 1690–1776," *Journal of British Studies* 25 (1980), 467–99.

25. James H. Merrell, *The Indians' New World: Catawbas and Their Neighbors from European Contact through the Era of Removal* (Chapel Hill: University of North Carolina Press, 1989); William Cronon, *Changes in the Land: Indians, Colonists, and the Ecology of New England* (New York: Hill and Wang, 1983); Timothy Silver, *A New Face on the Countryside: Indians, Colonists, and Slaves in South Atlantic Forests, 1500–1800* (New York: Cambridge University Press, 1990); Carolyn Merchant, *Ecological Revolutions: Nature, Gender, and Science in New England* (Chapel Hill: University of North Carolina Press, 1989).

26. Richard White, *The Roots of Dependency: Subsistence, Environment, and Social Change among the Choctaws, Pawnees, and Navajos* (Lincoln: University of Nebraska Press, 1983).

27. Russell Thornton, *American Indian Holocaust and Survival: A Population History since 1492* (Norman: University of Oklahoma Press, 1987); Thornton, "Aboriginal North American Population and Rates of Decline, ca. A.D. 1500–1900," *Current Anthropology* 38 (1997): 310–15; William M. Denevan, ed., *The Native Population of the Americas in 1492*, 2d ed. (Madison: University of Wisconsin Press, 1992).

28. William Bradford, *Of Plymouth Plantation*, ed. Harvey Wish (New York: Capricorn, 1962), 176.

29. Elizabeth A. Fenn, *Pox Americana: The Great Smallpox Epidemic of 1775–82* (New York: Hill and Wang, 2001); Colin G. Calloway, *One Vast Winter Count: The Native American West before Lewis and Clark* (Lincoln: University of Nebraska Press, 2003), 415–26.

30. Thornton, *American Indian Holocaust and Survival*, 94–99; Clyde D. Dollar, "The High Plains Smallpox Epidemic of 1837–38," *Western Historical Quarterly* 8 (1977): 15–38.

31. Miles, *Tribes of Britain*, 273.

32. Smout, *History of the Scottish People*, 253.

33. M. M. McKay, ed., "A Highland Minister's Diary," *Cornhill Magazine* 152 (July–Dec., 1935), 572 (full pagination 570–80).

34. Daniel William Kemp, ed., *Tours in Scotland in 1747, 1750, 1760 by Richard Pococke, Bishop of Meath* (Edinburgh: Scottish Historical Society, 1887), 94.

35. F. Fenner, D. A. Henderson, I. Arita, Z. Jezek, and I. D. Ladnyi, *Smallpox and Its Eradication* (Geneva: World Health Organization, 1988) 231; Smout, *History of the Scottish People*, 253–54; SAS 1: 263, 485; 7: 570; 17: 374.

36. James Dow McCallum, ed., *Letters of Eleazar Wheelock's Indians* (Hanover, N.H.: Dartmouth College Publications, 1932), 205, 211–16. Since Benjamin Rush believed that bleeding and purging patients were the best ways to cure them of just about any illness, it is questionable whether his presence could have helped Tobias.

37. Margaret Connell Szasz, *Scottish Highlanders and Native Americans: Indigenous Education in the Eighteenth-century Atlantic World* (Norman: University of Oklahoma Press, 2007), 185.

38. McKay, ed., "Highland Minister's Diary," 572–73.

39. Charles W. J. Withers, *Urban Highlanders: Highland-Lowland Migration and Urban Gaelic Culture, 1700–1900* (East Linton, Scotland: Tuckwell, 1998), 145–50; Miles, *Tribes of Britain*, 391.

40. Margaret Glen to Archibald Campbell, January 27, 1833, in Judith Hudson Beattie and Helen M, Buss, eds., *Undelivered Letters to Hudson's Bay Company Men on the Northwest Coast of America, 1830–57* (Vancouver: University of British Columbia Press, 2003), 32; 352; Thornton, *American Indian Holocaust and Survival*, 103–04.

41. Marianne McLean, *The People of Glengarry: Highlanders in Transition, 1745–1820* (Montreal: McGill-Queens University Press, 1991), 87; "On Emigration from the Scottish Highlands & Isles," by Edward S. Fraser; NLS, ms. 9646: 31.

42. Marjory Harper, *Adventurers and Exiles: The Great Scottish Exodus* (London: Profile, 2003), 199. *Scots Magazine* 36 (1774), 263–64, carried an account of conditions on board the *Nancy*.

43. D. C. Harvey, "Scottish Emigration to Cape Breton," in *Cape Breton Historical Essays*, ed. Don Macgillivray and Brian Tennyson (Sydney, Cape Breton Island, Canada: College of Cape Breton Press, 1980), 36.

44. Daniel Szechi, *1715: The Great Jacobite Rebellion* (New Haven, Conn.: Yale University Press, 2006), 13.

45. Linda Colley, *Captives* (New York: Pantheon, 2002), 188–92; Douglas Skelton, *Indian Peter: The Extraordinary Life and Adventures of Peter Williamson* (Edinburgh: Mainstream, 2004); Ferenc M. Szasz, "Peter Williamson and the Eighteenth-century Scottish-American Connection," *Northern Scotland* 19 (1999), 47–61.

46. James Axtell, "The Power of Print in the Eastern Woodlands," in James Axtell, *After Columbus: Essays in the Ethnohistory of Colonial North America* (New York: Oxford University Press, 1988), 86–99; *Minutes of debates in council on the banks of the Ottawa River, (commonly called the Miamia of the Lake) November—, 1791. Said to be held there by the chiefs of the several Indian nations, who defeated the army of the United States, on the 4th of that month. Present, various nations.* (Philadelphia, 1794), 11 ("pen and ink witch-craft"); Richard B. Sher, *The Enlightenment and the Book: Scottish Authors and Their Publishers in Eighteenth-century Britain, Ireland, and America* (Chicago: University of Chicago Press, 2006); Arthur Herman, *How the Scots Invented the Modern World* (New York: Crown, 2001).

47. Samson Occom, "A Short Narrative of My Life," in *The World Turned Upside Down: Indian Voices from Early America*, ed. Colin G. Calloway (Boston: Bedford, 1994), 56.

48. Donald E. Meek, *The Scottish Highlands: The Churches and Gaelic Culture* (Geneva: World Council of Churches, 1996), 15–18; Murray G. H. Pittock, *The Myth of the Jacobite Clans* (Edinburgh: Edinburgh University Press, 1999), ch. 2; Szechi, *1715*, 61.

49. Szasz, *Scottish Highlanders and Native Americans*, chs. 3–5; James Hunter, *The Last of the Free: A Millennial History of the Scottish Highlands and Islands* (Edinburgh: Mainstream, 1999), 174.

50. Hugh MacDiarmid, "Island Funeral," in *Selected Poetry*, ed. Alan Riach and Michael Grieve (New York: New Directions, 1993), 180.

51. Robert A. Dodgshon, *From Chiefs to Landlords: Social and Economic Change in the Western Highlands and Islands, c. 1493–1820* (Edinburgh: Edinburgh University Press, 1998).

52. Macinnes, *Clanship, Commerce, and the House of Stuart*, 144–48; Richards, *History of the Highland Clearances*, vol. 1, 52, 114, 122–25.

53. James Hunter, *Culloden and the Last Clansman* (Edinburgh: Mainstream, 2001), 174–75.

54. Macinnes, *Clanship, Commerce, and the House of Stuart*, 210–11, 217.

55. Hunter, *Making of the Crofting Community*, 45; Hunter, *Last of the Free*, 207–12.

56. T. M. Devine, *Scotland's Empire and the Shaping of the Americas, 1600–1815* (Washington, D.C.: Smithsonian Books, 2003), 120; Devine, *Transformation of Rural Scotland*.

57. *Colonial Records of Pennsylvania* 5: 146–47; Seneca and Onondaga quotes from Calloway, *American Revolution in Indian Country*, 7, 59.

58. Calloway, *American Revolution in Indian Country*, 190–96; William L. Saunders, ed., *The Colonial Records of North Carolina*, vol. 10 (Raleigh: State Printer, 1890), 773–84

59. White, *Roots of Dependency*, ch. 4.

60. Theda Perdue, *Cherokee Women: Gender and Culture Change, 1700–1835* (Lincoln: University of Nebraska Press, 1998).

61. John Wood Sweet, *Bodies Politic: Negotiating Race in the American North, 1730–1830* (Baltimore: Johns Hopkins University Press, 2003), ch. 1.

62. Saunt, *New Order of Things*.

63. R. A. Houston and W. W. J. Knox, eds., *The New Penguin History of Scotland* (London: Penguin, 2001), xxxi ("streets of Scots" quote); T. C. Smout, N. C. Landsman, and T. M. Devine, "Scottish Emigration in the Early Modern Period," in *Europeans on the Move: Studies on European Migration, 1500–1800*, ed. Nicholas Canny, 76–112 (Oxford, UK: Clarendon, 1994); Christopher Smout, "Culture of Migration: Scots as Europeans 1500–1800," *History Workshop Journal* 40 (1995): 108–17; Eric Richards, *Britannia's Children: Emigration from England, Scotland, Wales, and Ireland since 1600* (London: Hambledon and London, 2004), 27, 53.

64. David Armitage, "Making the Empire British: Scotland in the Atlantic World 1542–1707," *Past and Present* 155 (May 1997): 46.

65. R. J. Adam, ed., *Papers on Sutherland Estate Management, 1802–1816*, 2 vols. (Edinburgh: Scottish History Society, 1972), vol. 1, 16 (Strathnaver quote); NSAS 7: 214; 14: 347.

66. Withers, *Urban Highlanders*, Perth mill owner quote at 143; Devine, *Transformation of Rural Scotland*.

67. Devine and Mitchison, eds., *People and Society in Scotland*, vol. 1, 41–43.

68. Alex Murdoch, "Emigration from the Scottish Highlands to America in the Eighteenth Century," *British Journal for Eighteenth-century Studies* 21 (1998): 161–74.

69. Withers, *Gaelic Scotland*, ch. 5.

70. Quoted in Stuart Banner, *How the Indians Lost Their Land: Law and Power on the Frontier* (Cambridge, Mass.: Harvard University Press, 2005), 260.

71. Joseph Medicine Crow, *From the Heart of the Crow Country: The Crow Indians' Own Stories* (New York: Crown, 1992); N. Scott Momaday, *The Way to Rainy Mountain* (Albuquerque: University of New Mexico Press, 1969); Pekka Hämäläinen, *The Comanche Empire* (New Haven, Conn.: Yale University Press, 2008); John H. Moore, *The Cheyenne Nation: A Social and Demographic History* (Lincoln: University of Nebraska Press, 1987); Elliott West, "Called Out People: The Cheyennes and the Central Plains," *Montana, The Magazine of Western History* 48 (Summer 1998); Elliott West, *The Contested Plains: Indians, Goldseekers, and the Rush to Colorado* (Lawrence: University Press of Kansas, 1998).

72. Alice Littlefield and Martha C. Knack, eds., *Native Americans and Wage Labor: Ethnohistorical Perspectives* (Norman: University of Oklahoma Press, 1996).

73. Judith A. Ranta, *The Life and Writings of Betsey Chamberlain, Native American Mill Worker* (Boston: Northeastern University Press, 2003).

74. Devine and Mitchison, eds., *People and Society in Scotland*, vol. 1, 232.

75. Jenni Calder, *Scots in the USA* (Edinburgh: Luath, 2006), 124.

NOTES TO CHAPTER 3

1. Samuel Johnson and James Boswell, *A Journey to the Western Islands of Scotland and the Journal of a Tour to the Hebrides*, ed. Peter Levi (New York: Penguin, 1984), 308.

2. Fernand Braudel, *The Mediterranean and the Mediterranean World in the Age of Philip II*, 2 vols. (New York: Harper and Row, 1972), vol. 1, 34.

3. P. Hume Brown, ed., *Scotland before 1700 from Contemporary Documents* (Edinburgh: David Douglas, 1893), 10.

4. Martin Martin, *A Description of the Western Islands of Scotland circa 1695*, ed. Donald J. Macleod, (Edinburgh: Birlinn, 1994), esp. 19; R. Jamieson, ed., *Burt's Letters from the North of Scotland*, 2 vols. (Edinburgh: John Donald, 1974).

5. Daniel Defoe, *A Tour of the Whole Island of Great Britain*, ed. Pat Rogers (Exeter, UK: Webb and Bower, 1989; Promotional Reprint, 1992), 238.

6. General Wade, "Report, &, Relating to the Highlands, 1724," in *Historical Papers relating to the Jacobite Period, 1699–1750*, ed. Col. James Allardyce, 2 vols. (Aberdeen: New Spalding Club, 1895–1896), vol. 1, 139–40.

7. Norman Scarfe, ed., *To the Highlands in 1786: The Inquisitive Journey of a Young French Aristocrat* (Rochester, N.Y.: Boydell, 2001), 226; Tobias Smollett, *The Expedition of Humphrey Clinker* (Athens: University of Georgia Press, 1990), 244.

8. Johnson and Boswell, *Journey to the Western Islands*, 12, 314.

9. William Knight, ed., *Journals of Dorothy Wordsworth* (London: Macmillan, 1925), 362.

10. Michael Newton, *A Handbook of the Scottish Gaelic World* (Dublin: Four Courts Press, 2000).

11. "The Present Situation of the Highlands," NLS, ms. 2200: 60–60a; Wade, "Report, &, Relating to the Highlands, 1724," 132.

12. "Some Thoughts concerning the State of the Highlands of Scotland," *Culloden Papers . . . from the Originals in Possession of Duncan George Forbes, of Culloden* (London: T. Cadell and W. Davies, 1815), 298–99.

13. Johnson and Boswell, *Journey to the Western Islands*, 63.

14. William Smith, *An Historical Account of the Expedition against the Ohio Indians* (Philadelphia, 1765), 3; quoted in Patrick Griffen, *American Leviathan: Empire, Nation, and the Revolutionary Frontier* (New York: Hill and Wang, 2007), 68.

15. Grady McWhiney, *Cracker Culture: Celtic Ways in the Old South* (Tuscaloosa: University of Alabama Press, 1988).

16. Robert F. Berkhofer Jr., *The White Man's Indian: Images of the American Indian from Columbus to the Present* (New York: Vintage, 1979), 27–28.

17. Gordon M. Sayre, *Les Sauvages Américains: Representations of Native Americans in French and English Colonial Literature* (Chapel Hill: University of North Carolina Press, 1997), 144–46.

18. Scarfe, ed., *To the Highlands in 1786*, 161.

19. Martin J. Daunton and Rich Halpern, eds., *Empire and Others: British Encounters with Indigenous Peoples, 1600–1850* (Philadelphia: University of Pennsylvania Press, 1994), 4.

20. Colin G. Calloway, *Crown and Calumet: British-Indian Relations, 1783–1815* (Norman: University of Oklahoma Press, 1987), 94–95.

21. Thomas Pennant, *A Tour in Scotland, 1772* (London, 1776), 84; Scarfe, ed., *To the Highlands in 1786*, 172; Jamieson, ed., *Burt's Letters*, vol. 2, 299; John Loveday, *Diary of a Tour in 1732 through Parts of England, Wales, Ireland, and Scotland* (Edinburgh, 1890), 163.

22. Daniel Gookin, "Historical Collections of the Indians of New England," *Collections of the Massachusetts Historical Society for 1792* (repr., Towtaid, N.J., 1970), 15.

23. Thomas Garnett, *Observations on a Tour through the Highlands and Part of the Western Isles of Scotland*, 2 vols. (London: Cadell and Davies, 1800), vol. 1, 159–60;

Eric Richards, *A History of the Highland Clearances*. Vol. 2: *Emigration, Protest, Reasons* (London: Croom Helm, 1985), 3 (Clark quote); Arthur Herman, *How the Scots Invented the Modern World* (New York: Crown, 2001), 109.

24. Knight, ed., *Journals of Dorothy Wordsworth*, 224, 229, 234 ("Hottentotish"), 274–75, 316.
25. Gookin, "Historical Collections of the Indians of New England," 14; Samuel Cole Williams, ed., *The Memoirs of Lieutenant Henry Timberlake* (Johnson City, Tenn.: Watauga Press, 1927), 99; Francis Paul Prucha, ed., *Documents of United States Indian Policy* (Lincoln: University of Nebraska Press, 1975); 78 (Medill); L. R. Masson, ed., *Les Bourgeois de la Compagnie du Nord-Ouest*, 2 vols. (1889–1890; repr., New York: Antiquarian Society Press, 1960), vol. 1, 281; vol. 2, 413; Pennant, *Tour in Scotland*, 84; James Loch, *An Account of the Improvements on the Estates of the Marquess of Stafford* (London: Longmans, Hurst, Rees, Orme, and Brown, 1820), 51; Smollett, *Expedition of Humphrey Clinker*, 245.
26. James Axtell, ed., *The Indian Peoples of Eastern America: A Documentary History of the Sexes* (New York: Oxford University Press, 1981), 103–39; Gookin, "Historical Collections of the Indians of New England," 14; Scarfe, ed., *To the Highlands in 1786*, 172; Pennant, *Tour in Scotland*, 84; Loch, *Account of the Improvements*, 51, 63; Calloway, *Crown and Calumet*, 91–92.
27. J. P. Grant, ed., *Letters from the Mountains, being the correspondence with her friends between the years 1773 and 1803, of Mrs. Grant of Laggan*, 6th ed., 2 vols. (London: Longman, Brown, Green, and Longmans, 1845), vol. 1, 229–30; Anne Grant, *Memoirs of an American Lady; with Sketches of Manners and Scenery in America, as they existed previous to the Revolution*, 2d ed., 2 vols. (London: Longman, Hurst, Rees, and Orme, 1809).
28. Calloway, *Crown and Calumet*, 89–90; Robert Michael Ballanyne, *Hudson Bay, or, Everyday Life in the Wilds of North America during Six Years' Residence in the Territories of the Hon. Hudson Bay Company*, 4th ed. (London: Thomas Nelson and Sons, 1902), 32–33.
29. William Fraser, *The Emigrant's Guide, or Sketches of Canada, with some of the Northern and Western States of America, by a Scotch Minister, Thirty-six Years Resident in Canada—from 1831 to 1867* (Glasgow: Porteus Brothers, 1876–1877), 17; "Some Considerations by way of Essay, upon the means of Civilizing the Highlands & extinguishing Jacobitism in Scotland," NLS, ms. 5201: 17.
30. Gookin, "Historical Collections of the Indians of New England," 13 (quote); M. François Perrin du Lac, *Travels through the Two Louisianas and among the Savage Nations of the Missouri* (London: Richard Phillips, 1807), 66; John Ferdinand Dalziel Smyth, *A Tour in the United States of America . . . with a Description of the Indian Nations*, 2 vols. (London: G. Robinson, 1784), vol. 1, 341; Milo M. Quaife, ed., *John Long's Voyages and Travels in the Years 1768–1788* (Chicago: R. R. Donnelley and Sons, 1922), 40.
31. Arthur S. Morton, ed., *The Journal of Duncan McGillivray of the North West Company at Fort George on the Saskatchewan, 1794–95* (Toronto: Macmillan of

Canada, 1929), 63; Alexander Ross, *Adventures of the First Settlers on the Oregon or Columbia River,* ed. Milo M. Quaife (Chicago: R. R. Donnelley and Sons, 1923), 352.

32. Jamieson, ed., *Burt's Letters,* vol. 2, 130; see also Pennant, *Tour in Scotland,* 128.

33. Gookin, "Historical Collections of the Indians of New England," 13–14; Barry M. Gough, ed., *The Journal of Alexander Henry the Younger, 1799–1814,* 2 vols. (Toronto: Champlain Society, 1992), vol. 2, 333.

34. Wade, "Report, &, Relating to the Highlands, 1724," 132 (quote); Anne MacVicar Grant, *Essays on the Superstitions of the Highlanders of Scotland,* 2 vols. (London: Hurst, Res, Orme, and Brown, 1811), vol. 1, 127.

35. Morton, ed., *Journal of Duncan McGillivray,* 57.

36. On Cherokee clan vengeance see Theda Perdue, *Cherokee Women* (Lincoln: University of Nebraska Press, 1998), 50 (cosmic order quote); John Phillip Reid, *A Law of Blood: The Primitive Law of the Cherokee Nation* (New York: New York University Press), ch. 5; Rennard Strickland, *Fire and the Spirits: Cherokee Law from Clan to Court* (Norman: University of Oklahoma Press, 1975), 27–28. Among the Creeks: Claudio Saunt, *A New Order of Things: Property, Power, and the Transformation of the Creek Indians, 1733–1816* (New York: Cambridge University Press, 1999), 90–93.

37. Scarfe, ed., *To the Highlands in 1786,* 197–98.

38. Gookin, "Historical Collections of the Indians of New England," 19–20.

39. Elizabeth Thompson, ed., *The Emigrant's Guide to North America (Ceann-iùil an Fhir-Imrich do Dh'America Mu-Thuath)* (1841; translated Toronto: Natural Heritage Books, 1998), 55; Calloway, *Crown and Calumet,* 85.

40. Calloway, *Crown and Calumet,* 85–86.

41. Scarfe, ed., *To the Highlands in 1786,* xix, 223.

42. Quaife, ed., *John Long's Voyages and Travels,* 40.

43. Quoted in Newton, *Handbook of the Scottish Gaelic World,* 120.

44. Masson, ed., *Les Bourgeois de la Compagnie du Nord-Ouest,* vol. 2, 263–64; Calloway, *Crown and Calumet,* 102–106.

45. William Douglass, *A Summary, Historical and Political, of the First Planting, Progressive Improvements, and Present State of the British Settlements in North America,* 2 vols. (Boston, 1749, 1787), vol. 1, 22.

46. Nicholas Canny, "England's New World and the Old, 1480s–1630s," in *The Oxford History of the British Empire.* Vol. 1, *The Origins of Empire,* ed. Canny (New York: Oxford University Press, 1998), 154; Kim Sloan, *A New World: England's First View of America* (Chapel Hill: University of North Carolina Press, 2007), 153.

47. Julian Goodare, "The Statutes of Iona in Context," *Scottish Historical Review* 77 (Apr. 1998), 31–57.

48. Donald E. Meek, *The Scottish Highlands: The Churches and Gaelic Culture* (Geneva: World Council of Churches, 1996), 20–21 (1616 act); T. M. Devine, *Clanship to Crofters' War: The Social Transformation of the Scottish Highlands* (Manchester, UK: Manchester University Press, 1994), 100 (parish size).

49. *An Account of the Funds, Expenditure, and General Management of the Affairs of the Society in Scotland for Propagating Christian Knowledge* (Edinburgh: J. Paterson, 1796), 8–9; Robert Clyde, *From Rebel to Hero: The Image of the Highlander, 1745–1830* (East Linton, Scotland: Tuckwell, 1995), ch. 3; Charles W. J. Withers, *Gaelic Scotland: The Transformation of a Culture Region* (London: Routledge, 1988), quote at 405. For a full discussion of the work of the SSPCK in both the Highlands and America, see Margaret Connell Szasz, *Scottish Highlanders and Native Americans: Indigenous Education in the Eighteenth-century Atlantic World* (Norman: University of Oklahoma Press, 2007), especially ch. 3 for the society's birth.

50. "Observation about the Improvements and Reformation of the West Highlands made in the Year 1754," NLS, ms. 17504: 57–58, quoted in Heather Streets, "Identity in the Highland Regiments in the Nineteenth Century: Soldier, Region, Nation," in *Fighting for Identity: Scottish Military Experience, c. 1550–1900,* ed. Steve Murdoch and A. Mackillop (Leiden, the Netherlands: Brill, 2002), 217; "Some Considerations by way of Essay, upon the means of Civilizing the Highlands & extinguishing Jacobitism in Scotland," NLS, ms. 5201: 6; "Some Remarks on the Highland Clans and Methods proposed for Civilizing Them," NLS, Adv. ms. 16.1.14.

51. Allan I. Macinnes, *Clanship, Commerce, and the House of Stuart, 1603–1788* (East Linton, Scotland: Tuckwell, 1996), 159–60.

52. Annette M. Smith, *Jacobite Estates of the Forty-five* (Edinburgh: John Donald, 1982), 20.

53. "On the Condition of the Highland Peasantry before and since the Rebellion of 1745," by "B. G.," reprinted in Thomas Bakewell, *Remarks on a Publication by James Loch, Esq. entitled an Account of the Improvements on the Estates of the Marques of Stafford* (London: Longman, Hurst, Rees, Orme, and Brown, 1820), 62.

54. "Some Thoughts concerning the State of the Highlands of Scotland," *Culloden Papers . . . from the Originals,* 297–301; quote at 301.

55. Quoted in Devine, *Clanship to Crofters' War,* 86.

56. *Historical Papers relating to the Jacobite Period,* vol. 2, 514, 516–20, 522–27, 550, 554. Although the government recognized the martial spirit of bagpipes, there is little contemporary evidence to support the common view that bagpipes were outlawed; William Donaldson, *The Highland Pipe and Scottish Society 1750–1950* (East Linton: Tuckwell, 2000), 8.

57. Quoted in John Prebble, *Culloden* (Harmondsworth, UK: Penguin, 1967), 299.

58. Donald E. Meek, "Scottish Highlanders, North American Indians, and the SSPCK: Some Cultural Perspectives," *Records of the Scottish Church History Society* 23 (1989), 383–85, 391, 395; Meek, *The Scottish Highlands,* 18–19; *Account of the Funds, Expenditure, and General Management,* 50–51; Clyde, *From Rebel to Hero,* 63–64; Nancy C. Dorion, *Language Death: The Life Cycle of a Scottish Gaelic Dialect* (Philadelphia: University of Pennsylvania Press, 1981), 21–22.

59. SAS 2: 389; Buchanan, quoted in Szasz, *Scottish Highlanders and Native Americans,* 181; Withers, *Gaelic Scotland,* ch. 3 and SSPCK policy quote at 160.

60. Devine, *Clanship to Crofters' War,* ch. 8 and quote at 115.

61. Rev. John Walker's reports to the general assembly of the Kirk of Scotland, *Scots Magazine* 28 (1766), 680–88; 34 (1772), 289.

62. SAS 2: 389; 9: 601–602; 17: 384; NSAS 7: 187, 307, 401, 528; 11: 611–12; 14: 84, 199; 15: 7, 112, 156.

63. David J. Silverman, *Faith and Boundaries: Colonists, Christianity, and Community among the Wampanoag Indians of Martha's Vineyard, 1600–1871* (New York: Cambridge University Press, 2005), 219–20, 238.

64. Clyde, *From Rebel to Hero,* 68–84.

65. Meek, *Scottish Highlands,* 33–34; Clyde, *From Rebel to Hero,* 90.

66. "On Emigration from the Scottish Highlands and Isles," by Edward S. Fraser, NLS, ms. 9646: 111.

67. Johnson and Boswell, *Journey to the Western Islands,* 73.

68. Scarfe, ed., *To the Highlands in 1786,* 175, 197.

69. Meek, "Scottish Highlanders, North American Indians, and the SSPCK," 378–96; Frederick V. Mills, "The Society in Scotland for Propagating Christian Knowledge in British North America, 1730–1775," *Church History* 63 (1994), 15–30.

70. Michael Newton, *We're Indians Sure Enough: The Legacy of the Scottish Highlanders in the United States* (Richmond, VA.: Saorsa Media, 2001), 233.

71. *Account of the Funds, Expenditure, and General Management of the Affairs of the Society in Scotland for Propagating Christian Knowledge,* 27–29.

72. Laura M. Stevens, *The Poor Indians: British Missionaries, Native Americans, and Colonial Sensibility* (Philadelphia: University of Pennsylvania Press, 2004), 94; Meek, *Scottish Highlands,* 20.

73. *The Life of Rev. David Brainerd, chiefly extracted from his diary by President [Jonathan] Edwards* (Grand Rapids, Mich.: Baker, 1978), 64. On Brainerd's work see Szasz, *Scottish Highlanders and Native Americans,* 126–31.

74. Walter Pilkington, ed., *Journals of Samuel Kirkland: 18th-Century Missionary to the Iroquois, Government Agent, Father of Hamilton College* (Clinton, N.Y.: Hamilton College, 1980), 121, 181.

75. Szasz, *Scottish Highlanders and Native Americans,* 153–59, quote at 155.

76. NAS, SSPCK records, letter book containing the American correspondence of the society, 1799–1806, GD95/3/1:94.

77. *Mamusse wunneetupanatamwe Up-Biblum God naneeswe Nukkone Testament kah wonk Wusku Testament. Ne quoshkinnumuk nashpe wuttinneumoh Christ noh asoowesit John Eliot* (Cambridge, Mass.: Printeuoop nashpe Samuel Green kah Marmaduke Johnson, 1661–1663), Dartmouth College, Rauner Rare Book Library; Szasz, *Scottish Highlanders and Native Americans,* 123.

78. Meek, "Scottish Highlanders, North American Indians, and the SSPCK," 385–96; Szasz, *Scottish Highlanders and Native Americans,* chs. 5–6 and quote at

144; Sergeant quote from *A Letter from the Rev'd Mr. Sergeant of Stockbridge, to Dr. Colman of Boston* (Boston, 1743), 1; Michael C. Coleman, *American Indians, the Irish, and Government Schooling* (Lincoln: University of Nebraska Press, 2007).

79. Stevens, *Poor Indians*, 26; *Scots Magazine* 29 (1767), 499; Szasz, *Scottish Highlanders and Native Americans*, ch. 7, esp. 201, 208 (comparative sums raised) and 212–13 (much in common); Meek, *Scottish Highlands*, 22.

80. Eleazar Wheelock to William Hyslop, Dec. 1, 1760, NAS, GD95/12/2; GD95/3/1: 15–16, 46–51, 55–60; "Correspondence between the American Board of Commissioners for Foreign Missions and the S.S.P.C.K regarding the education of Indians at Moore's Indian school and Dartmouth College, 1890–1898," NAS, GD95/12/16; SSPCK Records, 1794–1892, Dartmouth College, Rauner Manuscripts DA-42 (see, for example, correspondence from President Nathan Lord, Apr. 20 and 26, 1832, folders 1–3; May 9, 1853, folders 1–5; SSPCK Secretary John Tawse, July 8, 1869, folders 1–6; President Asa Smith, Dec. 31, 1872, folders 1–7; President Bartlett, Mar. 9, 1892, folders 1–9); *Account of the Funds, Expenditure, and General Management*, 56–57, 60–61.

81. Pilkinton, ed., *Journals of Samuel Kirkland*, 279.

82. NAS, GD95/12/23–24.

83. Smollett, *Expedition of Humphrey Clinker*, 227; Richard B. Sher, *The Enlightenment and the Book: Scottish Authors and Their Publishers in Eighteenth-century Britain, Ireland, and America* (Chicago: University of Chicago Press, 2006), quote at 117.

84. James Buchan, *Crowded with Genius: The Scottish Enlightenment: Edinburgh's Moment of the Mind* (New York: HarperCollins, 2003), 131 (Spartans and Iroquois); P. J. Marshall and Glyndwr Williams, *The Great Map of Mankind: Perceptions of New Worlds in the Age of Enlightenment* (Cambridge, Mass.: Harvard University Press, 1982), Burke quote at 1; Troy O. Bickham, *Savages Within Empire: Representations of American Indians in Eighteenth-Century Britain* (Oxford: Clarendon Press, 2005), ch. 5.

85. George Dekker, "Historical Romance and the Stadialist Model of Progress," in *The American Historical Romance* (New York: Cambridge University Press, 1987), 73–98; Ferguson quote at 80 and 98; Herman, *How the Scots Invented the Modern World*, 221 (Ferguson may have found quote); Bickham, *Savages Within Empire*, 171 ("more than curiosities"), 199 ("first footsteps" quoted from *Scots Magazine* (1777), 434); H. M. Höpfl, "From Savage to Scotsman: Conjectural History of the Scottish Enlightenment," *Journal of British Studies* 17 (1978): 19–40. For Enlightenment attitudes toward Indians elsewhere see David J. Weber, *Bárbaros: Spaniards and Their Savages in the Age of Enlightenment* (New Haven, Conn.: Yale University Press, 2005).

86. Roy Harvey Pearce, *Savagism and Civilization: A Study of the Indian and the American Mind* (1953; repr., Berkeley: University of California Press, 1988), 82–91, 94–96 (quote at 82); Stewart J. Brown, ed., *William Robertson and the*

Expansion of Empire (New York: Cambridge University Press, 1997); Owen Dudley Edwards, "Robertsonian Romanticism and Realism," in Brown, ed., *William Robertson and the Expansion of Empire,* quote at 101.

87. Bruce P. Lenman, "'From Savage to Scot' via the French and the Spaniards: Principal Robertson's Spanish Sources," in *William Robertson and the Expansion of Empire,* 196–209, quotes at 208–209; Sher, *Enlightenment and the Book,* ch. 8; Berkhofer, *White Man's Indian,* 48–49. Patrick Griffen recognizes the influence of Scottish stadial theory in *American Leviathan,* 29–31, 66–69, 254–56.

88. Anthony F. C. Wallace, *Jefferson and the Indians: The Tragic Fate of the First Americans* (Cambridge, Mass.: Harvard University Press, 1999), quote at 11; Reginald Horsman, *Expansion and American Indian Policy 1783–1812* (1967; repr., Norman: University of Oklahoma Press, 1992).

89. H. Thomas Foster, ed., *The Collected Works of Benjamin Hawkins, 1796–1810* (Tuscaloosa: University of Alabama Press, 2003); Wallace, *Jefferson and the Indians.*

90. Prucha, ed., *Documents of United States Indian Policy,* 33; Coleman, *American Indians, the Irish, and Government Schooling,* 40.

91. Quoted in John Ehle, *Trail of Tears: The Rise and Fall of the Cherokee Nation* (New York: Doubleday, 1988), 254.

92. Theda Perdue and Michael D. Green, eds., *The Cherokee Removal: A Brief History with Documents,* 2d ed. (Boston: Bedford/St. Martin's, 2005), 115–21; Krisztina Fenyo, *Contempt, Sympathy, and Romance: Lowland Perceptions of the Highlands and the Clearances during the Famine Years, 1845–1855* (East Linton, East Lothian, Scotland: Tuckwell, 2000).

93. Linda Colley, *Captives* (New York: Pantheon, 2002), 188–92; Douglas Skelton, *Indian Peter: The Extraordinary Life and Adventures of Peter Williamson* (Edinburgh: Mainstream, 2004); Ferenc M. Szasz, "Peter Williamson and the Eighteenth-century Scottish-American Connection," *Northern Scotland* 19 (1999), 47–61.

94. Patrick Campbell, *Travels in the Interior Inhabited Parts of North America in the Years 1791 and 1792,* ed. H. H. Langton (Toronto: Champlain Society, 1937), 206.

95. Campbell, *Travels in the Interior Inhabited Parts of North America,* 164–70.

96. Carl F. Klinck and James J. Talman, eds., *The Journal of Major John Norton, 1816* (Toronto: Champlain Society, 1970), xvi ("Indian book"), xx (Thomas Scott letter), xxviii, 36 (father rescued); lxxxiii, lxxxvi (son in school and married); David Douglas, ed., *Familiar Letters of Sir Walter Scott,* 2 vols. (Edinburgh: David Douglas, 1894), vol. 1, 345–46; Calloway, *Crown and Calumet,* 113–14.

97. Tim Fulford, *Romantic Indians: Native Americans, British Literature, and Transatlantic Culture* (New York: Oxford University Press, 2006), 4, 6.

98. "Letter re: an American Indian, 1823," NLS, Acc. 10453; Richard Drinnon, *White Savage: The Case of John Dunn Hunter* (New York: Schocken, 1972), ch. 3; John Dunn Hunter, *Memoirs of a Captivity among the Indians of North America* (London, 1824; repr., ed. Richard Drinnon; New York: Schocken, 1973).

99. Granville Garter, ed., *The Collected Speeches of Sagoyewatha, or Red Jacket* (Syracuse: Syracuse University Press, 2006), 141–42.

100. Ross, *Adventures of the First Settlers,* 353.

101. "On the Condition of the Highland Peasantry," 62–63.

102. J. Hector St. John de Crèvecoeur, *Letters from an American Farmer,* ed. Susan Manning (New York: Oxford University Press, 1997), 202.

103. Masson, ed., *Les Bourgeois de la Compagnie du Nord-Ouest,* vol. 1, 318.

104. Translated and quoted in Newton, *Handbook of the Gaelic Scottish World,* 270.

105. *An Appeal on Behalf of the Scottish Settlers in British North America: A Sermon by John Jaffrey, A. M.* (Dundee: James Adam, 1831).

NOTES TO CHAPTER 4

1. Letter from Bouquet, camp at Edge Hill, Aug. 5, 1763, *The Papers of Henry Bouquet,* ed. Sylvester K. Stevens et al., 6 vols. (Pennsylvania Historical and Museum Commission, 1951–1954), vol. 6, 338–40, "Bouquet Papers," *Collections of the Michigan Pioneer and Historical Society,* vol. 19, 219–23; reprinted in *Gentleman's Magazine* for 1763, 487–88, and in Francis Parkman, *The Conspiracy of Pontiac,* 2 vols. (1851; New York: Dutton, 1908), vol. 2, 235–39. Sergeant Robert Kirk said the Indians broke the British square; *The Memoirs and Adventures of Robert Kirk, Late of the Royal Highland Regiment . . . Written by Himself* (Limerick: J. Ferrar printers, n.d.), 78.

2. British Museum, Add. Ms. 21949: 316, quoted in Ian Macpherson McCulloch, *Sons of the Mountains: The Highland Regiments in the French and Indian War, 1756–1767,* 2 vols. (Fleischmanns, N.Y.: Purple Mountain, 2006), vol. 1, 306.

3. Daniel Defoe, *A Tour of the Whole Island of Great Britain,* ed. Pat Rogers (Exeter, UK: Webb and Bower, 1989; Promotional Reprint, 1992), 238.

4. P. Hume Brown, ed., *Scotland before 1700 from Contemporary Documents* (Edinburgh: David Douglas, 1893), 60.

5. Defoe, *Tour of the Whole Island of Great Britain,* 238.

6. General Wade, "Report, &, Relating to the Highlands, 1727," in *Historical Papers relating to the Jacobite Period, 1699–1750,* ed. Col. James Allardyce, 2 vols. (Aberdeen: New Spalding Club, 1895–1896), vol. 1, 160.

7. Samuel Johnson and James Boswell, *A Journey to the Western Islands of Scotland and the Journal of a Tour to the Hebrides,* ed. Peter Levi (New York: Penguin, 1984), 64.

8. Norman Scarfe, ed., *To the Highlands in 1786: The Inquisitive Journey of a Young French Aristocrat* (Woodbridge, UK: Boydell, 2001), 172.

9. George Heriot, *Travels through the Canadas* (Rutland, Vt.: Tuttle, 1971), 421; Clarence Edwin Carter, ed., *The Correspondence of General Thomas Gage,* 2 vols. (New Haven, Conn.: Yale University Press, 1933), vol. 1, 13; Tom Hatley, *The Dividing Paths: Cherokees and South Carolinians through the Era of Revolution*

(New York: Oxford University Press, 1993), 9 (Stuart quote); Robbie Ethridge, *Creek Country: The Creek Indians and Their World* (Chapel Hill: University of North Carolina Press, 2003).

10. McCulloch, *Sons of the Mountains*, vol. 1, 28–34.

11. Emerson W. Baker and John G. Reid, "Amerindian Power in the Early Modern Northeast: A Reappraisal," *William and Mary Quarterly* 61 (2004): 1–28; Daniel Richter, "War and Culture: The Iroquois Experience," *William and Mary Quarterly* 40 (1983): 528–29 (quote); Colin G. Calloway, *New Worlds for All: Indians, Europeans, and the Remaking of Early America* (Baltimore: Johns Hopkins University Press, 1997), ch. 5; Ned Blackhawk, *Violence over the Land: Indians and Empires in the Early American West* (Cambridge, Mass.: Harvard University Press, 2006).

12. David Armitage, "The Scottish Diaspora," in *Scotland: A History*, ed. Jenny Wormald (New York: Oxford University Press, 2005), 287.

13. George P. Hammond, ed., *Narratives of the Coronado Expedition, 1540–1542* (Albuquerque: University of New Mexico Press, 1940), 105.

14. Steve Murdoch, ed., *Scotland and the Thirty Years' War, 1618–1648* (Leiden, the Netherlands: Brill, 2001), figures at 19–20, table 1; Alexia Grosjean, "A Century of Scottish Governorship in the Swedish Empire, 1574–1700," in *Military Governors and Imperial Frontiers, c. 1600–1800: A Study of Scotland and Empires*, ed. A. Mackillop and Steve Murdoch (Leiden, the Netherlands: Brill, 2003), 60–61; Steve Murdoch, "Scotsmen on the Danish-Norwegian Frontiers, c. 1580–1680," in *Military Governors and Imperial Frontiers*, 13; NLS, Miscellaneous Papers, ms. 1001 (ii): extract from Swedish army list showing Scots officers and soldiers serving Gustavus Adolphus in 1632.

15. R. A. Houston and W. W. J. Knox, eds., *The New Penguin History of Scotland* (London: Penguin, 2001), 202; John E. Willis Jr., *1688: A Global History* (New York: Norton, 2001), 95.

16. John Prebble, *Mutiny: Highland Regiments in Revolt 1743–1804* (Harmondsworth, UK: Penguin, 1977), 23–27, 34–35; Archibald Forbes, *The Black Watch: The Record of an Historic Regiment* (repr., Bowie, Md.: Heritage Books, 2002).

17. Adam Smith, *An Inquiry into the Nature and Causes of the Wealth of Nations*, ed. R. H. Campbell, A. S. Skinner, and W. B. Todd, 2 vols. (Oxford: Clarendon, 1976), vol. 2, 701.

18. Jeremy Black, *Culloden and the '45* (New York: St. Martin's, 1990), 162; Andrew Mackillop, *"More Fruitful than the Soil": Army, Empire, and the Scottish Highlands, 1715–1815* (East Linton, Scotland: Tuckwell, 2000), 8–9, 229; Andrew Mackillop, "For King, Country, and Regiment? Motive and Identity within Highland Soldiering, 1746–1815," in *Fighting for Identity: Scottish Military Experience c. 1550–1900*, ed. Steve Murdoch and A. Mackillop (Leiden, the Netherlands: Brill, 2002), 191–98; Allan I. Macinnes, *Clanship, Commerce, and the House of Stuart, 1603–1788* (East Linton, Scotland: Tuckwell, 1996), 165.

19. Colin G. Calloway, *The American Revolution in Indian Country* (New York: Cambridge University Press, 1995), 62.

20. Prebble, *Mutiny;* Mackillop, "For King, Country, and Regiment?" 185–211.

21. "Memorial Anent the Thieving and Depredations in the Highlands of Scotland (1747?)," in *Historical Papers relating to the Jacobite Period,* vol. 2, 500.

22. Stephen Brumwell, *Redcoats: The British Soldier and War in the Americas, 1755–1763* (New York: Cambridge University Press, 2002), 274; Prebble, *Mutiny,* 96–97.

23. Johnson and Boswell, *Journey to the Western Islands,* 103; John Prebble, *The Highland Clearances* (Harmondsworth, UK: Penguin, 1969), 21–22 ("old ardours" quote).

24. Prebble, *Mutiny,* 93–94; Robert Scott Stephenson, "With Swords and Plowshares: British and American Soldiers in the Trans-Allegheny West, 1754–1774," PhD diss., University of Virginia, 1998, 176–84.

25. Charles Withers, "The Historical Creation of the Scottish Highlands," in *The Manufacture of Scottish History,* ed. Ian Donnichie and Christopher Whatley (Edinburgh: Polygon, 1992), 149.

26. Describing such recruitment tactics, Thomas Garnett commented: "Though the feudal claims have been abolished, the highland chieftain has nearly the same power as ever over his vassals." Thomas Garnett, *Observations on a Tour through the Highlands and Part of the Western Isles of Scotland,* 2 vols. (London: Cadell and Davies, 1800), vol. 1, 166–67; Mackillop, *"More Fruitful than the Soil,"* 12.

27. Michael Brander, *The Scottish Highlanders and Their Regiments* (1971; New York: Barnes and Noble, 1996), 14; Robert Clyde, *From Rebel to Hero: The Image of the Highlander, 1745–1830* (East Linton, Scotland: Tuckwell, 1995), 150; Prebble, *Mutiny,* 271; Eric Richards, *A History of the Highland Clearances.* Vol. 1, *Agrarian Transformation and the Evictions, 1746–1886* (London: Croom Helm, 1982), 148–49; "State of Emigration from the Highlands of Scotland, its extent, causes, & proposed remedy," Mar. 21, 1803, NLS, Adv. ms. 35.6.18: 7, 21 (50,000 figure and every other male).

28. Michael Fry, *Wild Scots: Four Hundred Years of Highland History* (London: John Murray, 2005), 106 (Johnstone); "Memoire pour le ministre de la marine," Jan. 7, 1759, *Rapport de l'archiviste de la province de Québec,* 1924: 40; McCulloch, *Sons of the Mountains,* vol. 1, 103.

29. *Collections of the Georgia Historical Society,* 1873, 12; ("agree very well"); Allen D. Candler et al., eds., *The Colonial Records of the State of Georgia,* 32 vols. (Atlanta: State Printers, 1904–1989), vol. 2, 188; vol. 21 (1910), 11–14, 17–30, 72, 76 ("manly appearance"), 104, 120 (Oglethorpe in Highland dress), 372 ("Last Extremity"); vol. 27, 4 ("Share in the Slaughter"); Anthony W. Parker, *Scottish Highlanders in Colonial Georgia: The Recruitment, Emigration, and Settlement at Darien, 1735–1748* (Athens: University of Georgia Press, 1997), "Slaughter"

quote at 91; "warlike colonists" at 96; "Notes of the Genealogy of the House of Mackintosh," NLS, Farr manuscripts, ms. 9854: 221–23; Prebble, *Mutiny*, 85 (Black Watch recruits). See also Julie Anne Sweet, *Negotiating for Georgia: British-Creek Relations in the Trustee Era, 1733–1752* (Athens: University of Georgia Press, 2005), although she ignores the Highlanders.

30. Roger G. Kennedy, *Mr. Jefferson's Lost Cause: Land, Farmers, Slavery, and the Louisiana Purchase* (New York: Oxford University Press, 2003), 121.

31. Geoffrey Plank, *Rebellion and Savagery: The Jacobite Rising of 1745 and the British Empire* (Philadelphia: University of Pennsylvania Press, 2006), 98, 122–25, 153–57, 161, 168–69; Beckles Wilson, ed., *The Life and Letters of James Wolfe* (1909; repr., Cranbury, N.J.: Scholar's Bookshelf, 2005), 141.

32. Quoted in Clyde, *From Rebel to Hero*, 153.

33. Bruce Lenman, *The Jacobite Clans of the Great Glen, 1650–1784* (London: Methuen, 1984), ch. 9; Annette M. Smith, *Jacobite Estates of the Forty-five* (Edinburgh: John Donald, 1982), 224. The proceedings against Fraser of Lovat for high treason are in "The 1745 Rebellion Papers," PRO, TS 20/2: 121 (reel 7).

34. PRO, War Office Records, W. O. 4/53: 102; reproduced in NAC, microfilm C-12585: Papers relating to the 77th Regiment of foot.

35. Michael Newton, "Jacobite Past, Loyalist Present," *E-Keltoi: Journal of Interdisciplinary Celtic Studies* 5 (online), http://www.uwm.edu/Dept/celtic/ekeltoi/.

36. Prebble, *Mutiny*, 93.

37. McCulloch, *Sons of the Mountains*, provides a detailed account of the services of the Highland regiments in the war in America.

38. *Scoouwa: James Smith's Indian Captivity Narrative* (1799; reprinted Columbus: Ohio Historical Society, 1978), 117–19.

39. Brumwell, *Redcoats*, ch. 8; quote at 267–68; Lenman, *Jacobite Clans of the Great Glen*, ch. 9; Stephenson, "With Swords and Plowshares," ch. 4; Richard C. Cole, "Montgomerie's Cherokee Campaign, 1760: Two Contemporary Views," *North Carolina Historical Review* 74 (1997): 19–36; Forbes, *Black Watch*, 88; J. P. MacLean, *An Historical Account of the Settlements of Scotch Highlanders in America prior to the Peace of 1783, together with Notices of Highland Regiments and Biographical Sketches* (1900; repr., Bowie, Md.: Heritage Books, 2001), 283, gives much more modest casualty figures for the Black Watch. For medical conditions among the regiments at Staten Island see *Sir Jeffery, 1st Baron Amherst, Official Papers and Correspondence, 1740–83*, 202 reels (London: World Microfilm, 1979), reel 74: 21, 64–65, 68, 202, 207–208, 211–15; reel 75: 117; reel 76, pt. 1: 47, 172, 178–79, 185–89, 191; Amherst's order to Campbell, reel 76, pt. 1: 172.

40. Murray G. H. Pittock, *The Myth of the Highland Clans* (Edinburgh: Edinburgh University Press, 1995), 40; Johnson and Boswell, *Journey to the Western Islands*, 104.

41. Petition reprinted in Stephenson, "With Swords and Plowshares," 200.

42. Frederick A. Pottle, ed., *Boswell's London Journal, 1762–1763* (New Haven, Conn.: Yale University Press, 1950), 71–72.

43. "Bouquet Papers," *Collections of the Michigan Pioneer and Historical Society* 19: 218.

44. K. M. Brown, "From Scottish Lords to British Officers: State Building, Elite Integration, and the Army in the Seventeenth Century," in *Scotland and War AD 79–1918*, ed. N. Macdougall (Edinburgh: John Donald, 1991), 145–52.

45. Michael Newton, *We're Indians Sure Enough: The Legacy of the Scottish Highlanders in the United States* (Richmond, Va: Saorsa Media, 2001), 122.

46. Brumwell, *Redcoats*, 271–72.

47. On the murder and trial see James Hunter, *Culloden and the Last Clansman* (Edinburgh: Mainstream, 2001).

48. Mungo Campbell to Lord Milton, Jan. 18, 1757, May 8, 1757, NLS ms 16699, Fletcher of Saltoun Muniments, 95, 103, quoted in Stephenson, "With Swords and Plowshares," 171.

49. Johnson and Boswell, *Journey to the Western Islands*, 93.

50. James Glen to John Forbes, July 13, 1758, NAS, GD 45/2/44, quoted in Alex Murdoch, "James Glen and the Indians," in *Military Governors and Imperial Frontiers*, ed. Mackillop and Murdoch, 156.

51. H. P. Biggar, ed., *The Works of Samuel de Champlain*, 6 vols. (Toronto: Champlain Society, 1922–36), vol. 2, 90–101; Calloway, *New Worlds for All*, ch. 5; Patrick M. Malone, *The Skulking Way of War: Technology and Tactics among the New England Indians* (New York: Madison Books, 1991). On military adaptations see also Armstrong Starkey, *European and Native American Warfare, 1675–1815* (Norman: University of Oklahoma Press, 1998).

52. Wilson, ed., *Life and Letters of James Wolfe*, 63, 385.

53. Black, *Culloden and the '45*, 82–83.

54. Ian K. Steele, *Betrayals: Fort William Henry and the "Massacre"* (New York: Oxford University Press, 1990).

55. McCulloch, *Sons of the Mountains*, vol. 1, 137.

56. Matthew C. Ward, *Breaking the Backcountry: The Seven Years' War in Virginia and Pennsylvania, 1754–1765* (Pittsburgh: University of Pittsburgh Press, 2003), 55; Peter Way, "The Cutting Edge of Culture: British Soldiers Encounter Native Americans in the French and Indian War," in *Empire and Others: British Encounters with Indigenous Peoples, 1600–1850*, ed. Martin Daunton and Rick Halpern (Philadelphia: University of Pennsylvania Press, 1999), 123–48. For broader consideration of the use of terror by colonists as well as Indians during this period, see Peter Silver, *Our Savage Neighbors: How Indian War Transformed Early America* (New York: W. W. Norton, 2008).

57. The magazine had Kennedy married to an Indian and elevated to "king" of a tribe. Kennedy's capture by the Abenakis while on a mission to secure their neutrality helped trigger Robert Rogers's assault on Odanak in 1759. *Scots Magazine* 18 (1756), 559; *Journal of Cherokee Studies* 2 (1977): 331 n16; Stephen

Brumwell, *White Devil* (London: Weidenfield and Nicolson, 2004), 146–49 ("motley contingent" quote at 147), 152–59.

58. *Scots Magazine* 18 (1756), 559; Robert J. Allison, ed., *The Interesting Narrative of the Life of Olaudah Equiano, Written by Himself* (Boston: Bedford/St. Martin's, 2007), 80.

59. McCulloch, *Sons of the Mountains*, vol. 1, 72–73; Captain John Knox, *An Historical Journal of the Campaigns in North America for the Years 1757, 1758, 1759, and 1760*, ed. Arthur G. Doughty, 3 vols. (Toronto: Champlain Society, 1914), vol. 1, 267 (feared no quarter).

60. James Hunter, *A Dance Called America: The Scottish Highlands, the United States, and Canada* (Edinburgh: Mainstream, 1994), 65; William Fraser, *The Emigrant's Guide, or Sketches of Canada, with Some of the Northern and Western States of America, by a Scotch Minister, Thirty-six Years Resident in Canada— from 1831 to 1867* (Glasgow: Porteus Brothers, 1867), 10 ("sauvages d'Ecosse").

61. R. O. Alexander, ed., "The Capture of Quebec: A Manuscript Journal relating to the Operations before Quebec from 8 May, 1759, to 17 May, 1760, kept by Colonel Malcolm Fraser, then lieutenant in the 78th Foot (Fraser's Highlanders)," *Journal of the Society for Army Historical Research* 18 (1939), 135–68, quotes at 141, 142, 148.

62. Knox, *Historical Journal*, vol. 1, 73–74. I am grateful to Geoffrey Plank for drawing this incident to my attention.

63. Stanley Pargellis, ed., *Military Affairs in North America, 1748–1765: Selected Papers from the Cumberland Papers in Windsor Castle* (New York: Appleton-Century, 1936), 264; Captain James Murray quoted in Dale Idiens, "Early Collections from the North American Woodlands in Scotland," in J. C. H. King and Christian F. Feest, eds., *Three Centuries of Woodlands Indian Art: A Collection of Essays* (Altenstadt, Germany: ZFK Publishers, 2007), 12.

64. Plank, *Rebellion and Savagery*, 178–79.

65. Both the Black Watch Museum at Balhousie Castle in Perth and the National Museum of Scotland in Edinburgh have powder horns from the Seven Years' War on which soldiers etched maps of the American colonies or the region in which they were fighting. Black Watch Regimental Museum, Acc. # 1077/1, 1077/2.

66. Alfred Proctor James, ed., *Writings of General John Forbes relating to His Services in North America* (Menasha, Wis.: Collegiate Press, 1938), x (farthing), 117 (quote).

67. Paul David Nelson, *General James Grant: Scottish Soldier and Royal Governor of East Florida* (Gainesville: University Press of Florida, 1993), ch. 3, "into the woods" quote at 36; Philip M. Hamer, ed., *The Papers of Henry Laurens*, 16 vols. (Columbia: University of South Carolina Press, 1968–), vol. 3, 275–355; quotes at 279, 286, 307; Duane H. King and E. Raymond Evans, ed., "Memoirs of the Grant Expedition against the Cherokees in 1761," special issue, *Journal of Cherokee Studies* 2 (Sept. 1977); McCulloch, *Sons of the Mountains*, vol. 1, ch. 9; Brumwell, *White Devil*, 265 (Kennedy's role).

68. Edith Mays, ed., *Amherst Papers, 1756–1763: The Southern Sector: Dispatches from South Carolina, Virginia, and His Majesty's Superintendent of Indian Affairs* (Bowie, Md.: Heritage Books, 1999), 105–106, 121–23, 176.

69. Mays, ed., *Amherst Papers*, 83 ("barbarian savages"), 120 ("severely punished"); Hamer, ed., *Papers of Henry Laurens*, vol. 3, 333 ("hunted down").

70. Grant quoted in MacLean, *Historical Account of the Settlements of Scotch Highlanders*, 284; John Oliphant, *Peace and War on the Anglo-Cherokee Frontier, 1756–63* (Baton Rouge: Louisiana State University Press, 2001), 136 (McLemore), 132 (preference), 189 (duel). Hamer, ed., *Papers of Henry Laurens*, vol. 3, 344 (McGunningham). McGunningham is identified in William L. McDowell, ed., *Colonial Records of South Carolina: Documents relating to Indian Affairs, 1754–1765* (Columbia: South Carolina Department of Archives and History, 1970), 488, 495; McLemore in Hatley, *Dividing Paths*, 136, and in Duane King, ed., *The Memoirs of Henry Timberlake* (Cherokee, N.C.: Museum of the Cherokee Indian Press, 2007), 127 n.46.

71. Mays, ed., *Amherst Papers*, 139–43.

72. McCulloch, *Sons of the Mountains*, vol. 1, 315–18; Benjamin Franklin, "A Narrative of the Late Massacres in Lancaster County" (1764), in Leonard W. Labaree, ed., *The Papers of Benjamin Franklin*, 37 vols. (New Haven, Conn.: Yale University Press, 1959–), vol. 11, 47–69.

73. "General Account of the fighting with the Indians after the peace treaty of 1763 and of expeditions to occupy the newly ceded territory in America," Black Watch Regimental Archives, Balhousie Castle, Perth (hereafter BWRA).

74. "Journal of a Detachment of the 42nd Regiment, from Fort Pitt down the Ohio to the Country of the Illenoise," NAS, GD 298/196, 24, 27, 34, 36. The author of this journal is uncertain, although it has been attributed to Lieutenant James Eddington or the surgeon. Captain Stirling's "Detailed account of the voyage of the 42nd from Fort Pitt down the Ohio and up the Mississippi to occupy Fort Chartres in 1765" is in the Papers of General Sir Thomas Stirling, 1763–1801, BWRA, Blue Folder, 398, Accession #3428 (buffalo meat quote at 17). Both journals are printed in Robert G. Carroon, ed., *Broadswords and Bayonets: The Journals of the Expedition under the Command of Captain Thomas Stirling of the 42nd Regiment of Foot, Royal Highland Regiment (the Black Watch) to occupy Fort Chartres in the Illinois Country, August 1765 to January 1766* (Society of Colonial Wars in the State of Illinois, 1984). Robert Kirk also appears to have been a member of the expedition. Ian McCulloch and Timothy Todish, eds., *Through So Many Dangers: The Memoirs and Adventures of Robert Kirk, Late of the Royal Highland Regiment* (Fleischmanns, N.Y.: Purple Mountain, 2004), 101–13.

75. "Detailed account of the voyage," 17.

76. "Journal of a Detachment of the 42nd Regiment," 28, 34, 44, 89, 91; Carroon, ed., *Broadswords and Bayonets*, 29 (Stirling quote); extract of a letter from Captain Stirling to General Gage, Oct. 18, 1765, BWRA (copy from PRO, War Office Records, WO 17, 3051).

77. "Journal of a Detachment of the 42nd Regiment," 43; Carroon, ed., *Broadswords and Bayonets,* 34–36.

78. "Journal of a Detachment of the 42nd Regiment," 12.

79. Ibid., 29–30.

80. Ibid., 58–63. Stirling's account of the encounter is almost identical, although he notes that the Shawnee chief's hostility stemmed in part from fear that the British would take away his wife, "a white girl that had been taken captive . . . and whom he very much loved." "Detailed Account," BWRA, 3/15; 3/16; Carroon, ed., *Broadswords and Bayonets,* 39–41.

81. "Journal of a Detachment of the 42nd Regiment," 65, 81.

82. BWRA, Extract of a letter from Captain Stirling; "General account of the fighting with the Indians."

83. "Journal of a Detachment of the 42nd Regiment," 87, 89–90, 94, 99.

84. James Sullivan et al., *The Papers of Sir William Johnson,* 15 vols. (Albany: University of the State of New York, 1921–65), vol. 4, 743.

85. "Journal of a Detachment of the 42nd Regiment," 135, 144–46.

86. Reuben Gold Thwaites and Louise Phelps Kellogg, eds., *Documentary History of Dunmore's War, 1774* (Madison: Wisconsin Historical Society, 1905), 151–56.

87. Ira D. Gruber, ed., *John Peebles' American War: The Diary of a Scottish Grenadier, 1776–1782* (Gloucestershire, UK: Army Records Society, 1997).

88. John McAlpine, *Genuine Narratives and Concise Memoirs of some of the most Interesting Exploits and Singular Adventures of J. McAlpine, a Native Highlander, from the Time of his Emigration from Scotland to America, 1773* (1780; facs. repr., Greenock, Scotland: William Innes, 1883).

89. Patrick Campbell, *Travels in the Interior Inhabited Parts of North America in the Years 1791 and 1792,* ed. H. H. Langton (Toronto: Champlain Society, 1937), 227.

90. Mary Beacock Fryer, *Allan Maclean, Jacobite General: The Life of an Eighteenth-century Career Soldier* (Toronto: Dundurn, 1987); "A Brief Genealogical & Historical Account of the Family & Surname of MacLean from its settling in the Island of Mull and parts adjacent to the Year 1807," NLS, ms. 3018. On land grants to MacLean's recruits see Additional Instructions to William Tryon, Apr. 3, 1775, and Dartmouth to Lieutenant Governor Colden, Apr. 5 1775, PRO, CO 5/76.

91. Allan Maclean to Andrew Stuart, Oct. 24, 1779, NLS, Stuart Stevenson Papers, ms. 8250, ff. 34–36.

92. Colin G. Calloway, "Fort Niagara: The Politics of Hunger in a Refugee Community," in Calloway, *American Revolution in Indian Country,* ch. 5.

93. Correspondence and Papers of Governor General Sir Frederick Haldimand, 1758–91, British Museum, Add. Mss. 21762: 215, 234–35; 21763; 114–15.

94. Ibid., Add. Mss. 21763: 225–26.

95. Ibid., Add. Mss. 21763: 162.

96. Ibid., Add. Mss. 21763: 179.

97. Ibid., Add. Mss. 21764: 368.

98. PRO, CO 42/15: 370.

99. Haldimand Papers, British Museum, Add. Mss. 21756: 138.

100. Colin G. Calloway, *Crown and Calumet: British-Indian Relations, 1783–1815* (Norman: University of Oklahoma Press, 1987).

101. George M. Stanley, "The Scottish Military Tradition," in *The Scottish Tradition in Canada*, ed. W. Stanford Reid (Toronto: McClelland and Stewart, 1976), 147–48.

102. "Observations on the means of obtaining from the Highlands of Scotland an efficient & prominent Force for the Defence of Canada," NAC, CO 42/165: 469–70, reel B-134.

103. Scott A. McLean, ed., *From Lochnaw to Manitoulin: A Highland Soldier's Tour through Upper Canada* (Toronto: Natural Heritage Books, 1999), 24–25, 30, 35.

104. Prebble, *Highland Clearances*, 41–42.

105. Clyde, *From Rebel to Hero*, 156.

106. Prebble, *Highland Clearances*, 67.

107. "On Emigration from the Scottish Highlands & Isles," by Edward S. Fraser, NLS, ms. 9646: 115; Richards, *History of the Highland Clearances*, vol. 1, 151–53.

108. Prebble, *Highland Clearances*, 56; Alexander MacKenzie, *History of the Highland Clearances* (1883; repr., Edinburgh: Mercat Press, 1997), 144–48, 158–59, 321; Richards, *History of the Highland Clearances*, vol. 1, 155.

109. Sutherland to Duke Charles Gordon, Dec. 27, 1847, NLS, Sutherland Papers, Dep. 313/863.

110. James Loch, *An Account of the Improvement on the Estates of the Marquess of Stafford, in the Counties of Stafford and Salop, and on the Estate of Sutherland* (London: Longman, Hurst, Rees, Orme, and Brown, 1820), 57–59 (93rd veterans "fomenting" opposition); Duchess of Sutherland quoted in Craig, *On the Crofters' Trail*, 128; Sutherland refusals to serve: Prebble, *Highland Clearances*, 56; MacKenzie, *History of the Highland Clearances*, 144–47; Richards, *History of the Highland Clearances*, vol. 1, 155–56.

111. Henry Mayhew, *London Labour and the London Poor*, 4 vols. (London, 1861; repr., New York: Dover, 1968), vol. 3, 165.

112. Clyde, *From Rebel to Hero*, ch. 6; Major General David Stewart of Garth, *Sketches of the Character, Institutions, and Customs of the Highlanders of Scotland* (1822; new ed., Inverness: A. and W. Mackenzie, 1885), 287–93.

113. Mackillop, "For King, Country, and Regiment?" and Heather Streets, "Identity in the Highland Regiments in the Nineteenth Century: Soldier, Region, Nation," both in *Fighting for Identity*, 185–211, 213–36; Mackillop, "*More Fruitful than the Soil,*" 184–86.

114. Lenman, *Jacobite Clans of the Great Glen*, 220.

115. Mackillop, ed, "For King, Country, and Regiment?" 202–203.

116. Figures on Highland casualties in Michael Fry, *How the Scots Made America* (New York: St. Martin's, 2003), 207 (almost 150,000 killed); Fry, *Wild Scots*, 255 (128,000).

117. Colin G. Calloway, "'Army Allies or Tribal Survival': The 'Other Indians' in the 1876 Campaign," in *Legacy: New Perspectives on the Battle of the Little Bighorn,* ed. Charles E. Rankin (Helena: Montana Historical Society Press, 1996), 63–81.

118. Hunter, *Dance Called America,* 54; Edward P. Hamilton, ed., *Adventure in the Wilderness: The American Journals of Louis Antoine de Bougainville, 1756–1760* (Norman: University of Oklahoma Press, 1990), 149; Calloway, *Crown and Calumet,* 196–97, 206.

119. Michael Leroy Oberg, *Uncas, First of the Mohegans* (Ithaca, N.Y.: Cornell University Press, 2003); David Naumec, "Connecticut's Native Troops, 1775–1783," paper presented at the symposium titled "Northeastern Native Peoples and the American Revolutionary Era," Mashantucket Pequot, Ledyard, Conn., Sept. 23, 2005.

120. Stephen Warren, *The Shawnees and Their Neighbors, 1795–1870* (Urbana: University of Illinois Press, 2005), 46.

121. Lawrence M. Hauptman, *Between Two Fires: American Indians in the Civil War* (New York: Free Press, 1995), 47–48.

122. Thomas W. Dunlay, *Wolves for the Blue Soldiers: Indian Scouts and Auxiliaries with the United States Army, 1860–1890* (Lincoln: University of Nebraska Press, 1982).

123. John G. Bourke, *On the Border with Crook* (New York: Charles Scribner's Sons, 1891), 303, 316, 318.

124. Colin G. Calloway, "The Vermont Secretary and the Apache POWs: Redfield Proctor and the Case of the Chiricahuas," *Vermont History* 59 (1991): 166–79; Michael L. Tate, "Soldiers of the Line: Apache Companies in the U.S. Army, 1891–97," *Arizona and the West* 16 (1974): 343–64; Michael L. Tate, "From Scout to Doughboy: The National Debate over Integrating American Indians into the Military, 1891–1918," *Western Historical Quarterly* 17 (1986): 417–43; *Annual Report of the Secretary of War for 1891* (Washington, D.C.: GPO, 1891), 14–16.

125. Frederick E. Hoxie, ed., *Talking Back to Civilization: Indian Voices from the Progressive Era* (Boston: Bedford/St. Martins, 2001), 125–27.

126. Susan Applegate Krouse, *North American Indians in the Great War* (Lincoln: University of Nebraska Press, 2007), ch. 1; Whirlwind Horse quote at 33; Russel Lawrence Barsh, "American Indians in the Great War," *Ethnohistory* 38 (1991): 276–303; quotes at 276, 287, 288; Thomas A. Britten, *American Indians in World War I: At War and at Home* (Albuquerque: University of New Mexico Press, 1997).

127. Alison Bernstein, *American Indians and World War II: Toward a New Era in Indian Affairs* (Norman: University of Oklahoma Press, 1990); Kenneth William Townshend, *World War II and the American Indian* (Albuquerque: University of New Mexico Press, 2000); Tom Holm, *Strong Hearts, Wounded Souls: Native Americans of the Vietnam War* (Austin: University of Texas Press, 1996).

128. John Moses, *A Sketch Account of Aboriginal Peoples in the Canadian Military* (Ottawa: Minister of National Defence, 2004), chap. 6, 62–63, 67 (figures), 70 (McLeod); 71 (Patterson).

NOTES TO CHAPTER 5

1. Quoted in Kathryn E. Holland Braund, *Deerskins and Duffels: Creek Indian Trade with Anglo-America, 1685–1815* (Lincoln: University of Nebraska Press, 1993), 26.
2. Roger G. Kennedy, *Mr. Jefferson's Lost Cause: Land, Farmers, Slavery, and the Louisiana Purchase* (New York: Oxford University Press, 2003), 132.
3. Edward J. Cashin, *Lachlan McGillivray, Indian Trader: The Shaping of the Southern Colonial Frontier* (Athens: University of Georgia Press, 1992); Braund, *Deerskins and Duffels*, 56–57 (John McGillivray), 62 (Stuart quote), 87 (Stuart figures).
4. William S. Coker and Thomas D. Watson, *Indian Traders of the Southeastern Spanish Borderlands: Panton, Leslie and Company, and John Forbes and Company, 1783–1847* (Pensacola: University of West Florida Press, 1986); Braund, *Deerskins and Duffels*, ch. 9.
5. Governor John Nixon, quoted in Jennifer S. H. Brown, *Strangers in Blood: Fur Trade Company Families in Indian Country* (Norman: University of Oklahoma Press, 1980), 24.
6. John Nicks, "Orkneymen in the HBC," in *Old Trails and New Directions: Papers of the Third North American Fur Trade Conference*, ed. Carol M. Judd and Arthur J. Ray (Toronto: University of Toronto Press, 1980), 102–26; Peter C. Newman, *Empire of the Bay: The Company of Adventurers That Seized a Continent* (Toronto: Penguin, 1998), ch. 9.
7. Philip Goldring, "Lewis and the Hudson's Bay Company in the Nineteenth Century," *Scottish Studies* 24 (1980): 23–42; Allan I. Macinnes, Marjory-Ann D. Harper, and Linda G. Fryer, eds., *Scotland and the Americas, c. 1650–c. 1939: A Documentary Source Book* (Edinburgh: Scottish History Society, 2002), 148.
8. Newman, *Empire of the Bay*, 8; Robert Michael Ballantyne, *Hudson Bay, Everyday Life in the Wilds of North America during Six Years' Residence in the Territories of the Hon. Hudson Bay Company*, 4th ed. (London: Thomas Nelson and Sons, 1902), 26; Isaac Cowie, *The Company of Adventurers: A Narrative of Seven Years in the Service of the Hudson's Bay Company during 1867–1874 on the Great Buffalo Plains* (Toronto: William Briggs, 1913), 191–93.
9. Cowie, *Company of Adventurers*, 42–43; Michael Fry, *The Scottish Empire* (Edinburgh: Birlinn, 2001), 102 ("syndicate"); Heather Devine, "Roots in the Mohawk Valley: Sir William Johnson's Legacy in the Northwest Company," in *The Fur Trade Revisited: Selected Papers of the Sixth North American Fur Trade Conference*, ed. Jennifer S. H. Brown, W. J. Eccles, and Donald

P. Heldman (East Lansing: Michigan State University Press, 1994), 217–42; W. Stewart Wallace, ed., *Documents relating to the North West Company* (Toronto: Champlain Society, 1934), 35 ("Culloden roll-call"); also A. Innes Shand, quoted in Ferenc Morton Szasz, *Scots in the North American West, 1790–1917* (Norman: University of Oklahoma Press, 2000), 30; Newman, *Empire of the Bay*, 276–77 ("transcontinental chiefs" and list of names); Elaine Allan Mitchel, "The Scot in the Fur Trade," in *The Scottish Tradition in Canada*, ed. W. Stanford Reid (Toronto: McClelland and Stewart, 1976), ch. 3. Additionally, W. S. Wallace, "Strathspey in the Canadian Fur Trade," in *Essays in Canadian History*, ed. R. Flenley (Toronto: Macmillan of Canada, 1939), 278–95, considers the bewildering number of Grants in the business.

10. Malcolm McLeod, ed., *Peace River; a Canoe Voyage from Hudson's Bay to the Pacific by the late Sir George Simpson in 1828. Journal of the late chief factor, Archibald McDonald, who accompanied him* (Ottawa: J. Durie and Son, 1872), 2, 4, 16 (quote), 24. McDonald described Fraser as "a decent young man." Typically, Simpson complained on one occasion that "the Piper cannot find sufficient Wind to fill his Bag" and on another described him as "a piper & nothing but a piper." E. E. Rich, ed., *Simpson's 1828 Journey to the Columbia: Part of Dispatch from George Simpson Esqr. Governor of Rupert's Land to the Governor and Committee of the Hudson's Bay Company* (Toronto: Champlain Society, 1947), 248.

11. NAC, A-27, Papers of Thomas Douglas, fifth Earl of Selkirk, 8: 1201.

12. Frederick Merk, ed., *Fur Trade and Empire: George Simpson's Journal 1824–25*, rev. ed. (1931; Cambridge, Mass.: Harvard University Press, 1968), xiv.

13. W. S. Wallace, ed., *John McLean's Notes of a Twenty-five Years' Service in the Hudson's Bay Territory* (Toronto: Champlain Society, 1932), 332–34, 383–90, quote at 383.

14. "The Character Book of George Simpson, 1832," in *Hudson's Bay Miscellany, 1670–1870*, ed. Glyndwr Williams (Winnipeg: Hudson's Bay Record Society, 1975), 151–236. The individuals in the following paragraphs are discussed in the order they appear in the book.

15. Margaret Arnett MacLeod and W. L. Morton, *Cuthbert Grant of Grantown: Warden of the Plains of Red River* (Toronto: McClelland and Stewart, 1963).

16. Charles Mackenzie, "The Mississouri Indians: A Narrative of Four Trading Expeditions to the Mississouri, 1804–06," in *Les Bourgeois de la Compagnie du Nord-Ouest*, ed. L. R. Masson, 2 vols. (1889–1890; repr., New York: Antiquarian Press, 1960), vol. 1, 315–93.

17. Merk, ed., *Fur Trade and Empire*, 23.

18. J. M. Bumsted, ed., *The Collected Writings of Lord Selkirk, 1810–1820* (Vol. 2 of *The Writings and Papers of Thomas Douglas, Fifth Earl of Selkirk*) (Winnipeg: Manitoba Record Society, 1988), 22–23, 42 n420.

19. Alexander Mackenzie, *Journal of the Voyage to the Pacific*, ed. Walter Sheppe (New York: Dover, 1995; repr. of *First Man West: Alexander Mackenzie's Journal*

of His Voyage to the Pacific Coast of Canada in 1793 (Berkeley: University of California Press, 1962), memorial at 239.

20. Simon Fraser, "Journal of a Voyage from the Rocky Mountains to the Pacific Coast, 1808," in *Les Bourgeois de la Compagnie du Nord-Ouest* 1: 155–221. For Mackenzie's and Fraser's routes see William H. Goetzmann and Glyndwr Williams, *The Atlas of North American Exploration* (Norman: University of Oklahoma Press, 1992), 114–15, 118–19.

21. Mackenzie, *Journal,* 32–38.

22. Ibid., 219.

23. E. E. Rich, ed., *Colin Robertson's Correspondence Book, September 1817 to September 1822* (Toronto: Champlain Society, 1939), 56.

24. Mackenzie, *Journal,* 166.

25. W. Raymond Wood, ed., *Prologue to Lewis and Clark: The Mackay and Evans Expedition* (Norman: University of Oklahoma Press, 2003), 3, 185–90; Abraham P. Nasatir, ed., *Before Lewis and Clark: Documents Illustrating the History of the Missouri, 1785–1804,* 2 vols. (1952; repr., Lincoln: University of Nebraska Press, 1990), vol. 1, 94, 96–103, 107 (McKay's petition), 354–64 (Blackbird quote at 359), vol. 2, 410–16, 461–64 (proclamation at 461), 478, 490–503 (McDonnell quote at 503).

26. Alexander Ross, *The Fur Hunters of the Far West,* ed. Kenneth A. Spaulding (Norman: University of Oklahoma Press, 1956), 208–10.

27. For a biography and full study of the colony and conflicts at Red River see John Morgan Gray, *Lord Selkirk of Red River* (Toronto: Macmillan of Canada, 1964).

28. Thomas Douglas, fifth Earl of Selkirk, *A Sketch of the British Fur Trade in North America; with Observations relative to the North-West Company of Montreal* (London: James Ridgway, 1816), 119–20 (repr. in Bumsted, ed., *Collected Writings of Lord Selkirk);* "A Letter by Lord Selkirk on Trade between Red River and the United States," *Canadian Historical Review* 17 (1936): 418–23; NAC, A-27: Papers of Thomas Douglas, fifth Earl of Selkirk, vol. 1, 2 (seizing furs), 8 ("unprincipled association"); Alexander Ross, *The Red River Settlement: Its Rise, Progress, and Present State* (London: Smith, Elder, 1856), vi, 16–17.

29. Material on the conflict at Red River is found throughout NAC, Selkirk Papers. See also J. M. Bumsted, *Fur Trade Wars: The Founding of Western Canada* (Winnipeg: Great Plains Publications, 1999), and J. M. Bumsted, *Trials and Tribulations: The Red River Settlement and the Emergence of Manitoba, 1811–1870* (Winnipeg: Great Plains Publications, 2003), ch. 1.

30. NAC, Selkirk Papers 1: 21; 2: 235; NAC, CO 42/164: 489–90, reel B-133.

31. "Narrative of the History of the Red River Settlement from Sept. 1814 to June 1815," by Miles MacDonnell, NAC, Selkirk Papers, vol. 1: 207; NAC, CO 42/164: 203, 403, reel B-133; Ross, *Red River Settlement,* 33.

32. McDonnell's proclamation, Jan. 8, 1814, is in NAC, CO 42/165–66, reel B-133, reprinted in *Report of the Proceedings connected with the Disputes between*

the Earl of Selkirk and the North-West Company, at the Assizes, held at York, in Upper Canada, October 1818, from Minutes taken in Court (repr., London: B. McMillan, 1819), 98–99. On the pemmican proclamation and its consequences see Bumsted, *Fur Trade Wars,* ch. 5; on the Métis, see Gerhard J. Ens, *Homeland to Hinterland: The Changing Worlds of the Red River Métis in the Nineteenth Century* (Toronto: University of Toronto Press, 1996), ch. 1.

33. *Dictionary of Canadian Biography* (Toronto: University of Toronto Press, 1966—) vol. 7, 341–44; MacLeod and Morton, *Cuthbert Grant of Grantown,* chs. 3–4; "Diary of Chief Trader, John MacLeod, Senior, of Hudson's Bay Company, Red River Settlement," *Collections of the State Historical Society of North Dakota* 2 (1908), 128–29.

34. Newman, *Empire of the Bay,* ch. 22; NAC, Selkirk Papers 2: 307–309, 320; Ross, *Red River Settlement,* 35–36, 40.

35. NAC, Selkirk Papers, vols. 2 and 3. Captain D'Orsennen's Expedition to Red River, vol. 2, 367–90; proclamation, vol. 3, 413G–413J.

36. NAC, Selkirk Papers, vol. 5; *Report of the Proceedings connected with the Disputes between the Earl of Selkirk and the North-West Company, at the Assizes, held at York, in Upper Canada, October 1818. From Minutes taken in Court* (repr., London: B. McMillan, 1819); Bumsted, *Fur Trade Wars,* ch. 10; Gray, *Lord Selkirk of Red River,* chs. 10–13.

37. Carlos A. Schwantes, *The Pacific Northwest: An Interpretive History* (Lincoln: University of Nebraska Press, 1989), 63; Richard Somerset Mackie, *Trading beyond the Mountains: The British Fur Trade on the Pacific, 1793–1843* (Vancouver: University of British Columbia Press, 1997).

38. Ferenc Morton Szasz, *Scots in the North American West, 1790–1917* (Norman: University of Oklahoma Press, 2000), 45–48; Mackie, *Trading beyond the Mountains,* 73 (quote).

39. Kenneth A. Spaulding, ed., *On the Oregon Trail: Robert Stuart's Journey of Discovery, 1812–1813* (Norman: University of Oklahoma Press 1953), 3.

40. Elizabeth Vibert, *Traders' Tales: Narratives of Cultural Encounters in the Columbia Plateau, 1807–1846* (Norman: University of Oklahoma Press, 1997), 16–19, 119–27; Lewis O. Saum, *The Fur Trader and the Indian* (Seattle: University of Washington Press, 1965).

41. Saum, *Fur Trader and the Indian;* see, for example, Wallace, ed., *John McLean's Notes.*

42. Charles M. Gates, ed., *Five Fur Traders of the Northwest, Being the Narrative of Peter Pond and the Diaries of John MacDonnell, Archibald N. McLeod, Hugh Fairies, and Thomas Connor* (Saint Paul: Minnesota Historical Society, 1965), 123–85.

43. Christopher L. Miller and George R. Hamell, "A New Perspective on Indian-White Contact: Cultural Symbols and Colonial Trade," *Journal of American History* 73 (1986): 311–28.

44. Martha Wilson Hamilton, *Silver in the Fur Trade 1600–1820* (Chelsmford, Mass: Martha Hamilton Publishing, 1995), 49, 132; Carolyn Gilman ("national

badge"), pers. comm., June 22, 2006; Ian Bunyon, Jenni Calder, Dale Idiens, and Bryce Wilson, *No Ordinary Journey: John Rae, Arctic Explorer, 1813–1893* (Edinburgh: National Museum of Scotland and Montreal, McGill-Queens University Press, 1993), 67–91; Jenni Calder, "Changing Places: The Migrating Meaning of Objects," paper presented at the "Across the Great Divide" symposium, Edinburgh, July 19, 2003. I am grateful to Six Nations attorney Paul Williams for bringing the crowned heart/owl brooch connection to my attention.

45. Alison K. Brown, "A Social History of Four Beadwork Bands," in *Papers of the Rupert's Land Colloquium 2004,* ed. D. G. Malaher (Winnipeg: Centre for Rupert's Land Studies, University of Winnipeg, 2004), 229–40; Alison Brown, "Fur Trade Artefacts and Family Histories: Christina Massan's Beadwork," paper presented at the annual meeting of the American Society of Ethnohistory, Tulsa, Okla., Nov. 2007.

46. Daniel William Kemp, ed., *Tours in Scotland, 1747, 1750, 1760 by Richard Pococke* (Edinburgh: Scottish History Society, 1887), 139.

47. *The Annual Register* (London, 1758–) for 1763, 102.

48. Laura Peers, *The Ojibwa of Western Canada, 1780—1870* (Saint Paul: Minnesota Historical Society Press, 1994), 26 (quote), 36–37; Evan Haefeli, "On First Contact and Apotheosis: Manitou and Men in North America," *Ethnohistory* 54 (2007): 424–26; Timothy J. Shannon, "Dressing for Success on the Mohawk Frontier: Hendrick, William Johnson, and the Indian Fashion," *William and Mary Quarterly,* 3rd ser., 53 (1996): 13–42.

49. Sherry Farrell Racette, "Sewing Ourselves Together: Clothing, Decorative Arts, and the Expression of Métis and Half-breed Identity," Ph.D. diss., University of Manitoba, 2004, quotes at 83, 193, 309; Racette, "'A Shawl of Even Brighter Hue': Scottish Tartan and First Nations Women," paper presented at the annual meeting of the American Society of Ethnohistory, Tulsa, Okla., Nov. 2007.

50. [James Carnegie], Earl of Southesk, *Saskatchewan and the Rocky Mountains: A Diary and Narrative of Travel, Sport, and Adventure, during a Journey through the Hudson's Bay Company Territories, in 1859 and 1860* (Edinburgh: Edmonston and Douglas, 1875), 53–54.

51. Mark Van Doren, ed., *Travels of William Bartram* (New York: Dover, 1955), 394.

52. Dorothy Downs, "British Influences on Creek and Seminole Men's Clothing, 1733–1858," *Florida Anthropologist* 33 (June 1980): 46–65; Dorothy Downs, *Art of the Florida Seminole and Miccosukee Indians* (Gainesville: University Press of Florida, 1995), chs. 1–2, plate 22; J. Leitch Wright Jr., *Creeks & Seminoles: The Destruction and Regeneration of the Muscogulge People* (Lincoln: University of Nebraska Press, 1986), quote at 36.

53. Cowie, *Company of Adventurers,* 122–23; J. M. Bumsted, "The Scottish Diaspora: Emigration to British North America, 1763–1815," in *Nation and Province in the First British Empire,* ed. Landsman, 130.

54. "Some Account of the fur trade carried on by the North West Company," *Report of the Public Archives of Canada* (for 1928), 68.

55. Colin G. Calloway, *Crown and Calumet: British-Indian Relations, 1783–1815* (Norman: University of Oklahoma Press, 1987), ch. 7; Saum, *Fur Trader and the Indian.*

56. Ross, *Fur Hunters of the Far West,* 87, 194–95.

57. Ibid., 194.

58. Masson, ed., *Les Bourgeois de la Compagnie du Nord-Ouest,* vol. 2, 249.

59. Rich, ed., *Simpson's 1828 Journey to the Columbia,* Appendix A, 204–208.

60. Peter C. Mancall, *Deadly Medicine: Indians and Alcohol in Early America* (Ithaca, N.Y.: Cornell University Press, 1995).

61. "Reminiscences by the Honorable Roderick McKenzie," in *Les Bourgeois de la Compagnie du Nord-Ouest,* vol. 1, 12.

62. Arthur S. Morton, ed., *The Journal of Duncan McGillivray of the North West Company at Fort George on the Saskatchewan, 1794–95* (Toronto: Macmillan of Canada, 1929), 30, 35–36, 47, 53, 69, 72.

63. Morton, ed., *Journal of Duncan McGillivray,* 48, 51.

64. P. Hume Brown, ed., *Scotland before 1700 from Contemporary Documents* (Edinburgh: David Douglas, 1893), 285; Thomas Garnett, *Observations on a Tour through the Highlands and Part of the Western Isles of Scotland,* 2 vols. (London: Cadell and Davies, 1800), vol. 1, 168 ("too commonly used"). Also, T. M. Devine, *Clanship to Crofters' War: The Social Transformation of the Scottish Highlands* (Manchester: Manchester University Press, 1994), ch. 9, discusses illicit whiskey making between 1760 and 1840 as a "peasant enterprise." *Scots Magazine,* quoted in Arthur Herman, *How the Scots Invented the Modern World* (New York: Crown, 2001), 276.

65. Carolyn Podruchny, "Festivities, Fortitude, and Fraternalism: Fur Trade Masculinity and the Beaver Club, 1785–1827," in *New Faces of the Fur Trade: Selected Papers of the Seventh North American Fur Trade Conference,* ed. Jo-Anne Fiske, Susan Sleeper-Smith, and William Wicken (East Lansing: Michigan State University, 1998), 31–52; William Rorabaugh, *The Alcoholic Republic: An American Tradition* (New York: Oxford University Press, 1979).

66. Joseph McGillivray in Rich, ed., *Simpson's 1828 Journey to the Columbia,* Appendix A, 231.

67. Vibert, *Traders' Tales,* ch. 5 (Sellocks quote at 175); G. P. de T. Glazebrook, ed., *The Hargrave Correspondence, 1821–1843* (Toronto: Champlain Society, 1938), 153 (McTavish letter); Mary Black-Rogers, "Varieties of 'Starving': Semantics and Survival in the Subarctic Fur Trade, 1750–1850," *Ethnohistory* 33 (1986): 353–83; Peers, *Ojibwa of Western Canada, 1780–1870,* 64–65.

68. Glazebrook, ed., *Hargrave Correspondence,* 225.

69. Wallace, ed., *John McLean's Notes,* 328.

70. Ibid., 264.

71. Ibid., chs. 15 and 19, esp.179, 315, 326 ("extraordinary rate"), 355–56 ("What is to become?"), 358–59 (alternative).

72. Other traders also pondered this encounter. Saum, *Fur Trader and the Indian,* ch. 10.
73. W. Kaye Lamb, ed., *The Journals and Letters of Sir Alexander Mackenzie* (Cambridge, UK: Cambridge University Press for the Hakluyt Society, 1970), 65.
74. Alexander Ross, *Adventures of the First Settlers on the Oregon or Columbia River,* ed. Milo M. Quaife (Chicago: Donnelley and Sons, 1923), 314, 353–54; see also Ross, *Red River Settlement,* 80.
75. Masson, ed., *Les Bourgeois de la Compagnie du Nord-Ouest,* vol. 2, 412–14, 421.
76. Wallace, ed., *John McLean's Notes,* 350–51.
77. Jean Murray Cole, ed., *This Blessed Wilderness: Archibald McDonald's Letters from the Columbia, 1822–44* (Vancouver: University of British Columbia Press, 2001), 93.
78. W. Kaye Lamb, ed., *The Letters and Journals of Simon Fraser, 1806–1808* (Toronto: Macmillan of Canada, 1960), 271.
79. Ross, *Fur Traders of the Far West,* 188.
80. E. E. Rich, ed., *Journal of Occurrences in the Athabasca Department by George Simpson, 1820 and 1821, and Report* (Toronto: Champlain Society, 1938), 121–22, 376 (Chipewyans), 387 (Beaver).
81. Ibid., 400.
82. Merk, ed., *Fur Trade and Empire,* 96–99.
83. Ibid., 109–110.
84. Ibid., 179.
85. Ibid., 181.
86. Saum, *Fur Trader and the Indian,* 16.
87. Fry, *Scottish Empire,* 66.

NOTES TO CHAPTER 6

1. W. S. Wallace, ed., *John McLean's Notes of a Twenty-five Year's Service in the Hudson's Bay Territory* (Toronto: Champlain Society, 1932), 17.
2. Albert L. Hurtado, *Intimate Frontiers: Sex, Gender, and Culture in Old California* (Albuquerque: University of New Mexico Press, 1993); Anne McClintock, *Imperial Leather: Race, Gender, and Sexuality in the Colonial Conquest* (London: Routledge, 1995); Ann Laura Stoler, "Tense and Tender Ties: The Politics of Comparison in North American History and (Post) Colonial Studies," *Journal of American History* 88 (2001): 829–65, esp. 830–31.
3. Martha Hodes, ed., *Sex, Love, Race: Crossing Boundaries in North American History* (New York: New York University Press, 1999), 4.
4. David D. Smits, "'Abominable Mixture': Toward the Repudiation of Anglo-Indian Intermarriage in Seventeenth-century Virginia," *Virginia Magazine of History and Biography* 95 (1987): 157–92; Ann Marie Plane, *Colonial Intimacies:*

Indian Marriage in Early New England (Ithaca, N.Y.: Cornell University Press, 2000); Richard Godbeer, "Eroticizing the Middle Ground: Anglo-Indian Sexual Relations along the Eighteenth-century Frontier," in *Sex, Love, Race,* ed. Hodes, 91–111.

5. Andrea Smith, *Conquest: Sexual Violence and American Indian Genocide* (Cambridge, Mass.: South End, 2005).

6. Allan I. Macinnes, Marjory-Ann D. Harper, and Linda G. Fryer, eds., *Scotland and the Americas, c. 1650–c. 1939: A Documentary Source Book* (Edinburgh: Scottish History Society, 2002), 108.

7. Simon Fraser of Lovat to Sir William Johnson, Feb. 23, 1759, Huntington Library, PU 1790; my thanks to Geoffrey Plank for providing me with a copy of this letter.

8. Mark Van Doren, ed., *Travels of William Bartram* (1928; repr., New York: Dover, 1955), 170.

9. Jacqueline Peterson and Jennifer S. H. Brown, eds., *The New Peoples: Being and Becoming Métis in North America* (Lincoln: University of Nebraska Press, 1985); Thomas N. Ingersoll, *To Intermix with Our White Brothers: Indian Mixed Bloods in the United States from Earliest Times to the Indian Removals* (Albuquerque: University of New Mexico Press, 2005).

10. Russel Lawrence Barsh, "German Immigrants and Intermarriage with American Indians in the Pacific Northwest," in *Germans and Indians: Fantasies, Encounters, Projections,* ed. Colin G. Calloway, Gerd Gemünden, and Susanne Zantop (Lincoln: University of Nebraska Press, 2002), 125.

11. Roy Porter, *English Society in the Eighteenth Century,* rev. ed. (New York: Penguin, 1990), 148; Jennifer S. H. Brown, *Strangers in Blood: Fur Trade Company Families in Indian Country* (Norman: University of Oklahoma Press, 1980), 79, 131; Sylvia Van Kirk, *Many Tender Ties: Women in Fur Trade Society, 1670–1870* (Norman: University of Oklahoma Press, 1980), 52; R. A. Houston and W. W. J. Knox, eds., *The New Penguin History of Scotland* (London: Penguin, 2001), 221; *Annual Register* (for 1763), 166. Nicholas Maclean-Bristol, *Warriors and Priests: The History of the Clan Maclean, 1300–1570* (East Linton, Scotland: Tuckwell, 1995), 85–86, refers to "the vagaries of Gaelic secular marriage" and discusses the limitations in marriage contracts between clans.

12. Quoted in Adele Perry, *On the Edge of Empire: Gender, Race, and the Making of British Columbia, 1849–1871* (Toronto: University of Toronto Press, 2000), 61.

13. Theda Perdue, *"Mixed Blood" Indians: Racial Construction in the Early South* (Athens: University of Georgia Press, 2003), 25; Clara Sue Kidwell, "Indian Women as Cultural Mediators," *Ethnohistory* (1992): 97–107. On the role of marriage in incorporating Europeans into Caddo society see Julianna Barr, *Peace Came in the Form of a Woman: Indians and Spaniards in the Texas Borderlands* (Chapel Hill: University of North Carolina Press, 2007), 69–71.

14. Theda Perdue, *Cherokee Women: Gender and Culture Change, 1700–1835* (Lincoln: University of Nebraska Press, 1998), 83.

15. Ibid., 49, 54; John Phillip Reid, *A Law of Blood: The Primitive Law of the Cherokee Nation* (New York: New York University Press, 1970), 39–41.

16. J. Leitch Wright Jr., *Creeks and Seminoles: The Destruction and Regeneration of the Muscogulge People* (Lincoln: University of Nebraska Press, 1986), 62; Andrew K. Frank, *Creeks and Southerners: Biculturalism on the Early American Frontier* (Lincoln: University Press, 2005), 3.

17. Perdue, *Cherokee Women,* 82; cf. Claudio Saunt, Barbara Krauthamer, Tiya Miles, Celia E. Naylor, and Circe Sturm, "Rethinking Race and Culture in the Early South," *Ethnohistory* 53 (2006): 399–405, quote at 401.

18. Alfred Proctor James, ed., *Writings of General John Forbes relating to His Service in North America* (Menasha, Wis.: Collegiate, 1938), 233.

19. J. Russell Snapp, *John Stuart and the Struggle for Empire on the Southern Frontier* (Baton Rouge: Louisiana State University Press, 1996), 55–57, 87; W. Stitt Robinson, ed., *North and South Carolina Treaties, 1756–1775,* vol. 14 of *Early American Indian Treaties and Laws, 1607–1789,* gen. ed. Alden T. Vaughan (Bethesda, Md.: University Publications of America, 2003), 336; John L. Nichols, "John Stuart, Beloved Father of the Cherokees," *Highlander Magazine,* 31 (Sept/Oct. 1993); John Bartlett Meserve, "Chief Dennis Bushyhead," *Chronicles of Oklahoma,* 14 (1939), 391 n1; Brent Alan "Yanusdi" Cox, *Heart of the Eagle: Dragging Canoe and the Emergence of the Chickamauga Confederacy* (Milan, Tenn.: Chenanee Publishers, 1999), 199.

20. John L. Nichols, "Alexander Cameron, British Agent among the Cherokee, 1764–1781," *South Carolina Historical Magazine* 97 (1996): 94–114; wife and children at 100.

21. Robinson, ed., *North and South Carolina Treaties,* 276, 278, 305–307, 309–10, 328.

22. K. G. Davies, ed., *Documents of the American Revolution, 1770–1783,* 21 vols. (Shannon: Irish University Press, 1972–1982), vol. 12, 194; vol. 17, 232–34; William L. Saunders and Walter Clark, eds., *The Colonial and State Records of North Carolina,* 30 vols. (Raleigh: Secretary of State, 1886–1914), vol. 10, 767; Co5/82: 114; Stuart to Gage, Jan. 18, 1775, Clements Library, University of Michigan, Gage Papers, vol. 125.

23. Nichols, "Alexander Cameron," 100; Cox, *Heart of the Eagle, 169.*

24. Correspondence and Papers of Governor General Sir Frederick Haldimand, 1758–91, British Museum, Additional Mss. 21762: 203; William S. Coker and Thomas D. Watson, *Indian Traders of the Southeastern Spanish Borderlands: Panton, Leslie, and Company and John Forbes and Company, 1783–1847* (Pensacola: University of West Florida Press, 1986), 162; *American State Papers, Class II: Indian Affairs* (Washington D.C.: Gales and Seaton, 1832–1834), vol. 1, 327.

25. *American State Papers, Class II: Indian Affairs,* vol. 1, 532.

26. Carl F. Klinck and James J. Talman, eds., *The Journal of Major John Norton, 1816* (Toronto: Champlain Society, 1970), 58, 76.

27. Duane H. King, ed., *The Memoirs of Lt. Henry Timberlake* (Cherokee, N.C.: The Museum of the Cherokee Indian Press, 2007), 128, n. 150.

28. Klinck and Talman, eds., *Journal of Major John Norton*, 113–14; Charles J. Kappler, ed., *Indian Affairs: Laws and Treaties*, 2 vols. (Washington, D.C.: Government Printing Office, 1904), vol. 2, 34, 73–74, 83–84, 91.

29. Klinck and Talman, eds., *Journal of Major John Norton*, 60.

30. Ibid., 120.

31. Snapp, *John Stuart and the Struggle for Empire*, 45–53.

32. Dorothy Downs, "British Influences on Creek and Seminole Men's Clothing, 1733–1858," *Florida Anthropologist* 33 (June 1980): 52; "Letters of Benjamin Hawkins, 1796–1806," *Collections of the Georgia Historical Society*, 9 (1916), 168.

33. Edward J. Cashin, *Lachlan McGillivray, Indian Trader: The Shaping of the Southern Colonial Frontier* (Athens: University of Georgia Press, 1992), 306; Coker and Wilson, *Indian Traders of the Southeastern Spanish Borderlands*, 24 (residence with Farquhar).

34. Claudio Saunt, *A New Order of Things: Property, Power, and the Transformation of the Creek Indians, 1733–1816* (New York: Cambridge University Press, 1999), ch. 3, 88.

35. Cashin, *Lachlan McGillivray*, 257.

36. Perdue, *"Mixed Blood" Indians*, 59; Cashin, *Lachlan McGillivray*, 307–308; Saunt, *New Order of Things*, quote at 89.

37. Antonio J. Waring, *Laws of the Creek Nation* (Athens: University of Georgia Press, 1960), 21.

38. Cashin, *Lachlan McGillivray*, 308–10.

39. Thomas H. Foster, ed. *The Collected Works of Benjamin Hawkins, 1796–1810* (Tuscaloosa: University of Alabama Press, 2003), 29–31; Claudio Saunt, *Black, White, and Indian: Race and the Unmaking of an American Family* (New York: Oxford University Press, 2005), quotes at 4, 11.

40. Van Kirk, *Many Tender Ties*, 6–7; Brown, *Strangers in Blood*, 51–52.

41. Glyndwr Williams, ed., *Andrew Graham's Observations on Hudson's Bay 1767–1791* (London: Hudson Bay Record Society, 1969), 248, 299. A seventy-five-page handwritten manuscript listing the items presented to the Edinburgh Royal Society is in Edinburgh University Library in MS DC. I. 57.

42. Van Kirk, *Many Tender Ties*, 174, 276–77 n5; Williams, ed., *Andrew Graham's Observations*, 341, 344–45.

43. Paul Kelbie, "200 Years On, Cree Indians Go Home to Orkneys," *Independent* (London) (Sept. 6, 2004).

44. W. Stewart Wallace, ed., *Documents relating to the North West Company* (Toronto: Champlain Society, 1934), 210–11.

45. Patrick Campbell, *Travels in the Interior Inhabited Parts of North America in the Years 1791 and 1792*, ed. H. H. Langton (Toronto: Champlain Society, 1937), 117, 225.

46. Brown, *Strangers in Blood*, 51.

47. Ibid., 70–80, 96–107.

48. R. O. Alexander, ed., "The Capture of Quebec: A Manuscript Journal relating to the Operations before Quebec from 8 May, 1759, to 17 May, 1760, kept by Colonel Malcolm Fraser, then Lieutenant in the 78th Foot (Frasers Highlanders)," *Journal of the Society for Army Historical Research* 18 (1939): 136; Brown, *Strangers in Blood*, 90–94; Howard R. Lamar, ed., *The New Encyclopedia of the American West* (New Haven, Conn.: Yale University Press, 1998), 672.

49. Margaret Arnett McLeod and W. L. Morton, *Cuthbert Grant of Grantown: Warden of the Plains of Red River* (Toronto: McClelland and Stewart, 1963), 67, 73, 85.

50. Van Kirk, *Many Tender Ties*, 88.

51. Ibid., ch. 7.

52. Brown, *Strangers in Blood*, 98.

53. Marjorie Wilkins Campbell, *McGillivray, Lord of the Northwest* (Toronto: Clarke, Irwin, 1962), 49; Brown, *Strangers in Blood*, 90; Colin G. Calloway, *Crown and Calumet: British-Indian Relations, 1783–1815* (Norman: University of Oklahoma Press, 1987), 179–80.

54. E. E. Rich, ed., *Journal of Occurrences in the Athabasca Department by George Simpson, 1820 and 1821, and Report* (Toronto: Champlain Society, 1938), 392, 396.

55. Brown, *Strangers in Blood*, 115–30; Van Kirk, *Many Tender Ties*, 161–62; R. Harvey Fleming, ed., *Minutes of Council, Northern Department of Rupert Land, 1821–31* (Toronto: Champlain Society, 1940), 411 (letter to McTavish).

56. Christine Welsh, "Women in the Shadows: Reclaiming a Métis Heritage," in *New Contexts of Canadian Criticism*, ed. Ajay Heble, Donna Palmateer Pennee, and J. R. (Tim) Struthers (Peterborough, Ont.: Broadview, 1997), 56–66, esp. 62–63.

57. Morag MacLachlan, ed., *The Fort Langley Journals, 1827–30* (Vancouver: University of British Columbia Press, 1998), 16; Brown, *Strangers in Blood*, 133; Van Kirk, *Many Tender Ties*, 182–88, 198–99; G. P. de T. Glazebrook, ed., *The Hargrave Correspondence 1821–1843* (Toronto: Champlain Society, 1938), 86 (McMillan's "Scotch Lassie"); Welsh, "Women in the Shadows," 63–64 (Margaret); John C. Jackson, *Children of the Fur Trade: Forgotten Métis of the Pacific Northwest* (Missoula: Mountain Press, 1995), 265 (Nancy's tragic trip to the Columbia).

58. Roxann Wheeler, *The Complexion of Race: Categories of Difference in Eighteenth-century British Culture* (Philadelphia: University of Pennsylvania Press, 2000), 33.

59. E. E. Rich, ed., *Colin Robertson's Correspondence Book, September 1817 to September 1822* (Toronto: Champlain Society, 1939), cxxi–cxxiii; Van Kirk, *Many Tender Ties*, 204–205. Simpson's opinions on Robertson are expressed in the first lines of "The Character Book of Governor George Simpson, 1832," in Glyndwr Williams, ed., *Hudson's Bay Miscellany 1670–1870* (Winnipeg: Hudson's Bay Record Society, 1975), 169. On another occasion Simpson described him as

"an uncertified bankrupt [who] from his extravagant habits cannot be worth a guinea should he live a thousand years." NAC, A-27: Papers of Thomas Douglas, fifth Earl of Selkirk, vol. 7, 1145. On McTavish snubbing Métis families see Williams, ed., *Hudson's Bay Miscellany*, 157–58, 171 n3.

60. D. Geneva Lent, *James Sinclair and the Hudson's Bay Company* (Seattle: University of Washington Press, 1963), 6–7.

61. Wallace, ed., *John McLean's Notes*, 220–21.

62. NAC, Selkirk Papers, vol. 1, 12; see also Alexander Ross, *The Red River Settlement: Its Rise, Progress, and Present State* (London: Smith, Elder, 1856), vi, 17.

63. L. G. Thomas, "Fur Traders in Retirement," *The Beaver* (Winter 1979), 14–21; Patricia A. McCormack, "Lost Women: Native Wives in Orkney and Lewis," paper presented at the annual meeting of the American Society for Ethnohistory, Tulsa, Okla., Nov. 2007; Brown, *Strangers in Blood*, 142; Van Kirk, *Many Tender Ties*, 141–42; T. M. Devine, *Scotland's Empire and the Shaping of the Americas, 1600–1815* (Washington, D.C.: Smithsonian Books, 2003), 202.

64. Miles Macdonnell Papers, NAC, MG 19, E4, quoted in Brown, *Strangers in Blood*, 101.

65. Brown, *Strangers in Blood*, 145.

66. David G. Mandlebaum, "The Plains Cree," *Anthropological Papers of the American Museum of Natural History* 37, part 2 (1940): 167.

67. [James Carnegie], Earl of Southesk, *Saskatchewan and the Rocky Mountains: A Diary and Narrative of Travel, Sport, and Adventure, during a Journey through the Hudson's Bay Company Territories, in 1859 and 1860* (Edinburgh: Edmonston and Douglas, 1875), quote at 359; Lady Ishbel, quoted in Ferenc Morton Szasz, *Scots in the North American West, 1790–1917* (Norman: University of Oklahoma Press, 2000), 54; Alexander Morris, ed., *The Treaties of Canada with the Indians of Manitoba and the North-West Territories* (Toronto: Belfords, Clarke and Co., 1880; reprinted Saskatoon: Fifth House Publishers, 1991), 293.

68. NAC, Selkirk Papers, vol. 7, 1139.

69. Jenni Calder, *Scots in Canada* (Edinburgh: Luath, 2003), 89–90.

70. Fleming, ed., *Minutes of Council*, 32–35, 314–15.

71. Van Kirk, *Many Tender Ties*, 33, 35, 234, 236–37; Ross, *Red River Settlement*.

72. Sylvia Van Kirk, "'What If Mama Is an Indian?' The Cultural Ambivalence of the Alexander Ross Family," in *New Peoples*, ed. Peterson and Brown, 207–17; Sherry Farrell Racette, "Sewing Ourselves Together: Clothing, Decorative Arts, and the Expression of Métis and Half-breed Identity," Ph.D. diss., University of Manitoba, 2004, 191.

73. Van Kirk, *Many Tender Ties*, 87.

74. Jennifer Brown, "Ultimate Respectability: Fur Trade Children in the 'Civilized World,'" *The Beaver*, (Winter 1977), 4–10, (Spring 1978), 48–57; Brown, *Strangers in Blood*, 156.

75. Isaac Cowie, *The Company of Adventurers: A Narrative of Seven Years in the Service of the Hudson's Bay Company during 1867–1874 on the Great Buffalo Plains*

(Toronto: William Briggs, 1913), 63; Peter C. Newman, *Empire of the Bay: The Company of Adventurers That Seized a Continent* (Toronto: Penguin, 1998), 158.

76. Brown, *Strangers in Blood*, 182–83.

77. Lent, *West of the Mountains*, 42–46.

78. Brown, *Strangers in Blood*, 184.

79. Jackson, *Children of the Fur Trade*, 48–49.

80. MacLachlan, ed., *Fort Langley Journals*, 76; Jean Murray Cole, ed., *This Blessed Wilderness: Archibald McDonald's Letters from the Columbia, 1822–44* (Vancouver: University of British Columbia Press, 2001), 9–10, 24, 112 (long quote), 139; Brown, *Strangers in Blood*, 185–90.

81. William S. Lewis and Naojiro Murakimi, eds., *Ranald MacDonald: The Narrative of his early life on the Columbia under the Hudson's Bay Company's regime; of his experiences in the Pacific Whale Fishery; and of his great Adventure to Japan; with a sketch of his later life on the Western Frontier, 1824–1894* (Portland: Oregon Historical Society Press, 1990); Frederik L. Schodt, *Native American in the Land of the Shogun: Ranald MacDonald and the Opening of Japan* (Berkeley: Stone Bridge, 2003); Elizabeth B. Custer, "An Out-of-the-Way Outing," *Harper's Weekly* (July 18, 1891), 534–35.

82. Jean Barman and Bruce M. Watson, "Fort Colvile's Fur Trade Families and the Dynamics of Race in the Pacific Northwest," *Pacific Northwest Quarterly* 90 (1999): 140–53; esp. 142–43, 145, 149–50. Joseph McDonald's recollection is in Robert Bigart, ed., *"I Will Be Meat for My Salish": The Montana Writers Project and the Buffalo of the Flathead Indian Reservation* (Helena: Montana Historical Society Press, 2002), 104. Thanks to Dan Runnels from the Colville reservation for this source. David M. Buerge, ed., *West Coast Journeys, 1865–1879: The Travelogue of a Remarkable Woman by Caroline C. Leighton* (Seattle: Sasquatch, 1995), 49–50; Szasz, *Scots in the North American West*, 72–76. James Hunter's book, *Glencoe and the Indians* (Edinburgh: Mainstream, 1996; published in America as *Scottish Highlanders, Indian Peoples: Thirty Generations of a Montana Family* (Helena: Montana Historical Society Press, 1997), traces the McDonald family from the Highlands to Montana and provides many details on Angus, Christina, Duncan, and their descendants (Glengarry frock and Scotch habits quotes at 132, 149).

83. Szasz, *Scots in the North American West*, 70–72; Juana Fraser Lyon, "Archie McIntosh, the Scottish Indian Scout," *Journal of Arizona History* 7 (Autumn 1966): 103–22; Martin F. Schmitt, ed., *General George Crook: His Autobiography* (Norman: University of Oklahoma Press, 1986), 147, quote at 245.

84. Brown, *Strangers in Blood*, 211.

85. McLeod and Morton, *Cuthbert Grant of Grantown*.

86. Judith Hudson Beattie and Helen M. Buss, eds., *Undelivered Letters to Hudson's Bay Company Men on the Northwest Coast of America, 1830–57* (Vancouver: University of British Columbia Press, 2003), 340–42, 459–60, quote at 342.

87. Elizabeth Vibert, *Traders' Tales: Narratives of Cultural Encounters in the Columbia Plateau, 1807–1846* (Norman: University of Oklahoma Press, 1997), 160.

88. Maria Campbell, *Halfbreed* (Lincoln: University of Nebraska Press, 1973), 14.

89. Emily Levine, ed., *With My Own Eyes: A Lakota Woman Tells Her People's History—Susan Bordeaux Bettelyoun and Josephine Waggoner* (Lincoln: University of Nebraska Press, 1998), 44. I am grateful to Alyce Spotted Bear for sharing this with me.

90. McClintock, *Imperial Leather: Race, Gender, and Sexuality in the Colonial Conquest,* 46–48; Ronald Hym, *Empire and Sexuality: The British Experience* (Manchester, UK: Manchester University Press, 1990), ch. 5, quote at 207; Margaret MacMillen, *Women of the Raj* (London: Thames and Hudson, 1988), 110–11.

91. Brown, *Strangers in Blood,* 111–14, 156, 208–09, 237; Perry, *On the Edge of Empire: Gender, Race, and the Making of British Columbia, 1849–1871,* esp. chs. 2, 4, 6.

92. MacLeod interviewed and quoted by James Hunter, *Scottish Exodus: Travels among a Worldwide Clan* (Edinburgh: Mainstream, 2005), 239; Van Kirk, *Many Tender Ties,* 240–41.

NOTES TO CHAPTER 7

1. Eric Richards treats the insurrection of 1792 in *A History of the Highland Clearances.* Vol. 1, *Agrarian Transformation and the Evictions, 1746–1886* (London: Croom Helm, 1982), ch. 9; Eric Richards, *The Highland Clearances: People, Landlords, and Rural Turmoil* (Edinburgh: Birlinn, 2002), ch. 6.

2. Norman Scarfe, ed., *To the Highlands in 1786: The Inquisitive Journey of a Young French Aristocrat* (Woodbridge, UK: Boydell, 2001), 223.

3. John Prebble, *The Highland Clearance* (Harmondsworth, UK: Penguin, 1969) 21; J. M. Bumsted, *The People's Clearance: Highland Emigration to British North America, 1770–1815* (Edinburgh: Edinburgh University Press, 1982), 175.

4. Eric Richards, *Britannia's Children: Emigration from England, Scotland, Wales, and Ireland since 1600* (London: Hambledon and London, 2004), quotes at 27 and 176; Jeanette M. Brock, *The Mobile Scot: A Study of Emigration and Migration, 1861–1911* (Edinburgh: John Donald, 1999); James Hunter, *Scottish Exodus: Travels among a Worldwide Clan* (Edinburgh: Mainstream, 2005).

5. David Armitage, "The Scottish Diaspora," in *Scotland: A History,* ed. Jenny Wormald (New York: Oxford University Press, 2005), 272.

6. Ivan Doig, *Dancing at the Rascal Fair* (New York: Harper and Row, 1987), 94.

7. D. Masson, "The Gael in the Far West," *Transactions of the Gaelic Society of Inverness* 3 (1873), 26–45.

8. John C. Weaver, *The Great Land Rush and the Making of the Modern World, 1650–1900* (Montreal: McGill-Queens University Press, 2003); Cole Harris,

"How Did Colonialism Dispossess? Comments from an Edge of Empire," *Annals of the Association of American Geographers* 94 (2004): 165–82.

9. "On Emigration from the Scottish Highlands and Isles," by Edward S. Fraser, NLS, ms. 9646: iii; "State of Emigration from the Highlands of Scotland, its extent, causes, & proposed remedy," Mar. 21, 1803, NLS, Adv. ms. 35.6.18; "On Emigration," 1803, NLS, Adv. ms. 73.2.15: 1–3.

10. Jack M. Bumsted, "The Scottish Diaspora: Emigration to British North America, 1763–1815," in *Nation and Province in the First British Empire: Scotland and the Americas, 1600–1800,* ed. Ned C. Landsman (Providence, R.I.: John Carter Brown Library, 2001), 134; Peter Womack, *Improvement and Romance: Constructing the Myth of the Highlands* (London: Macmillan, 1989), 115–16; James Loch, *An Account of the Improvements on the Estates of the Marquess of Stafford, in the Counties of Stafford and Salop, and on the Estate of Sutherland* (London: Longman, Hurst, Rees, Orme, and Brown, 1820), xvi–xvii. (A copy of Loch's *Account* is also in NLS, Sutherland Papers, Dep. 313/1016.)

11. SAS 11: 598.

12. Ibid., 2: 391; 10: 470; Richards, *History of the Highland Clearances,* vol. 1, ch. 6.

13. Duane Meyer, *The Highland Scots of North Carolina, 1732–1776* (Chapel Hill: University of North Carolina Press, 1957), chs. 5–7; J. P. MacLean, *An Historical Account of the Settlements of Scotch Highlanders in America prior to the Peace of 1783, together with Notices of Highland Regiments and Biographical Sketches* (1900; repr., Bowie, Md.: Heritage Books, 2001), ch. 5; William L. Saunders and Walter Clark, eds., *The Colonial and State Records of North Carolina,* 30 vols. (Raleigh: Secretary of State, 1886–1914), 4: 489–90, 7: 543–44; 8: 526; A. Murdoch, ed., "A Scottish Document concerning Emigration to North Carolina," *North Carolina Historical Review* 67 (1990): 438–49; Alex Murdoch, "Emigration from the Scottish Highlands to America in the Eighteenth Century," *British Journal for Eighteenth-century Studies* 21 (1998): 164–67 ("not far from the *Indians*" at 166); Barbara De Wolfe, ed., *Discoveries of America: Personal Accounts of British Emigrants to North America during the Revolutionary Era* (New York: Cambridge University Press, 1997), 27–37.

14. Murdoch, "Emigration from the Scottish Highlands to America," 161–74; T. C. Smout, N. C. Landsman, and T. M. Devine, "Scottish Emigration in the Seventeenth and Eighteenth Centuries," in *Europeans on the Move: Studies on European Migration 1500–1800,* ed. Nicholas Canny (New York: Clarendon, 1994), 90–112; Meyer, *Highland Scots of North Carolina,* chs. 2–3; De Wolfe, ed., *Discoveries of America,* vol. 3 (125,000); Bernard Bailyn, *Voyagers to the West: A Passage in the Peopling of America on the Eve of the Revolution* (New York: Knopf, 1986), 26, suggests that as many as forty thousand Scots left for America between the Seven Years' War and the Revolution; Bumsted, *People's Clearance,* 9–10, 229, offers more conservative estimates.

15. Murdoch, ed., "Scottish Document concerning Emigration to North Carolina," 449; [Scotus Americanus] *Informations [sic] concerning the Province*

of North Carolina Addressed to Emigrants from the Highlands and Western Isles of Scotland by an Impartial Hand (Glasgow, 1773); the text is available online at the website of the North Carolina Colonial Records Project, North Carolina Office of Archives and History, http://www.ah.dcr.state.nc.us/sections/hp/colonial/Bookshelf/Tracts/Informations/Default.htm.

16. *Scots Magazine* 33 (1771), 325, 500; 35 (1773), 557; 36 (1774), 221; De Wolfe, ed., *Discoveries of America*, 30, 37, 170–86; NLS, Delvine Papers, ms. 1306: 54–55, 67–68, 72. Eric Richards, *A History of the Highland Clearances.* Vol. 2, *Emigration, Protest, Reasons* (London: Croom Helm, 1985), 194 (10 percent estimate).

17. "Observes or Remarks upon the Lands and Islands which Compose the Barrony called Harris, the property of Norman McLeod of MacLeod Esq., 1772," NLS, Lee Papers, ms. 3431: 177–83.

18. Hunter, *Scottish Exodus*, 91.

19. Samuel Johnson and James Boswell, *A Journey to the Western Islands of Scotland and the Journal of a Tour to the Hebrides*, ed. Peter Levi (New York: Penguin, 1984), 101–105, quotes at 102–103.

20. Viola Root Cameron, comp., *Emigrants from Scotland to America 1774–1775: Copied from a Loose Bundle of Treasury Papers in the Public Record Office* [PRO,T 47/12] (London, 1930; repr., Baltimore: Genealogical Publishing, 1965), quotes at 6–7 (Gordon), 12–13 (McDonald), 25 (Stornaway), 91 (Glenurchy emigrants). Thomas Garnett, *Observations on a Tour through the Highlands and Part of the Western Isles*, 2 vols. (London: Cadell and Davies, 1800), vol. 1, 185, reported similar reasons for emigration.

21. SAS 1: 488; Saunders and Clark, eds., *Colonial and State Records of North Carolina*, vol. 9, 1159.

22. *Scots Magazine* 37 (1775), 340, 690.

23. NLS, Session Papers, Herman Collection, vol. 8, Petition of John Maclauchlane, July 3, 1782, quoted in T. M. Devine, *The Transformation of Rural Scotland: Social Change and the Agrarian Economy, 1660–1815* (Edinburgh: John Donald, 1994), 72–73.

24. NSAS 14: 342; Sir Walter Scott, *Manners, Customs, and History of the Highlanders of Scotland* (1816; repr., New York: Barnes and Noble, 2004), 27.

25. James Hunter, *The Making of the Crofting Community*, new ed. (Edinburgh: John Donald/Birlinn, 2000), 70.

26. Johnson and Boswell, *Journey to the Western Islands*, 97.

27. William Knight, *The Journals of Dorothy Wordsworth* (London: Macmillan, 1925), 244.

28. SAS 10: 470.

29. "On Emigration from the Scottish Highlands & Isles," by Edward S. Fraser, NLS, ms. 9646: 35 ("sheep must come"); Prebble, *Highland Clearances*, 21.

30. Alex MacNab to Archibald MacRae, Oct. 18, 1793, NLS, Acc. 6945; "On Emigration from the Scottish Highlands & Isles," 77.

31. James Hunter, *A Dance Called America: The Scottish Highlands, the United States, and Canada* (Edinburgh: Mainstream, 1994), 39–41; Smout, Landsman, and Devine, "Scottish Emigration in the Seventeenth and Eighteenth Centuries," 106–11; Bumsted, *People's Clearance*, ch. 3, quotes at 63; Bumsted, "Scottish Diaspora"; Meyer, *Highland Scots of North Carolina*, 55–56; Stephen J. Hornsby, "Patterns of Scottish Emigration to Canada, 1750–1870," *Journal of Historical Geography* 18 (1992), 397–416; Marjory Harper, *Adventurers and Exiles: The Great Scottish Exodus* (London: Profile, 2003); Ian Adams and Meredyth Somerville, *Cargoes of Despair and Hope: Scottish Emigration to North America 1603–1803* (Edinburgh: John Donald, 1993).

32. Hunter, *Making of the Crofting Community*, ch. 2; A. J. Youngson, *After the Forty-five: The Economic Impact on the Scottish Highlands* (Edinburgh: Edinburgh University Press, 1973), 128–29; 134–39; NLS, ms. 6602: 21–28; bound with *Observations on the Report of the Committee of the House of Commons appointed to enquire into the State of the British Fishery*, 1786, NLS, LC 2605. Garnett, *Observations on a Tour through the Highlands*, vol. 1, 186–88, described kelp manufacturing at the end of the eighteenth century.

33. Bumsted, *People's Clearance*, 98.

34. Charles Fraser-Mackintosh, ed., *Letters of Two Centuries, chiefly connected with Inverness and the Highlands, from 1616 to 1815* (Inverness: Mackenzie, 1890), 312.

35. J. G. Fyfe, ed., *Scottish Diaries and Memoirs 1746–1843* (Stirling, Scotland: Eneas Mackay, 1942), 564–65.

36. "State of Emigration from the Highlands of Scotland, its extent, causes, & proposed remedy," Mar. 21, 1803, NLS, Adv. ms. 35.6.18: 5–7, 18–19, 21, 33–34; "On Emigration," 1803, NLS, Adv. ms. 73.2.15: 3; "On Emigration from the Scottish Highlands & Isles," 171. Dorothy Wordsworth expressed the same fear; Knight, ed., *Journals of Dorothy Wordsworth*, 343.

37. Robert Clyde, *From Rebel to Hero: The Image of the Highlander, 1745–1830* (East Linton, Scotland: Tuckwell, 1995), 163–64; Allan I. Macinnes, *Clanship, Commerce, and the House of Stuart, 1603–1788* (East Linton, Scotland: Tuckwell, 1996), 217, 223.

38. Bumsted, *People's Clearance*, 66.

39. Youngson, *After the Forty-five*, ch. 6; Bumsted, "Scottish Diaspora," 139; Bumsted, *People's Clearance*, 143–45; Allan I. Macinnes, Marjory-Ann D. Harper, and Linda G. Fryer, eds., *Scotland and the Americas, c. 1650–c. 1939: A Documentary Source Book* (Edinburgh: Scottish History Society, 2002), 22, 46; *Scots Magazine* 64 (1802), 705; "State of Emigration from the Highlands of Scotland," 20–21, 26 ("torrent of depopulation"); "On Emigration," 1803, NLS, Adv. ms. 73.2.15: 1–3 ("race of Highlanders" at 3); "On Emigration from the Scottish Highlands and Isles," by Edward S. Fraser, NLS, ms. 9646; Hunter, *Making of the Crofting Community*, 58–62; Adams and Somerville, *Cargoes of Despair and Hope*, 169–71.

40. Thomas Douglas, Earl of Selkirk, *Observations on the Present State of the Highlands of Scotland, with a view of the Causes and Probable Consequences of Emigration* (London: Longman, Hurst, Rees, and Orme, 1805). The second edition of Selkirk's "Observations" is reprinted in J. M. Bumsted, ed., *The Collected Writings of Lord Selkirk, 1799–1809* (Winnipeg: Manitoba Record Society, 1984), 100–240.

41. Hunter, *Dance Called America*, 106–107; Womack, *Improvement and Romance*, 118; Harper, *Adventurers and Exiles*, ch. 2; Bumsted, *People's Clearance*, 218; Hunter, *Making of the Crofting Community*, 81–82.

42. Richards, *Highland Clearances*, 63–64.

43. NAC, CO 42/165 (reels B-133–134), 469–70.

44. Letter from Patrick Sellar to James Loch, in Loch, *Account of the Improvements*, appendix 7: 53–54; "On the Condition of the Highland Peasantry before and since the Rebellion of 1745," by "B.G.," reprinted in Thomas Bakewell, *Remarks on a Publication by James Loch, Esq. entitled an Account of the Improvements on the Estates of the Marquess of Stafford* (London: Longman, Hurst, Rees, Orme, and Brown, 1820), 57, 63.

45. On the Sutherland clearances see Richards, *History of the Highland Clearances*, vol. 1, chs. 11–12; Richards, *Highland Clearances*, chs. 8–11; R. J. Adam, ed., *Papers on Sutherland Estate Management 1802–1816*, 2 vols. (Edinburgh: Scottish History Society, 1972); NLS, Sutherland Papers, Dep. 313.

46. Quote in Clyde, *From Rebel to Hero*, 28–29.

47. NLS, Sutherland Papers, Dep. 313/1015–1016.

48. Ibid., 313/1128, #21; letter from Patrick Sellar to James Loch, in Loch, *Account of the Improvements*, appendix 7: 53–54; sheep figures in Sutherland: Richards, *Highland Clearances*, 72–73, and NSAS 15: 218.

49. Richards, *Highland Clearances*, 128.

50. Eric Richards, *Patrick Sellar and the Highland Clearances: Homicide, Eviction, and the Price of Progress* (Edinburgh: Edinburgh University Press, 1999). Sellar described himself as a "convert" to the policy of improvement; letter to Loch in Loch, *Account of the Improvements*, appendix 7: 56.

51. Adam, ed., *Papers on Sutherland Estate Management*, vol. 1, 156.

52. Ibid., 175–76.

53. Ian Grimble, *The Trial of Patrick Sellar: The Tragedy of Highland Evictions* (London: Routledge and Paul, 1962); Richards, *Patrick Sellar and the Highland Clearances*, ch. 10; Adam, ed., *Papers on Sutherland Estate Management*, vol. 1, 151–68.

54. Sellar was "*n céard dubh,*" the black rogue, who when he died should have his "dung-like" carcass spread like manure on a field; Donald Meek, ed., *Tuath Is Tighearna, Tenants and Landlords: An Anthology of Gaelic Poetry of Social and Political Protest from the Clearances to the Land Agitation (1800–1890)* (Edinburgh: Scottish Academic Press, 1995), 54–55, 190–91. Eric Richards describes Sellar as "the target of the accumulated and ritualized indignation

of posterity against the clearances." His grave in Elgin Cathedral is regularly desecrated, and he became the object of electronic graffiti in the global mail system. Richards, *Highland Clearances,* 9–10.

55. Loch, *Account of the Improvements,* xi, 48, 50–53, 60, 63–64; NLS, Sutherland Papers. Loch also quoted in John Prebble, *The Royal Jaunt: George IV in Scotland, August 1822* (1988; repr., Edinburgh: Birlinn, 2000), 165; Prebble, *Highland Clearances,* 56. Loch's papers for 1819 and 1820 are in NLS, Sutherland Papers, Dep. 313/1139–1140.

56. Adam, ed., *Papers on Sutherland Estate Management,* vol. I, II; Richards, *Patrick Sellar and the Highland Clearances,* 224, NLS, Sutherland Papers, Dep. 313/1026, 1128: #13.

57. Richards, *Highland Clearances,* 165; NSAS 15: 147.

58. Karl Marx, *Capital.* Vol. I, *A Critique of Political Economy: The Process of Capitalist Production,* trans. from the 4th German ed. (London: Allen and Unwin, 1928), 807–13.

59. Alexander MacKenzie, *History of the Highland Clearances* (1883; repr., Edinburgh: Mercat, 1997), 37, 101 (quote); Prebble, *Highland Clearances,* 63; Hunter, *Making of the Crofting Community,* 144. Memories of the church's complicity in the clearances endured well into the twentieth century. For example, Murdo McCuish's grandmother, who was eleven at the time of the clearances and died in 1929, told him that the minister came around "advising people that it was God's will they should leave." David Craig, *On the Crofters' Trail: In Search of the Clearance Highlanders* (London: Jonathan Cape, 1990), 56–57.

60. T. M. Devine, *Clanship to Crofters' War: The Social Transformation of the Scottish Highlands* (Manchester, UK: Manchester University Press, 1994), 41.

61. Richards, *History of the Highland Clearances,* vol. 2, chs. 12–13.

62. NLS, Sutherland Papers, Dep. 313/1128: #20, #25.

63. Both quoted in Prebble, *Royal Jaunt,* 30–31.

64. NLS, Sutherland Papers, Dep. 313/1139: #57, #63; 1468: 170, 311.

65. Macleod's "Gloomy Memories in the Highlands of Scotland" are reprinted in MacKenzie, *History of the Highland Clearances.*

66. Michael Fry, *Wild Scots: Four Hundred Years of Highland History* (London: John Murray, 2005), xii; Richards, *Highland Clearances,* 119.

67. See, for example, "Sutherland Improvements" and "Statement respecting Improvements in Sutherland," NLS, Sutherland Papers, Dep. 313/1016, 1139; NSAS 15: 115–17.

68. Harriet Beecher Stowe, *Sunny Memories of Foreign Lands* (London, 1854), 219–28; quoted in Richards, *History of the Highland Clearances,* vol. I, 181–82.

69. NSAS 7: 435.

70. Richards, *Highland Clearances,* 72, 81–82.

71. Richards, *History of the Highland Clearances,* vol. I, 231; vol. 2, 183, 230; Harper, *Adventurers and Exiles,* 48.

72. Hunter, *Making of the Crofting Community*, 87.
73. NSAS 7: 186, 221–22.
74. Richards, *Highland Clearances*, ch. 13.
75. Ibid., 245–46, 259–74.
76. Henry Cockburn, *Circuit Journeys* (1886), 67; quoted in Richards, *Highland Clearances*, 244.
77. Quoted in Richards, *Highland Clearances*, 21.
78. Harper, *Adventurers and Exiles*, 44.
79. Richards, *History of the Highland Clearances*, vol. 2, 250; *Report of the Select Committee on Emigration (Scotland)*, Parliamentary Papers, 1841, VI.
80. Fyfe, ed., *Scottish Diaries and Memoirs, 1746–1843*, 564–65, 569, 573.
81. T. M. Devine, *The Great Highland Famine: Hunger, Emigration, and the Scottish Highlands in the Nineteenth Century* (Edinburgh: John Donald, 1988), chs. 6–7 and quote at 181; Hunter, *Making of the Crofting Community*, ch. 4. The Duke of Sutherland spent £18,000 on famine relief and helped 380 of his tenants to emigrate in 1847.
82. Krisztina Fenyo, *Contempt, Sympathy, and Romance: Lowland Perceptions of the Highlands and the Clearances during the Famine Years, 1845–1855* (East Linton, Scotland: Tuckwell, 2000).
83. Henry Mayhew, *London Labour and London Poor*, 4 vols. (London, 1861; repr., New York: Dover, 1968), vol. 3, 162, 164–71.
84. Margaret Bennett, *Oatmeal and the Catechism: Scottish Gaelic Settlers in Quebec* (Montreal: McGill-Queens University Press, 1998), 2; Harper, *Adventurers and Exiles*, 50–51.
85. Craig, *On the Crofters' Trail*, 195.
86. On Grosse Isle, Cape Breton, and the hardships and horrors of Highland emigration generally see Hunter, *Dance Called America*, chs 5–6. Catherine Parr Traill, *The Backwoods of Canada: being letters from the Wife of an Emigrant Officer* (London: Nattali and Bond, n.d.), 19–20, 36–37. Lucille H. Campey, *After the Hector: The Scottish Pioneers of Nova Scotia and Cape Breton, 1773–1852* (Toronto: Natural Heritage Press, 2004), offers a more optimistic view.
87. NSAS 7: 216, 306.
88. Hunter, *Making of the Crofting Community*, 131.
89. W. S. Wallace, ed., *John McLean's Notes of a Twenty-five Years' Service in the Hudson's Bay Territory* (Toronto: Champlain Society, 1932), 289–90; Meek, ed., *Tuath Is Tighearna*, 69–73, 199–202, 315.
90. Wormald, ed., *Scotland: A History*, 218.
91. *Report of the Commissioners of Inquiry into the Condition of the Crofters and Cottars of the Highlands and Islands of Scotland* (Napier Commission), Parliamentary Papers 1884, xxxii–xxxvi; Richards, *History of the Highland Clearances*, vol. 1, 237; Richards, *Highland Clearances*, ch. 18; Hunter, *Making of the Crofting Community*, chs. 8–11.
92. Hunter, *Making of the Crofting Community*, 77, 90.

93. Sorley MacLean, quoted in James Hunter, *Last of the Free: A Millennial History of the Highlands and Islands* (Edinburgh: Mainstream, 1999), 339.

94. Hugh MacLennan, *Scotchman's Return: and Other Essays* (Toronto: Scribner, 1960), 7, quoted in James Hunter, *On the Other Side of Sorrow: Nature and People in the Scottish Highlands* (Edinburgh: Mainstream, 1995), 25.

95. Thomas Grierson, *Autumnal Rambles among the Scottish Mountains* (Edinburgh, 1850), 104–106, quoted in Richards, *Highland Clearances*, 231.

96. See ch. 3, pp. 78–79. Bruce P. Lenman, "'From Savage to Scot' via the French and Spaniards: Principal Robertson's Spanish Sources," in *William Robertson and the Expansion of Empire*, ed. Stewart J. Brown (New York: Cambridge University Press, 1997), 208–209.

97. Francis Paul Prucha, ed., *Documents of United States Indian Policy* (Lincoln: University of Nebraska Press, 1975), 22–23.

98. Arthur H. DeRosier Jr., *The Removal of the Choctaw Indians* (Knoxville: University of Tennessee Press, 1970). Donna L. Akers, *Living in the Land of Death: The Choctaw Nation, 1830–1860* (East Lansing: Michigan State University Press, 2004), ch. 2, provides a Choctaw account of Choctaw removal.

99. Quoted in Ronald N. Satz, *American Indian Policy in the Jacksonian Era* (Lincoln: University of Nebraska Press, 1971), 41.

100. James D. Richardson, *A Compilation of the Messages and Papers of the Presidents, 1789–1902*, 10 vols. (New York: Bureau of National Literature and Art, 1903), vol. 2, 280–83.

101. Theda Perdue and Michael D. Green, eds., *The Cherokee Removal: A Brief History with Documents* (New York: Bedford/St. Martin's, 1995), 125–26.

102. Benjamin W. Griffith Jr., *McIntosh and Weatherford, Creek Indian Leaders* (Tuscaloosa: University of Alabama Press, 1988); Andrew K. Frank, *Creeks and Southerners: Biculturalism on the Early American Frontier* (Lincoln: University of Nebraska Press, 2005), ch. 6; Frank, "The Rise and Fall of William McIntosh: Authority and Identity on the Early American Frontier," *Georgia Historical Quarterly*, 86 (2002), 18–48; Michael D. Green, *The Politics of Indian Removal: Creek Government and Society in Crisis* (Lincoln: University of Nebraska Press, 1982), 54–57, 69–97; Grace M. Schwartzman and Susan K. Barnard, "A Trail of Broken Promises: Georgians and Muskogee/Creek Treaties," *Georgia Historical Quarterly* 75 (1991): 697–718; Charles J. Kappler, ed., *Indian Affairs: Laws and Treaties*, 2 vols. (Washington, D.C.: Government Printing Office, 1904), vol. 2, 86, 109, 156, 196–97, 215. Documents relating to McIntosh's killing are in *American State Papers, Class II, Indian Affairs*, 2 vols. (Washington, D.C.: Gales and Seaton, 1834), vol. 2, 760–74.

103. Alison Cathcart, "Crisis of Identity? Clan Chattan's Response to Government Policy in the Scottish Highlands c. 1580–1609," in *Fighting for Identity: Scottish Military Experience c. 1550–1900*, ed. Steve Murdoch and A. Mackillop (Leiden, the Netherlands: Brill, 2002), 163–84.

104. Perdue and Green, eds., *Cherokee Removal*, 105–14.

105. Andrew Jackson, "State of the Union Address, Dec. 6, 1830," in Richardson, ed., *Papers of the Presidents*, vol. 2, 519–23; extracts reprinted in Perdue and Green, eds., *Cherokee Removal*, 119–20.

106. Perdue and Green, eds., *Cherokee Removal*, 159.

107. Alexander Mackenzie's popular and polemic book, *The History of the Highland Clearances*, first published in 1883, denounced the evictions as bitter payment for the patriotism Highlanders had demonstrated during the wars against France.

108. Ibid., 254.

109. Perdue and Green, eds., *Cherokee Removal*, 105.

110. Satz, *American Indian Policy in the Jacksonian Era*, 53–56 (enlightened policy quote); Medill in Prucha, ed., *Documents of United States Indian Policy*, 77–78.

111. Hunter, *Last of the Free*, 260; Tom F. Cunningham, *The Diamond's Ace: Scotland and the Native Americans* (Edinburgh: Mainstream, 2001), 14.

112. Cunningham, *Diamond's Ace*, 14.

113. Gary Moulton, ed., *The Papers of Chief John Ross*, 2 vols. (Norman: University of Oklahoma Press, 1984), vol. 2, 321. The Choctaws made a donation of $710 the same year to aid the famine-stricken Irish; Joy Porter, "The North American Indians and the Irish," *Irish Studies Review*, 11 (2003), 270, n.3.

114. Fenyo, *Contempt, Sympathy, and Romance*.

NOTES TO CHAPTER 8

1. James Hunter, *Glencoe and the Indians* (Edinburgh: Mainstream, 1996), 126.

2. John C. Weaver, *The Great Land Rush and the Making of the Modern World, 1650–1900* (Montreal: McGill-Queens University Press, 2003).

3. Eric Richards, *A History of the Highland Clearances*: Vol. 1, *Agrarian Transformation and the Evictions, 1746–1886* (London: Croom Helm, 1982), 76–80, 123; Robert A. Dodgshon, *From Chiefs to Landlords: Social and Economic Change in the Western Highlands and Islands, c. 1493–1820* (Edinburgh: Edinburgh University Press, 1998), 151–53.

4. Malcolm Gray, *The Highland Economy, 1750–1850* (Edinburgh: Oliver and Boyd, 1950), 66.

5. T. M. Devine, *Clanship to Crofters' War: The Social Transformation of the Scottish Highlands* (Manchester, UK: Manchester University Press, 1994), 38 and ch. 5; Charles Jedrej and Mark Nutall, *White Settlers: The Impact of Rural Repopulation in Scotland* (Luxembourg: Harwood Academic, 1996), 158 (quote); Eric Richards, *The Highland Clearances: People, Landlords, and Rural Turmoil* (Edinburgh: Birlinn, 2002), 247–48; NSAS 7: 180–81.

6. Richard White, *Remembering Ahanagran: Storytelling in a Family's Past* (New York: Hill and Wang, 1998), 50.

7. Nancy Shoemaker, *A Strange Likeness: Becoming Red and White in Eighteenth-century North America* (New York: Oxford University Press, 2004), 29.

8. Barbara De Wolfe, ed., *Discoveries of America: Personal Accounts of British Emigrants to North America during the Revolutionary Era* (New York: Cambridge University Press, 1997), 17.

9. "Observes or Remarks upon the Lands and Islands which Compose the Barrony called Harris, the Property of Norman MacLeod of MacLeod, Esq.," 1772, NLS, Lee Papers, ms. 3431: 179–80.

10. William R. Brock, *Scotus Americanus: A Survey of the Sources for Links between Scotland and America in the Eighteenth Century* (Edinburgh: Edinburgh University Press, 1982), 170.

11. Bernard Bailyn, *Voyagers to the West: A Passage in the Peopling of America on the Eve of the Revolution* (New York: Knopf, 1986), 134–47; Allen D. Candler et al., eds., *The Colonial Records of the State of Georgia*, 32 vols. (Atlanta: State Printer, 1904–1989), vol. 2, 336–39, 366.

12. "On Emigration from the Scottish Highlands & Isles," by Edward S. Fraser, NLS, ms. 9646: 67.

13. Anthony Parker, *Scottish Highlanders in Colonial Georgia: The Recruitment, Emigration, and Settlement at Darien, 1735–1748* (Athens: University of Georgia Press, 1997); Candler, ed., *Colonial Records of the State of Georgia*, vol. 2, 110, 188, 366, 380; vol. 21 (1910), 11–14, 17–30. Information on the Darien settlers is also included in Lillian Hawes and Albert S. Britt, eds., "The Mackenzie Papers," *Georgia Historical Quarterly* 56 (1972): 535–83, and 57 (1973): 85–144.

14. Allan I. Macinnes, Marjory-Ann D. Harper, and Linda G. Fryer, eds., *Scotland and the Americas, c. 1650–c. 1939: A Documentary Source Book* (Edinburgh: Scottish History Society, 2002), 102, 266–67; "Notes of the Genealogy of the House of Mackintosh," NLS, Farr Manuscripts, ms. 9854: 223.

15. Harvey H. Jackson, *Lachlan McIntosh and the Politics of Revolutionary Georgia* (Athens: University of Georgia Press, 1979), quote at 13. Lilla M. Hawes, ed., "The Papers of Lachlan McIntosh, 1774–1779," *Collections of the Georgia Historical Society* 12 (1957). The treaties of Fort Pitt and Hopewell are in Colin G. Calloway, ed., *Early American Indian Documents: Treaties and Laws, 1607–1789*, vol. 18, *Revolution and Confederation* (Bethesda, Md.: University Publications of America, 1994), 167–69, 393–408.

16. Edward J. Cashin, *Lachlan McGillivray, Indian Trader: The Shaping of the Southern Colonial Frontier* (Athens: University of Georgia Press, 1992). On McGillivray's opposition see Hawes, ed., "Papers of Lachlan McIntosh," 140–42.

17. Claudio Saunt, *A New Order of Things: Property, Power, and the Transformation of the Creek Indians, 1733–1816* (New York: Cambridge University Press, 1999), ch. 3.

18. William S. Coker and Thomas D. Watson, *Indian Traders of the Southeastern Spanish Borderlands: Panton, Leslie and Company, and John Forbes and Company,*

1783–1847 (Pensacola: University of West Florida Press, 1986), 228–29, 366, 370, and ch. 12, quote at 229; map of 1805 cessions at 264; figures 265, 271–72; Joel W. Martin, "Cultural Contact and Crises in the Early Republic: Native American Religious Renewal, Resistance, and Accommodation," in *Native Americans and the Early Republic,* ed. Frederick E. Hoxie, Ronald Hoffman, and Peter J. Albert (Charlottesville: University Press of Virginia, 1999), 244–46 (quote).

19. Roger G. Kennedy, *Mr. Jefferson's Lost Cause: Land, Farmers, Slavery, and the Louisiana Purchase* (New York: Oxford University Press, 2003), part 2.

20. Robert A. McGeachy, "Captain Lauchlin Campbell and Argyllshire Emigration to New York," *Northern Scotland* 19 (1999), 21–46.

21. *Calendar of New York Colonial Manuscripts Indorsed Land Papers, 1643–1803* (Albany: State Printers, 1864), quote at 325.

22. Robert Scott Stephenson, "With Swords and Plowshares: British and American Soldiers in the Trans-Allegheny West, 1754–1774," Ph.D. diss., University of Virginia, 1998), 208–20.

23. *Calendar of New York Colonial Manuscripts Indorsed Land Papers,* 317–22, 325–33, 344–54, 357–76, 379–89, 395–98, 404–406, 411, 419–22, 426–32.

24. Ibid., 387–89, 523. See also 519–23, 539, 545, 623.

25. Ibid., 333.

26. Ibid., 398. See also 397, 429, 463.

27. Ibid., 329, 350–53, 359, 364, 366, 368, 370, 372–75, 381, 383–89, 405, 411, 419, 427, 432, 437, 440–41, 451–53, 519, 521–23, 525, 532, 536, 539, 541, 545, 550, 557, 566, 571–74, 578, 582–83, 588, 593, 615, 623.

28. Colin G. Calloway, *The Western Abenakis of Vermont, 1600–1800: War, Migration, and the Survival of an Indian People* (Norman: University of Oklahoma Press, 1987), ch. 10.

29. "A Journal of the Managers of the Scotch American Company of Farmers," in *The Upper Connecticut: Narratives of Its Settlement and Its Part in the American Revolution,* 2 vols. (Montpelier: Vermont Historical Society, 1943), vol. 1, 181–203; "Journal of Colonel Alexander Harvey of Scotland and Barnet, Vermont," *Proceedings of the Vermont Historical Society* 55 (1921–1923): 199–262.

30. Duncan Fraser, "Sir John Johnson's Rent Roll of the Kingsborough Patent," *Papers and Records of the Ontario Historical Society* 52 (1960), 176–89.

31. Marianne McLean, *The People of Glengarry: Highlanders in Transition, 1745–1820* (Montreal: McGill-Queens University Press, 1991), 82–90; James Sullivan et al., *The Papers of Sir William Johnson,* 15 vols. (Albany: University of the State of New York, 1921–1965), vol. 7, 1026; vol. 12, 1023, 1041, 1111 (quote at 1111).

32. Fintan O'Toole, *White Savage: William Johnson and the Invention of America* (New York: Farrar, Straus, and Giroux, 2005), 308.

33. Heather Devine, "Roots in the Mohawk Valley: Sir William Johnson's Legacy in the Northwest Company," in *The Fur Trade Revisited: Selected Papers of the Sixth North American Fur Trade Conference, Mackinac Island, Michigan, 1991,* ed.

Jennifer S. H. Brown, W. J. Eccles, and Donald P. Heldman (East Lansing: Michigan State University Press, 1994), 217–42.

34. "Letter-Book of Captain Alexander McDonald of the Royal Highland Emigrants, 1775–1779," *Collections of the New York Historical Society* 15 (1882), 224, 354.

35. Patrick Campbell, *Travels in the Interior Inhabited Parts of North America in the Years 1791 and 1792*, ed. H. H. Langton (Toronto: Champlain Society, 1937), 227.

36. Ibid., 228, 231.

37. McLean, *People of Glengarry*, 90–97.

38. Ibid., ch. 7–9; quote at 125.

39. Ibid., 213.

40. John G. Reid, "The Conquest of 'Nova Scotia': Cartographic Imperialism and the Echoes of a Scottish Past," in *Nation and Province in the First British Empire: Scotland and the Americas, 1600–1800*, ed. Ned C. Landsman (Providence, R.I.: John Carter Brown Library, 2001), 39–59.

41. Marjory Harper, *Adventurers and Exiles: The Great Scottish Exodus* (London: Profile, 2003), 198–99; Marjory Harper and Michael E. Vance, eds., *Myth, Migration, and the Making of Memory: Scotia and Nova Scotia c. 1700–1990* (Edinburgh: John Donald, 1999).

42. Alexander MacKenzie, *History of the Highland Clearances* (1883; repr., Edinburgh: Mercat, 1997), 389–96.

43. John McAlpine, *Genuine Narratives and Concise Memoirs of some of the most Interesting Exploits and Singular Adventures of J. McAlpine, a Native Highlander, from the time of his Emigration from Scotland to America 1773* (Greenock, Scotland, 1787), 69–70; Rory Steel to Colin MacDonald, Oct. 22, 1791, NLS, Adv. ms. 73.2.13.

44. Campbell, *Travels in the Interior Inhabited Parts of North America*, 46, 49, 55–56.

45. Lucille H. Campey, *After the* Hector: *The Scottish Pioneers of Nova Scotia and Cape Breton 1773–1852* (Toronto: Natural Heritage Books, 2004); D. C. Harvey, "Scottish Immigration to Cape Breton," in *Cape Breton Historical Essays*, ed. Don Macgillivray and Brian Tennyson (Sydney, Canada: College of Cape Breton Press, 1980), 31–40.

46. R. C. MacDonald, *Sketches of Highlanders: with an account of Their early Arrival in North America; Their Advancement in Agriculture, and some of their Distinguished Military Services in the War of 1812, &c; with Letters, containing useful Information for Emigrants from the Highlands of Scotland to the British Provinces* (Saint John, New Brunswick: Henry Chubb, 1843), appendix v.

47. Charles W. Dunn, *Highland Settler: A Portrait of the Scottish Gael in Nova Scotia* (Toronto: University of Toronto Press, 1953), 30; James Hunter, *Scottish Exodus: Travels among a Worldwide Clan* (Edinburgh: Mainstream, 2005), 158, 164. In 1849 the Duke of Sutherland, who assisted many of his tenants in emigrating

to Nova Scotia and Cape Breton, intervened on behalf of some who ran into difficulties paying the emigrant tax in Nova Scotia and Prince Edward Island. NLS, Sutherland Papers, Dep. 313/878.

48. Rusty Bitterman, "The Hierarchy of the Soil: Land and Labor in a 19th-Century Cape Breton Community," *Acadiensis* 18 (1988), 33–55.

49. Harvey, "Scottish Immigration to Cape Breton."

50. Chrestien LeClerq, *New Relation of Gaspesia, with the Customs and Religion of the Gaspesian Indians,* trans. and ed. William F. Ganong (Toronto: Champlain Society, 1910), 104–106.

51. Arthur J. Ray, *I Have Lived Here since the World Began: An Illustrated History of Canada's Native People* (Toronto: Lester, 1996), 146–47 (including Pemeenauweet's petition); Harper and Vance, eds., *Myth, Migration, and the Making of Memory;* L. F. S. Upton, *Micmacs and Colonists: Indian-White Relations in the Maritimes, 1713–1867* (Vancouver: University of British Columbia Press, 1979), 89–92, 134, 188–92 (facsimile of Peemeenauweet's petition); Olive P. Dickason, *Canada's First Nations* (Norman: University of Oklahoma Press, 1992), 230.

52. Upton, *Micmacs and Colonists,* 95; *Journals and Proceedings of the House of Assembly of the Province of Nova Scotia,* 1844–1845, appendix 16: 69–70; 1847, appendix 19: 99–102; 1849, appendix 45: 355–58.

53. Upton, *Micmacs and Colonists,* 138; Bitterman, "Hierarchy of the Soil," 43–44.

54. Upton, *Micmacs and Colonists,* 95–96 ("paid in full"); examples of Highland settlers who paid for their lands, as well as the amounts they paid, are in *Journals and Proceedings of the House of Assembly of the Province of Nova Scotia,* 1860: 214–15; 1862, appendix 29: 1–4, appendix 30: 1; 1863, app. 16: 1–7.

55. W. S. Wallace, ed., *John McLean's Notes of a Twenty-five Years' Service in the Hudson's Bay Territory* (Toronto: Champlain Society, 1932), 369; Robert Michael Ballantyne, *Hudson Bay, or Everyday Life in the Wilds of North America during Six Years' Residence in the Territories of the Hon. Hudson Bay Company,* 4th ed. (London: Thomas Nelson and Sons, 1902), 60; E. E. Rich, ed., *Colin Robertson's Correspondence Book, September 1817 to September 1822* (Toronto: Champlain Society, 1939), 45.

56. Alexander Ross, *The Red River Settlement: Its Rise, Progress, and Present State* (London: Smith, Elder, 1856), vi; J. M. Bumsted, *Trials and Tribulations: The Red River Settlement and the Emergence of Manitoba 1811–1870* (Winnipeg: Great Plains Publications, 2003), 12.

57. Laura Peers, *The Ojibwa of Western Canada 1780–1870* (St. Paul: Minnesota Historical Society Press, 1994), 63.

58. *The Falcon: A Narrative of the Captivity and Adventures of John Tanner during Thirty Years' Residence among the Indians in the Interior of North America* (1830; New York: Penguin, 1994), 192–93.

59. NLS, Sutherland Papers, Dep. 313/744, 1128: #26–28.

60. *Dictionary of Canadian Biography* (Toronto: University of Toronto Press, 1966–), vol. 6, 440–44.

61. Arthur J. Ray, *Indians in the Fur Trade: Their Role as Hunters, Trappers, and Middlemen in the Lands Southwest of Hudson Bay, 1670–1870* (Toronto: University of Toronto Press, 1974), 99–104; Peers, *Ojibwa of Western Canada*, 63–70.

62. L. R. Masson, ed., *Les Bourgeois de la Compagnie du Nord-Ouest*, 2 vols. (1889–1890; repr., New York: Antiquarian, 1960), vol. 1, 269; "Diary of Chief Trader, John MacLeod, Senior, of Hudson's Bay Company, Red River Settlement," *Collections of the State Historical Society of North Dakota*, 2 (1908), 129–30; Gerhard J. Ens, *Homeland to Hinterland: The Changing Worlds of the Red River Métis in the Nineteenth Century* (Toronto: University of Toronto Press, 1996).

63. NAC, A-27: Papers of Thomas Douglas, fifth Earl of Selkirk, 2: 198 (population estimate).

64. NAC, Selkirk Papers 1: 127–28; Ross, *Red River Settlement*, 12 ("no claim" quote); 160 ("turbulent").

65. NAC, Selkirk Papers 1: 147–48.

66. Ibid., 128, 207 II; J. M. Bumsted, *Fur Trade Wars: The Founding of Western Canada* (Winnipeg: Great Plains Publications, 1999), 39 (Cutnose).

67. NAC, Selkirk Papers 1: 137–38. Selkirk favored the establishment of an independent Indian buffer zone between British and American Territory; Bumsted, *Fur Trade Wars*, 95. In this he was in line with the strategy of the British government; see Colin G. Calloway, *Crown and Calumet: British-Indian Relations, 1783–1815* (Norman: University of Oklahoma Press, 1987).

68. Peers, *Ojibwa of Western Canada*, 90.

69. *Inverness Journal*, quoted in J. M. Bumsted, ed., *The Collected Writings of Lord Selkirk, 1810–1820*, vol. 2 in *The Writings and Papers of Thomas Douglas, Fifth Earl of Selkirk* (Winnipeg: Manitoba Record Society, 1988), xix; McGillivray to Bathurst: NAC, Selkirk Papers 2: 235, and NAC, CO 42/164: 489–90, reel B-133.

70. NAC, Selkirk Papers 1: 207 xix; NAC, CO 42/164: 203, 403, reel B-133; Ross, *Red River Settlement*, 33.

71. NAC, Selkirk Papers 1: 207 xix, 207 xxxi, 207 xxxvi; NAC, CO 42/164: 212, reel B-133.

72. NAC, Selkirk Papers 8: 1277.

73. Bumsted, *Fur Trade Wars*, 142; Bumsted, *Trials and Tribulations*, 17; Bumsted, ed., *Collected Writings of Lord Selkirk 1810–1820*, 113.

74. NAC, Selkirk Papers 2: 307 (quote); Ross, *Red River Settlement*, 35.

75. NAC, Selkirk Papers 2: 320H, 321.

76. Ibid., 2: 386–87, 390; 3: 401, 403, 503; 4: 539.

77. Ibid., 4: 521, 542; 7: 1035–1035B; Ross, *Red River Settlement*, 10–12 (treaty), 158–59; Jenni Calder, *Scots in Canada* (Edinburgh: Luath, 2003), 100–101; Bumsted, *Fur Trade Wars*, 191; Bumsted, *Trials and Tribulations*, 139–43 (aboriginal title);

Peers, *Ojibwa of Western Canada,* 92–93, 123–39, 198. The Selkirk Treaty of 1817 is in Derek G. Smith, ed., *Canadian Indians and the Law: Selected Documents, 1663–1972* (Toronto: McClelland and Stewart, 1975), 197–98 and in Alexander Morris, ed., *The Treaties of Canada with the Indians of Manitoba and the North-West Territories* (Toronto: Belfords, Clarke and Co., 1880; reprinted Saskatoon: Fifth House Publishers, 1991), 13–15, 298 (map and Indian signatures), 299–300.

78. NAC, Selkirk Papers 6: 1014L (colony chief); 7: 1051–1051A ("poor," "truth," and "talons").

79. John West, *The Substance of a Journal during a residence at the Red River Colony, British North America in the years 1820–1823* (Vancouver: Alcuin Society, 1967), 17–18, 22–23, 36, 64, 67, 109; Ray, *Indians in the Fur Trade,* 218 (seasonal farm labor).

80. Eleanor M. Blain, "The Bungee Dialect of the Red River Settlement," MA thesis, University of Manitoba, 1989; Blain, "Bungee," http://www.thecanadianencyclopedia .com; S. Osborne Scott and D. A. Mulligan, "The Red River Dialect," *The Beaver* (Dec. 1951), 42–45.

81. "Untitled Pamphlet on Indian Education," in Bumsted, ed., *Collected Writings of Lord Selkirk, 1810–1820,* 1–6.

82. Winona Stevenson, "The Red River Indian Mission School and John West's 'Little Charges,' 1820–1833," *Native Studies Review* 4 (1988), 129–65; West, *Substance of a Journal,* 24, 95–96, 109–110.

83. Quoted in Bumsted, *Trials and Tribulations,* 52.

84. Stevenson, "Red River Indian Mission School," 139; Peers, *Ojibwa of Western Canada,* 136–37.

85. NAC, Selkirk Papers 8: 1173.

86. Ibid., 6: 1014L; 7: 1028G, 1095, 1097C; Masson, ed., *Les Bourgeois de la Compagnie du Nord-Ouest,* vol. 1, 129 (grasshoppers).

87. Bumsted, *Trials and Tribulations,* 40–41. On Dickson see Louis Arthur Tohill, "Robert Dickson, British Fur Trader on the Upper Mississippi," *North Dakota Historical Quarterly* 3 (1928–1929), 5–49, 83–128, 183–203.

88. "Letters of W. F. Wentzel," in Masson, ed., *Les Bourgeois de la Compagnie du Nord-Ouest,* vol. 1, 130.

89. See, for example, Robert Dickson's report, NAC, Selkirk Papers 7: 1042–51.

90. R. Harvey Fleming, ed., *Minutes of Council, Northern Department of Rupert's Land, 1821–31* (Toronto: Champlain Society, 1940), 394–95; NAC, Selkirk Papers 7: 1028H, 1028K, 1131.

91. NAC, Selkirk Papers 7: 1135–36, 1139.

92. Ibid., 7: 1133.

93. Ibid., 7: 1134, 1157–57B.

94. Peers, *Ojibwa of Western Canada,* 130.

95. NAC, Selkirk Papers 7: 1098; G. P. de T. Glazebrook, ed., *The Hargrave Correspondence, 1821–1843* (Toronto: Champlain Society, 1938), 19.

96. Simpson to Roderick McKenzie, in Masson, ed., *Les Bourgeois de la Compagnie du Nord-Ouest*, vol. 1, 59. By the time Simpson wrote his "character book" in 1832 (after he had lived at Red River), he had nothing good to say about Donald McKenzie and called him "one of the worst and most dangerous men I ever was acquainted with." The two men had clashed, in part, on the question of Métis wives. McKenzie was outraged at the treatment of his niece, Nancy or Matooskie, by George McTavish and made his views known. Glyndwr Williams, ed., *Hudson's Bay Miscellany 1670–1870* (Winnipeg: Hudson's Bay Record Society, 1975), 179–80.

97. Wallace, ed., *John McLean's Notes*, 372.

98. NAC, Selkirk Papers 8: 1174, 1175, 1179; Bumsted, *Trials and Tribulations*, 55–57; Bumsted, *Floods of the Centuries: A History of Flood Disasters in the Red River Valley, 1776–1997* (Winnipeg: Great Plains Publications, 1997).

99. Williams, ed., *Hudson's Bay Miscellany 1670–1870*, 156, 160.

100. Glazebrook, ed., *Hargrave Correspondence*, 58, 122, 143.

101. Wallace, ed., *John McLean's Notes*, 373–74.

102. Glazebrook, ed., *Hargrave Correspondence*, 143 ("wonders"), 161 (church).

103. Ibid., 158, 160 ("swarm of children"), 164, 166, 182 ("suffered dreadfully"), 207; Bumsted, *Trials and Tribulations*, 69–70.

104. Glazebrook, ed., *Hargrave Correspondence*, 207. Simpson, who participated in expeditions to the Arctic from 1837 to 1839, died five years later by his own hand (or so it seemed) after he had killed two traveling companions "in a fit of insanity." Ibid., 329–30, 340, 344–45, 360.

105. Irene Sprye, "The Great Transformation: The Disappearance of the Commons in Western Canada," in Richard Allen, ed., *Man and Nature on the Prairies* (Regina: Canadian Plains Research Center, University of Regina, 1976), 35–36; James B. Hartman, "The Churches of Early Winnipeg," *Manitoba History*, 46 (Spring/Summer 2003), 20–33.

106. NAC, Selkirk Papers 8: 1228, 1280; Bumsted, *Trials and Tribulations*, 39 (ethnic composition of 1818 total), 103 (flu epidemic); Ballantyne, *Hudson Bay*, 61. Sprye, "The Great Transformation," 25, gives slightly different population figures.

107. Ballantyne, *Hudson Bay*, 61.

108. Laura Peers, "On Missionaries, Artists, Bears, and 'Grandfathers': Peter Rindisbacher's Paintings, John White's Collection, and the Red River Ojibwa." In J. C. H. King and Christian F. Feest, eds., *Three Centuries of Woodlands Indian Art: A Collection of Essays* (Altenstadt, Germany: ZFK Publishers, 2007), 105–6.

109. Ross, *Red River Settlement*, 80.

110. William L. Saunders and Walter Clark, eds., *The Colonial and State Records of North Carolina*, 30 vols. (Raleigh: Secretary of State, 1886–1914), vol. 9, 1159.

111. Thomas Douglas, Earl of Selkirk, *Observations on the Present State of the Highlands of Scotland, with a view of the Causes and Probable Consequences of Emigration* (London: Longman, Hurst, Rees, and Orme, 1805), 191.

112. Ross, *Red River Settlement*, 50. Highlanders hunting on the northern Plains may have found Indian travois—two wooden poles attached to a horse—very much like a "cart without wheels" used in the Great Glen in the eighteenth century. Norman Scarfe, ed., *To the Highlands in 1786: The Inquisitive Journey of a Young French Aristocrat* (Woodbridge, UK: Boydell, 2001), 171.

113. Catherine Parr Traill, *The Backwoods of Canada: Being Letters from the Wife of an Emigrant Officer* (London: Nattali and Bond, n.d.), 186–89 (corn), 208 (moccasins), 315–20 (maple sugar); Elizabeth Thompson, ed., *The Emigrant's Guide to North America (Ceann-iùil an Fhir-imrich Do Dh'America Mu-Thuath)* (1841; trans.; Toronto: Natural Heritage Books, 1998), 33 (moccasins), 80–81 (corn), 88–90 (sugar).

114. De Wolfe, ed., *Discoveries of America*, 8.

115. Donald E. Meek, ed., *Tuath Is Tighearna, Tenants and Landlords: An Anthology of Gaelic Poetry of Social and Political Protest from the Clearances to the Land Agitation (1800–1890)* (Edinburgh: Scottish Academic Press, 1995), 67, 198.

116. Traill, *Backwoods of Canada*, 47.

117. Mrs. C. P. Traill, *The Canadian Settler's Guide*, 7th ed. (Toronto: *Toronto Times*, 1857), 29.

118. Hunter, *Scottish Exodus*, 206.

119. D. Masson, "The Gael in the Far West," *Transactions of the Gaelic Society of Inverness* 3 (1873), 31–32.

120. James Loch, *An Account of the Improvements on the Estates of the Marquess of Stafford* (London: Longman, Hurst, Rees, Orme, and Brown, 1820), 37; appendix 7: 53–54.

121. Timothy Silver, *A New Face on the Countryside: Indians, Colonists, and Slaves in South Atlantic Forests, 1500–1800* (New York: Cambridge University Press, 1990), 172–85; Virginia DeJohn Anderson, *Creatures of Empire: How Domestic Animals Transformed Early America* (New York: Oxford University Press, 2004); Peter Karsten, "Cows in the Corn, Pigs in the Garden, and 'the Problem of Social Costs': 'High' and 'Low' Legal Cultures of the British Diaspora Lands in the 17th, 18th, and 19th Centuries," *Law and Society Review* 32(1) (1998): 63–91; *Journals and Proceedings of the House of Assembly of the Province of Nova Scotia*, 1849, appendix 45: 356; Grady McWhiney, *Cracker Culture: Celtic Ways in the Old South* (University: University of Alabama Press, 1988), ch. 3.

122. Rosemary Ommer, "Primitive Accumulation and the Scottish *Clann* in the Old World and the New," *Journal of Historical Geography* 12 (1986), 121–41; cf. Allan MacNeill, "Scottish Settlement in Colonial Nova Scotia," *Scottish Tradition* 19 (1994), 60–79.

123. Selkirk, *Observations on the Present State of the Highlands of Scotland*, 198; Patrick C. T. White, ed., *Lord Selkirk's Diary 1803–1804: A Journal of His Travels in British North America and the Northeastern United States* (Toronto: Champlain Society, 1958), 35, 39.

124. "Journal of a Tour to the Southern States by Lady Liston, 1797," NLS, Liston Papers, ms. 5697: 12, 25 (Lady Liston looked with contempt on the Catawbas,

26–27); Michael Newton, "In Their Own Words: Gaelic Literature in North Carolina," *Scotia* 25 (2001), 1–28; David Hackett Fischer, *Albion's Seed: Four British Folkways in America* (New York: Oxford University Press, 1989), 818. Masson, "Gael in the Far West," 28, 30, repeats the account of emigrant Highlanders and their slaves "who regularly worshipped in the Gaelic language."

125. John McGregor, *British America,* 2 vols. (Edinburgh: Blackwood, 1832), vol. 2, 184–87.

126. Thanks to Michael Macdonald for bringing this pattern to my attention.

127. Masson, "Gael in the Far West," 28–29, 37–38, 41.

128. Papers of the Calder Family from Creich Sutherland: letters of Neil Calder, 1888–1893, to his brother John, NLS, Acc. 9000/2: letters of Mar. 28, Sept. 14, Nov. 17, 1890, and July 2, 1891. Calder found the Indians in New Mexico "quite a different class of Indians from those in the Indian territory."

129. McWhiney, *Cracker Culture,* 43; McGregor, *British America,* vol. 1, 297; vol. 2, 183–84.

130. Selkirk, *Observations on the Present State of the Highlands of Scotland,* 211.

131. M. G. Parks, ed., *Western and Eastern Rambles: Travel Sketches of Nova Scotia by Joseph Howe* (Toronto: University of Toronto Press, 1973), 152–53.

132. Campey, *After the* Hector, 138 (description of St. Mary's district); Moorsom, quoted in Dunn, *Highland Settler,* 108; John McGregor said almost exactly the same thing: McGregor, *British America,* vol. 2, 184.

133. Quoted in Harper, *Adventurers and Exiles,* 367.

134. For an example of how Indian people preserved traditional ways on reservations see Frederick E. Hoxie, "From Prison to Homeland: The Cheyenne River Indian Reservation before World War I," *South Dakota History* 10 (1979), 1–24. Some Indian people at this time participated in the market economy but used the proceeds of their labor to strengthen their communities and preserve their cultural independence; Brian C. Hosmer, *American Indians in the Marketplace: Persistence and Innovation among the Menominees and Metlakatlans, 1870–1920* (Lawrence: University Press of Kansas, 1999).

135. I. Whitaker, "Some Traditional Techniques in Modern Scottish Farming," *Scottish Studies* 3 (1959), 163–68, quote at 164; quoted in Dodgshon, *From Chiefs to Landlords,* 234; Ignatia Broker, quoted in Colin G. Calloway, *First Peoples: A Documentary Survey of American Indian History,* 3rd ed. (Boston: Bedford/St. Martin's 2008), 490.

136. Thompson, ed., *Emigrant's Guide to North America,* 4.

137. Ibid., ch. 6, esp. 30–31, 35, 36.

138. Ibid., 1–12.

139. Ibid., 11 (quote), 52–54, 62–66, 69–70.

140. "State of Emigration from the Highlands of Scotland, its extent, causes, & proposed remedy," Mar. 21, 1803, NLS, Adv. ms. 35.6.18: 5–6, 18–19.

141. Thompson, ed., *Emigrant's Guide to North America,* 56.

142. Harper, *Adventurers and Exiles*, 76–80.

143. William Fraser, *The Emigrant's Guide, or Sketches of Canada, with some of the Northern and Western States of America, by a Scotch Minister, Thirty-six years in Canada—from 1831 to 1867* (Glasgow: Porteus, 1867), 17.

144. Sprye, "The Great Transformation," 21–45, quotes at 36, 39

145. Wayne Norton, *Help Us to a Better Land: Crofter Colonies in the Prairie West* (Regina, Sask.: Canadian Plains Research Center, University of Regina, 1994); Hunter, *Scottish Exodus*, 283.

146. Masson, "Gael in the Far West," 26; Luther Standing Bear, *Land of the Spotted Eagle* (1933; repr., Lincoln: University of Nebraska Press, 1978), 248.

NOTES TO CHAPTER 9

1. Grace Steele Woodward, *The Cherokees* (Norman: University of Oklahoma Press, 1963), 60–67; Samuel Cole Williams, ed., *Early Travels in the Tennessee Country, 1540–1800* (Johnson City, Tenn.: Watauga, 1928), 122–29, 138–41; Grant's quote at 133 n. 29. When the Cherokees sailed home from London, Cuming stayed behind to answer charges of fraud and embezzlement. He was later sentenced to debtor's prison and confined to a poorhouse; he died in London in 1775.

2. Michael Fry, *The Scottish Empire* (Edinburgh: Birlinn, 2001).

3. David Armitage argues that the creation of a "British" empire demanded that Scots and English "arrive at mutually accepted methods of integration" and that colonization provided "the opportunity for such convergence." David Armitage, "Making the Empire British: Scotland in the Atlantic World 1542–1707," *Past and Present* 155 (May 1997), 49–50.

4. James Hunter, *On the Other Side of Sorrow: Nature and People in the Scottish Highlands* (Edinburgh: Mainstream, 1995), 109–11.

5. Rayna Green, "The Tribe Called Wannabee," *Folklore* 99 (1988), 30–35.

6. Krisztina Fenyo, *Contempt, Sympathy, and Romance: Lowland Perceptions of the Highlands and the Clearances during the Famine Years, 1845–1855* (East Linton, Scotland: Tuckwell, 2000), 167.

7. Edward Said, *Orientalism* (New York: Vintage, 1979); Homi Bhabha, "Of Mimicry and Man: The Ambivalence of Colonial Discourse," in *Tensions of Empire: Colonial Cultures in a Bourgeois World*, ed. Frederick Cooper and Ann Laura Stoler (Berkeley: University of California Press, 1997), 152–59.

8. Frederick A. Pottle, ed., *Boswell's London Journal, 1762–1763* (New Haven, Conn.: Yale University Press, 1950), 46.

9. Neil Davidson, *The Origins of Scottish Nationhood* (London: Pluto, 2000).

10. A. Mackillop and Steve Murdoch, eds., *Military Governors and Imperial Frontiers, c. 1600–1800: A Study of Scotland and Empires* (Leiden, the Netherlands: Brill, 2003).

11. Martha McLaren, *British India and British Scotland, 1780–1830: Career Building, Empire Building, and a Scottish School of Thought on Indian Governance* (Akron: University of Akron Press, 2001); Andrew Mackillop, "Fashioning a 'British' Empire: Sir Archibald Campbell of Inverneil and Madras, 1785–9," in *Military Governors and Imperial Frontiers*, ed. Mackillop and Murdoch, ch. 10; Niall Ferguson, *Empire: The Rise and Demise of the British World Order and the Lessons for Global Power* (New York: Basic, 2003), 33–34 (East India Company percentages).

12. Tim Hanson, "Gabriel Johnston and the Portability of Patronage in the Eighteenth-century North Atlantic World," in *Military Governors and Imperial Frontiers*, ed. Mackillop and Murdoch, ch. 6, quote at 122.

13. Mackillop and Murdoch, eds., *Military Governors and Imperial Frontiers*, xx, 130.

14. James Hunter, *Culloden and the Last Clansman* (Edinburgh: Mainstream, 2001), 194–95.

15. Mackillop and Murdoch, eds., *Military Governors and Imperial Frontiers*, xlii.

16. Ibid., xiv.

17. Murray G. H. Pittock, *The Invention of Scotland: The Stuart Myth and the Scottish Identity, 1638 to the Present* (New York: Routledge, 1991), 102; Marinell Ash, *The Strange Death of Scottish History* (Edinburgh: Ramsay Head Press, 1980); see also Colin Kidd, *Subverting Scotland's Past: Scottish Whig Historians and the Creation of an Anglo-British Identity, 1689–c. 1830* (New York: Cambridge University Press, 1993), chs. 11–12.

18. David Armitage, "The Scottish Diaspora," in *Scotland: A History*, ed. Jenny Wormald (New York: Oxford University Press, 2005), 297; Linda Colley, *Britons: Forging the Nation, 1707–1837* (New Haven, Conn.: Yale University Press, 1992), 125; Kidd, *Subverting Scotland's Past*, ch. 9; Colin Kidd, *British Identities before Nationalism: Ethnicity and Nationhood in the Atlantic World, 1600–1800* (New York: Cambridge University Press, 1999); Murray G. H. Pittock, *Celtic Identity and the British Image* (Manchester, UK: Manchester University Press, 1999); Murray Pittock, *Inventing and Resisting Britain: Cultural Identities in Britain and Ireland, 1685–1789* (New York: St. Martin's, 1997).

19. Peter Womack, *Improvement and Romance: Constructing the Myth of the Highlands* (London: Macmillan, 1989), 147–48, 176, 178; Allan Massie, *The Thistle and the Rose: Six Centuries of Love and Hate Between Scots and English* (Edinburgh: John Murray, 2005), ch. 3.

20. J. Hector St. John de Crèvecoeur, *Letters from an American Farmer*, ed. Susan Manning (New York: Oxford University Press, 1997), 61, 66–82.

21. Bernard Aspinall, "The Scots in the United States," in *The Scots Abroad: Labour, Capital, Enterprise, 1750–1914*, ed. R. A. Cage (London: Croom Helm, 1985), 80–110, quotes at 80–81. See also Charles A. Hanna, *The Scotch-Irish, or the Scot in North Britain, North Ireland, and North America*, 2 vols. (New York: Putnam's

Sons, 1902); Arthur Herman, *How the Scots Invented the Modern World* (New York: Crown, 2001), ch. 14; Jim Hewitson, *Tam Blake and Co.: The Story of the Scots in America* (Edinburgh: Canongate, 1993); Ferenc Morton Szasz, *Scots in the North American West, 1790–1917* (Norman: University of Oklahoma Press, 2000).

22. Charlotte Erickson, *Invisible Immigrants: The Adaptation of English and Scottish Immigrants in Nineteenth-century America* (Coral Gables, Fla.: University of Miami Press, 1972); Matthew Frye Jacobson, *Whiteness of a Different Color: European Immigrants and the Alchemy of Race* (Cambridge, Mass.: Harvard University Press, 1998); Noel Ignatiev, *How the Irish Became White* (New York: Routledge, 1995), 59.

23. Michael Newton, "Becoming Cold-hearted like the Gentiles around Them: Scottish Gaelic in the United States, 1872–1912," *E-Keltoi: Journal of Interdisciplinary Celtic Studies* 2; http://www.uwm.edu/Dept/celtic/ekeltoi/.

24. Susan Bryant Dakin, *A Scotch Paisano in Old Los Angeles: Hugo Reid's Life in California, 1832–1852, Derived from His Correspondence* (Berkeley: University of California Press, 1939); Szasz, *Scots in the North American West*, 66–67.

25. Jenni Calder, *Scots in the USA* (Edinburgh: Luath, 2006), 154–55.

26. Hewitson, *Tam Blake and Co.*, 182; Douglas D. Scott, P. Willey, and Melissa A. Connor, *They Died with Custer: Soldiers' Bones from the Battle of the Little Bighorn* (Norman: University of Oklahoma Press, 1998), 94. Thanks to Barrie Dacre-Cox for bringing the Forbes plaque to my attention.

27. Andrew C. Isenberg, *The Destruction of the Bison: An Environmental History, 1750–1920* (New York: Cambridge University Press, 2000).

28. Terry G. Jordan, *North American Cattle-ranching Frontiers: Origins, Diffusion, and Differentiation* (Albuquerque: University of New Mexico Press, 1993), 42–55, 113, 182, 283; Forrest McDonald and Grady McWhinney, "The Antebellum Southern Herdsman: A Reinterpretation," *Journal of Southern History* 41 (1975), 147–66, and critique by Rowland Berthoff, "Celtic Mist over the South," *Journal of Southern History* 52 (1986), 423–46.

29. Lawrence M. Woods, *British Gentlemen in the Wild West* (New York: Free Press, 1989), ch. 5; Szasz, *Scots in the North American West*, ch. 5; W. Turrentine Jackson, *The Enterprising Scot: Investors in the American West after 1873* (Edinburgh: Edinburgh University Press, 1968).

30. James Hunter, *Scottish Exodus: Travels among a Worldwide Clan* (Edinburgh: Mainstream, 2005), 225–32; John C. Ewers, *The Blackfeet: Raiders on the Northwestern Plains* (Norman: University of Oklahoma Press, 1958), 263–66; Hugh A. Dempsey, *Crowfoot, Chief of the Blackfeet* (Norman: University of Oklahoma Press, 1972), chs. 7 and 9.

31. Alexander Morris, ed., *The Treaties of Canada with the Indians of Manitoba and the North-West Territories* (Toronto: Belfords, Clarke and Co., 1880; reprinted Saskatoon: Fifth House Publishers, 1991), 245–75, 368–75, quotes at 255, 273.

32. Alan J. Turner, "Scottish Settlement of the West," in *The Scottish Tradition in Canada*, ed. W. Stanford Reid (Toronto: McClelland and Stewart, 1976),

ch. 5, quote at 80; Morris, ed., *The Treaties of Canada with the Indians of Manitoba and the North-West Territories.*

33. D. Masson, "The Gael in the Far West," *Transactions of the Gaelic Society of Inverness* 3 (1873), 40.

34. Fenyo, *Contempt, Sympathy, and Romance.*

35. Colin G. Calloway, *The American Revolution in Indian Country* (New York: Cambridge University Press, 1995), 292–301.

36. Anthony F. C. Wallace, *Jefferson and the Indians: The Tragic Fate of the First Americans* (Cambridge, Mass.: Harvard University Press 1999), quote at 18; Linda Colley, *Captives* (New York: Pantheon, 2002), quotes at 236.

37. Colin G. Calloway, "Army Allies or Tribal Survival? The 'Other Indians' in the 1876 Campaign," in *Legacy: New Perspectives on the Battle of the Little Bighorn*, ed. Charles E. Rankin (Helena: Montana Historical Society Press, 1996), 62–81.

38. Dawes and Roosevelt quoted in Colin G. Calloway, *First Peoples: A Documentary Survey of American Indian History*, 3d ed. (Boston: Bedford/St. Martins, 2008), 378; Morgan quoted in Michael C. Coleman, *American Indians, the Irish, and Government Schooling* (Lincoln: University of Nebraska Press, 2007), 51.

39. Emily Greenwald, *Reconfiguring the Reservation: The Nez Percés, Jicarilla Apaches, and the Dawes Act* (Lincoln: University of Nebraska Press, 2002); Bonnie Lynn-Sherow, *Red Earth: Race and Culture in Oklahoma Territory* (Lawrence: University Press of Kansas, 2004), ch. 7.

40. Collier quoted in Francis Paul Prucha, ed., *The Great Father: The United States Government and the American Indians*, 2 vols. (Lincoln: University of Nebraska Press, 1984), vol. 2, 951.

41. On the assault on Indian culture in the late nineteenth and early twentieth centuries see, for example, David Wallace Adams, *Education for Extinction: American Indians and the Boarding School Experience, 1875–1928* (Lawrence: University Press of Kansas, 1995); Brenda Child, *Boarding School Seasons: American Indian Families, 1900–1940* (Lincoln: University of Nebraska Press, 1998); Frederick E. Hoxie, *The Final Promise: The Campaign to Assimilate the Indians, 1888–1920* (Lincoln: University of Nebraska Press, 1984); Francis Paul Prucha, ed., *Americanizing the American Indian: Writings by the "Friends of the Indian," 1880–1900* (Lincoln: University of Nebraska Press, 1978).

42. Renato Rosaldo, *Culture and Truth: The Remaking of Social Analysis* (Boston: Beacon, 1993), ch. 3, quote at 69; Renato Rosaldo, "Imperialist Nostalgia," *Representations* 26 (Spring 1989), 107–22.

43. Howard Gaskill, ed., *The Poems of Ossian and Related Works, by James Macpherson* (Edinburgh: Edinburgh University Press, 1996); Hugh Blair, *A Critical Dissertation on the Poems of Ossian, Son of Fingal* (London: Becket and de Hondt, 1763), 2; Tim Fulford, *Romantic Indians: Native Americans, British Literature, and Transatlantic* Culture (New York: Oxford University Press, 2006), 7–8; Hunter, *On the Other Side of Sorrow*, 89–95, quotes at 93, 95.

44. Hugh Trevor-Roper, "The Invention of Tradition: The Highland Tradition of Scotland," in *The Invention of Tradition*, ed. Eric Hobsbawm and Terence Ranger (New York: Cambridge University Press, 1983), 15–41, quotes at 15–16, 25.

45. Hugh Trevor-Roper, *The Rise of Christian Europe* (London: Thames and Hudson, 1965), 9.

46. Burt described kilts as large plaids "set in Folds and girt around the Waist to make of it a short Petticoat that reaches half-way down the Thigh, and the rest is brought over the Shoulders, and then fastened before." R. Jamieson, ed., *Burt's Letters from the North of Scotland*, 2 vols. (Edinburgh: John Donald, 1974), vol. 2, 186–88; Trevor-Roper, "Invention of Tradition," 20–22. Poet Robert Southey also attributed the philibeg to Rawlinson; Robert Southey, *Journal of a Tour in Scotland in 1819*, ed. C. H. Herford (London: John Murray, 1929), 140.

47. Hugh Cheape, *Tartan: The Highland Habit*, 2d ed. (Edinburgh: National Museum of Scotland, 1995); Michael Fry, *Wild Scots: Four Hundred Years of Highland History* (London: John Murray, 2005), 180–86.

48. Col. James Allardyce, ed., *Historical Papers relating to the Jacobite Period, 1699–1750*, 2 vols. (Aberdeen: New Spalding Club, 1895–1896), vol. 2, 514, 516–20, 522–27, 550, 554.

49. Cheape, *Tartan*, 72; Thomas Pennant, *A Tour in Scotland, 1769* (1771; repr., Edinburgh: Birlinn, 2000), xv–xvi, 125; Norman Scarfe, ed., *To the Highlands in 1786: The Inquisitive Journey of a Young French Aristocrat* (Woodbridge, UK: Boydell, 2001), 174–75; Samuel Johnson and James Boswell, *A Journey to the Western Islands and Highlands of Scotland*, ed. Peter Levi (New York: Penguin, 1984), quote at 69.

50. Trevor-Roper, "Invention of Tradition," 24 (quote); T. M. Devine, *Clanship to Crofters' War: The Social Transformation of the Scottish Highlands* (Manchester, UK: Manchester University Press, 1994), 87.

51. Charles Withers, "The Historical Creation of the Scottish Highlands," in *The Manufacture of Scottish History*, ed. Ian Donnachie and Christopher Whatley (Edinburgh: Polygon, 1992), 146.

52. Robert Clyde, *From Rebel to Hero: The Image of the Highlander, 1745–1830* (East Linton, Scotland: Tuckwell, 1995), 132; Major General David Stewart of Garth, *Sketches of the Character, Institutions, and Customs of the Highlanders of Scotland* (1822; new ed., Inverness: Mackenzie, 1885), 278–82.

53. "On the Condition of the Highland Peasantry before and since the Rebellion of 1745," by "B. G." in Thomas Bakewell, *Remarks on a Publication by James Loch, Esq., entitled An Account of the Improvements on the Estates of the Marques of Stafford* (London: Longman, Hurst, Rees, Orme, and Brown, 1820), 71.

54. For a broader discussion of emerging British identity and nationhood see Colley, *Britons: Forging the Nation 1707–1837*, and Kidd, *British Identities before Nationalism*.

55. Clyde, *From Rebel to Hero*, 121.

56. Hunter, *On the Other Side of Sorrow*, 101.

57. Brian D. Osborne, *The Last of the Chiefs: Alasdair Ranaldson Macdonell of Glengrarry 1773–1828* (Glendaruel, Scotland: Argyll, 2001).

58. Trevor-Roper, "Invention of Tradition," 28–29; David Stewart of Garth, *Sketches;* Eric Richards, *A History of the Highland Clearances.* Vol. 1, *Agrarian Transformation and the Evictions, 1746–1886* (London: Croom Helm, 1982), 224.

59. John Prebble traces the events in *The King's Jaunt: George IV in Scotland, August 1822* (1988; repr., Edinburgh: Birlinn, 2000). Newspaper announcements of the order of march and descriptions of the events are in NLS, Sutherland Papers, Dep. 313/779. Trevor-Roper, "Invention of Tradition," 29.

60. Trevor-Roper, "Invention of Tradition," 29–31.

61. Clyde, *From Rebel to Hero*, 112; Prebble, *King's Jaunt*, 103; Steven Parissien, *George IV: Inspiration of the Regency* (New York: St. Martin's, 2001), 209 (Wilkie portrait); Celeste Ray, *Highland Heritage: Scottish Americans in the American South* (Chapel Hill: University of North Carolina Press, 2001), 155.

62. R. R. McIan, *The Clans of the Scottish Highlands* (London: Ackermann, 1845).

63. Womack, *Improvement and Romance*, 46.

64. Clyde, *From Rebel to Hero*, 128.

65. Pittock, *Invention of Scotland;* Murray Pittock, *The Myth of the Jacobite Clans* (Edinburgh: Edinburgh University Press, 1995), ch. 5; Lawrence James, *Warrior Race: The British Experience of War from Roman Times to the Present* (London: Little, Brown, 2001), 209.

66. Michael Newton, *A Handbook of the Scottish Gaelic World* (Dublin: Four Courts, 2000), 65; Prebble, *King's Jaunt*, 177.

67. Heather Streets, "Identity in the Highland Regiments in the Nineteenth Century: Soldier, Region, Nation," in *Fighting for Identity: Scottish Military Experience, c. 1550–1900,* ed. Steve Murdoch and A. Mackillop (Leiden, the Netherlands: Brill, 2002), 213–36.

68. Richard J. Finlay, "Queen Victoria and the Cult of Scottish Monarchy," in *Scottish History: The Power of the Past,* ed. Edward J. Cowan and Richard J. Finlay (Edinburgh: Edinburgh University Press, 2002), ch. 10; James, *Warrior Race,* 209 (Balmoral quote); Prebble, *Highland Clearances,* 146.

69. William Donaldson, *The Highland Pipe and Scottish Society 1750–1950* (East Linton, Scotland: Tuckwell, 2000), 461–66.

70. Cheape, *Tartan,* 69–70.

71. Simon Schaama, *Landscape and Memory* (New York: Knopf, 1995), 466–69.

72. Hunter, *On the Other Side of Sorrow,* 101–103.

73. Womack, *Improvement and Romance,* 85, 111–14; Hunter, *On the Other Side of Sorrow,* 104–105.

74. Womack, *Improvement and Romance,* 174–75.

75. Charles W. J. Withers, *Gaelic Scotland: The Transformation of a Culture Region* (New York: Routledge, 1988), 66–72.

76. T. C. Smout, *Nature Contested: Environmental History in Scotland and Northern England since 1600* (Edinburgh: Edinburgh University Press, 2000), 133–34.

77. Devine, *Clanship to Crofters' War*, 97.

78. Eric Richards, *The Highland Clearances: People, Landlords, and Rural Turmoil* (Edinburgh: Birlinn, 2002), 4, 248, 282, 288–90; Hunter, *On the Other Side of Sorrow*, 111–12, 154.

79. Hunter, *On the Other Side of Sorrow*, ch. 6.

80. John McGrath, *The Cheviot, the Stag, and the Black, Black Oil* (London: Eyre Methuen, 1974), 48.

81. Andrew Hook, *From Goosecreek to Gandercleugh: Studies in Scottish-American Literary and Cultural History* (East Linton, Scotland: Tuckwell, 1999), 110–13.

82. Hunter, *On the Other Side of Sorrow*, 105–106.

83. Fulford, *Romantic Indians*, 196.

84. James Fenimore Cooper, *The Last of the Mohicans* (1826; repr., New York: Penguin, 1994), 414–15.

85. Gordon M. Sayre, *The Indian Chief as Tragic Hero: Native Resistance and the Literatures of America, from Moctezuma to Tecumseh* (Chapel Hill: University of North Carolina Press, 2005).

86. Colin G. Calloway, ed., *After King Philip's War: Presence and Persistence in Indian New England* (Hanover, N.H.: University Press of New England, 1997).

87. J. Hector St. John de Crèvecoeur, *Letters from an American Farmer* (New York: Penguin, 1981), 123.

88. Lester J. Cappon, ed., *The Adams-Jefferson Letters: The Complete Correspondence between Thomas Jefferson and Abigail and John Adams*, 2 vols. (Chapel Hill: University of North Carolina Press, 1959), vol. 2, 310–11.

89. Rev. Jedediah Morse, *A Report to the Secretary of War of the United States, on Indian Affairs* (New Haven, Conn.: Converse, 1822), 64–75.

90. Alexis de Tocqueville, *Democracy in America*, ed. J. P. Mayer (New York: Doubleday, 1969), 321.

91. Joseph S. Wood, *The New England Village* (Hanover, N.H.: University Press of New England, 1997).

92. Judith A. Ranta, *The Life and Writings of Betsey Chamberlain, Native American Mill Worker* (Boston: Northeastern University Press, 2003). Jeanne Guillemin, *Urban Renegades: The Cultural Strategy of American Indians* (New York: Columbia University Press, 1975), examines this phenomenon among Mi'kmaq workers in twentieth-century Boston.

93. Trudy Ann Parker, *Aunt Sarah, Woman of the Dawnland* (Lancaster, N.H.: Dawnland, 1994), 261. On Indian basket making in New England see Ann McMullen and Russell G. Handsman, eds., *A Key into the Language of Woodsplint Baskets* (Washington, Conn.: American Indian Archaeological Institute, 1987).

94. Renée Bergland, *The National Uncanny: Indian Ghosts and American Subjects* (Hanover, N.H.: University Press of New England, 2000); Philip J. Deloria, *Playing Indian* (New Haven, Conn.: Yale University Press, 1998), 191.

95. Szasz, *Scots in the North American West*, 126–31; Mae Reed Porter and Odessa Davenport, *Scotsman in Buckskin: Sir William Drummond Stewart and the Rocky Mountain Fur Trade* (New York: Hastings, 1963), 178–81, 198–99; Lisa Strong, "American Indians and Scottish Identity in Sir William Drummond Stewart's Collection," *Winterthur Portfolio* 35 (Summer/Autumn 2000), 127–55; Henry Liebersohn, *Aristocratic Encounters: European Travelers and North American Indians* (New York: Cambridge University Press, 1998), "affinity" quote at 1.

96. Now extremely valuable, the items of Cree and Blackfoot clothing became a source of bitter controversy in 2006 when the American Indian Movement tried to block their sale by the current Earl of Southesk and Sothebys. "Native Americans on the Warpath over Earl's Art Treasures," *Scotland on Sunday* (Apr. 30, 2006). Most of the collection was purchased at auction by the Royal Alberta Museum.

97. William H. Truettner, ed., *The West as America: Reinterpreting Images of the Frontier, 1820–1920* (Washington, D.C.: Smithsonian Institution Press, 1991); Jules David Prown et al., eds., *Discovered Lands, Invented Pasts: Transforming Visions of the American West* (New Haven, Conn.: Yale University Press/Yale University Art Gallery, 1992).

98. L. G. Moses, *Wild West Shows and the Images of American Indians, 1883–1933* (Albuquerque: University of New Mexico Press, 1996), 119; Calder, *Scots in the USA*, 153; Sam A. Maddra, *Hostiles? The Lakota Ghost Dance and Buffalo Bill's Wild West* (Norman: University of Oklahoma Press, 2006), chs. 6–8.

99. Steven Conn, *History's Shadow: Native Americans and Historical Consciousness in the Nineteenth Century* (Chicago: University of Chicago Press, 2004), quote at 36.

100. Alan Trachtenberg, *Shades of Hiawatha: Staging Indians, Making Americans, 1880–1930* (New York: Hill and Wang, 2004), 26; Mick Gidley, *Edward S. Curtis and the North American Indian, Incorporated* (New York: Cambridge University Press, 1998); Sherry L. Smith, *Reimagining Indians: Native Americans through Anglo Eyes, 1880–1940* (New York: Oxford University Press, 2000).

101. Thomas H. Guthrie, "Good Words: Chief Joseph and the Production of Indian Speech(es), Texts, and Subjects," *Ethnohistory* 54 (2007), 509–54.

102. Trachtenberg, *Shades of Hiawatha*, 196–97.

103. Lucy Maddox, *Citizen Indians: Native American Intellectuals, Race, and Reform* (Ithaca, N.Y.: Cornell University Press, 2005).

104. Ethel Boissevan, "Narragansett Survival: A Study of Group Persistence through Adopted Traits," *Ethnohistory* 6 (1959), 347–62; Ann McMullen, "What's Wrong with This Picture? Context, Conversion, Survival, and the Development of Regional Cultures and Pan-Indianism in Southeastern New England," in *Enduring Traditions: The Native Peoples of New England*, ed. Laurie Weinstein (Westport, Conn.: Bergin and Garvey, 1994), 123–50.

105. Richard J. Finlay, *Modern Scotland, 1914–2000* (London: Profile, 2004), 90–94, 104; Fry, *Wild Scots*, 270–71, 276–77.

106. Charles Wilkinson, *Blood Struggle: The Rise of Modern Indian Nations* (New York: Norton, 2005).

107. Iain Moncreiffe of that Ilk, *The Highland Clans: The Dynastic Origins, Chiefs, and Background of the Clans and of Some Other Families Connected with Highland History,* rev. ed. (New York: Potter, 1982), 156.

NOTES TO EPILOGUE

1. Edward W. Said, *Culture and Imperialism* (New York: Vintage, 1994); cf. Murray G. H. Pittock, *Celtic Identity and the British Image* (Manchester, UK: Manchester University Press, 1999), 6.
2. See, for example, http://stinet.dtic.mil/dticrev/a400144.pdf (bombing range); Richard J. Finlay, *Modern Scotland, 1914–2000* (London: Profile, 2004), 290.
3. Michael Lawson, *Dammed Indians: The Pick-Sloan Plan and the Missouri River Sioux, 1944–1980* (Norman: University of Oklahoma Press, 1982); Donald L. Fixico, *Termination and Relocation: Federal Indian Policy, 1945–1960* (Albuquerque: University of New Mexico Press, 1986); Donald L. Fixico, *The Invasion of Indian Country in the Twentieth Century: American Capitalism and Tribal Natural Resources* (Niwot: University Press of Colorado, 1999); Emily Benedek, *The Wind Won't Know Me: A History of the Navajo-Hopi Land Dispute* (Norman: University of Oklahoma Press, 1999).
4. John McGrath, *The Cheviot, the Stag, and the Black, Black Oil* (London: Methuen, 1974), quote at vi.
5. Finlay, *Modern Scotland, 1914–2000,* 295.
6. Eric Richards, *A History of the Highland Clearances.* Vol. 2, *Emigration, Protests, Reasons* (London: Croom Helm, 1985), 126.
7. Charles Jedrej and Mark Nutall, *White Settlers: The Impact of Rural Repopulation in Scotland* (Luxembourg: Harwood Academic, 1996), 120.
8. Michael Fry, *Wild Scots: Four Hundred Years of Highland History* (London: John Murray, 2005), 320–24.
9. Robert McCrum, Robert MacNeil, and William Cran, *The Story of English,* 3d ed. (New York: Penguin, 2003), xx.
10. David Craig, *On the Crofters' Trail: In Search of the Clearance Highlanders* (London: Jonathan Cape, 1990), 178.
11. Nancy Dorion, *Language Death: The Life Cycle of a Scottish Gaelic Dialect* (Philadelphia: University of Pennsylvania Press, 1981), 24–28, 38–41, 50; "The Highlands and Islands Education Trust: Historical Report," Dartmouth College, Rauner Library, 5, 8, 11.
12. Brenda J. Child, *Boarding School Seasons: American Indian Families, 1900–1940* (Lincoln: University of Nebraska Press, 1998), 28.
13. Quoted in Jedrej and Nutall, *White Settlers,* 73. For broader consideration of the historical assault on Gaelic and the continuing threats to its survival, focused on the east Sutherland region of the Highlands, see Dorion, *Language Death.*
14. Quote from Anne (née McLean) Calloway in family history.

15. Jack M. Bumsted, "The Scottish Diaspora: Emigration to British North America, 1763–1815," in *Nation and Province in the First British Empire: Scotland and the Americas, 1600–1800*, ed. Ned C. Landsman (Providence, R.I.: John Carter Brown Library, 2001), 141.

16. Charles W. Dunn, *Highland Settler: A Portrait of the Scottish Gael in Nova Scotia* (Toronto: University of Toronto Press, 1953), 35.

17. Fry, *Wild Scots*, 317–18.

18. David McCrone, *Understanding Scotland: The Sociology of a Nation*, 2d ed. (New York: Routledge, 2001), 28.

19. Bruce Granville Miller, *Invisible Indigenes: The Politics of Nonrecognition* (Lincoln: University of Nebraska Press, 2003), 206.

20. Pittock, *Celtic Identity and the British Image*.

21. The late Lakota scholar, Vine Deloria Jr., discussed the phenomenon in his 1984 essay, "The Popularity of Being Indian: A New Trend in Contemporary American Society," reprinted in *Spirit & Reason: The Vine Deloria Jr., Reader*, ed. Barbara Deloria, Kristen Foehner, and Sam Scinta (Golden, Colo.: Fulcrum, 1999), 230–40.

22. McGrath, *Cheviot, the Stag, and the Black, Black Oil*, xix–xx; Jedrej and Nuttall, *White Settlers;* James Hunter, *On the Other Side of Sorrow: Nature and People in the Scottish Highlands* (Edinburgh: Mainstream, 1995), 168 (Skye population increase), 172 (quote); James Hunter, *Last of the Free: A Millennial History of the Highlands and Islands of Scotland* (Edinburgh: Mainstream, 1999), 378–79; Eric Richards, *Britannia's Children: Emigration from England, Scotland, Wales, and Ireland since 1600* (London: Hambledon and London, 2004), 274 (1990s' increase).

23. Hunter, *Last of the Free*, 379.

24. Angus Calder, *Scotlands of the Mind* (Edinburgh: Luath, 2002), 37–38.

25. Benedict Anderson, *Imagined Communities: Reflections on the Spread of Nationalism* (London: Verso, 1983), 15.

26. William Ferguson, *The Identity of the Scottish Nation: An Historic Quest* (Edinburgh: Edinburgh University Press, 1998); Colin Kidd, *British Identities before Nationalism: Ethnicity and Nationhood in the Atlantic World, 1600–1800* (New York: Cambridge University Press, 1999).

27. R. A. Houston and W. W. J. Knox, eds., *The New Penguin History of Scotland* (London: Penguin, 2001), 357.

28. See, for example, Andrés Reséndez, *Changing National Identities at the Frontier: Texas and New Mexico, 1800–1850* (New York: Cambridge University Press, 2005).

29. Cf. Joy Porter, "The North American Indians and the Irish," *Irish Studies Review* 11 (2003), 264–71. "Given the wealth of colonial experience that links Ireland and Native America, it is perhaps surprising that when Irish culture has engaged with Indian culture it has so often been through the prism of an imagined or invented Indian colonial identity. The Irish have mainly engaged with Indian culture by co-opting it or 'playing Indian.'" (quote at 268).

30. James Loch, *An Account of the Improvements on the Estates of the Marquess of Stafford* (London: Longman, Hurst, Rees, Orme, and Brown, 1820), 2.

31. Edward J. Cowan, "The Myth of Scotch Canada," in *Myth, Migration, and the Making of Memory: Scotia and Nova Scotia c. 1700–1990*, ed. Marjorie Harper and Michael E. Vance (Edinburgh: John Donald, 1999), 49–72, Highland games at 62; Michael Kennedy, "'Lochaber No More': A Critical Examination of Highland Emigration Mythology," in *Myth, Migration, and the Making of Memory*, ed. Harper and Vance, 267–97; Canadian boat song at 273–74; Edward A. MacCardy, *A Literary Enigma—The Canadian Boat-Song: Its Authorship and Associations* (Stirling, Scotland: E. Mackay, 1935).

32. Celeste Ray, *Highland Heritage: Scottish Americans in the American South* (Chapel Hill: University of North Carolina Press, 2001), 2.

33. James Hunter, *Scottish Exodus: Travels among a Worldwide Clan* (Edinburgh: Mainstream, 2005), 18.

34. John W. Sheets, "Finding Colonsay's Emigrants and a 'Heritage of Place,'" and Paul Basu, "Pilgrims to the Far Country: North American 'Roots-Tourists' in the Scottish Highlands and Islands," both in *Transatlantic Scots*, ed. Celeste Ray (Tuscaloosa: University of Alabama Press, 2005), chs. 10–11; Paul Basu, "Hunting Down Home: Reflections on Homeland and the Search for Identity in the Scottish Diaspora," in *Contested Landscapes: Movement, Exile, and Place*, ed. Barbara Bender and Margot Winer (New York: Berg, 2001), ch. 20 (338–48); Paul Basu, "My Own Island Home: The Orkney Homecoming," *Journal of Material Culture* 9 (2004): 27–42.

35. Salman Rushdie, *Imaginary Homelands: Essays and Criticism, 1981–1991* (London: Granta, 1991), 9–21, quotes at 10, 12.

36. Marjory Harper, ed., *Emigrant Homecomings: The Return Movement of Emigrants, 1600–2000* (Manchester, UK: Manchester University Press, 2005), 3, 7–8, 10.

37. Calder, *Scotlands of the Mind*, 192; Marjory Harper, *Adventurers and Exiles: The Great Scottish Exodus* (London: Profile, 2003), ch. 9; Harper and Vance, eds., *Myth, Migration, and the Making of Memory*.

38. Jeffery C. Alexander, Ron Eyerman, Bernard Giesen, Neil J. Smelser, and Piotr Sztompka, *Cultural Trauma and Collective Identity* (Berkeley: University of California Press, 2004); Francesca Polletta and James M. Jasper, "Collective Identity and Social Movements," *Annual Review of Sociology* 21 (2001): 283–305, quote at 285.

39. Cf. Jedrej and Nutall, *White Settlers*, 120.

40. Neal Acherson, *Stone Voices: The Search for Scotland* (New York: Hill and Wang, 2002), 174–75.

41. Clyde Kluckhohn and Dorothea Leighton, *The Navaho* (Cambridge, Mass.: Harvard University Press, 1956), 9.

42. Alexander et al., eds., *Cultural Trauma and Collective Identity*.

43. Charles W. J. Withers, *Urban Highlanders: Highland-Lowland Migration and Urban Gaelic Culture, 1700–1900* (East Linton, Scotland: Tuckwell, 1998),

chs. 3, 5–7; Joan Weibel-Orlando, *Indian Country, L.A.: Maintaining Ethnic Community in Complex Society* (Urbana: University of Illinois Press, 1991).

44. Harper, *Adventurers and Exiles*, ch. 9; Harper and Vance, eds., *Myth, Migration, and the Making of Memory;* Ray, *Highland Heritage,* quote at 8.

45. Craig, *On the Crofters' Trail*, cited in Michael Fry, *How the Scots Made America* (New York: St. Martin's, 2003), 162–63; James Hunter, *The Making of the Crofting Community*, new ed. (Edinburgh: John Donald/Birlinn, 2000), quote at 26. My own conversations with American Scots do not lead me to share Michael Fry's conclusion drawn from Craig's findings: "A paradox of modern mourning about clearance is that it all comes from descendants of those who stayed behind." Fry, *Wild Scots*, 228.

46. Rusty Bitterman, "On Remembering and Forgetting: Highland Memories within the Maritime Diaspora," and Michael Kennedy, "'Lochaber No More': A Critical Examination of Highland Emigration Mythology," both in *Myth, Migration, and the Making of Memory*, ed. Harper and Vance, 253–65 and 267–97.

47. Michael Vance, "Powerful Pathos: The Triumph of Scottishness in Nova Scotia," in *Transatlantic Scots*, ed. Ray, 156–79; Ian McKay, "Tartanism Triumphant: The Construction of Scottishness in Nova Scotia, 1933–1954," *Acadiensis* 21 (Spring 1992), 5–48.

48. Cowan, "Myth of Scotch Canada," quote at 56.

49. Quoted in Paul Basu, "Roots Tourism as Return Movement: Semantics and the Scottish Diaspora," in *Emigrant Homecomings*, ed. Harper, ch. 7, quotes at 135–37, 140, 144.

50. Circe Sturm, *Blood Politics: Race, Culture, and Identity in the Cherokee Nation of Oklahoma* (Berkeley: University of California Press, 2002), 207.

51. Circe Sturm, "States of Sovereignty: Race Shifting, Recognition, and Rights in Cherokee Country," in *Beyond Red Power: American Indian Politics and Activism since 1900*, ed. Daniel M. Cobb and Loretta Fowler (Santa Fe: School for Advanced Research Press, 2007), 228–42.

52. Sturm, *Blood Politics*, 14.

53. Ray, *Highland Heritage*.

54. Ray, *Transatlantic Scots*, 38, 81.

55. Celeste Ray, "Bravehearts and Patriarchs: Masculinity on the Pedestal in Southern Scottish Heritage Celebration," in *Transatlantic Scots*, ch. 9, quote at 233.

56. Peter Womack, *Improvement and Romance: Constructing the Myth of the Highlands* (London: Macmillan, 1989), 178–79.

57. Philip J. Deloria, *Playing Indian* (New Haven, Conn.: Yale University Press, 1998).

58. James Hunter, *A Dance Called America: The Scottish Highlands, the United States, and Canada* (Edinburgh: Mainstream, 1995), 87; Grant Jarvie, "The North American Emigré, Highland Games, and Social Capital in International Communities," in *Transatlantic Scots*, ed. Ray, ch. 7.

59. Hunter, *Scottish Exodus*, 25.

60. Morris W. Foster, *Being Comanche: A Social History of an American Indian Community* (Tucson: University of Arizona Press, 1991), 131.

61. "The Wreck of the Swan," in *Hugh MacDiarmid: Selected Poetry*, ed. Alan Riach and Michael Grieve (New York: New Directions, 1993), 228.

62. Hunter, *On the Other Side of Sorrow*, 79.

63. John G. Gibson, *Old and New World Highland Bagpiping* (Montreal: McGill-Queens University Press, 2002; repr., Edinburgh: Birlinn, 2005).

64. *Pipe Band Magazine* (July/August 1962), 27. My thanks to Michael Macdonald for bringing Jim Forbes's pipe band to my attention and for providing me with a copy of this article.

65. J. M. Bumsted, "Scottishness and Britishness in Canada, 1790–1914," in *Myth, Migration, and the Making of Memory*, ed. Harper and Vance, 91.

66. Jenni Calder, *Scots in the USA* (Edinburgh: Luath, 2006), 213; Jenni Calder, "Changing Places: The Migrating Meaning of Objects," paper presented at the "Across the Great Divide" symposium, Edinburgh, July 19, 2003.

67. Colin McArthur, *Brigadoon, Braveheart, and the Scots: Distortions of Scotland in Hollywood Cinema* (London: Tauris, 2003).

68. Ascherson, *Stone Voices: The Search for Scotland*, 41.

69. Harper and Vance, eds., *Myth, Migration, and the Making of Memory*, quote at 37; David McCrone, Angela Morris, and Richard Kiely, *Scotland—The Brand: The Making of Scottish Heritage* (Edinburgh: Edinburgh University Press, 1995).

70. Fry, *How the Scots Made America*, 228.

71. Edward Cowan, "Tartan Day in America," in *Transatlantic Scots*, ed. Ray, ch. 12.

72. David Lowenthal, *The Heritage Crusade and the Spoils of History* (New York: Viking, 1996), 78, 128, 165.

73. Ascherson, *Stone Voices*, 41.

Index

LaVergne, TN USA
27 July 2010
190988LV00001B/81/P

9 780195 340129